WRITE BLACK,
WRITE BRITISH

WRITE BLACK, WRITE BRITISH

From Post Colonial to Black British Literature

Edited by Kadija Sesay

HANSIB

First published in the United Kingdom in 2005
by Hansib Publications Limited
PO Box 226, Hertford SG14 3WY
www.hansib-books.com

ISBN 1 870518 06 3

Cover design by Benjamin Wachenje

Contents

Part One: Writers in Prose-Fiction

Part Two: Writers in Verse

Part Three: Locating Writers
in History, Culture, and Society

Acknowledgements

My first thanks must go to the two bodies who, without which this book physically could not have happened, and they are Hansib Publications; much respect to Arif Ali and his commitment and dedication he has made to Black publishing in Britain. Also to Arts Council England, London for providing me with a bursary which allowed me time and resources to undertake work on this book.

Many thanks to the contributors for their patience, understanding, faith and belief in me to get this project completed. Amongst those contributors, special thanks go to Vicki Arana and Maria Helena Lima. Their hard work, efforts and support are ensuring that Black British writers are known, seen and read in literature departments across the USA with their conferences, summer schools that they organise and their invitations to writers, and of course, their writing. They also give me continued support and encouragement in every element of the work that I do.

For research, reading and editorial assistance, many thanks to Susan Yearwood, Marika Preziuso and Midori Saito and to Benjamin Wachenje for the cover design.

To Courttia Newland – we kind of started this journey together from *IC3* days and talked of the need first, for a conference, which became Write Black, Write British in 2001 and then a non-fiction book focusing on individual Black British writers. And to the writers themselves, featured within the book who have and continue to produce such stimulating and extraordinary work that compiling this anthology made me proud of our African diasporic heritage.

To Deirdre Osborne a dear friend and another advocate of Black British writers and playwrights in her teaching and writings. Staying at her apartment provided me with much needed space for final edits and space to discuss the book with her.

My family of friends in Washington DC who give me support and encouragement when I'm there and where I did a lot of the work in the summer of 2003, Clement Goddard, Juliette Bethea, Clayton Spitzer, Juanita, Mel and Victor (at Millennium B & B) and of course, my late night/early morning IM buddie, Divajamiewalker!

Thanks also to all those around me who continue to provide much love and support my family who support me in everything I do, especially my parents and Saffiatu my sister.

Contributors

R. Victoria Arana is Professor of English at Howard University, Washington D.C., (USA) where she directs the Graduate Program in English and teaches research and critical methods, British literature, 'Black' British travel writing, 'Black' British writers, & post-colonial critical theory and literature. She co-edited (with Lauri Ramey) Black British Writing (Palgrave Macmillan).

Sandra Courtman is a Senior Lecturer in English Literature at Staffordshire University (UK). She has published a number of articles based on doctoral research on the apparent paucity and marginality of West Indian women's writing in Britain in the 1960s and 1970s. She recovered and edited a rare Jamaican woman's autobiography, Joyce Gladwell's Brown Face, Big Master (Macmillan Caribbean Classic, 2003). She has published a multi-disciplinary collection, Beyond the Blood, the Beach and The Banana: New Perspectives in Caribbean Studies (Jamaica: Ian Randle, 2004).

Pilar Cuder-Domínguez is Associate Professor at the University of Huelva (Spain), where she teaches British and English-Canadian Literature. She is the author of Margaret Atwood: A Beginner's Guide (2003), and the (co)editor of four collections of essays (La mujer del texto al contexto, 1996; Exilios femeninos, 2000; Sederi XI, 2002; and Espacios de Género, 2004). Her current research, funded by the Canadian Department of Foreign Affairs and International Trade, deals with Canadian women's transnational poetics.

Eric Doumerc teaches English at the University of Toulouse-Le Mirail in Toulouse, southwestern France. His main research interests are Black British and Caribbean performance poetry, and political and cultural developments in the post-independence English-speaking Caribbean. He received his PhD in English from the University of Toulouse-Le Mirail in 1997. He has published articles on dub poetry, Louse Bennett and the Mento Traditon as well as reviews for the Society for Caribbean Studies Newsletter.

Kwame Dawes, Distinguished Poet in Residence, Louise Frye Scudder Liberal Arts Professor, and Founder and Director of the South Carolina Poetry Initiative at the University of South Carolina, (US). He has published nine collections of poetry since 1994 including Progeny of Air (Peepal Tree Press, 1994), winner of the Forward Poetry Prize (UK) for best first collection, Mapmaker (Smith Doorstop, 2000) a chapbook of poems, won the Poetry Business Contest in the UK for 2000. Other awards include the Hollis Summers Poetry, Prize Pushcart Prize and the Silver Musgrave Medal. Dawes collection of poems Wisteria will appear in 2005. Dawes is the programming director of the Calabash International Literary festival.

Fatimah Kelleher has an MA from SOAS (UK). She has taught pre-colonial African history at the Horniman Museum for Birkbeck College and facilitates creative writing and performance workshops. She has appeared as a performance artist in the UK and abroad including the 2002 poetry International at the South Bank performing a commissioned piece written in English and Hausa as part of a themed event, entitled, 'Babel' and has had her poetry published in SABLE LitMag.

Mahlete-Tsige Getachew read Philosophy, Politics and Economics at Oxford, and went on to do an MPhil in Philosophy at Cambridge, and is now a PhD student at York (UK). She has had fiction and essays published in Inky Foot (Macmillan 1997), IC3 (Hamish Hamilton 2000), and James Bond and Philosophy (Open Court 2006, forthcoming).

Laura Griggs studied English Literature at Leicester University before completing her MA in English Literary Research, also at Leicester (UK). Her specialist area is literary and cultural representations of the Medusa figure, particularly with reference to contemporary women's poetry and feminist theory. Laura lives in Birmingham and is a contributor to literary journal SABLE LitMag.

Dave Gunning is currently putting the finishing touches to his PhD thesis at the University of Leeds, (UK). His research focuses on the relations between the registers of anti-racism and the form and content of Black British literatures.'

Maria Helena Lima is a Brazilian who is an Associate Professor of English at SUNY-Geneseo, (USA). She has published on Jamaica Kincaid, Michelle Cliff, Merle Collins and 'The Politics of Teaching Black and British' in Black British Writing, (Palgrave 2004). An article on Black British Women Writers and an interview with Kadija George Sesay in Obsidian III's special issue on Black British Writing (Fall 2004). She has also published reviews of contemporary Black British fiction in SABLE, Wasafiri, and Humanitas. She is currently working on a book of interviews, Black Britons Writing.

Koye Oyedej is a research PhD student in Literatures of the Nigerian Diaspora at the School Of Oriental and African Studies, (UK). He has contributed to a number of publications including the New Nation and the Nottingham Evening Post. His short stories and poetry have appeared in IC3 (Penguin 2000) and The Fire People (Payback Press 1998). He is currently a contributing editor for SABLE LitMag.

 Molly Thompson completed her PhD at the University of Exeter in 2003 and currently teaches part-time at Bath Spa University College (UK). Her doctoral research focused on the representation of the Black feminine body in writing by Black women in Britain.

 Tracey Walters is an Assistant Professor of literature in the departments of Africana Studies and English at Stony Brook University (UK). She publishes in the area of Black British literature and African American literature. She is currently completing her manuscript: 'Writing the Classics Black: The Political and Aesthetic Function of African American Women's Classical Revision'.

 Patrick Williams is Professor of Literary and Cultural Studies at Nottingham Trent University (UK), where he teaches in the areas of race, national identity and post-colonial studies. His publications include: Colonial Discourse and Postcolonial Theory (Harvester Wheatsheaf Press 1993/Columbia University Press 1994), Introduction to Post-colonial Theory (Prentice Hall, 1996), Ngugi wa Thiong'o (Manchester University Press, 1999), Edward Said (SAGE Publications Ltd. 2000), Post-colonial African Cinemas (MUP, forthcoming).

 Emily Wroe received a PhD in Contemporary Black British Literature from the University of Gloucestershire in 2004. She has published an article on Lawrence Scott's novel 'Aelred's Sin' in Beyond the Blood, the Beach and the Banana: New Perspectives in Caribbean Studies by Dr Sandra Courtman. (Jamiaca: Ian Randle, 2004).

 Susan Yearwood is a post-graduate student in Creative Writing at Sheffield Hallam University (UK). She has read and attended a variety of conferences in the Caribbean and Europe. She has contributed articles to Humanitas: The Journal of the George Bell Institute and has an essay in Black British Writing. She is currently a contributing editor for SABLE LitMag.

"Literature is the most beautiful of countries."

- Jose Marti

Foreword

The first years of the 21st century see black Britain at an interesting time in terms of fashioning self-identities. Anecdotal evidence seems to suggest a mood of confidence and creative opportunism amongst some black professional Britons as the possibilities of being able to claim a distinctive and simultaneous blackness and Britishness begins to emerge.

In 1998 events and activities were put on across the country in commemoration of the 50th anniversary of the landing of the Empire Windrush with its hopeful settlers from the Caribbean. Those collective acts of memorialising that marked the iconic Windrush moment formed a significant part of the process of becoming embedded in British culture whilst re-constructing and re-defining what 'British' means. This is not to say that the struggles over racism, discrimination, culture and representation are over because clearly they are not. I am simply noting the obvious: there have been significant developments in the ways in which we think about and represent our selves, and our communities of interest.

The texts under discussion in this volume are both about specific kinds of experience and the universality of experiences. For too long writing about black people has been thought of as 'special interest' or worse still, 'special pleading'. This last two or three years has dispelled the myth that people of African or Asian descent do not read books. The hunger for interesting, challenging work is apparent: but it is also true that a wider public has an appetite for novels and poetry written and performed by diaspora peoples. It would be invidious to focus on one or two authors as being exemplars here but the critical acclaim, publicity and prizes that a handful of authors have received means that there must be plenty more to look forward to as new writers emerge.

Why is it important to develop more critical discourses on black cultural production? I think it's necessary to move beyond simply celebrating what we have achieved. The drive to engage in different kinds of literary criticism has a momentum that will ensure that we continue to document and disseminate, to analyse critically and rigorously black styles, texts and representations in history and in contemporary society. I hope though, that we will not become totally enthralled by fixed critical terms and frameworks but that we are always sensitive to ongoing debates and alternative modes of articulating the politics of black cultural production.

To refer to the essays in this collection as being about 'black' anything is not without its problems. The works cited and analysed undermine any claim to a fixed, unified or singular approach to the predicaments we have encountered now and in the past. Indeed, the very notion of diaspora is problematised by the testing of its limitations and constraints, even whilst the need for some kind of connectivity is often affirmed.

Many African diaspora scholars and intellectuals have spoken of the importance of recognition - of issues, problems, achievements, gaps and absences - and the necessity for a sense of historical rootedness for black people in this country. Laying claim to a historical and a literary tradition is particularly important for us in racially stratified societies where the acquisition of a certain kind of skill with the written word and an identifiable intellectual progression are seen as key markers of a civilised culture. There is an increasingly significant number of texts being written by black scholars and intellectuals about diaspora writing and this collection of essays is a valuable addition to that body of work.

Lola Young

*Lola Young is a freelance arts and heritage consultant
and a Crossbench member of the House of Lords.*

Introduction

The title, *Write Black, Write British* is taken from a conference of the same name organised by SAKS Media/SAKS Publications, publishers of SABLE LitMag, in 2001.

Courttia Newland and myself had just co-edited *IC3:The Penguin Book of New Black Writing* in Britain the year before and on the journey, had discovered, discussed and decided on how else we could raise the profile of Black British literature. In spite of over 100 contributions of poetry, memoirs, fiction and essays across three generations included in it, there were huge gaps – there was so much more we wanted to cover, so many topics, areas, histories that we wanted to discuss and fill the book with – and could have filled another book with.

But we also realised the need, particularly from the readings of the memoirs, that a critical text of the work of Black writers in Britain was specifically relevant and needed – a text that focused on the histories, sociologies and economic drives from whence these writers came; from whence their ideas, and identities came.

Before that even, was a much needed forum for networking and discussion, a place and space to continually create and develop new work.

We came up with the idea of the conference, that basically reflected the sections within *IC3*, the settlers, explorers and the crusaders.

It took place finally at the Barbican Centre on 27-28 September, where *The Companion to Black British Literature and Culture* edited By Alison Donnell was also launched. During the conference I announced that the papers would be published in a book, with no real idea of when and how, just that what had taken place needed to be documented. They are not all included here; two of the 'crusading' contributors and panellists who represent what the future of Black British literature could look like, are Koye Oyedeji and Mahlete-tsige Getachew, who have taken their ideas from four years ago and now, as PhD research students, present them here as stronger, well researched, more mature arguments and in fact, challenge the concept of what this book is about.

So why 'from Post Colonial to Black British?' For me, there is a generation of writers who more clearly fall into that category of what is termed, 'post colonial' and some of those writers, will also (happily) be referred to as Black British, particularly if they can benefit from what is often seen as a new catch-all sexy terminology. But can the Black British writers discussed in individual chapters here also be termed as post colonial? I don't think so. They are writers born in Britain, educated in Britain and because of heritage and parentage, their 'take' on Britain is viewed through different glasses from those born elsewhere, and possibly raised and or educated here. And it is not always because they want it that way, but because they are forced into it. They are reminded constantly that they are 'not of here' even though they believe and feel that they are, so they consider the 'hybridity' of themselves and their situation in a way that does not refer to their 'alienness' and even a different kind of 'otherness' than their 'post colonial' writer peers. I am not suggesting here that the term 'post colonial' is an outmoded one, but for many emerging writers, a shift away from this canon to a development of another one. Such books as *Extravagant Strangers* edited by Caryl Phillips and *Other Black, Other British,* edited by Robert Lee tell me that this is so – prime examples of how inconsequential 'labelling' and categorising can be. Dare I even admit it? I don't even refer to myself as Black British, I'm African British and for many of us, that is not so much as new terminology, but one that was not acknowledged in literature that we read or even in the African diasporic environment we found ourselves in.

My aim as always is to make whatever I do as easy to navigate as possible. Therefore, this book is divided into three sections, Writers in Prose Fiction, Writers in Verse, Locating Writers in History Culture and Society.

In section one, six writers are featured who have have all broken major ground in contemporary British Literature. It opens with an essay on Diran Adebayo who was the recipient of the first SAGA prize set up by Marsha Hunt. Lambasted by many (writers) that such a prize was only open to those who were born, or whose parents/grandparents were born in Britain, totally missed the point of what she was trying to say and do. It was important for markers to be made that stories from such writers did herald a difference.

Emily Wroe focuses on Adebayo's second book, in which he combines elements of Black British lifestyle with that of his African myth-telling heritage of Yoruba deities. Newland too in a yet unpublished novel has dug deep into African mysticism, driving forward how it interplays with the future. Arana's in depth portrayal here of the author himself and his work reflect the myriad of lifestyles and topics that one young Black British male, commonly referred to as an 'urban writer' experiences and encompasses and with the amount of work that Newland has produced in a relatively short writing career, is one of those writers who exceptionally shows how unlimiting Black British writers are. This will be even more evident in his forthcoming short story collection, *Music For the Off Key*. Newland catches his critics off guard with the urban label that he has been given.

Ross's complicated novel structure is typical of her – another one of Britain's most talented writers. In *Orange Laughter* the madness of Tony is probably, one of the most significant elements of the society that we live in today – that of young, Black males being interred, physically and mentally. In Tony, her protagonist, we see the talent and creativity reflective of today's generations of too many young Black men being lost in madness. Again, although Jackie Kay is one of our most prolific writers in various genres, it is probably her short story collection, *Why Don't You Stop Talking?* that is the most emblematic of her work, and in this essay, Patrick Williams discusses how well she reflects the multifarious society that we live in.

Levy's work has matured so much from her first title, she created her own level playing field. Lima's study of Levy's work perhaps is one that most clearly shows the identity journey of those born Black in Britain. It has taken her to her fourth (award winning) novel to get people to wake up and see that there is another Britain within Britain. And it has the colour of Black in it.

Although Zadie Smith took the publishing world by storm on both sides of the Atlantic, few in Britain, will not forget that this was built on several years of writing that came from Black British women, years of building and developing to enable writers of her generation to emerge and move directly into the mainstream. In her own way, Thompson demonstrates her acknowledgement of this, with her discussion on 'roots' and 'routes' – and the tenuousness of both. In Section Two, Writers in Verse, all four poets come from a strong performance background.

All four, probably speak even louder than even our novelists of what Britain in Black really does look like as they are some of the most popular writers on the national and global circuit and all four regularly represent Britain through their work with the British Council (Some of the biographies at the end of this book have generally been provided from this source).

Agbabi, one of the most popular performance poets in the country today, has not only raised her own game, but quite distinctly, her nomination as a 'New Generation Poet' says performance poetry has permanence, as much as any 'page poet'. Smartt, as Agbabi, came thorough the nurturing of Centerprise in East London, and her career as a performance poet, is stamped with her multi-media performances that sing of her Barbadian origins, although in this essay chapter, Laura Griggs focuses on Smartt's popular Medusa series.

Zephaniah, is known primarily as a performance poet too, and performs across the globe.

Eric Doumerc looks at each element of his poetic life, the content of which probably speaks more so than many of the diversity of cultures in Britain today, whereas Evaristo, as Dave Gunning shows, brilliantly documents our history here in her verse novels and her poetry collections.

Section 3, reflects the places; historical, social, economical, geographical and spiritual that these writers and their works have emerged from. The first three 'historical' and chronological contributions from Sandra Courtman, Victoria Arana and Fatimah Kelleher, provide us with specificities and overviews of writing in Britain from the 70s through to the beginning of this decade. My discussion with Sandra in regards to representation here, is an important note for all the pieces within the book and our place in Britain. The decision was made to only use the term 'migrant' and not 'immigrant' because of it's negative connotations and in fact, I found that people often use the term intermittently. It has only remained in a few cases because of the context in which it is in, for example when Kwame Dawes has referred to other people's terminology of 'immigrant literature'.

Kwame Dawes essay chapters first appeared in *Wasafiri*. His two discussions, one on Black British fiction, the other on poetry, are the kind that will be continually referenced for years to come. I agree with him in the comment he made to me after we updated the poetry piece that he "should have been harder on the establishment" although kudos must go here, to his own publishers in the UK, Peepal Tree Press, probably the only publisher in the UK today, willing to take the risk of publishing new and performance based poets of African and Asian descent in Britain.

Tracey Walters discusses that ongoing question, which prompted this book – what is Black British literature? She and many others continually asked that throughout the the conference, 'Teaching Black British Literature', convened by Professor Arana at Howard University in 2001.

Pilar Cuder's comparitive on Evaristo and Roy looks at one of the most important identity aspects of people born in Britain of a different heritage – where is home, and how do you find it? Especially when you thought that you were already there.

The last two essays in this book take us to a different look and probably, in the end, a different book. As previously mentioned, Getachew and Oyedeji have taken the Black British ball and ran with it – directly challenging every idea raised in this book. Forget the questions, 'What is a Black Briton?' and 'what does their literature look like?' They ask and attempt some answers at why it is, as it is, why is it marginalised and how do we climb out of these margins?

Getachews' comparison's to other Black cultural entities such as hip-hop tells us that as writers we are not thinking big enough, global enough or innovative enough to become permanent leading lights and that if this is not changed, literature by Black writers in Britain will forever remain in the margins.

Oyedeji pulls us in another direction and questions if the term should even exist as the mere existence of these writers work (and he looks at this in reference to Adebayo and Evaristo) proclaims that the only commonality here is that fact that they are both writers!

This book has been a long time in coming, and in the meantime, numerous changes – such as writers publishing more books and winning major awards, have occurred. Yet once again, like *IC3*, although it shows the breadth of work, it is always just as evident of who and what has been inadvertently left out.

Kadija Sesay

Part One: Writers in Prose-Fiction

Towards a 'non-ghettocentric Black Brit vibe': A Trickster Inspired Approach to Storytelling in Diran Adebayo's *My Once Upon A Time*

Emily Wroe

ALTERNATIVE ROUTES OUT OF 'THE GHETTO'

This essay considers the trickster figure and formal trickster strategies in Diran Adebayo's second novel, *My Once Upon A Time*.[1] It suggests that Adebayo adopts and adapts trickster figures and strategies from African (Eshu Elegbara) and African-American (the Signifying Monkey) traditions within a novel reflecting London's socio-cultural environment in order to emphasise a 'non-ghettocentric' Black British identity and to create his own individual trickster tale for the contemporary world.[2] I argue that the narrative itself reflects the trickster's energy through its intricate intertextuality, mapping and revising a network of contemporary and older Black vernacular texts alongside literature from the western canon. Drawing upon Henry Louis Gates' theory of the linguistic and stylistic principals of the Black tradition, I highlight how the 'double-voicedness' of Adebayo's narrative critiques and overrides stereotypical and static perceptions of individual and cultural identity.

In *My Once Upon A Time*, the trickster figure emphasises the value of previous Black traditions to a younger generation of Black Britons for whom, like young African-Americans, such traditions may be unknown or undervalued and who turn to 'street' culture and its values as a mode of identification and expression and as a model of power, resistance and survival.[3] Through his protagonist Boy – an Everyman representative of the young Black Western male living in an urban environment – Diran Adebayo is saying something important about the reasons for and consequences of becoming 'caught in the rap-trap'.[4] This refers to the way in which men, like Boy, who consider themselves trapped in urban environments abandoned by the government, and who also feel neglected by their own communities, will do anything to 'escape the ghetto'.[5] The rap-trap, then, also describes a state of mind moulded by inner-city living and encouraged by certain hiphop artists whose music glamorises the 'gangsta's' life-style and confirms the 'dog-eat-dog' attitudes of many young people.[6]

For Adebayo, young Black Westerners underachieve emotionally because of the pressures of living in urban environments and the demands placed upon them to authenticate their 'Blackness' by conforming to the 'street notion' of the Black male that is a Western invention.[7] The novel shows how the street demands a particular kind of behaviour for young Black Westerners many of whom are not stereotypical gangsters but ordinary young men who want to improve their lives. At the same time as the novel considers the reasons for emotional and economic/social underachievement among young Black males, it also dispels the 'gangsta' stereotype affixed to Black youth in which deviancy or delinquency is deemed 'natural' or 'characteristic'. Men like Boy adopt the mask of menace in order to survive the 'mean city streets' and as a response to dominant mechanisms of power. While there is no doubt that the novel acknowledges that the kind of mindset that governs Boy's actions is a product of and – as hooks argues – a reflection of white supremacist capitalist patriarchy, it is equally critical of the counter-productivity of intra-racial misunderstandings and Black-on-Black violence.[8] Intra-racial conflict and mistrust between diverse groups in the Black community, alongside the dominant society's discriminatory practices, mark the narrative's urban landscape.

In response to the belief that there is no alternative route out of the 'ghetto', the novel foregrounds Black Diasporean achievement, searches for a specific kind of spirituality and argues for a particular form of resistance to oppression through learning and knowledge. While Adebayo's novel shares an affinity with works by Victor Headley (*Yardie*, 1992) and Courttia Newland (*The Scholar*, 1997 and *Society Within*, 1999) – insofar as they all reflect upon the way in which an individual's situation can cause them to act in the worst possible way – Adebayo also explores, through mythical figures, such as the divine trickster, the value of older (spiritual and philosophical) knowledge and how this can serve as an alternative guide to coping with socio-economic pressures.[9]

The trickster figure and 'his' energies, then, assist the author in establishing a pluralist approach to identity and culture.[10] I refer, of course, to the trickster's borderdwelling status, his/her ability to shift shape and form – all traits which create ambiguity and contradictions. The multifariousness and fluidity of the trickster aid the author in his task of undoing stereotypical and reductive perceptions of Black identities and UK culture. Trickster concepts and trickster figures are not only used to redefine UK culture but as a mode of narration that challenges the so-called superiority of narrative forms from the western world and the kinds of reductive and arbitrary epistemological and ontological myths they create. Adebayo joins the ranks of trickster novelists such as Toni Morrison and Ishmael Reed who use tricksters to simultaneously undermine or deflate cultural norms and pretensions and to reinforce and promote African Diasaporean achievement.

HYBRID STRATEGIES OF TRANSFORMATION

My Once Upon A Time is what Jeanne Rosier Smith would refer to as a 'full-blown trickster novel' because it employs trickster strategies formally as well as using a trickster character to convey a message concerning personal and cultural identity.[11] Generic flexibility is just one example of how the novel engages in formal trickery. *My Once Upon A Time* incorporates a cross-section of genres such as fairy-tale, romance, fable, detective/gumshoe or suspense novel, tragedy, tragi-comedy, dilemma tale, *bildungsroman* and confessional (also linked to quest narrative) and as such, like the trickster, resists generic compartmentalisation. As Rosier-Smith notes, "trickster cannot be pinned down to any one form, shape or position", thus "he or she continually disrupts the status quo" and "embodies an expansive, dynamic cultural identity rather than a reductive, static one".[12] One of the narrative's intertexts, Shakespeare's *Troilus and Cressida*, which is famous for its generic instability, draws attention to earlier challenges to generic labelling from within the western canon. It makes sense that Adebayo adopts and adapts *Troilus and Cressida* as a model since it too reflects trickster-like formal energies.[13] As the intertextual relationships with *Troilus and Cressida* and African/African-American folklore and canonical literature suggests, Adebayo dons the mask of trickster and thus transgresses the boundaries between 'Black and white' and 'high and low' traditions, boundaries which present different kinds of literature as being naturally incompatible.[14]

We can approach the novel, then, in terms of Gates's concept of doublevoicedness, which influenced by Mikhail Bakhtin's analysis of language, refers to the double heritage and thus "double-accented, double-styled hybrid construction" of "each Black text written in the Western language".[15] Gates theorises double-voicedness through the African-American trickster's (the signifying monkey's) act of Signifyin(g). Signifyin(g) is a "Black rhetorical strategy peculiar to the Black vernacular tradition" and refers to "a set of practices that encode Black difference by transforming 'mainstream literary and linguistic practices'".[16] While Adebayo's narrative works within and revises western forms (the novel) and traditions (Romance), it also asserts its difference from western literary conventions by drawing upon and adapting vernacular texts from the African Diaspora. In this way, the novel calls attention to the myth of the west's superiority and absolute knowledge.

The act of Signifyin(g), involving repetition with a difference, begins with the title *My Once Upon A Time* which – as Adebayo states – is partly a conscious echo of the fairy-tale tradition.[17] Boy's story calls upon Cinderella's tale – if he finds the girl for his client, his own wish to work with the Race Man (a divine/human Black leader, committed to racial uplift) will be granted. In this sense, the novel re-vises western storytelling conventions and creates a new fairy-tale for contemporary Britain, focussing upon Black issues and experiences that re-write the landscape (historical, political, cultural and literary). For Adebayo, the title riffs upon the Spaghetti Westerns created by Sergio Leone ('Once Upon a Time in the West' and 'Once Upon a Time in America'), with the 'my' referring to the way in which the author repeats with a difference the operatic baroque and slightly surreal style of Leone's European Western. Adebayo's nightmarish cityscape is familiar and strange at the same time. There are a few identifiable London landmarks and buildings alongside the use of local languages (Cockney and a blend of Black British Englishes) which name the city but, apart from these the setting remains anonymous, creating the sensation that it could also be any city in the world. Importantly, and in relation to the earlier point about non-ghettocentricism, the author's homage to Leone – implicit in the title and the novel – is linked to his refusal to conform to a blueprint for Black British writers that expects, and insists on, 'gritty' social realism. Although Adebayo does not regard his novel as a direct response to the western canon, the very fact that it retrieves older learning from the African diaspora and pursues its own style presents a challenge to both the conventions of the street and the canon.

The novel's double-voicedness – the way in which it is Signifyin(g) upon crosscultural traditions – is particularly evident through its epigraphs. One of these (also the riddle that Boy – a small time private investigator – must think through in order to solve his latest case) is taken from The Book of Ecclesiastes (Chapter 7) in the Old Testament which in the New King James Version is headed 'The Value of Practical Wisdom':

> Adding one thing to another to discover the scheme of things –
> Still searching but not finding
> I found one man amongst a thousand
> but a woman amongst all those have I not found.[18]

The last two lines of the biblical epigraph apply to Boy's assignment, while the first two lines relate to the novel's structure and the act of interpretation. The novel itself is organised around the first line of the note: part one is headed 'adding one thing to another', while part two changes the biblical riddle slightly by heading the section 'to discover the *theme* of things'. This highlights the way the reader joins the protagonist – in fact almost becomes the protagonist – on his mission to solve the case via the riddle.[19] There is an important existential point being made within this form of chiasmic word-play which links to Boy's pursuit of a better life. Love and its offshoots – sacrifice, honour and trust – is the key to Boy's quest. The third epigraph, 'For they are the best of us/Those who love, and believe' denotes the novel's main concern, which is emotional (under)achievement. However slippery the themes of the novel appear to be, it is clear that the epigraphs all reflect its premise that the 'good life' involves the pursuit of love.

The way in which Adebayo organises the narrative around this subtly adapted biblical phrase is the first indication that he is Signifyin(g) upon the book of Ecclesiastes alongside ancient Yoruba religious belief and notions of chivalry and love characteristic of the Romance tradition (for example, 'courtly love is based upon the idea that love is an ennobling, even spiritual experience').[20] He looks at the consequences of wickedness and folly through both Judeo-Christian and Yoruba lenses within a contemporary context. This is a further example of how the novel employs a trickster aesthetic; it crosses and therefore blurs the boundaries between two distinct but – as the novel seems to imply – compatible systems of belief. The content of *My Once Upon A Time* also follows a fairly similar pattern to that found in Ecclesiastes (which also falls into two parts);

for example, chapters 1 to 6 offer 'a philosophical treatise on life and the absurd', while the remaining chapters provide 'an ethical discussion on how one should live one's life as a result'.[21] Part one of the novel is peppered with Boy's philosophical musings about life and its absurdities; for example, through the metaphors of cricket and *Troilus and Cressida*. Part two of the novel demonstrates how to live one's life by setting Boy up as an example to us all: that is, how to live one's life is mediated through how not to live one's life.

The novel, then, is an extended proverb, which like the Book of Ecclesiastes, restructures accepted truths about – in this context – identity and a fulfilling life. Boy's reaction to his latest case demonstrates a contemporary materialistic view of happiness:

> I locked the door, stuffed his note in my pocket, then contemplated this mad money in front of me, as welcome as pussy in midwinter. Yeah, looked like I was finally coming in from the cold ... Could it be that I was finally getting overs.[22]

'Getting overs' puns on the rules of cricket – a sport greatly admired by Boy for its genteel, graceful and sports-manly qualities. 'Getting overs' for Boy means, in one sense, making enough cash to escape the mean city streets and, in another, it relates to a serious desire for inner self-improvement. Adebayo disrupts the negative and stereotypical images of Black males as delinquents or criminals by depicting his protagonist as someone with 'brains', feelings and a determination for change, and also by acknowledging the possibility of change when everything seems hopeless. The way in which Boy's own view of life (reality) is refigured as he attempts to solve the client's case exemplifies this and further reflects the kind of restructuring characteristic of Ecclesiastes that the novel is Signifyin(g) upon. The Book of Ecclesiastes uses contradictions as a teaching tool, as does the novel, in that Boy's actions often contradict his aspirations – for example, the desire to live a better life which is overshadowed at the end. The novel, again like Ecclesiastes, is philosophical in nature rather than religious and this is evident in the question the client poses concerning heaven and hell that I comment on later. This technique (a series of reactions to a question) is found in the biblical work and importantly reflects on the Black vernacular tradition (call and response). Reading the epigraphs in relation to the novel reveals the complex intertextual weaving across traditions, reflecting trickster's energy.

(RE)INTERPRETING THE FOLK HEROIC

Alongside those trickster energies such as generic instability and the Signifiyin(g) Monkey's language, is its didactic function. As Jacqueline Fulmer notes:

> Despite the different guises, one aspect of folklore's continuing influence involves its didactic function. While its context varies through time, altering its appearance along the way, folklore's influence on art continues to advise audiences about desirable and undesirable patterns of behaviour.[23]

However, as John W. Roberts states, the actions of trickster figures in traditional African cultures are

> not designed to provide a model of adaptive behaviour in a literal sense. Rather folk heroic literature offers a conception of attributes and actions that a group perceives as the most advantageous for maintaining and protecting its identity in the face of a threat to values guiding action. Folk heroic literature always portrays the exceptional actor whose exploits offer the group a glimpse of its own possibilities in handling similar situations in everyday life and specific situations.[24]

I will now discuss, by way of a traditional trickster figure, how Adebayo adopts and adapts the folk heroic in order to offer the group (by which I mean young Black Britons) possibilities for handling life situations in Britain and beyond. *My Once Upon A Time* questions a self-centred approach to life and implicitly encourages the individual to consider the wider picture, to consider others in families, communities and societies. Roberts' discussion of African socio-religious law and custom, which emphasises communal welfare before individual gain (a value associated with the western world), respect for a hierarchy of social and religious powers and harmony in social relationships, argues that "trickster's actions offered Africans a model of behaviour that allowed for the development and maintenance of behavioural patterns that facilitated individual and communal well-being without violating or threatening communal identity".[25] In a society with a rigid hierarchy and harsh natural environment, people who do not share the privileges and power of those at the top of the social scale could "contest irrational authority" and demonstrate their worth and ability through trickster tales.[26]

In *My Once Upon A Time*, it is the divine trickster figure from Yoruba mythology, Esu-Elegbara (also spelt Eshu-Elegbara), who commands the plot and who attempts to help Boy, by way of the trick, read the signs pertaining to his own destiny. Eshu comes to assist Boy in his personal quest to 'get overs' and thus signals the way in which the novel provides a metaphorical model for adaptive behaviour. As the novel's first epigraph – from a Yoruba invocation – implies, Eshu appears to have a small part to play in the story (he is, like many tricksters, characteristically elusive) when in fact he pulls Boy's strings and crucially, represents the path to divine insight:

> Eshu Elegba
> Master of Potentiality
> He's the tiny, tiny guy
> Returning with the last stragglers
> from the market of the night.
> He's close, close as the shoulder of the road.[27]

At the beginning of the narrative, Eshu comes to Boy in the guise of a client looking for a private investigator to help him find 'a woman of substance' – a lady with whom he can share his country idyll.[28] He passes Boy the first of two coded messages that is repeated throughout the narrative and which echoes a line from a Wu Tang Clan track: "Tell me, Boy, what do you believe in, heaven or hell?"[29] We might view the way in which the story is set to a song in terms of a spin on operatic conventions. This opening scene establishes the 'feel' and tone for the remainder of the story. Its mystery and ambiguity stem from the client and the assignment he gives to Boy. His behaviour and mannerisms, his request and his two cryptic messages (including the biblical riddle as discussed earlier in Part II) both intrigue and disturb the protagonist and reader. For example, 'the client' knows Boy's name without asking, uses trick terms and carries himself with a certain air or quality that has become unfamiliar in the menacing world Boy lives in, where every 'brother' on the 'crimeside' is forever on his guard. The tricksy client and the task reflect a commingling of trickster and romance traditions: for example, the trickster sets in motion a quest echoing those knightly quests in romance stories where the hero faces such things as magic and contests for the sake of a heroine who is the focus for courtly love. These stories, like the trickster tale, have a strong moral content.

Adebayo's use of the traditional Yoruba trickster figure serves three particular interrelated functions which I outline below. Firstly, Eshu or the client symbolises the kind of cross-cultural contact, exchange and transformation that the narrative embodies in its attempt to override stereotypes. The client's signet ring, marked with the sign of the monkey, signals this cross-cultural connection and metamorphosis, and more specifically, African diasporean identity. Although Eshu often appears with his companion the monkey in Yoruba mythology, Gates explains that in the African myths of the New World the monkey becomes a central character. The second and third functions relate to form (style and language) and the act of interpretation: while Adebayo is Signifyin(g) upon Yoruba mythology – as we have already seen – the African-American trickster's act of signifying drives his narrative. Gates explains that the trickster figure differs in the African-American context because the signifying monkey functions primarily as "a vehicle for narration itself", the trope of literary revision rather than "a character in a narrative".[30] The following part of my discussion will elaborate upon the way in which Eshu Elegbara serves as a guiding force of interpretation while the signifying monkey's energy describes the novel's narrative strategy.

As I indicated earlier, the client's role (he masks his true identity as the divine trickster Eshu) is to help Boy interpret and realise his destiny by way of the trick. Boy is tricked into thinking that the case he is working on is about his client's pursuit of love, when in fact it is to do with his own search for happiness. Eshu's relation to destiny and his ability to assist in the outcome of a human's fate is, as Gates says of the Yoruba and Fon trickster figures, "inscribed in his role as the guiding force of interpretation itself".[31] As is the case for Yoruba and Fon peoples who consult their sacred texts in an attempt to ascertain their destinies, Boy can only begin to read his text of fate by way of the divine messenger. Gates' descriptions of the complex processes of mediation and translation involved in Ifa and Fa divination is significant in that in each process the supplicant's destiny is not literally revealed, nor is one's dilemma or the uncertainty of one's future resolved; rather the supplicant must attempt to interpret the densely metaphorical, ambiguous and indeterminate lyric poems or riddles that the *babalawo* (priest) translates from the visual signs he receives from the gods. The note that the client passes to Boy is a riddle of this sort and is somehow analogous to Boy's life and his quest to 'get overs'. Although Boy is suspicious of his client, and despite his love of riddles, he more or less ignores the note which is the key to his future.

It is not until he is well in pursuit of a suitable female for his client that he pays closer attention to the note, at which stage he muses:

> Perhaps I was not meant to take this note so literally, but I was surely supposed to draw some aid, to understand something from it. And this, fitted. If I am the man [the 'one man amongst a thousand'], this man ... Could it be? I stared at the rich, old lettering. I had been selected to complete a task in the great tradition. A pride I had not felt in some time percolated through me.[32]

The 'great tradition' here refers to the western heroic tradition in which the actions of knights and soldiers – real and fictional, such as Richard Lionheart, Cyrano de Bergerac and Troilus reflect the kinds of values Boy admires and aspires to: honour, bravery and chivalry.[33] However, the author's voice is also perceptible here in that the other utterance within the words 'great tradition' refers to Boy's as yet unconscious initiation into the ancient African tradition of his descendants. This phrase is just one example of the double-voicedness of Adebayo's text in Gates' and Bakhtin's sense of the word. The fact that Boy is unconscious of the fables and myths of African culture is evident in the closing pages when Eshu attempts to give him further clues to his own destiny by referring to a Yoruba legend concerning 'The Alafin of Ife'. Significantly, Boy remarks, "I was irked because I had so many legends under my belt, but not these."[34] Had he known this legend, he may have played the trickster's game better.

Alongside *Troilus and Cressida*, Edmond Rostand's *Cyrano de Bergerac* is a key intertext that the narrative is Signifyin(g) upon or repeats with a difference in order to explore the 'corrosion' of love, particularly between Black men and Black women, in contemporary Britain. The riddle: "one man amongst a thousand have I found. But a woman amongst those have I not found", has something to do with Boy's own approach to love, women and relationships. Boy, like Cyrano, believes that love has forsaken him: "I found I rarely welcomed the whole loss-leading business of intimacies with women. Most of the time now, when surplus built up, I went out and paid for its release".[35] The reasons for his lack of faith in male/female relationships is extremely different from and more complex than Cyrano's. It has to do with a history of negative and stereotypical representations of the Black male and the damaging psychological effects this produces on the psyche: low self-esteem and depression are two of the symptoms related to this that Boy attempts to protect himself from by avoiding long-term intimacy. However, in case of doubts arising about whether or not Adebayo's novel is misogynistic – the plot, for example, like *Troilus and Cressida*, centres on the exchange of a woman – Boy actually reflects on the possibility of his owns gender-biases and makes a concerted effort to keep an 'open mind' about the women he meets throughout his mission.[36]

It would also be an injustice to label a novel misogynistic which attempts to explore and understand the misunderstandings and mistrust between Black women and Black men. Lincia, a strong-minded business women and single-parent, whom Boy spots in a supermarket and arranges to meet with a view to her becoming 'the woman', conveys to Boy a negative impression of Black men. Boy reflects:

> I surmised from her crack about Black men's time, that she was probably a frustrated intimate. A lady who considered herself down but who found herself frequently exasperated by the imperfections of those less together than her. Slack Blacks, perhaps, was her issue. I would have to come across as competent and ambitious tonight to get her onside. Let 'driven' be my watchword. [37]

Boy's tricksy comment reveals something of the cunning and deception he feels is necessary if men like him – without the 'proper' credentials – are to stand a chance in the dating-game. For example, he poses as an accountant to both Lincia and Candy Bon-Bons so that he can win their trust and get them to buy his story about the mission. Boy is a modern-day trickster figure who, like the slaves in America and the Caribbean, uses the trickster's cunning and wit to survive. Gaining trust through subterfuge is central to the trickster's individual survival and as such offers a model for the protection of both personal and cultural identity; hence the language of Signification (naming by indirection) central to African-American culture. Boy also dons a variety of linguistic masks depending on his situation providing a further example of the way in which the novel's multivocality (another trickster trait) foregrounds language as 'heteroglossia' rather than single or unitary.[38] For Boy, trickery is essential not only in terms of surviving the deprivation of the streets and oppression from the 'keepers' of the state but, as his behaviour towards the women suggests, as a means of enticing the opposite sex.

The task to find a woman is a scam insomuch as the gods (Eshu and The Race Man) have already chosen the girl (named Girl) who is Boy's soul-mate. Taken together, the character names, Boy and Girl, pun on a conventional literary theme where 'boy meets girl' and both 'live happily ever after'. The book complicates this notion by exploring and questioning the extent to which oppressive forces damage individual and communal growth – in the context of the story, communal means any kind of human relationship (between men and women, families and communities). Eventually the gods intervene and reveal 'the woman' to Boy. Girl represents all that Boy has longed for: that is, his quest to achieve "great purpose" or "glory" in life is embodied in Girl's spiritual energy and grace rather than in material gain.[39]

The Boy meets Girl scenario therefore calls upon that idealised notion of love reflected in courtly love. After their initial meeting, the narrative moves from the dark and menacing space of the city into an idyllic landscape. The fantasy landscape perhaps describes "chivalric behaviour in a magical world" in conflict with reality.[40] With its "Nigerian associations and symbols", the landscape also reflects a country (in Africa) that Boy dreams about but cannot shape into consciousness.[41] The conflict between fantasy and reality, which the narrative's form eschews by blending traditions and styles, is presented in the climax of the plot. When it comes to the moment at which he must leave Girl and collect his money, Boy, already irked by the realisation that the client's task has been a scam all along and unable to bear further mockery, makes the fatal mistake that prevents him from achieving the task and joining the Race Man. Despite Eshu's warning encoded in the story of 'The Alafin of Ife', which centres on a disloyal warrior who tries to cheat the king, Boy cannot see beyond his own sense of loss. Self-discipline and integrity – chivalric qualities he endeavours to possess – elude him at this crucial moment in which he 'murders' the divine trickster (only now revealed to the reader as Eshu) and fails the task.

Boy's disappointment (also the reader's) at failing the task is the primary didactic function of Adebayo's contemporary trickster tale. This is where a direct comparison with African-American animal trickster tales is useful. Roberts remarks that these tales: 'served to remind enslaved Africans not only of the value of behaviours that they associated with the trickster but also of the consequences of acting like the dupe'.[42] As a contemporary trickster tale, *My Once Upon A Time* warns of the consequences for the individual who lacks discipline in that Boy's lack of selfdiscipline leads him to underachieve at an emotional level, in spite of his talents and his intellect. His reaction is symptomatic of the urban male emotionally hardened by city living. The didactic function of Adebayo's trickster tale is clear: the task or the trick set by the divine trickster is a test of Boy's self-discipline in an overwhelming situation. As Eshu tries to tell Boy, "you must remain loyal to the deal. Only then can we know of your situa ...".[43] How Boy deals with the assignment and what he learns about himself through trying to solve it, is the primary function of the trick. The issue of Boy's 'situation' is significant in that it relates to two literary models that disrupt both the 'myth' of Black male underachievement and notions of heroism (medieval and contemporary). Furthermore, it is the signifying monkey's language, his energy that drives the disruption. In other words the narrative is Signifiyin(g) upon Yoruba mythology and Shakespeare's *Troilus and Cressida* in order to challenge the destructive ideology of the street and the oppressing culture largely responsible for it.

I close this discussion of *My Once Upon A Time* by demonstrating how the narrative deflates myths concerning Black male underachievement by Signifiyin(g) upon Shakespeare's Troilus and Cressida which acknowledges that political and social factors do determine individual action and can destroy relationships. I will also suggest that Adebayo draws on the subversive energy underpinning Shakespeare's text alongside the trickster's influence in order to question medieval and contemporary notions of heroism such as those inscribed in street culture and the Romance tradition.

The tragic fall of Boy is anticipated earlier – in the novel via the debate between Lincia and Boy over whether individual action is determined by character or situation. Boy turns to Shakespeare's *Troilus and Cressida* to support his own philosophy that situation has more to do with individual behaviour and action than character. In Boy's interpretation of the play, Troilus 'loses it' when he learns of Cressida's faithlessness despite the fact that the brave knight once professes – as Boy puts it – "Oh, I'm a lover, not a fighter".[44] In the play, after discovering Cressida's ambiguous attentions to Diomedes,

Troilus embarks on a killing spree in the battle-fields outside the walls of Troy. According to Boy, politics undermine Troilus's character as the strong and brave knight he once was (the Trojan camp hands Cressida over to the Greeks in exchange for their respected warrior Antenor just as Boy should bring Girl to the client in exchange for the money and a new life). Boy parallels his task with the chivalric missions of knights but, like Troilus, he loses 'reason' and positive notions of chivalry and honour to the senses. Boy's commentary and interpretation of the play, of course, predicts his own performance at the end of the task.

Boy's determination to "move up the chambers" – a phrase adopted by the Wu Tang Clan from Shaolin myth which refers to physical and mental improvement – is undermined by his situation.[45] Boy's actions (the murder of Eshu) stem from his past and present in the area of the Rest where opportunities for 'his kind' are few or precarious and where the mentality is to protect oneself at any cost. While the novel acknowledges that Boy is a product of his environment, like Shakespeare's play, it reflects upon male pride and competitiveness: "a need to validate one's male sense of self-confidence through violence against other males".[46] Boy is constantly under pressure to protect himself by validating his masculinity in a world guided by the 'kill or be killed' ethos of contemporary gangsterism, a need that is itself linked to white male supremacy. Shakespeare's play deflates notions of heroism by showing how 'chivalry "masked savage and unregenerative self-interest"' and 'knighthood legitimated and rewarded rapacity' as it "glorified bravery and martial prowess".[47] Likewise, in *My Once Upon A Time* the honour and bravery of the street hero is deflated through the "fuckries and foolishness" of his actions .[48] There is no glory in the killing of the divine trickster, nor the futile intra-racial murders of Candy Bon-Bons and Boy's brother Junior which happen "because we don't care for us either".[49] Boy's pointed comment refers to the way in which Black life is not only inconsequential to sections of the dominant culture but also to those diverse peoples of the Black community whose political solidarity could effect change, and yet even with this insight he still kills the client. This latter point also references back to the ultimate message in Adebayo's first novel, *Some Kind of Black*, in which the Black community organisations which could have affected change became fractionalised.

Adebayo's novel does not by any means make light of the way in which an individual's situation often determines their action or behaviour but it does suggest that it is possible to transform reductive perceptions of reality as fixed and unchangeable by looking to other mythical and/or spiritual models such as the divine trickster in Yoruba mythology, the philosophical messages in the bible and the rap lyrics of the Wu Tang Clan. The novel encourages nurturing of the inner self (soul, mind, imagination or spirit) and does not allow its narrative or life itself to become consumed and hardened by stark realities: Boy's motto "reality rules, cos the city ain't pretty" is in this sense over-turned.[50] This is not escapism from social reality but a belief in the possibility of alternative realities (hence the response to the Wu Tang Clan refrain 'we don't believe in heaven so we're living in hell'). For example, the divine trickster-like figure, the Race Man, does not buy the 'situation' theory wholly – as his response to Boy's complaint about the city reveals: "yes, it gets tasty, and yes, it gets nasty but it isn't relevant at the deep end of the day. The city is a poor excuse for a better man, do you understand."[51] The presence of the divine trickster who is "the metaphor for the act of Black interpretation", and who signifies open-endedness and disclosure, reminds the reader and Boy that 'reality' is subject to constant change and revision. Race Man's final piece of advice – echoing the conclusion to Ecclesiastes – is: "one's striving must simply be to live the best life one can. You are life; deeply linked to all that lives."[52] When Boy bemoans how unfair and unkind life is, Race Man admonishes him, reminding him of how lightly he has got off despite his misdemeanours, and that if you sin, someone somewhere pays – not necessarily the sinner.[53](This is where the issue of moral retribution comes in to play, a belief, says Reginald Martin, "which underlies much of Black writing; that in the face of overwhelming, oppressive odds and arrogance, there is a magic talisman, a "force out there" which is "fair and retributive".[54] Boy shows an awareness of this karma-like concept when he says: "always the same: you're trying to move on, and some old shit drags you back down ... I wondered if it was possible to somehow bypass this trouble; to leave it behind me, too, in the distance".[55] For Boy, the 'bypass' away from trouble – at least away from moral, emotional and intellectual underachievement – is to think outside the philosophy of the street and look to higher models such as the divine trickster who awakens the would-be hero to his own potential.

NOTES AND REFERENCES

1   Adebayo, Diran, *My Once Upon A Time* (London: Abacus, 2000)

2   'Caught in the Rap Trap', *The Guardian*, 22 August 2000, http://books.guardian.co.uk [accessed August 2002]

3   As the BBC2 television documentary 'the hip-hop generation' (Wednesday, 25 June 2003) confirmed, hip-hop music (frequently subsumed within the term 'gansta rap') defines today's youth culture. Frequently berated because of its often sexist, misogynistic, and violent lyrics and images, hiphop is the most influential form to emerge from street culture and extremely popular among young Britons, Black and white alike

4   'Caught in the Rap Trap' is the title of an essay in which Adebayo considers the increasing ghettoisation of Black youngsters. There are echoes here of Patience Agbabi's poem 'The Rap-Trap' not only in the title, but also in terms of the way in which it questions the values conveyed in rap-music from within its structures. Agbabi's poem, like Adebayo's novel, adopts the rhythms, word-play and storytelling techniques characteristic of rap music (closely associated with hip-hop) and simultaneously questions the negative and reductive values and attitudes in street culture. Kadija Sesay, (ed), *Burning Words, Flaming Images: Poems and Short Stories by Writers of African Descent*, (Hackney: S.A.K.S. Publications, 1996), pp.113-114

5   'Thug Life – The Crisis Facing Young Black Men', Channel 4 Dispatches report by Geoff Schumann, Sunday 26 October 2003. Schumann visited housing estates in South London talking to young Black men to try and find out why they were killing each other. A disproportionate number of Black people are both victims and perpetrators of gun crime which rose by 30% in 2002. The national statistics agency puts this figure slightly higher at 36% with crimes involving firearms at 7, 362 in 2000/01 and 9, 974 in 2001/2002 http://www.statistics.gov.uk. When one boy stated that, like his friends, he was raised to show consideration, kindness and respect for others Schumann asked "what happened", the boy replied: "street life" which colludes with the way in which Adebayo's novel demonstrates how the city moulds the behaviour of its inhabitants

6   The street or rap term 'gangsta' re-appropriates the standard English word 'gangster'. It relates not simply to a criminal or anti-social behaviour but to the causes of contemporary 'gangsterism'. 'Gangsta' culture refers to a style that evolved in the ghetto culture of America in the 1980s – a culture, says Nelson George, besieged by drug related criminality and reflective of the 'go-go capitalism of Reagan's America (and its corporate greed)'. The term is politically fuelled and should not be read simply in terms of a glamorisation of criminality. As Michael Eric Dyson states 'gangsta rap is largely an indictment of mainstream and bourgeois Black institutions by young people who do not find conventional methods of addressing personal and social calamity useful'. However, Schumann's report (cited above) emphasises the influence rap crews have on the youth. 53% of young people agreed that violent lyrics effects their behaviour. The report suggested that the pressure to keep-up with the image of a 'bling-bling' (materially rich) lifestyle portrayed by the 'gangsta' image encouraged theft and violence. See Nelson George, *Hip Hop America* (New York: Penguin, 1998), pp.41 – 42 and Michael Eric Dyson, *Between God and Gangsta' Rap: Bearing Witness to Black Culture* (Oxford University Press USA, 1996), p.185

7   Adebayo, 'Caught in the Rap-Trap'

8   bell hooks, 'Sexism and Misogyny: Who Takes the Rap?" *Race and Ethnicity Collection* in Z magazine, February 1994, www.eserver.org.com [accessed 26 June 2003]. hooks's point is highly significant in that it dispels the myth that 'the gangsterism these young Black males embrace emerged from some unique Black experience'

9   See Andy Wood's article 'Contemporary Black British Urban Fiction: A 'Ghetto Perspective?', *Wasafiri* 36, Summer (2002), p.18 – 22

10 Although the trickster in most cultures is androgynous, Adebayo's tricksters or trickster-like figures only ever appear in male form (Boy, Eshu and The Race Man)

11 Jeanne Rosier Smith, *Writing Tricksters; Mythic Gambols in American Ethnic*

Literature (Los Angeles: University of California Press, 1997), p.49

[12] Rosier Smith, *Writing Tricksters*, p.156

[13] David Bevington remarks that *Troilus and Cressida* 'is an experimental play, characterised throughout by an intermingling of mode, tone, genre and style. Such an open-ended play needs to be read inclusively, rather than being racked on some Procrustean bed of generic classification'. See his introduction in *The Arden Shakespeare: Troilus and Cressida*, (2001), p.7

[14] Sami Ludwig, 'The Realist Trickster as Legba: Howells's Capitalist Critique', Mosaic 34, no.1 (March 2001), 173 – 84 (p.173)

[15] Henry Louis Gates Jr, 'Criticism in the Jungle' in *Black Literature and Literary Theory*, ed.by Henry Louis Gates Jr, (New York and London: Routledge, repr 1990) p.4 and M.M.Bahktin, 'From 'Discourse in the Novel', The Dialogic Imagination, ed. by M. Holquist, in *Modern Literary Theory: A Reader* (GB: Edward Arnold, 1989), p.205

[16] Henry Louis Gates Jr, *The Signifying Monkey: A Theory of African-American Literary Criticism* (Oxford University Press, 1988) p.51 and Jennifer Andrews, 'Reading Toni Morrison's *Jazz*: Rewriting the Tall Tale and Playing with the Trickster in the White American and African-American Humour Traditions', *Canadian Review of American Studies* 29, No 1(1999), p.90

[17] Author interview with Diran Adebayo, Cheltenham Festival of Literature, 17 October, 2003

[18] *The Holy Bible*, (Nashville: Thomas Nelson, 1987), pp. 653 – 54

[19] Traditional trickster tales are also communal experiences involving interaction – as Rosier Smith notes "novels use storytelling to set up dialogue among characters and with the reader, thereby lending a sense of orality to the written text". *Writing Tricksters*, p.23

[20] Martin Gray, *A Dictionary of Literary Terms*, 2nd edn, (Beirut: Longman York Press, 1992), p.74

[21] Bruce M. Metzger, *The Oxford Companion to the Bible* (Oxford University Press, 1993), p.177

[22] Adebayo, D. *My Once Upon A Time* (London: Abacus, 2000)

[23] Jacqueline Fulmer, "Men Ain't All" – A Reworking of Masculinity in Tales From the Hood, or, Grandma Meets the Zombie, *Journal of American Folklore* 115, no.457 (SUM/FAL 2002), 422 – 42 (p.424)

[24] Roberts, *From Trickster to Badman*, p.6

[25] Ibid. p.28

[26] Roberts introduces Susan Feldman who speaks of this kind of contestation as 'the traditional right of the individual'. *From Trickster to Badman*, p.28

[27] Epigraph

[28] Adebayo, D. *My Once Upon A Time* (London: Abacus, 2000), p.11

[29] Boy believes he has the answer to this – it being a line from a key *Wu Tang Clan* classic and answers 'we don't believe in heaven 'cos we're living in hell' (OT 8). Towards the end of the story Boy discovers that the answer to the refrain is 'we don't believe in heaven so we're living in hell' which destabilises the notion that reality cannot be re-configured: 'it couldn't always be 'cos' could it ... because that would just be to hate how it is, but we have to think to the way it should be. We have to love that ... How else could it get better' (OT 295)

[30] Henry Louis Gates Jr, 'The Blackness of Blackness: A Critique of the Sign and the Signifying Monkey', in *Black Literature and Literary Theory*, p.287

[31] Gates, *The Signifying Monkey*, p.23

[32] Adebayo, D. My Once Upon A Time (London: Abacus, 2000), p.150

[33] It has been pointed out to me that the reference to 'the great tradition' calls upon F.R. Leavis (1948) book of the same name. Although the novel implicitly challenges the

damaging elitist notion of a Canon of great 'English' works, I interpret Boy's use of the phrase as a desire to complete a knightly and thus honourable task

[34] Adebayo, D. *My Once Upon A Time* (London: Abacus, 2000), p.330

[35] Ibid. p.23

[36] Ibid. p.139

[37] Ibid. p.93

[38] Heteroglossia describes a diversity of voice/language/point of view in conflict with each other. Bakhtin reveals how the novel presents diverse social languages interacting through the characters' speeches, shifts in narration and changes in points of view thereby creating tension, contradiction and disruption to 'concrete socio-ideological language consciousness'. `From 'Discourse in the Novel', p.200 & 205. Like Ishmael Reed before him, Adebayo creates his own syncretic literary model. He draws on a variety of language-levels and discourse possibilities which reflects Bakhtin's concept of language. He blends slang expressions with 'standard' discourse, uses a variety of Black British Englishes along with 'standard English' and his discourse is taken from the streets, popular music, television and film as well as diverse types of literature.

[39] Adebayo, D. *My Once Upon A Time* (London: Abacus, 2000), p.153

[40] Gray, *A Dictionary of Literary Terms*, p.251

[41] Bruce King, 'My Once Upon a Time', *World Literature Today* 74, no.3 (Summer 2000), 591 (p.591)

[42] *From Trickster to Badman*, p.38

[43] Adebayo, D. *My Once Upon A Time* (London: Abacus, 2000), p.334

[44] This is perhaps a contemporary take on Troilus's 'why should I war without the walls of Troy/That find such cruel battle here within?/Each Trojan that is master of his heart/Let him to field; Troilus, alas, hath none', *The Arden Shakespeare*, p.132

[45] The Wu Tang Clan are an American hip-hop band from Staten Island in New York popular with Boy in his gang days. Their lyrics are gritty, immediate, often complex and always politically charged – rapping stories of the street and Black history. The Wu Tang's rhymes are directed at mobilising the oppressed in and beyond the Projects. They seem particularly concerned with the 'seeds' (the younger generation) and their stories offer nourishment and encouragement in a language and medium the urban youth can relate to. They discourage intra-racial violence and their knightly war is not against the white race but the laws, legislations and ideologies that thwart African-Americans and other oppressed groups. Parallel to Adebayo's message, some of their tracks suggest that the youth need to overcome spiritual, cultural and socio-political ignorance and to find creative and productive channels for their anger and frustration

[46] Bevington, 'Introduction', *Arden: Troilus & Cressida*, p.31

[47] Ibid. p.16

[48] Adebayo, D. *My Once Upon A Time* (London: Abacus, 2000), p.288

[49] Ibid. p.288

[50] Ibid. p.6

[51] Ibid. p.179

[52] Compare with: 'if effort and toil, if even piety and justice avail so little, the only profitable attitude to adopt is to live in the world as one finds it, to be moderate in all things (even piety), and to enjoy the good pleasure that life gives, for even this is a gift, and fulfilment may not come with success'. Metzger, *The Oxford Companion to the Bible*, p.177

[53] Adebayo, D. *My Once Upon A Time* (London: Abacus, 2000), p.181

[54] *Ishmael Reed & The New Black Aesthetic Critics* (London: Macmillan, 1988), p.81

[55] Adebayo, D. *My Once Upon A Time* (London: Abacus, 2000), p.149

Significant corporeality: bodies and identities in Jackie Kay's fiction

Patrick Williams

> "We are in the presence of three contingent dimensions of significant corporeality: anatomical sex, gender identity and gender performance." (Judith Butler, *Gender Trouble*)[1]

> "Stomping, stamping, hooting, whistling, cheering. They want more of him. ...They want more blood. He dives back down again. He has barely come out. When he plays his trumpet, his left leg is uncontrollable. It bends and cracks like a tree in the wind. His foot going out and coming in. His eyes shut tight to keep out the light. He is the music. The blood dreaming. The long slow ache. All the light is in the music -- soaring, flying."[2]

Joss Moody in concert: a great performer; something of a jazz legend, in fact. Loosely based on the American jazzman Billy Tipton, and transposed to Scotland, Joss is, however, a more consummate performer than anyone realised, since on his death he is discovered to be a woman – or at least anatomically female. The shocking revelations, the questions about Joss's identity – who or what was he 'really'? – have profound implications for those close to him – the closer, the more profound – in terms of their own sense of identity, of who they, in turn, might 'really' be. This "troubling" (in Judith Butler's terms) of gender identity is the product of Joss Moody's transgendered performance – and performance is of course the term most frequently associated with Butler's radical perspective on the social constitution of gendered identities. Against that background, the first part of this chapter will explore the interweaving voices in Jackie Kay's prize-winning novel *Trumpet* as they meditate on the production or performance of identity and – especially in relation to Joss Moody – on bodies which perform.

    Trumpet is itself a bravura performance of a kind not typical in novels, but one that makes sense – might even have been anticipated – in the context of Jackie Kay's earlier poetry and plays. It is constructed from the interweaving voices and narratives of a wide range of characters – Joss's widow Millie, his adopted son Coleman, his mother, a childhood friend, the registrar, funeral director, band members, fans. The inhabiting and voicing of characters has been one of the most impressive aspects of Jackie Kay's poetry, from the three women in *Adoption Papers* to Black and mixed race figures such as Sarah Bateman, Christian Sanderson, and Gambia in more recent work. Here, the range of first person and third person focalised voices is supplemented by other forms – letters, newspaper editorials, music company publicity handouts – in a multi-vocal, multi-perspectival narrative. One of the reasons for this inter-weaving multi-vocality is no doubt that Jackie, as she stated in an interview, "wanted to write a novel whose structure was very close to jazz itself."[3] Most of the characters or voices are concerned with the question of identity – Joss's, inevitably, and, for those who recognise the implications of the revelation, their own.

Judith Butler's provocative – and influential – thesis in *Gender Trouble* is that gender is not simply the historically – or culturally - mutable construct foisted onto 'real' (coherent, stable, pre-existing, fully sexually-differentiated) subjectivities, as earlier feminist theory argued; the idea that "for instance, within the sex/gender distinction, sex poses as 'the real' and the 'factic', the material or corporeal ground upon which gender operates as an act of cultural *inscription*."[4] For Butler, it is not that some 'essence' of identity is expressed by what someone does or 'is', rather that identity is only constituted because it is repeatedly enacted by individuals. In other words, it is the very doing or performing of the forms or styles of gender that creates the effect of gendered identity.

One of the targets of Butler's conceptualisation of identity is the older, but very tenacious, model of subjectivity: the idea that we are fully self-conscious, autonomous individuals, able to make unconstrained choices about our lives, and possessing something like a 'real' or true identity, a core being which survives despite life's vicissitudes. One of the problems with Butler's attack on that model is that although most of us (including Butler, I would imagine), live day-to-day as if we were that sort of person, many of us are aware of the things – unconscious desires, historical or social forces, insidiously influential ideologies and discourses – which make us other than the fully rational or autonomous people we would like to believe we are. There is something like the same disparity between radical position and 'core' belief in the novel. On the one hand, in a way that accords very well with Butler's theories, Joss's life and performance destabilise notions of gender, and even identity more widely. On the other and in a manner which it is hard to imagine Butler accepting, the novel in general – positions taken by Millie and Coleman in particular – supports the idea of a true identity to be discovered, uncovered or asserted in spite of everything. A similar partial utilisation of strategies that Butler outlines and promotes, and the simultaneous retention of the categories which she critiques, has been noted in relation to Angela Carter's fiction.[5]

The performance of gender is, however, as Butler notes, one of the dimensions of "significant corporeality." In this perspective, gender only matters (is significant), and has meaning (signifies), in so far as it is "corporeal" or embodied. It is as body (female, and later dead) that Joss constitutes the greatest disturbance of the meaning of gender – or at least of people's ordinary understandings of it. The novel's moments of greatest shock are those of living revelation (to Millie), and post-mortem (to the funeral director, and then to Coleman) of the bodily fact of Joss's femaleness – the absence of penis, the presence of breasts. For the funeral director, who thinks he has "seen it all" already, it is a life- (and career-) altering moment: "It had never happened to him before. He had never had a man turn into a woman before his very eyes. He felt it to be one of those defining moments in his life that he would be compelled to return to again and again."[6] Joss's bodily performance has been flawless throughout his life – and even beyond it: as a fully-dressed corpse he still manages to convince the funeral director, who thinks he knows a thing or two about bodies. Flawless? Well, almost: at the same time, Joss's smooth, unmarked skin and full lips, his high voice and 'girlish' laugh occasion comments and mark the limits and the weak points of this bodily enactment. The comments also occasion a very bodily rebuttal: Big Red McCall, Joss's drummer, blind himself to the real meanings of what he is seeing and hearing, loyally beats up anyone foolish enough to notice these significant corporeal moments.

An additional performative dimension is that of style: "The effect of gender is produced through the stylisation of the body and, hence, must be understood as the mundane way in which bodily gestures, movements, and styles of various kinds constitute the illusion of an abiding gendered self."[7] Style and stylisation are central to the ways in which Joss pursues his embodiment of masculinity. In addition to the mundane – the carefully put-on layers of clothing to disguise the breasts, the rolled-up socks inside the boxer shorts – there is the fact that, "The man had style. He wore unusual shirts that had five cufflinks, specially ordered. Beautifully stitched. He never looked like he'd just got out of bed. His trousers always creased."[8] The cufflinks could, however, be seen as another potential weak point (or weak link) in Joss's performance: on the one hand, they might be regarded as an emphatic (over-) statement of masculinity, since women don't wear them; on the other, such an 'unnatural' profusion of quasi-jewellery (who wears <u>five</u> sets of cufflinks??) risks suggestions of effeminacy, undermining all the careful construction.

And these are not the only occasions of slippage: before she knows the (anatomical) truth about Joss, Millie has several moments of unwitting insight: "He tells me his name is Joss Moody, and I ask him if that is his real name. He is offended... Of course it is his real name, what am I talking about? I tell him it sounds like a stage name, like a name someone would make up in anticipation of being famous...At night, I watch Joss walk up the street, hands in his pockets. He has a slow, deliberate walk, like he's practised it."[9] Both of these encapsulate the power of the performance to maintain its air of authenticity despite certain individuals' ability to in fact see through it – if not to follow up their insights.

Other aspects of the style and stylisation of Joss include going to the barber's and even more so, shaving. The latter is made as elaborate, ritualised and masculine as possible, with special shaving soap, brush, razor, and shaving mirror and the ritual in turn becomes part of Coleman's life. However, whereas Millie's attitude manages to make elements like these of her husband's existence simply ordinary, for Coleman they constitute the biggest lie, greatest betrayal, the source of his angry uncertainty about himself and his past: "See that is what I mean. I'm going to have to go back over my whole life with a fine-tooth comb and look for signs like that."[10]

Joss's performance of gender also has its aspects of non-performance, which again mark its limits. not going to hospital; not using public urinals; not sunbathing or going swimming on holiday – all of these are acts which would expose the anatomical truth in different ways. Ironically, protecting the 'truth' of the body in the end becomes more important than protecting the body itself: when Joss becomes seriously – eventually terminally – ill, to Coleman's utter incomprehension he will not see a doctor, still less allow himself to be hospitalised.

If the right clothes are important in Joss's transgendered performance, they are equally crucial to the tabloid journalist Sophie Stones' effort to make herself into "the woman I'd like to be. I know

I'm not there yet, but the clothes can lie. Was that it with Joss Moody? That the clothes could lie?"[11] As usual, Sophie's attempt to understand Joss is a failure: in fact, something like the opposite is true, and clothes are the means to truth – the truth which matters most to Joss, the truth of music.

> If it wasn't for his horn he would be dead and gone. Years ago. Dead in his spirit, and still living. It doesn't matter a damn he is somebody he is not. None of it matters. The suit is just the suit the body holds. The body needs the suit to wear the horn. Only the music knows everything. Only the dark sweet heart of the music.[12]

"The body needs the suit to wear the horn" – this more than anything gives a clue as to the driving force behind Joss's choice of a transgendered life. Music for him possesses power, pain and pleasure, beyond anything else. Joss performs gender in order to perform music. He performs his identity in order to enter a different performative space, where that identity no longer has substance or importance, where the corporeal is in fact no longer significant.

> The music is in his blood. His cells. But the odd bit is that down at the bottom, the blood doesn't matter after all. None of the particulars count for much... All his self collapses – his idiosyncracies, his personality, his ego, his sexuality, even, finally, his memory. All of it falls away like layers of skin unwrapping. He unwraps himself with his trumpet... The horn ruthlessly strips him bare till he ends up with no body, no past, nothing.[13]

The musical performance as locus of truth – "Never lying. Telling it like it is."[14] – takes on an added importance in the context of a life where a crucial part cannot quite be told like it is, where a kind of lie is lived daily. In its dissolution of individual ego and identity, the music grants access to a wider identity – transhistorical, transcultural, potentially universal? This, it would seem, is a performance without the weak links, slippages, inconsistencies or anxieties which attend the daily (trans)gendered versions and where the style and stylisation, the ritual and repetition, function in more empowering and liberatory modes.

At one level, Joss embodies or enacts a lifetime of "subversion of identity" in Judith Butler's terms, a breaking of the bounds of normality. (Sophie Stones, in her usual perceptive and understanding way, calls him a "pervert"). At the same time, the aim of this subversion is the creation of (the appearance of) absolute normality: the happily married couple, the nuclear family with their adopted, but much loved, child. Here, there may be something of what Butler describes as "a transgendering that *reidealises* certain bourgeois forms of heterosexual exchange."[15] However, whether or not the form of their relationship problematically reconfirms bourgeois or heterosexual norms, for Joss and (especially) Millie, it *is* normal, not unusual. Even the daily ritual of Millie wrapping Joss in bandages to disguise his breasts is ordinary for her. "That was it. Other than that, they didn't exist. Not really."[16] (Interestingly enough, they 'don't exist' to such an extent that they form no part of Joss and Millie's lovemaking, since Millie says, "That was the closest I came to them, wrapping them up."[17] The fact that it is *his* breasts is another sign of the normalisation that has taken place: for Millie, Joss is always 'he', regardless of the circumstances. Even looking at photos of Joss – now, in everyone's eyes *"this person who is obviously a woman, once you know"* – Millie still can't see 'her', and doesn't feel she ever will. In the same sort of way, she can't see their relationship as lesbian: for her, that is just an inappropriate label that some people want to impose on her and Joss. Rather than simply being a refusal to face facts on Millie's part, this reluctance to accept reductive categorisation brings Millie closer to another aspect of Judith Butler's theorising. Butler is perhaps best known as the major figure in queer theory. One of the aims of queer is to unsettle meanings, categories or labels that appear unhelpful or restrictive:

> "Claiming a queer identity is an effort to speak to and from
> the differences and silences that have been suppressed by the
> homo-hetero binary, an effort to unpack the monolithic
> identities 'lesbian' and 'gay', including the intricate always
> lesbian and gay sexualities are inflected by heterosexuality,
> race, gender and ethnicity."[18]

This deliberate undecidability of identity – which queer theory (slightly paradoxically, perhaps) would regard as a truer image of how people really are – has recently been theorised as 'fuzzy gender', following the mathematical category of fuzzy logic.[19] In a manner reminiscent of Eve Sedgwick's 'homo-social continuum', the fuzzy model offers a spectrum of positions, varying shades of 'grey', approximations to the privileged sex/gender norms (here seen as unattainable and polarised). Again for Millie, rejection of labelling is not a denial of truth – she is, for example, explicit about the passionate mutuality of their sex life.

Hennessy's quote reminds us of something which we might have expected to be foregrounded, but in many ways the novel almost sidelines – the question of race. Joss and Coleman are both mixed race – Joss brought up by his white Scottish mother, Coleman obviously by Joss and Millie, after his adoption. However, despite the racial identity of two of the three main characters, race is not central to the questioning of identity which takes place. In that, there is the possibility that the novel is echoing the lack of attention to racial issues which correspond to the reason why queer theory has been criticised. That, however, does not seem – to be what is happening in *Trumpet*. If the novel is indeed structured like jazz, then race is one of the motifs which occurs quietly, occasionally, at first, only to figure as solo, crescendo, thematic resolution in the letter "to be read after my death" that Joss leaves for Coleman. What the letter contains is the narrative of Black identity which Coleman has repeatedly asked Joss for and Joss, just as repeatedly, denied:

> "He said, you make up your own bloodline Coleman. Make it up, and trace it back. Design your own family tree... It drove me mad. Which one? I said. Which one is true? It doesn't matter a damn, he said. You pick. You pick the one you like best, and that one is true."[20]

Coleman is sure Joss is wrong in this. In a sense he is both right and wrong. In the context of performative identities and even performative families (the relationship of Joss, Millie and Coleman to one another is not strictly 'natural') the kind of choice and agency Joss advocates, a refusal to be constrained or conditioned by accident of birth or biology, is important. In other ways, this advice flies in the face of what Joss has said to Coleman about the importance of history, of knowing 'our' stories, the ones that matter. As Joss paradoxically says to Coleman, "there's more future in the past than there is in the future,"[21] emphasising the importance of Black history generally, but also the contribution of Black people to particular histories such as music. Beyond mere knowing, Joss's musical performances encapsulate that history (and others):

> "So when he takes off, he is the whole century galloping to its

close. The wide moors. The big mouth. Scotland. Africa. Slavery. Freedom."[22]

In the end, Joss decides that his father's story *is* worth telling, remembering, taking into the future. What had previously been for him just the story of any Black man in the diaspora now becomes an important link between fathers and sons (parents and children) – however paradoxically constituted – all of whom have gone by different names: Joss's father is renamed John Moore when he comes to Scotland; John Moore's daughter Josephine becomes Joss Moody; Joss's son Coleman is born William Dunsmore. Whether it is the apparently unexceptional nature of John Moore's story that makes it seem not worth telling for so long, Joss finally hands on the narrative to Coleman and also frees him in terms of what he chooses to remember from the past – familial and racial. No doubt, one Black person's standing in for the whole of the African diaspora can make them appear 'just like all the rest', of little or no account; but from a slightly different perspective, it can of course confer a remarkable representational status on the individual and their narrative and who and what they are becomes anything but insignificant. In something of the same way, the novel's downplaying of the 'obvious' issue of race can make it seem as if it doesn't matter very much; clearly, though, it matters a great deal.

Joss Moody's death raises all manner of questions about truth, authenticity, reality and identity. Coleman's desire to know more about the racial family history is just one aspect of his own and others' quests for certainty and stability in relation to their own identities, as well as knowledge in relation to Joss. Coleman is in an unusual situation – at the same time as he is forced to reassess his personal and familial history and question his identity, he is also simultaneously trying to find out more about his father, while explaining and narrating his father to the journalist Sophie Stones. At one point, he wants to ask her one of the novel's key questions: "Do you think this is the truth?" but angrily decides that it doesn't matter if it is or it isn't, because his father lived a lie – and by implication forfeited any claim to have the truth told about him. This suits Sophie Stones perfectly, since, despite her occasional declarations of wanting to find out "what made her tick", all she wants is a certain kind of information or fact that will fit the narrative – Joss Moody as 'weirdo' or pervert. Factual information, of course, has its limitations. As one of the series of letters (presumably sent to a newspaper, though it isn't made clear) says:

> "We question this notion that somebody who lives their life as a man and is discovered to be female at the time of death was really a woman all along. What is 'really' in this context? What is the force of that reality?" (Transvestites Anonymous Group)[23]

Like Coleman's unspoken question, this is crucial: establishing what constitutes the real; assessing 'the force of that reality', are the essential epistemological and ethical tasks for readers of the novel (if not of the hypothetical newspaper). In one important area, as we have already seen, 'the force of that [anatomical] reality' is less significant than the force of music for Joss. (Again, revealingly, trying to work out Joss's motivation, Sophie Stones refuses this truth, since it does not fit her reductive, tabloid-framed categories of 'real' human behaviour: "All for the sake of playing a trumpet... Balls. I'm not buying it."[24]

It is at this point that the novel marks one of its significant divergences from Judith Butler's theorising. For Butler, part of the force of the concept of performativity is that it does away with the idea of the voluntaristic agency of the subject – consciously choosing and being in control of who or what we are. While there are a number of well-established theories that would go part of the way with Butler (feminism, psychoanalysis, Marxism), her Foucauldian perspective reduces identity to the performance of powerful pre-existing scripts, discourses which speak to you, rather than being spoken by you. That process is relatively easy to see in operation, as most of us daily perform the powerful scripts of the dominant versions of gendered ideology in our society. It is, however, less easy to see as a description of someone who is determinedly *not* following those scripts. In this context, unless music is granted a quite extraordinary power over Joss (and at a time when he has not yet become Joss) – for example, more than the historically-grounded, institutionallyconfirmed, socially – or ideologically-articulated discourses of 'normal' gender identity – it is hard to understand how Joss does not actively or consciously choose to become who he is, as well as what kind of performance is necessary to achieve that becoming. This critical transitional moment in Joss's life remains obscure, even to Millie, and despite all the attempts by her and others to reconstitute that life. However, a clue as to the form that the transition might have taken is offered in Joss's account of his father:

"Life, he told me, was like a fork of lightning. He could see
exactly where one decision violently parted company with another
and a new future flared up before him."[25]

The role of clarity of perception and decisive choice in constructing
a particular future represents a subjectivity significantly at odds with
that outlined by Butler, but without which *Trumpet* would arguably
make less sense.

As indicated earlier, the relationship between jazz and identity is
important. Coleman recalls Joss: "He goes into this long thing about
jazz being improvised and being different versions of the same
thing"[26] – which sounds like a reasonable approximation of how
Joss might understand himself and his identities. At its most extreme
or powerful, music allows for, or enforces, a dissolution of identity
beyond normal limits; it also allows a degree of knowledge,
including self-knowledge, which is preternatural, for example:

"The place down there: it forces him to witness his own death. He
watches open-mouthed the card he's going to be dealt. He watches
himself in flashback. ... The face of his undertaker scares him the
most. Albert Holding."[27]

As well as this access to the realm of the true, real or authentic, jazz
permits or encourages a kind of inauthenticity: Coleman's
recollection continues,

"Then he looks sad, he says something about people being only
talented for one moment in time... The ones that have a short time
can't believe it when their talent runs out, so they scramble to get
it back, impersonate themselves. Mimic. Parody. Act themselves.
He says jazz can get away with that better than most stuff. He
looks sad then. Like he's a conman or something."[28]

Although there is no suggestion that Joss has ever descended to this
level of self parody, the idea that he might be seen as inauthentic in
other ways clearly saddens him.

Jackie Kay's recent collection of short stories *Why Don't You
Stop Talking?*[29] approaches bodies and identities in ways which are
both similar to, and different from *Trumpet*. Again, these are
strongly voiced or inhabited characters. Half the stories are in the
first person; the other half in the focalised third person. These are

very much embodied identities, though none approximates Joss Moody's style or stylisation in that embodiment. There is also nothing as bodily transgressive as Joss's performance (unless we count the very strange events of 'Shell'), but bodies are more generally a problem for the narrators or focalised central characters. Here, bodies are overweight, unloved, unattractive, ageing and dying. It may or may not be significant that with just one exception – the (token) male in 'Shark! Shark!' – these are all women's bodies. It may or may not be significant that the most loved body (we assume) – that of the lesbian narrator in "Married Women" with her series of lovers – is the one least present in the story.

In this realm of unhappy corporeality, it is noteworthy that the nearest thing to a state of happiness is represented by the eponymous Physics and Chemistry, whose relationship appears to be only occasionally fully physical. It is also noteworthy that they represent the clearest example of a particular kind of identity performance in the collection. For years, they have been living the role of respectable spinsters and schoolteachers, and – with occasional Shirley Bassey-induced lapses – generally living up to that image of respectability. Nevertheless, the performance itself is not necessarily completely convincing: most of their colleagues in the staffroom know, or believe they know, but it is not until the complaint of a homophobic parent results in both of them losing their jobs, that the pressure to perform is removed. In their new incarnation as Plain and Purl (they open a wool shop together), they become happier and more physical, (demonstrative and sexual), and less 'performatively' (i.e. spinsterly) or 'inauthentically' dressed.

A different kind of performance of identity is represented by 'Timing'. It is one of the noticeable aspects of the narrators and central characters in *Why Don't You Stop Talking?* that a number of them are slightly – or more than slightly – odd, and here the narrator's personal sense of stability depends on a highly ritualised performance of routine: seeing the same people in the same places in the same order as she goes to work every day; obsessively cleaning and tidying, such as disinfecting the toilet after every use. This rigid world is disturbed by physicality and passion when she witnesses 'the Kiss of the Century' as two women embrace by the river. This singular event disrupts the repetitive performances, and spontaneity and emotion begin to creep into her life; though in some ways she perhaps does no more than exchange an obsession with cling-film and 'Flash with added bleach' for an obsession with the women kissing. In keeping with several of the stories, however, there is no positive outcome for the narrator: hoping every day to see the two women again, she eventually comes across one of them on her own, but her attempt at a conversational gambit merely results in the other woman looking at her as if she were mad.

The only story in the collection is which in any way foregrounds race is 'Out Of Hand' – and even here, the treatment is low-key. Rose McGuire Roberts was one of the *Windrush* generation – quite literally: she arrived on it in June 1948. Over the next 50 years, racism has been a daily feature of Rose's existence and while in some senses it is just stuff she puts up with (despite being a highly qualified ward sister, she is always given the bedpans to empty), at the same time, racist abuse – patients telling her to "get back to the jungle" – constitutes a trauma she cannot articulate. Eventually, even her escape from daily racism -the cinema – is poisoned when at the time of the 1958 race riots she is told to "Go back to your country" – having, like so many, thought that England might be her own country. In many ways, however, what matters most about Rose is what she shares with the central characters of 'The Oldest Woman in Scotland' and 'A Guid Scots Death' – their (female) bodies, aged by a lifetime of hard work; their problems with children and grandchildren; above all, their memories – flying in the face of the passage of time, the ageing of bodies.

In several of the short stories, the focus is on body parts: the tongue in *Why Don't You Stop Talking?*, hands in 'Out of Hand', breasts in 'Big Milk'. In the latter, the narrator is doubly separated from what Kleinian psychoanalysis might see as the "good breast". The fact that her lover has had a baby has resulted in a lack of access to the lover's body in general and the breasts in particular. Ironically, the narrator was not previously particularly interested in her lover's breasts before the baby began its two-year monopoly of them, but is now obsessed: "Worse than a man," says her lover. In turn, this loss reminds her of her original deprivation – the maternal breast, then the mother altogether: "I was never breast-fed myself. My mother spoon fed me for two weeks then left. I never saw her again."[30] In addition to bringing about the separation of the narrator's body from that of her lover, the baby affects both the narrator's relationship to her own body, and her sense of who she is:

"The baby has converted me into a bland, boring, possessive
lover who doesn't know her arse from her elbow. There are bits

of my body that I can only remember in the dark. They are not touched."[31]

Suddenly, the narrator's sense of self-identity appears dependent on some kind of reestablished relationship to the original withheld maternal breast and on a whim she sets off to find her birthmother (and her breasts) in Scotland. This, however, is another tale with no clear or positive resolution. Having driven all day, the narrator arrives tired and thirsty at the mother's cottage, where there are two emblematic bottles of milk on the doorstep. She drinks from one but it is stale and sour; the other is the same. She knocks at the cottage door but there is no answer; peering through the letterbox all she sees is darkness. The maternal body and all it signifies continues to be absent, denied, irrecoverable.

While the importance of 'voiced' characters in Jackie Kay's work has already been mentioned, *Why Don't You Stop Talking?* includes fascinating and very different examples of oral performance. In the title story of the collection, the narrator, one of many mixed race characters in the book, is someone whose physical excess is matched by her verbal access. Very overweight, and doing nothing about it – except periodically feel paranoid – the narrator also has "One of those tongues that gets me into a load of trouble. I can't help myself. I just come out with what is in my head and it has caused me terrible problems all my life."[32] At the same time, her identity as someone who speaks her mind seems to her to be vindicated, "because nine times out of ten I'm right."[33] This sense of 'right speaking' is, however, tempered by the self knowledge that she is also prone to 'rant', for example at her former boyfriend. In the same sort of ambivalent manner, verbal excess is very much bound up with her physicality: saying too much is strongly linked to "my time of the month," while trying not to say too much is "as hard as bursting for a piss;"[34] at the same time there is the implication that the verbal excess is not 'really' her: "Sometimes it even feels like the words are not my decisions, like somebody else is talking with my tongue."[35] Whether it is the result of this kind of ambivalent awareness; whether it is the fact that the narrator, like many of the characters in the collection, is living on the edge (of normality, self-control, reason, or whatever); whether it is related to the feeling that "my tongue is going to get me killed"; whether it is connected to a desire to become one of "the silent ones" who the narrator feels have power in the world – whatever the cause, still nothing quite prepares the reader for the sudden shocking punishment meted out to the transgressive body part.

The conclusion of the narrator in *Why Don't You Stop Talking?*, that silence is more powerful than speech, is not one which is shared by the narrator of 'In between talking about the elephant.' In this intense, moving story, speech – or rather a special kind of narrative performance – is almost the most powerful thing there is, though bodies also matter terribly. The tone of the narrative is intense; the narrator's thoughts and actions appear not altogether usual: this looks like another 'on the edge' narrative – and in some ways it is. Unlike the other stories, however, there is a more 'normal' motivation here. In their 24th floor apartment overlooking the city, two women tell one another stories and facts about elephants as one of them slowly dies. At its most positive, this performance fights for life – like Scheherazade telling her 1001 stories in order to stave off the threat of imminent death. The ability of the linguistic performance to preserve life in the face of death is the most striking proof of the power of both language and performance. There is performative power, too, in the repetitive ritualised form that these narrative sessions have taken. Less optimistically, the subject is chosen "because elephants know all about sorrow" – and many examples concern the dignity in suffering and profound emotional attachments of these remarkable animals. Still less – optimistically, the stories represent a way of filling the time before the inevitable moment with significance – elephants matter. If the narratives of elephant emotion, suffering and death might seem to risk anthropomorphism, in a neat reversal the narrator performs an elephant ritual around her lover's dead body, and prepares herself to attempt the same fidelity in death as demonstrated by these 'lesser' animals.

The dying body in 'In between talking about the elephant' – desperately, lovingly, intimately nurtured – is the antithesis of that of the narrator in 'A Guid Scots Death', kept alive by medical intervention in the shape of wires, drips, tubes, oxygen masks and depersonalised human contact, where her major concern is that she should not die without the minimal dignity of her false teeth. Both are among the numerous bodies in the collection which are 'problematic', if not – in Kristevan terms – "abject": in other words, those bodies which society does not like the look of; which it undervalues, marginalises or ignores, as it increasingly and obsessively, valorises the young, the beautiful, the thin, the visibly healthy.

Equally important is the fact that these bodes are subject neither to sentimentalising nor over easy celebration, nor an equally over easy discourse of victimhood. Their corporeality may be altogether ordinary (and problematic) it is none the less significant for all that.

NOTES AND REFERENCES

[1] Butler, Judith, *Gender Trouble*, (London: Routledge, 1990)

[2] Kay, Jackie, *Trumpet*, (London: Picador, 1998) p.134

[3] Kay, Jackie, interview with *Bold Type*,Volume 3.1 'THERAPY' April, 1999

[4] Butler, J., *Gender Trouble*, (London: Routledge, 1990) p.186

[5] Trevenna, J., 'Gender as Performance: questioning the 'Butlerification' of Angela Carter's fiction', *Journal of Gender Studies*, 11/3/2002

[6] Kay, Jackie, *Trumpet*, (London: Picador, 1998) p.111

[7] Butler, J., *Gender Trouble*, (London: Routledge, 1990) p.179

[8] Kay, Jackie, *Trumpet*, (London: Picador, 1998) p.172

[9] Ibid. pp.13, 15

[10] Ibid. p.48

[11] Ibid. p.49

[12] Ibid. p.135-6

[13] Ibid. p.135

[14] Ibid. p.132

[15] Butler J., *Bodies That Matter*, (London: Routledge, 1993), p.240

[16] Kay, Jackie, *Trumpet*, (London: Picador, 1998) p.240

[17] Ibid. p.239

[18] Hennessy, R., 'Queer Theory, Left Politics', in Makdisi et al. eds, *Marxism beyond Marxism*, London, Routledge, 1995, p.216

[19] Tauchert, A., 'Fuzzy Gender: between female-embodiment and intersex', *Journal of Gender Studies*, 11/1/2002

[20] Kay, Jackie, *Trumpet*, (London: Picador, 1998), p.58-59

[21] Ibid. p.190

[22] Ibid. p.136

[23] Ibid. p.159-60

[24] Ibid. p.127

[25] Ibid. p.274

[26] Ibid. p.163

[27] Ibid. p.132-3

[28] Ibid. p.163

[29] Kay, J., *Why Don't You Stop Talking?*, (London: Picador, 2002)

[30] Ibid. p.29

[31] Ibid. p.30

[32] Ibid. p.41

[33] Ibid. p.40

[34] Ibid. p.42

[35] Ibid. p.41

'Pivoting the Centre': The Fiction of Andrea Levy[1]

Maria Helena Lima

> "The country where I live, among people so unaware of our shared past that all they would see if they were staring at my aunt would be a Black woman acting silly." – Andrea Levy[2]

Readers already familiar with some of the post-colonial rewritings of the conventions of the novel of development feel comfortably 'at home' when reading Andrea Levy's coming-of-age novels. For Levy immerses us in the stories of development of girls born in England to Jamaican parents, who struggle to (re)create their identities and allegiances as they grow up on a London council estate, in the sixties and seventies, among systemic racism and skinhead violence. *Every Light in the House Burnin'* (1994) and *Never far from Nowhere* (1996) focus on the renegotiation of identities fundamental both to migration itself and to the novels that attempt to recreate the subjectivities of children of migrants and on the patterns of migration and displacement that colonisation initiates, and that neocolonial conditions have unfortunately helped maintain.

Levy's more recent novels, *Fruit of the Lemon* (1999) and the Orange Prize and Whitbread novel-of-the-year award winner *Small Island* (2004), are historical narratives that offer "a critical return", in Antoinette Burton's formulation, "to the connections between metropole and colony, race and nation", exploring the extent to which "empire was not just a phenomenon 'out there,' but a fundamental and constitutive part of English culture and national identity at home."[3] *Fruit of the Lemon* powerfully corrects the protagonist's view, probably shared by many Black Britons of her generation (Levy herself was born in London in 1956), that "[her] history started when the ship carrying [her] parents sailed from Jamaica and docked in England [significantly] on Guy Fawkes night."[4] Faith has to travel to Jamaica to learn the history of her ancestors, in all its complexity, in order to acknowledge the African, Irish, Scot, English components of her identity. After reading *Small Island*, moreover, readers will not be able to see 'home' and 'empire' as two separate spaces, leaving unchallenged the fiction of a pre-existing England, herself constituted outside and without imperialism. Like scholars writing in the wake of what Burton characterises as "the imperial turn", Levy unmasks the instabilities of linear historical narratives, exposing the fiction of an insular "British (=white)" culture. "The nation", Burton writes, "is not only not antecedent to empire, but as both a symbolic and material site the nation [...] has no originary moment, no fixity outside of the various discourses of which it is itself an effect."[5] In each of her novels, Levy's characters become progressively more involved in deconstructing the official version of Englishness. As Gilbert Joseph, one of the protagonists of *Small Island* puts it, "I was ready to fight this master race theory. For my father was a Jew and my brother is a black man. [...] If this war is not won, then you can be certain that nothing here will ever change."[6]

If we were to compare Levy's protagonists' development to that of the writer herself, this is a journey she is perhaps taking personally. It seems as if a return to the past is required for her protagonists to be able to move on. When I asked Levy precisely this question about *Fruit of the Lemon*, she answered that "for [her] the starting point of writing books has always been about wanting to make the unseen visible, wanting to show the experience of [her] parents' generation and the children that came after, having to live in this country, quite a hostile environment, and how [they] cope with that."[7] *Fruit of the Lemon*, for Levy, is about "trying to show a life – an ordinary life." In an essay she wrote for *The Guardian* entitled "This is my England," Levy tells her readers about the ordinary in her own childhood:

> At school, they taught me to read, write and do arithmetic (well, with that one, heaven knows they tried). I studied Shakespeare and the Metaphysical poets. I learned to play the piano, and could sing and accompany myself to Greensleeves. I learned history – focusing on Gladstone and Disraeli – where at one time I truly did know all about the repeal of the Corn Laws and free trade. (None of this was unusual to my parents. It was what they had learned in their schools in Jamaica). I was educated to be English. Alongside me – learning, watching, eating and playing – were white children. But those white children would never have to grow up to question whether they were English or not.[8]

The white English children – regardless of class – felt entitled to the national identity whereas the children of Jamaican parents have had to carve out a space for themselves. This struggle has been evidenced on the streets and in the evolution of Black British writing. Because identities and cultures are constantly reconstituting themselves, the issue of belonging has been central to Levy's female protagonists: for how long, they all seem to be asking, will young Black Londoners have to answer to the white=English questions about their origin, identity and place in that society?

EARLY NOVELS OF DEVELOPMENT

Instead of thinking of identity as an already accomplished fact, which the new cultural practices would then represent, Levy's novels require that we think of identity as a "production," as Stuart Hall writes, which is "never complete, always in process, and always constituted within, not outside, representation."[9] Given the skewed structures of growing up in postcolonial societies, of attempting whatever social rank or position in the racial colour structure, it is not surprising that Caribbean people of all kinds, of all classes, experience the question of identity as an open question.[10] It is towards some form of identity, then, that Levy's characters seem to be moving in her coming-of-age novels, as she continues to explore the genre's traditional questions about the relationship between origin, experience, subjectivity and social structures. Caribbean writers 'at home' and in the Diaspora have used the *bildungsroman* to represent their quest for personal and national identity, to explore precisely the complexities and contradictions of growing up in a region where (post-)colonial and racial relationships exacerbate an already oppressive patriarchal situation. In 'Decolonizing Genre: Jamaica Kincaid and the Bildungsroman' I've tried to understand how Caribbean women writers have modified the conventions of the European novel of development, to offer their own counter-narratives to "progressive development" and "coherent identities".[11] The answers Levy offers initially are, not surprisingly, dependent on her characters' skin colour: the darker ones may want to go back to Jamaica where they hope to belong, and only the light-skinned seem to feel entitled to stay in London.

It used to be that to be Black and British was to be unnamed in the official discourse. "The construction of a national British identity," according to Heidi Mirza, has been "built upon a notion of a racial belonging, upon a hegemonic white ethnicity that never speaks its presence. But we live here," Mirza writes, "many are born here, all [four] million of us 'ethnic minority' people, as we are collectively called in the official Census surveys."[12] Black people in the UK have long had a significance – as representatives of otherness, as symbolic markers of the limits of Englishness – that Black British historiography has only recently begun to acknowledge. In fact, it was colonialism itself that provided the opportunity for Britons of all classes to conceive of the nation and to experience themselves as members of a "national culture."[13] Although the presence of Caribbean peoples, Asians and Africans in the metropolis changes its politics, its intellectual traditions and cultural ideologies, at the same time, that presence has not been sufficiently represented, not to mention validated. Empire was, as we have noted, not just a phenomenon "out there", but a fundamental and constitutive part of English culture and identity at home. As 'mother' country, however, England has left many of its children (by virtue of empire) orphaned, since it has rejected them as 'other', not-English, when they arrive from their Caribbean islands, as in Levy's protagonists' parents' case, in search of a better life.

In *Every Light in the House Burnin'*, Levy offers us a loving depiction of Angela's father, Winston Jacobs, who was born in Jamaica but came to England in 1948 on the S.S. Empire Windrush, with 492 other Jamaicans, in search of better opportunities. The Windrush pioneers, as Onyekachi Wambu writes, "were coming 'home', to a place that was rapidly changing." To this crucial moment in British history Levy triumphantly returns in her last novel, addressing "the open hostility of their new hosts" while searching for suitable jobs and housing. For after the Second World War there was great demand for labour in Britain as the nation began to rebuild her broken cities. As British citizens holding British passports, West Indians were actively recruited to work, through advertisements placed in West Indian newspapers by London Transport, the British Hotels and Restaurants Association, the NHS, and similar organisations. They came to work in jobs traditionally of low status and low pay. Working for London Transport, Mr. Jacobs is primarily depicted as the breadwinner: although he is not loving and openly affectionate to his children, the narrator seems to feel closer to him than to her mother.[14] The central presence in *Every Light in the House Burnin'* is not the mother (or a mother-substitute), as in many of the Caribbean novels by women I have studied: it is her dying father whom the narrator wishes to understand. It is the father who complains about "Every light in the house burnin", if he sees a light on in a room that nobody is in.[15]

From its title and throughout Levy's narrative, then, the importance of home is emphasised. As in other Caribbean novels, the house stands for the nation the migrant is only superficially, and seemingly temporarily, allowed to occupy thanks to the 'charity' of the mother country. Significantly, Angela's main family outing every year is a visit to the Ideal Home Exhibition, where they would spend time fantasising future house preferences, only to end up in the red-brick flat built in the thirties to house the poor, that they've always occupied: "We can't afford those houses--it's just talk," the father would tell Angela to stop her from believing the dream that they would one day own their homes.[16]

While the father is depicted in heroic strokes, one time saving Angela from a huge black dog, almost Superman-like in her recollection,[17] her mother Beryl is the squelcher of dreams, telling Angela art college is not for her: "People like us don't get famous. […] You'll be disappointed. I had big ideas when I was your age, but you soon grow up. [...] "Your teacher is not like us. She doesn't know."[18] Beryl has become so restrained that she can only write to Angela about the father's real condition.[19] At the same time, however, she refuses to give up on her Jamaican cooking, against Angela's secret wish "that her mum's cooking was more like school dinners."[20]

When the Jacobs children's 'friends' remind them that their dads have said they are "not English," calling them "wogs," "coons," "nig-nogs," and "Blackie," telling them to go back to the jungle where they come from, all their mother would answer is, : "You're not Black and you're not white. That's what we are – we're not Black and we're not white.... You born here. That's what matter."[21] Levy seems to be implying here that birth in the metropolis can worsen the ambivalence of the colonised condition captured in Franz Fanon's title *Black Skin, White Masks*. She also tells her readers that it is not only the West Indian migrant who still has a problem figuring out who she is. When Angela's aunt is visiting from Jamaica, she looks at the 'darker' niece, Patricia, and wonders who she looks like: "You must be like your mummy's side of the family," she concludes.[22] When asked whether she misses "back home," Beryl answers that she has everything she needs. The aunt tells them how they "hear awful things back home about how coloured people treated bad [in London]. Living in one room. People not wantin' to give jobs if you from Jamaica." It is the dad's turn to agree that it happens to other Jamaicans: that they don't have any trouble, for they "just keep ourselves to ourselves."[23]

While Angela's parents' "strategy [has been] to keep as quiet as possible in the hope that no one would know that they had sneaked into the country," she feels entitled to what England has to offer. Angela knows the society better than her parents: "I had grown up in its English ways. I could confront it, rail against it, fight it, because it was mine – a birthright."[24] But is it really a birthright, or Angela has to earn it? For she remembers when her mother takes her to get her hair straightened at age twelve, "After all the pain here was my reward. Straight hair. Manageable hair. Not my hair, but hair like my friends – not different."[25] At the beauty parlour she feels "pale in the company [of Black women], out of place, as white here as I felt Black among the pasty-faced English."[26] Are her parents to blame that Angela has never been in the company of many Black people before? That the only other Black child in Angela's school is Ada, a girl whose parents came from Africa, and they are also the only other Black family in their church?[27] In order to protect her children Beryl tells them to lie about Sunday dinners – that they have chicken, never sausages. "How can you explain your family conventions – the secrecies, the codes, the quirks, to someone who's never lived them," Angela wants to know.[28]

While Angela's memories of her mother are of her "hiding" either in the kitchen or in her room studying for an Open University degree, Beryl's resignation, omissions, and silences cannot simply be dismissed as internalised racism. She was a certified teacher when she left Jamaica, but would have to study for a similar degree to be good enough to teach the English children. At the same time, however, Beryl seems to care more for appearances and protocol than anything else. When Patricia, the "darker" sister who "was always miserable"[29] and who the narrator sometimes wished did not belong to the family, got married at age 18, their "mum was horrified she was getting married in black – more by the suit than the pregnancy."[30] Yvonne, the light-skinned older sister, became a trained nurse and went to live in New Zealand, according to the narrator, "the furthest away she could get."[31] Is she also implying where Yvonne could pass? Their brother John became the wanderer, moving all the time: "He travelled all round Europe by himself. Then to Africa on a huge truck with others. Then he went to live on a kibbutz in Israel."[32]

The similarities between the oppression of the African and that of the Jew have been explored in Caribbean fiction before. The protagonist of Michelle Cliff's *Abeng* (U.S./Jamaica 1984), for example, becomes interested in the history of the Holocaust because she feels a connection between the Jews and herself--the indigenous inhabitants of her island (Jamaica) were also victims of genocide. Clare even wonders whether her own mother who rejects her, would have been different if colonisation had not happened. The teachers at Clare's school dodge all her questions about the Holocaust, talking instead about "the London blitz and the heroism of the British."[33] When Clare asks them again, their answers are vague, "crystalising into one judgement: Jews were expected to suffer".[34] The teachers even attempt a parallel between the suffering of the Jews and "the primitive religiosity of Africans, which had brought Black people into slavery".[35] Concluding that both Jews and Africans are "flawed in irreversible ways," the teacher in *Abeng* stresses the "duty of white Christians as the 'ordained' protectors of other peoples"- it is the white men's burden.[36] Missionary understanding of Black peoples, according to Catherine Hall, depended on the assumption that "negroes" who were not Christians were savage and barbaric, whereas those who had been converted and had experienced the discipline of the missionary church, particularly with a white pastor, were new men, respectful, industrious, domesticated, aware of their responsibilities to authority, rightly seeking their political, economic and legal rights as subjects.[37] Levy's vicar subscribes to such missionary understanding of Black peoples, rejecting a child's question about "all darkies [being] dirty": "'Now Ada and Angela and their families are coloured, but that doesn't make them any different to you or me. We are all God's children and in the sight of God, everyone is equal.'"[38]

There is, however, irony and a strange form of humour in Mr. Jacobs' death since mother and daughter are not with him when he dies, and the nurses get him a rabbi rather than a minister from the Church of England [his religion] because of his name. It seems the family cat, Willie, gets more sympathy and care at the end: the last chapter in the novel, "The Death" describes how much Mr. Jacobs loved the cat and how he cries when she disappears: "He's taken the day off work just to look for her. He says even if he just finds her body, at least he could give her a decent burial."[39]

Of the four Jacobs children, readers feel that only Angela develops into a mature young woman who seems to know who she is and to what she is entitled. And this could be mostly due to narrative point of view, since we only hear Angela's voice as she tells her family story. By juxtaposing her past and present life, reliving her childhood years while helping her mother take care of her terminally-ill father and cope with the inadequacies of the National Health Service, Levy's persona seems to come to terms with herself, her family and her place in British society.

In *Never far from Nowhere*, Levy's second novel, we get to hear the voice of both sisters, since she alternates chapters from the point of view of the light-skinned artist-figure, Vivien, and Olive, her big, unhappy, "darker" sister. Both Vivien and Olive are born (on a council estate in North London's Finsbury Park) also of Jamaican parents who came over on a ship in the fifties. By choosing the form of the 'double' *bildungsroman*, two female protagonists rather than one, Levy emphasises the ways in which English society, by rigidly discriminating because of colour and class, limits the full development of all its children.

When Caribbean women writers have used the form before, the double *bildungsroman* has served to inscribe the question of who does and does not get to speak in the post-colonial society or novel. In Zee Edgell's *Beka Lamb* (U.S./Belize, 1982) and Cliff's *Abeng*, for example, Beka and Clare – each novel's protagonist – only introduce the questions that will eventually allow voices like Zoe's and Toycie's, their poor and dark best friends when they were children, to be heard without being filtered through the privileged classes or consciousness. Edgell and Cliff use Toycie and Zoe to establish that Beka and Clare have ties both in the world of colonial privilege and in the working class "native" world. Having Beka and Clare look at their friends' lives and character leads them to question the colonising forces within their own lives. Toycie and Zoe thus function as both educators and voices of reality: their lives serve only to make Beka's and Clare's better. Offering a critique of a post-colonial society in which roles ordinarily are rigidly defined, the double *bildungsroman*, then, traces the way in which the harmony and innocence of childhood, where class and colour do not seem to make much of a difference, are destroyed by a coloniser's culture which assigns radically different fates to people based on skin colour.

Rose Charles, the mother in *Never far from Nowhere*, appears to have accepted this value system, including the oppression it deals the migrant class. Although Rose knows that she and her husband are not the only people who came from Jamaica in the fifties, she likes to think that "because they are fair-skinned they are the only decent people who came. The only ones with 'a bit of class.'[40] And she believes that the English would recognise this."[41] She even prefers "a nice cup of tea" to rum.[42] But Rose has worked two jobs all her life – she helps prepare and serve meals at the local school and sell tea at the hospital – with no hope of advancement. Still, she doesn't believe in Black people, not seeing herself as Black. Her "dark" daughter, Olive, remembers how her mother used to talk to her about what she thought of the Black people there, "looking me straight in my Black face":

> 'I'm Black,' I used to say, when I was old enough to butt in.
> 'Don't be silly, Olive, you're not coloured.'
> 'No, Mum, I'm Black.'
> 'No Olive, you're not Black, and that's enough of this stupidness.'
> 'Well I'm not white, I have to be something.'
> 'You're not white and you're not Black – you're you.'[43]

Rose would also complain to Vivien about Olive: "That child will be the death of me – I don't know where she came from, she's the devil's child, the devil's."[44]

Although Olive believes that her mother and Vivien think she worries about colour too much, she ultimately feels they cannot know because they have not lived her life, "they haven't gone through what I've gone through."[45] When she and Vivien are children, for example, Olive tells her mother there are no Black girls in their school, and the mother just smiles and says that that was good.[46] For this and other reasons, Olive always thinks of it as Vivien's school: "My teacher at the primary school said I'd never come to anything because I couldn't stick at things. [...] They all looked surprised when I passed and nodded and smiled when I got into Lady Stanhope."[47] Olive doesn't get any exam when she leaves, but she says she does not care because she has always hated that school. Olive loves going to clubs to "forget who [she] was during the day."[48] She always has a lot of bad dreams, frustrating dreams, [foreshadowing] dreams of ending up in the wrong country. Olive's dreams symbolise her unhappiness; they convey how unable she is to control the things that make her unhappy:

> I was standing painting a picture. A canvas was propped up on the table in front of the window. And I was really excited by what I

was painting. I can't remember what it was – just something out of the window. Something yellow and bright. I was nearly finished. Then I took the paintbrush to add the final touches here and there. As the brush hit the canvas it lifted paint off. Every time I touched the canvas with the brush, more little bits would come off until it was beginning to look unfinished again. I couldn't believe it and kept dabbing, and it just made it worse and worse.[49]

Figured in this dream, I believe, is the difficulty that Olive finds in (re-)creating her identity and her place in English society against the normative whiteness embedded in the culture. She needs to figure out a way of belonging, and of fitting in. For this reason, falling in love with a man like Peter Flynn, who is white, seems right to Olive, since after talking about workers' rights, exploited labour and the right to strike, he talks about "Black people were exploited and how [they] should get together with the workers to overthrow all oppression."[50] Peter is a postman, and he likes Rose because she is working-class. (Although when he says that to her, she looks at him like he has just spat in her face). Olive should have run from him after hearing that "women were special because they were bearers of children, the givers of life."[51] But unfortunately she doesn't, and once they start having sex, that is all he wants to do. Fittingly, it is only during Olive's pregnancy that her mother feels close to her: "Mum stopped shouting at her altogether and started smiling instead."[52] Readers could assign Rose's smile to the link that motherhood forges, that tie that patriarchy wants us to believe binds daughters to mothers naturally and seamlessly, but a more cynical view would account for Rose's satisfaction in that Olive may be contributing to the family's whitening.

If the child who is born stands for the new citizen/nation, as it is already a convention in other post-colonial novels, the fact that it is an extremely difficult birth figures perhaps the hardships involved in trying to bridge the two worlds. For the doctor tells Olive that if she were giving birth a hundred years ago, she would have died from losing so much blood: "Amy, we called her. [...] It was like an omen. It means beloved."[53] But Amy inherits Peter's pale skin, and Olive hates it when people ask her whose baby she is. Olive tells Amy that she is Black:

'I liked being Black. I wanted to be Black. [...] That I am Black and so is my daughter.'

'You mustn't say that, Olive – she'll grow up confused,'[her mother responds].
And I said – I said at last: 'No, I grew up confused – she's growing up Black.'[54]

Vivien, the younger sister, does not want to end up like Olive. She does not want to be "at home all day surrounded by steaming nappies, watching a baby playing on the floor," too tired to even get dressed.[55] As the chapters alternate between Vivien's and Olive's point of view, readers cannot help but wonder whether Olive exists in the narrative only as a foil to Vivien. For Vivien is the lucky one, while "Olive is the black sheep of the family."[56] Only Vivien seems to know how the system works: "A-stream girls went to university and studied English or History. B-stream girls made good wives and C-stream girls...well, Olive was a C-stream girl."[57] Rose is not as pleased as Vivien would expect, however, when she gets into college: "I thought you'd be pleased that one of your daughters is doing something with her life."[58] But Rose has her set notions about who should attend Art College:

'Art College is for ruffians. Scruffy people go to Art College. What good is art? You can't get a job drawing people. [...] You want to go to university, Vivien. Clever people go to university. You'll meet a better class of person at university.'[59]

Rose could not take Vivien to college because she had to work to replace someone who was sick. While Rose wants a better life for her daughter, she also knows how alienating this new environment will be to her. Vivien also remembers that her mother "never came to [her] prize days at school":[60]

As I packed I kept looking round my bedroom wanting to feel nostalgic, wanting to remember all the fun times. But none came [...]
She never stuck up for me--if kids teased me, if teachers were nasty--take no notice, she'd say, "it doesn't matter."[61]

The truth is Rose is afraid she won't know what to say to Vivien's new friends in the college environment.
For isn't Vivien ashamed her family is from Jamaica, telling her boyfriend Eddie she is from Mauritius because she does not want

anyone to think they are Black? Vivien's friends reassure her she is "not really a darkie. ... You're one of us. ... You look Spanish or Italian anyway."[62] She snaps at Olive for using the word 'Black': "I mean I knew we weren't wogs or coons but I never thought we were Black."[63] The more education Vivien gets, the more her boyfriend Eddie's cockney background alienates him. All she sees Eddie do is "drink beer, play darts and hang around with his dad": " 'You've got so high and bloody mighty, Vivien, since you've been [in college]... Don't forget where you come from – you're just a working class girl.'" When Eddie talks to Vivien about love, she is not sure how she feels: " 'I enjoyed making love – that was fun.'"[64] But when Vivien asks him if he doesn't want to do something with his life, Eddie tells her he can't be anyone else: " 'I can't be all clever or arty. I'm me. So is that good enough for you or not?' [...] The choice had become my old life or the new. I looked at Eddie and said, 'No, it's not good enough.'"[65]

Olive's relationship with Peter fails for a very different reason. He is the one who changes once the baby is born, not coming home for days. Olive does not even care when he tells her he has met another woman whom he has been seeing for months, that she has "a flat and two children and he [is] moving in straight away."[66] When her mother tells her "not many men would care if they saw their children," but Peter is "an English man, he's decent,"and she should try to win him back for this reason, Olive does not agree.[67] After going on the dole, almost all of Olive's money goes to pay the gas bill, and she is still dependent on her mother.

When Olive aimlessly walks around the city (and later when she learns how to drive), she does not individually reinscribe it, as Michel de Certeau would want her to, for London does not feel like her city. To walk through a city, according to de Certeau, is to "actualize" the city as a function of time and narrative and thus to de-emphasise its qualities of planned and static and organising "place" in favour of active and spontaneously reorganised "space."[68] Although when "Britain's imperial chickens came home to roost,"[69] London was the place most visibly changed – its racial demographics saw a disproportionate decline in white dominance compared to those of the nation as a whole – Olive's "walk" through the city reveals that power does not lie in numbers alone. For this reason, I cannot agree with John Ball's conclusion (about Hanif Kureishi's London) that with this so-called "reinvasion of the centre," the directionality of imperialism is reversed: "Where once London reached out expansively into 'the world,' Ball writes, "now the world began to shrink in upon London."[70] The racist treatment the metropolitan police give Black folk is only one evidence that while the 'centre' may have been taken over by 'otherness,' power is not evenly shared by all its citizens.

When the cops stop Olive for a traffic violation and because she is Black, plant ganja in her bag to take her to jail, it is racism plain and simple. When her lawyer tells her to plead guilty, "even if you didn't do it, you're certainly guilty," readers see the British [In] Justice System in action: for the police, Olive is guilty of being Black.[71] But she cannot agree to take the punishment for something she has not done: "plead guilty: you'll only get a fine--twenty, thirty pounds--and then you can get on with your life." "The solicitor's England is a nice place where people are polite to her, smile at her," Olive concludes. "But my England shakes underneath me with every step I take."[72] Because England is not exactly her England, Olive decides she is going to leave it for Jamaica:

> Live in the sun and watch Amy playing on beaches. I'm going
> to live somewhere where being Black doesn't make you different.
> Where being Black means you belong. In Jamaica people will
> be proud of me. I've had enough of this country. What has it
> ever done for me except make me its villain. Well, I won't take
> it any more.[73]

Of course Olive's Jamaica exists only in tourist brochures and in her imagination.

Differently from what Carol Boyce Davies suggests, the desire for home that migration creates produces an imaginary home for the child of Jamaicans, but it does not produce a rewriting of home for Olive's mother. Home for her has not become a "contradictory, contested space":[74]

> 'I tell her, how you go back? You were born here, it's all you
> know. How you go back? I can go back but you children can't.'
> Her face became crimson. 'You don't know what it's like there.
> I know! I know! You children have had it easy. [...] But in
> Jamaica life is hard. You children don't know.'[75]

We can contrast the distance Levy creates between the two worlds to the one also represented in terms of class/colour in Merle Hodge's

Crick Crack, Monkey (Trinidad, 1972) by the two different aunts' households. For the estrangement Tee feels in Tantie's yard when she comes to visit, after having lived for a while in Aunt Beatrice's very middle-class house is very similar to the one Vivien experiences in her first visit home from college:

> "everything seems to her raw and desolate. I kept looking around. I was nervous. Jumpy. Like a lost tourist. 'How long you staying, Vivien?' Mum asked. I felt like a distant relation come to visit. Out of place."[76]

If such is the nature of Vivien's displacement when she comes home from College for a visit, is she only trying to fool herself in believing that she and Olive have "had the same chances, started from the same place?" Vivien tells Olive: "You act as if I was born in Buckingham Palace and you were born here."[77] Olive cannot be optimistic about Vivien's future however: "You think you've escaped now, don't you, because of your precious college. You think everything will be all right for you."[78]

> Vivien thinks she's escaped, with all her exams and college and middle-class friends. She thinks she'll be accepted in this country now. One of them. But I know more about life than her. Real life. Nothing can shock me now. But Vivien, one day she'll realize that in England, people like her are never far from nowhere. Never.[79]

Of course Olive is jealous that Vivien seems to have had all the choices because of her light skin, but in a way, what the novel's title seems to convey is the thin line the Black British need to walk in a society that has never fully embraced them. At least, not yet. Olive goes through Vivien's life listing what she sees: "teacher's pet...little miss goody-goody who never did anything wrong...Mum and Dad's favourite, precious little brown-eyed girl."[80] But she feels sorry for Vivien because she does not feel Vivien knows who she is anymore, despite her certificates for exams passed and merits for jobs well done, despite her prospects.[81] Not surprisingly, it is only inside their council flat that Vivien is not sure where she belongs by virtue of colour/class:

> I looked at the old photograph of Olive and me on the wall. Two little girls with identical yellow bows in our hair and happy,

smiling chubby cheeks. But now Olive's arms were folded on the
world. She was angry with everything, with everyone. And I had
grown too big for our council flat, but not sure where else I would
fit. Where did we belong? I answered my mum the only way I
could. I said, 'I don't know.'[82]

For when a white-haired old woman on the train back to college
asks her where she is from, after wondering "what country she
would want [her] to come from," Vivien tells her without further
hesitation, "My family are from Jamaica." [...] "But I am English."[83]
  Of course there are some readers who will be optimistic about this
ending and argue that Levy has managed to reconceptualise
Englishness as she claims it for one of her protagonists. The Vivien
in this reading will hope that her daughter will not feel that English
people hate migrants and their children. This Vivien will try to
repress the memory of the times when she herself was young and she
would look at her parents as they sat exhausted in chairs, thinking
how lucky this country was to have them:

> How grateful people should be that they came here and did such
> responsible jobs. [...] My parents helped this country, I thought.
> [...] But even when I was young, when I was still having my cheek
> pulled by passers-by and people winked at me on the tube, even
> then I knew that English people hated us.[84]

The Vivien in this version of the novel will continue to try to undo
stereotypes about "most people living in council houses not working
at all," telling more of her friends that they are "talking absolute
crap since both her mother and father worked" and they have lived
on a council estate "all their lives".[85]
  My first reading of Levy's novels criticised her for failing to
destabilise the whiteness implied in the identity 'English.'[86] I thought
then that Levy had, uncritically, kept whiteness right at the centre
since only the very light skinned characters seem to have had a
chance to belong in that society. I even criticised Levy for not
offering enough of a critique of the political success of the British
National Party and the rise in racial violence and racial harassment
in her novels. Now that I am re-reading both novels in light of her
third and fourth – and after our interview – I'm thinking that Levy's
choice to figure Englishness as a specific race, language, and moral
authority which excludes Blacks, has been intentionally slanted. All

her readers are to realise the injustice of such society and work together to change it.

REWRITING BRITISH HISTORY

Fruit of the Lemon and *Small Island* continue this process of excavation and cultural recreation. For the retrieval of counter memories, of subjugated knowledges, which are thought to lack a history, functions, as Mirza notes, as a challenge to the taken-for-granted normative assumptions of prevailing discourses.[87] By exposing the fallacy of perpetual whiteness through their focus on peoples who juggle multiple ethnicities and histories, Black British authors like Levy have begun to effect changes in the perception of English national identity. For with the loss of the Empire, an apparent loss of identity has settled upon England and a search for what constitutes English culture seems to be taking place. What will an alternative national imaginary be for the English? Now is the moment for novels like Levy's to serve as catalysts for such soul-searching re-imagining and redefinition.

For the fantasy that what is truly English is the countryside has definitely outlived its usefulness. That idea of England has not been accessible to the majority of people, so why keep the fiction. When Faith, *Fruit of the Lemon*'s protagonist, and her brother Carl took trips to the countryside, they would be "greeted with fences and gates and barbed wire. They never knew how to actually get onto 'that green and pleasant land.'"[88] The village where Faith's friend Simon's parents live is indeed "quintessentially English,"[89] but their weekend visit there only serves to further alienate Faith. The fact that Faith is the only Black face in the Tudor pub they enter to have a bitter, after a long walk, is yet one more sign that the countryside – the quintessentially English – does not really belong to her people. She is immediately asked where she comes from – because of her Black face:

'And whereabouts are you from, Faith?'
'London,' I said.
The man laughed a little. 'I meant more what country are you from?' I didn't bother to say I was born in England, that I was English, because I knew that was not what he wanted to hear.
'My parents are from Jamaica.'[90]

It is Faith's luck that the man had just come back from vacationing in Jamaica and that he had met another Bunyan, a dreadlocked one, with whom he took a photograph, "with [his] arm around him. Me and my brother Winston." When asked what she thought of that, Faith stops being polite and offers a possible reason why they share a not very common last name:

> 'Well, the thing is, that would have been his slave name, you see.'
> Then before I really knew what I was saying I'd said, 'Your family
> probably owned his family once.' [...]
> And I giggled a smile at Mr. Bunyan. But he still stared at me like
> I'd just spat in his face.[91]

After explaining that his family had no slave-owning connections in the Caribbean, Mr. Bunyan brings up a "wayward vicar" as a possibility. "We had a lot of vicars in our family. Some vicar just going round sowing his seed. Producing lots of little dark babies. That sort of thing happened all the time."[92]

Because "that sort of thing happened all the time," what we find out when trying to understand, for lack of a better term, the Black British reality is that the old static order, the colonial, or post-colonial, model has become somewhat obsolete because the usual categories no longer apply. "Race," as Caryl Phillips argues, "can no longer define nationality, and neither does it define the individual." We should be able to "explain our new hybrid selves," he claims, "without recourse to the simplistic discourse of race."[93] For "when you look at family trees – anybody's family tree – people's individual histories," as Levy writes in 'This is my England' "the question of identity becomes very complicated." She explains further:

> It would be nice and simple if we were all pure. If we all came
> from where our parents, grandparents and beyond came from. If
> we all just took on our forefathers' culture. Wouldn't it be nice if
> we could say that all Africans are Black and all English are white?
> [...] We would all fit into our separate boxes, and in times of
> change, such as those that we are now living through, we could
> retreat into them and lick our wounds. But it is not like that. Any
> history book will show that England has never been an exclusive
> club, but rather a hybrid nation. The effects of the British Empire
> were personal as well as political. And as the sun has finally set on
> the Empire, we are now having to face up to all of these realities.[94]

Levy acknowledges that there are many Black people with backgrounds similar to hers who do not wish to be called English. But national identity, Levy emphasises, is not a personal issue. It is political. "Englishness must never be allowed to attach itself to ethnicity. The majority of English people are white, but some are not." [95]

For Faith, Levy's protagonist, this realisation entails its own share of pain. After witnessing the aftermath of a horrible racist attack on the Black clerk of a bookstore in her Islington neighborhood, Faith falls into such a depression that she even stops going to work (a job at the BBC she had fought for) and covers all the mirrors around her: "I didn't want to be Black anymore. I just wanted to live." [96] The attack makes Faith remember the time her brother Carl came home "with bruises on his eyes, his face, his arms. The bruises took weeks to heal and turned bits of his skin blue. He never told anyone what happened." [97] Probably Carl did not trust that the police would handle the investigation well. Probably he thought he would be considered a suspect before being recognised as a victim. Faith had witnessed the devastation brought to the bookstore – "a woman with a bleeding head, a panting, furious Simon and a terrified me":

> Books were strewn over the floor and an unmistakable stench of piss came from somewhere. A half-full bag of shit was splattered on the table – while the other half of its contents slid down the bookcase of gay and lesbian books. And the Black and Third World fiction was spray-painted with 'Wog.'[98]

The policeman tells Faith and Simon that all the "'leftie bookshops are getting done.' He had a sneer in his tone. 'They say they're National Front, but they're not, they're just a bunch of thugs,'"[99] ignoring the fact that witnesses have just described the attackers' green jackets and that "the shop had been sprayed with angry red paint. All over it said NF, NF, NF."[100] Even if Faith's parents had faced racism and discrimination when they first came to London, "they knew they were Jamaican. They knew where they came from and they knew where they wanted to go [back to]."[101] Faith, on the other hand, had shown no interest in her parents' life before they came to England. In their words, "[Faith's] eyes would roll in [her] head when they began to speak about the place they had once called home."[102] Fortunately, in an attempt to forget the hatred she has witnessed, Faith is persuaded to leave for Jamaica to meet her extended family for the first time. Her trip to Jamaica "wraps [her] in a family history, [...] swaddl[ing] her tight in its stories," reminding her of who she is.[103] The knowledge Faith brings back to London empowers her to share that story and the voice readers hear at the end of Levy's novel not only cannot ever be silenced again, but promises some kind of deserved retribution:

> Let those bully boys walk behind me in the playground. Let them tell me, 'You're a darkie. Faith's a darkie.' I am the granddaughter of Grace and William Campbell. I am the great-grandchild of Cecilia Hilton. I am descended from Katherine whose mother was a slave. I am the cousin of Afria. I am the niece of Coral Thompson and the daughter of Wade and Mildred Jackson. Let them say what they like. Because I am the bastard child of Empire and I will have my day."[104]

When readers take that journey to Jamaica with Faith (the whole second half of the novel), they travel back into her family past, recovering the complex history of her ancestors. Her great-great-grandfather, for example, came from the north-west of Scotland. James Campbell's family "was made to move from the lush green glen, out to the coastland where they had to stop farming and start fishing."[105] Because they could not catch enough fish to feed a growing family, in the summer months James would go to Glasgow to find work. It is there that he is offered the promise of a better life in Jamaica, working on a sugar estate. There James marries Amy, "the daughter of a woman who was born a slave. Her family had worked on the estate for many years – as slaves, as apprentices, and then as free [people] working in return for small plots of land and lodging."[106] Amy used to say to everyone that her husband, "the white man, was one day going to take her and her [four] children to Scotland to live in a small stone house, in a beautiful lush green glen where the sun shone all day, even through rain."[107] That day never came and that version of Scotland only lives in the memory of Faith's Jamaican relatives – the same relatives who, unlike her parents, do not hesitate to tell her about slavery.

One of the horrors of slavery, as Levy explains, is "a psychological horror. To tell people that their past is not even worthy of history – it's not even worthy of being remembered. That a family history is not worthy of being passed down because there's a fear of something that happened there – this is horror."[108] According to Levy, this collective forgetting happens much more for the people who came to

England and had to assimilate than for the people who stayed 'home' in the Caribbean.

Another character in *Fruit of the Lemon* – Constance – chooses not to forget who she is, but she seems to lose her son (and herself) in the process. Always spoiled as a child because she is very light-skinned, Constance is sent to England to attend the school where her grandfather is the headmaster. But when Germany invades Poland and war is declared in Europe, she cannot safely return to Jamaica. "In Jamaica," aunt Coral tells Faith," we just have a little inconvenient blackout and [Constance] is in England being shot and bombed. [...] There was not [even] enough for her to eat in England."[109] Of course after World War II a lot of newly-wed white English women came to Jamaica with their Black Jamaican husbands, "men who had been stationed in England, in the army and in the Royal Air Force during the War."[110] Constance stays in England to complete a university degree in English, but she brings back a curiosity about her history and her people. That yearning prompts her to leave a good job to live with a group of Rastafarians who call England [the white world] Babylon. Although she could have chosen to pass as a white Jamaican, Constance takes her son Kofi to Africa to recover their heritage. She changes her name to Afria and only dresses in African garb. While Kofi is young, everything seems to work well, but when he is seventeen, Kofi cuts off his waist-length dreadlocks, moves to the USA, and changes his name to Edmund. "Poor Constance" begins to drink to forget. "Remembering," Levy emphasises, "always brings its share of pain to African Diasporan peoples – in Jamaica or in London."[111]

Whereas Andrea Levy's earlier novels are somewhat autobiographical coming-of-age narratives, *Small Island* constitutes a much more ambitious project of remembering, a historical novel that for the first time offers an account from the point of view of both the white and the Black British of a crucial period in England's history, the moment when the children of the Empire came "home" to the mother country. By juxtaposing the past and the present of two couples – one Jamaican, one English (=white) – Levy's narrative unfolds to an elegant and careful construction of observed detail, truthful voices, and a meticulous layering of social observation recreating the 1940s social fabric, its conflicts, its racist attitudes and some of its victories. While "still English," as she tells Christie Hickman in a recent interview, Levy has "this wonderfully rich heritage which [she] would like more people to understand and acknowledge."[112] Her own father and his twin brother, who had been among the thousands of West Indians serving in the wartime RAF, were among the first wave of Jamaican migrants to arrive at Tilbury on the SS Empire Windrush in 1948.

The consequences of such arrivals is the focus of Levy's fourth novel, a history she examines from all sides with roughly the same number of chapters for each of the four protagonists – Queenie and Bernard, Hortense and Gilbert – each written in its unique first-person-voice. Although Levy chooses to name each chapter, they would have been easily identified without resorting to that since the protagonists' voices are distinctively their own. These are not alternate chapters, however. Readers will follow significant events and turning points from each character's point of view. Levy manages to convey, for example, how the working class Midland girl to whom readers are introduced in the Prologue – Queenie – shares with the Jamaican Hortense similar aspirations to improve herself when moving to London. "I should have been a lady," Queenie thinks, "But I was stuck on a stinking farm."[113] The first-born child of Wilfred and Lillie Buxton, "christened Victoria yet called for ever Queenie,"[114] behaves as if she has "the whole world at her feet,"[115] never hesitating to please herself first. When her aunt Dorothy brings her to London, "to make a good catch of [her],"[116] Queenie begins elocution and deportment lessons twice a week and is given a new outfit every Saturday afternoon. Unfortunately, however, Dorothy dies too soon and, rather than going back to the farm, Queenie settles for Bernard Bligh, the first man who courts her. Bernard is not only older than Queenie, but so boring that she even "[looks] forward to the war" to escape her routine at home.[117]

Sex with her husband brings Queenie neither joy, nor children, so she uses all her energy to take care of survivors: "Population, we called them at the rest centre. The bombed-out who'd had the cheek to live through the calamity of a world blown to bits."[118] Very early on Queenie realises other shortcomings in Bernard: he is not only selfish but extremely class-conscious and even racist. Only when he feels shamed into joining the war effort, does Bernard become "part of their fighting machine—they were sending him overseas."[119] It is also the war that brings Michael Roberts, Hortense's Jamaican cousin, to Queenie's door, a RAF Sergeant who brings back the feeling Queenie experienced at the Empire Exhibition: "I was lost in Africa again [...], a little girl in a white organza frock with blood rising in my cheeks turning me red. He was coloured."[120]

   In order to figure precisely the complexity of feelings evoked by the presence of British colonials in the metropolis, Levy recreates the 1924 British Empire Exhibition in the novel's Prologue. Intended as a popular celebration of Britain's global achievement, the Exhibition's official guide was quite explicit about its purpose: "to make the different races of the British Empire better known to each other, and to demonstrate to the people of Britain the almost illimitable possibilities of the Dominions, Colonies, and Dependencies together." As Queenie later remembers it, the 1924 Empire Exhibition is "The Empire in little. The palace of engineering, the palace of industry, and building after building that housed every country we British owned. [...] Practically the whole world there to be looked at."[121] Although initially terrified, the child Queenie becomes intrigued by the African man she meets at the Exhibition, an experience Levy wants to frame the whole novel – readers soon find out why. By 1948, the present of the narrative, if you were not wearing the RAF's blue uniform, you would be dismissed as merely a Black man. But Michael Roberts is not only wearing the uniform; he gives Queenie what Levy describes as "picture-house smiles."[122] She is instantly drawn to him: "His lips plump as sausages – would you bounce off them or would they soften when kissed?"[123] It does not take long for Queenie's curiosity to be satisfied:

> She was so desirable he polished her with hot breath – his tongue lapping between her legs like a cat with cream. It wasn't me. This woman watching his buttocks rise and fall sucked at every finger on his hand. She clawed his back and cried out until his mouth lowering down filled hers with his eager tongue. It wasn't me. This woman panted and thrust and bit.[124]

This one night of passion some time in 1944 ends without a proper farewell. Queenie is even hit by a flying bomb the next day, a moralist reader would say as punishment. Others may criticise Levy for reproducing some of the stereotypes about Black male sexuality. Queenie's multiple orgasms, in my reading, are simply the result of years of involuntary sexual repression: someone has finally awakened her body to its full potential. We know she's not made pregnant then, but only realise the extent of the author's withholding of information later. We are as surprised by Queenie's pregnancy as her husband Bernard, when it is finally disclosed.

   According to Bonnie Greer, family is both theme and metaphor in

Levy's novel – "the story of the Jamaican family in London, and the metaphor of Empire, the Big Family, which turns out to be a betrayer and, in some cases, destroyer."[125] The Big Family is both Black and white. The two couples find out that the Empire has forged them a common destiny, but readers only realise what that entails at novel's end. What brings these two couples together is fate, one might say, but what truly unites them redefines British identity (and history) forever. "If ever there was a novel which offered a historically faithful account of how its characters thought and behaved" in the period, Mike Phillips writes, "*Small Island* is it."[126] Levy recalls long days spent in the RAF Museum, the Imperial War Museum and local community centre archives. "The novel took four and a half years to research," she told her audience at the Museum of London on July 14, 2004. "Some of the best research," Levy added, "was talking to the people who lived through the time." Mike Phillips (also at the Museum of London as her interlocutor) again emphasised Levy's grip on the language of the characters: "Queenie sounds like a Londoner brought up in the early part of the last century. Bernard sounds like a man who served in the Far East. Hortense and Gilbert sound absolutely Jamaican."[127]

Gilbert Joseph is one of the six thousand West Indians who volunteered for the RAF, serving as a driver rather than the pilot he imagined he would become. At the Museum of London, Levy chose to read what she called "Gilbert's rant on the mother country," to underscore the disappointment such volunteers felt at not being welcome. What follows is only a selection:

> Then one day you hear Mother calling – she is troubled, she need your help. Your mummy, your daddy say go. Leave home, leave familiar, leave love. Travel seas with waves that swell about you as substantial as concrete buildings. Shiver, tire, hunger – for no sacrifice is too much to see you at Mother's needy side. This surely is adventure. After all you have heard, can you imagine, can you believe, soon, soon you will meet Mother?

> The filthy tramp that eventually greets you is she. Ragged, old and dusty as the long dead. Mother has a blackened eye, bad breath and one lone tooth that waves in her head when she speaks. Can this be that fabled relation you heard so much of? This twisted-crooked weary woman. This stinking cantankerous hag. She offers you no comfort after your journey. No smile. No welcome. Yet,

she looks down at you through lordly eyes and says, 'Who the bloody hell are you?'[128]

Carefully researched, *Small Island*'s 'Before' chapters (the events leading to 1948, the narrative present), allow readers to explore both Black and white characters' lives, understanding their motivations and fears. The war years are mostly relived in personal recollections, like what Gilbert hears when stationed at a military camp in Virginia: "we West Indians, being subjects of his Majesty King George VI, had, for the time being, superior black skin. We were allowed to live with white soldiers, while the inferior American negro was not."[129] Through Bernard's service in India, we learn not only of the horrors of Partition but also the damages of British rule. Levy's irony makes it so very clear: "The railways! How am I forgetting? A gift from the British to an ignorant people. Just like your Lancashire cloth. Better than homespun, my mother says. Better." Or "[...] the rule of law – let us not forget the rule of law. Look here – are we not defending quality British goods from thieving Indians? Without your rule of law what are we?"[130] In real life the improbable indeed happens, so why should readers demand more verisimilitude of fiction than of life? Why couldn't Bernard be there to witness it all? Levy so humanises her racist protagonist that we actually feel sorry for him when he does not come home at the end of the war because of his ignorance about syphilis: "Wasn't even a miracle. I never had that awful disease. The pustule [on his penis] has probably been picked up from some straying insect after all. Or something gone septic. Nothing to do with that little madness in India."[131] Only Bernard would take two years to come home after the war.

How many babies like Queenie's were given up to be raised by "proper" parents, and by that Levy means Black? England in the forties is indeed a [white] mother who does not know how to treat her offspring and rejects them. Winston Churchill's words at the novel's end serve as a coda of sorts, but can also function as an epigraph (because we will reread it), illuminating the whole world Levy so powerful creates: "Never in the field of human conflict has so much been owed by so many to so few."

While Levy's earlier fiction explores the issue of belonging through her young Black Londoner protagonists having to answer to the white=English questions about their origin, identity and place in society, *Small Island* mixes it all up in a sobering way. The novel is much more than a social history of Black people in Britain at a pivotal point of the country's economic and political development. The novel pivots the centre, for very little of hegemonic whiteness is left at the novel's end – and this is not the reason why we cry.

When I asked Levy whether she also sees a social function in literature, her answer was, "absolutely – that's why I write!" She chooses realist conventions because of her faith in the power of representation – because of her belief that if you can represent reality, you can attempt to change it. Levy explains further:

> I write because I would like to change the world. I wasn't a great reader until I discovered storytelling. For me it is about wanting change. I don't say that all writers have to do that – that all writing should do that. Certainly the literature I like to read, by the end I like to understand something better. It's a noble ambition. If I read a James Baldwin story, there's no essay that could have been as powerful. You have to understand the craft of story as well. You can't just be angry or want to say something about something – that's just not good enough for me. I want it to be a story.[132]

Of course I concluded the 2002 interview with the question about Levy's chosen title, *Fruit of the Lemon*. Is it something that the English really did, I asked her, or is it about the colonial need to be more English than the English themselves? Is it the unpalatable in Jamaica's history, despite the beauty of the island?

> I had the title a very long time. The lemon is a bitter fruit of a very beautiful tree. The story of eating the lemon is true. Her aunt thought that's what the English did with them. Maybe she got confused with grapefruit. But my mother did eat lemons with a spoon (and sugar of course). So the lemon became this sort of symbol, from a song my mom used to sing, 'Lemon tree very pretty, lemon flower sweet but the fruit of the lemon is impossible to eat.'[133]

The song, according to Levy, is very much like the Caribbean.

Not only about the Caribbean, I wish I had added then, for, in England, old misconceptions unfortunately remain. A survey carried out recently for *The Observer* showed that nine out of ten respondents thought the rise in multiculturalism in England was linked with negative issues, such as increased crime and social tension. According to columnist Mary Riddel, "two in 10 [also] said they would not want anyone in their family to marry someone of a different race."[134] *The Guardian*'s Roy Greenslade even wonders whether some British newspapers have actually changed much since 1968, "the year Enoch Powell delivered his infamous 'rivers of blood' speech advocating a virtual end to black and commonwealth immigration along with a policy of assisted repatriation," in light of their responses to John Townend's (another Tory MP) comment that "'coloured immigrants' had ruined 'our homogeneous Anglo-Saxon society' and were responsible for raising crime."[135] For it is precisely concern over "the future of white identities," as Catherine Hall points out, "particularly in relation to black, which underpins the current debate on national identity, a term now regularly used by British politicians, which provides the backdrop for the discussions over the construction of 'Fortress Europe.'"[136] Europe's boundaries are swiftly being consolidated to prevent more migrants from coming in and to continue to make life very hard for the ones already in the country. The citizenship exam now in place could indeed lead to better integration if everyone in England recognises, as Mary Riddell writes, "we all need citizenship lessons."[137] The unease of Blair's cabinet over race and national identity has escalated since the publication of the 2000 Runnymede Trust report, *The Future of Multi-Ethnic Britain*, which called for an end to "Englishness."[138]

Nations are in part imagined communities, depending for their credibility and identity both on the legitimacy of government and the state apparatus and on invented traditions, manufactured myths, and shared perceptions of the social order that are usually not more than oversimplified stereotypes. Novels, as Benedict Anderson writes, are central to the construction of such imagined communities and national imaginaries. "Communities," according to Anderson, "are to be distinguished by the style in which they are imagined."[139] Although questions of identity and of freedom still compel the literature by Black Britons, Levy's novels have successfully reconfigured the many affiliations of a more fluid "British" sense of self. England needs more writers like Andrea Levy to continue to expose what Antoinette Burton characterises as "the complicity of history writing in patrolling the borders of national identity."[140]

"Made in Britain" is the title of the report Andrea Levy wrote for *The Guardian* to celebrate the coming together in a photograph of 50 contemporary British writers of Caribbean, Asian, and African descent gathered in front of the British Library, a new "Great Day" photo inspired by the one Art Kane took of American Jazz Musicians in 1958 Harlem. "Britain," Levy writes, "is finally beginning to gather up its more distant voices and listen to the rich stories that they have to tell, stories that are as central to the history of Britain and of British literature as anything that we are more familiar with."[141] It is Britain that gains, Levy notes, "where else in the world would this particular grouping of writers have any meaning?"

NOTES AND REFERENCES

[1]   In Bettina Aptheker's formulation, to "pivot the center" is to centre in another experience. Aptheker's paradigm avoids the dualistic opposition of centre/margin and enables historians to explore reality in concentric narratives. See *Tapestries of Life: Women's Work, Women's Consciousness and the Meaning of Daily Life* (Amherst: University of Massachusetts Press, 1989), chap. 1

[2]   Andrea Levy, *Fruit of the Lemon* (London: Review, 1999), p.326

[3]   Antoinette Burton, "Introduction: On the Inadequacy and the Indispensability of the Nation," *After the Imperial Turn: Thinking with and through the Nation*, ed. Antoinette Burton (Durham, N.C.: Duke University Press, 2003) p.2-3

[4]   Levy, *Fruit of the Lemon*, 325

[5]   Burton, "Introduction,"p.5

[6]   Andrea Levy, *Small Island* (London: Review, 2004), p.110

[7]   Andrea Levy, unpublished interview, March 5, 2002

[8]   Andrea Levy, 'This is my England,' *The Guardian* (February 19, 2000)

[9]   Stuart Hall, 'Cultural Identity and Diaspora,' *Identity, Community, Culture, Difference*, ed. Jonathan Rutherford, (London: Lawrence & Wishart, 1990), p.222

[10] Stuart Hall, 'Negotiating Caribbean Identities,' *New Left Review*, no. 209 (January/February 1995), p.7

[11] Maria Helena Lima, 'Decolonizing Genre: Jamaica Kincaid and the Bildungsroman,' *Genre*, vol. xxvi, no. 4 (winter 1993), pp.431-59

[12] Heidi Safia Mirza, 'Introduction: Mapping a Genealogy of Black British Feminism,' *Black British Feminism: A Reader*, ed. Heidi Safia Mirza, (London and New York: Routledge, 1977), p.3

[13] See Perry Anderson, 'Components of the National Culture,' *English Questions* (London: Verso, 1992), pp.48-104

[14] Levy's father died from lung cancer in 1987

[15] Andrea Levy, *Every Light in the House Burnin'*, (London: Review, 1994), p.33

[16] Ibid. p.42

[17] Ibid. p52

[18] Ibid. p.192

[19] Ibid. p.67

[20] Ibid. p.44

[21] Ibid. p.57-9

[22] Ibid. p.121

[23] Ibid. p.126

[24] Ibid. p.88

[25] Ibid. p.172

[26] Ibid. p.166

[27] Ibid. p.141

[28] Ibid. p.228

[29] Ibid. p.21

[30] Ibid. p.218

[31] Ibid. p.219

[32] Ibid. p.219

[33] Michelle Cliff, *Abeng*, (New York: Dutton, 1984), p.70

[34] Ibid. p.70

[35] Ibid. p.70 36 Ibid. p.71

[37] Catherine Hall, 'Gender Politics and Imperial Politics: Rethinking the Histories of Empire,' Engendering History: Caribbean Women in Historical Perspective, Verene Shepherd, Bridget Brereton & Barbara Bailey, eds., (New York: St. Martin's Press, 1995), p.56

[38] Levy, Every Light, p.145

[39] Ibid. p.250

[40] The father, Charles Newton, dies when the two girls are very young. All his life Mr. Newton works as a mechanic for the London Transport, and he dies of pneumonia, after being pensioned off for emphysema: "I was surprised at how mother missed him, even though all through his life she complained that he wasn't good for anything" (*Never far from Nowhere*, p. 4)

[41] Levy, Andrea, *Never far from Nowhere*, (London: Review, 1996), p.7

[42] Ibid. p.230

[43] Ibid. p.7

[44] Ibid. p.42

[45] Ibid. p.8

[46] Ibid. p.24

[47] Ibid. p.25

[48] Ibid. p.30

[49] Ibid. p.6

[50] Ibid. p.39

[51] Ibid. p.40

[52] Ibid. p.77

[53] Ibid. p.97

[54] Ibid. p.8

[55] Ibid. p.99

[56] "Without Olive [mother and I] didn't know what to do. There was no reason to tut or roll our eyes – there was no reason to slam doors, no fights to get away from" (Ibid., p.6 and p.235)

[57] Ibid. p.00

[58] Ibid. p.229

[59] Ibid. p.213

[60] Ibid. p.237

[61] Ibid. p.239

[62] Ibid. p.88

[63] Ibid. p.172

[64] Ibid. p.212

[65] Ibid. p.268

[66] Ibid. p.142

[67] Ibid. p.210

[68] de Certeau, Michel 'Walking in the City,' *The Practice of Everyday Life*, trans. Steven Kendall, (Berkeley: University of California Press, 1984), 117-19

[69] Porter, Roy, *London: A Social History*, (London: Hamish Hamilton, 1994), quoted in John Clement Ball, 'The Semi-Detached Metropolis: Hanif Kureishi's London,' *ARIEL: A Review of International English Literature*, 27: 4 (October 1996), p.8

[70] Ball, John Clement 'The Semi-Detached Metropolis,' p.8

[71] *Injustice* documents the struggles for justice by the families of Black people who have died in police custody in a six-year period (2001 documentary by Ken Fero and Tariq Mehmood). Unfortunately police violence has not stopped, and there is a second documentary in the works, according to email communication from Ken Fero. Contributions are welcome: www.injusticefilm.co.uk

[72] Levy, *Never far from Nowhere*, p.272

[73] Ibid. p.272

[74] Boyce Davies, Carol, *Black Women, Writing and Identity*, (London and New York: Routledge, 1994), p.113

[75] Levy, *Never far from Nowhere*, p.280

[76] Ibid. p.274

[77] Ibid. p.277

[78] Ibid. p.278

[79] Ibid. p.273

[80] Ibid. p.277

[81] Ibid. p.276

[82] Ibid. p.281

[83] Ibid. p.282

[84] Ibid. p.5

[85] Ibid. p.204

[86] I submitted a different version of this section of the paper to the 16th Annual West Indian Literature, University of Miami at Coral Gables (May 1997), but was unable to attend

[87] Heidi Mirza, *Black British Feminism*, p.5

[88] Levy, *Fruit of the Lemon*, p.56

[89] Ibid. p.115

[90] Ibid. p.130

[91] Ibid. p.131

[92] Ibid. p.131

[93] Phillips, Caryl, *A New World Order: Essays* (New York: Vintage International, 2002), p.132

[94] Levy, 'This is my England,' *The Guardian* (February 19, 2000)

[95] See http://books.guardian.co.uk/Print/0,3858,3965021,00.html

[96] Levy, *Fruit*, 160

[97] Ibid. p.157

[98] Ibid. p.152

[99] Ibid. p.54

[100] Ibid. p.151

[101] Ibid. p.332

[102] Ibid. p.332

[103] Ibid. p.326

[104] Ibid. p.327

[105] Ibid. p.241

[106] Ibid. p.242

[107] Ibid. p.242

[108] Levy, unpublished interview, 2002

[109] Levy, *Fruit*, p.314

[110] Ibid. p.249

[111] Levy, unpublished interview, 2002

[112] Hickman, Christie 'Andrea Levy: Under the skin of history,' (*Independent*, 06 February 2004)

[113] Levy, *Small Island*, 204

[114] Ibid. p.195

[115] Ibid. p.6

[116] Ibid. p.207

[117] Ibid. p.221

[118] Ibid. p.230

[119] Ibid. p.237

[120] Ibid. p.240

[121] Ibid. p.3

[122] Ibid. p.241

[123] Ibid. p.245

[124] Ibid. p.248

[125] Greer, Bonnie, 'Empire's child,' *The Guardian* (January 31, 2004)

[126] Phillips, Mike, 'Roots manoeuvre,' *The Guardian* (February 14, 2004)

[127] Phillips, Mike, in dialogue with Andrea Levy, who read and talked about her work at the Museum of London, on February 14, 2004, at 6:30pm

[128] Levy, *Small Island*, p.116

[129] Ibid. p.110

[130] Ibid. p.317

[131] Ibid. p.352

[132] Levy, unpublished interview, 2002

[133] Ibid

[134] Mary Riddell, 'Teach Us all to be British,' *The Observer* (10 February 2002), p.26

[135] Greenslade, Roy, 'Rivers of Newsprint…,' *The Guardian* (April 2, 2001), Media p.5

[136] Hall, Catherine, 'Gender Politics and Imperial Politics,' pp.48-9

[137] Riddell, 'Teach Us All,' p.26

[138] Runnymede Trust, *The Future of Multi-Ethnic Britain: Report of the Commission on Multi-Ethnic Britain* (London: Profile Books, 2000), p.15

[139] Anderson, Benedict, *Imagined Communities: Reflections on the Origin and Spread of Nationalism* (London & New York, Verso, 1991 [1983]), p.6

[140] Burton, Antoinette, Introduction, p.8

[141] Levy, Andrea, 'Made in Britain', *The Guardian* (September 18, 2004)

Courttia Newland's Psychological Realism and Consequentialist Ethics

R. Victoria Arana

Courttia Newland has been hailed as, "Britain's brightest black writer" publishing today[1]. His first novel, *The Scholar*, published in 1997, almost instantly earned him high critical praise from reviewers nationwide. Since then he has produced two more successful novels – *Society Within* and *Snakeskin* – and a sheaf of short stories which are currently being collated into a collection entitled, *Music for the Off Key* to be published by Peepal Tree Press (forthcoming). His theatrical works play to full houses, nowadays – and to enthusiastic young audiences. But the media hype has missed the mark, according to Newland himself: "The publicity and interest highlighted the fact *that* I am writing: rather than concentrating on what I'm writing. The persona, which has developed from this publicity is one of "a working class, Black, city boy made good"; I want my books to be famous, not me, not my life."[2] His wish has a strong probability of fulfillment.

Newland's storytelling is fast-paced and stylish, and his fictional world reflects a segment of contemporary Britain that has not been similarly scrutinised in fiction since Charles Dickens wrote his best-selling novels about lovable street urchins, sneaky blackguards, and the Empire's wanton perpetuation of poverty and crime in and around London. Like Dickens' great masterpieces *Oliver Twist*, *Dombey and Son*, and *Great Expectations*, Newland's works "tackle the essentially modern problem of the discontents of an urban civilization"[3]. Both Newland and Dickens, with a deep love for humanity of all types and degrees, have triumphed in depicting a changeable and changing urban civilization—and in rendering it with a nuanced solicitude calculated to foster deeper understanding of new cultural conditions in England. But to characterise Newland as a Dickens knock-off for the new millennium would be misleading. Newland's works possess none of Dickens' signature sentimentalism, romantic eccentricity, or restive overstatement. Nevertheless, the comparison is useful. It enables readers to appreciate Newland's importance as a social observer and commentator, particularly in an era when, around the world, metropolitan culture's discontents are not only vulnerable emotionally and economically, but many of them are resentful or desperate – and some, potentially lethal. Newland, like Dickens, portrays a world peopled by heterogeneous characters alive with energy, vitality and wit, whose daily dilemmas are dramatised with humor and compassion as well as intelligence, veracity and psychological insight. Newland's work possesses the maturity, the seemingly effortless verbal dexterity and the intellectual *gravitas* of a major artist.

However much Newland may wish that critical interest should concentrate on his works and not on himself, readers today (especially those brought up on cultural studies) pay close attention to the socio-political origins of creative works and are interested in discovering as much as possible about the connections between the author's life and his productions. Courttia Newland's background does indeed throw light on his creative writing, for it accounts – at least in part – for the realism of his representation of young Black aspiration.

Most of Newland's writing, so far, concerns a large cast of characters whose cultural backgrounds are comparable to his own. Courttia was born on August 25, 1973, at Queen Charlotte's Hospital in Hammersmith, West London, to Marlene Denny and Owen Newland. Courttia's father, who was born in Jamaica, had emigrated to England with his father, Enos Nolan. Marlene, born in Barbados, was only fifteen years old when she gave birth to Courttia. The couple's second child, Jerome, was born three years later. When the couple separated, Courttia's grandfather, Enos Nolan and his uncle Trevor Denny became the most influential men in the young boy's life, cultivating in him a sturdy sense of self. As Newland himself explains, both his first name (*Courttia*) and his surname (*Newland* rather than *Nolan*) have variant family stories. One of them is that 'the birth certificate guy/girl spelt the name [Nolan] wrong or misheard the name or something stupid like that and wrote it down wrong'[4] The family did not mind since they, like Courttia himself, preferred the deeper meanings of *new land* to those of *no lan*'[5] About his first name, *Courttia*, Newland explains that his father and one of his father's friends made it up:

> My dad wanted something that sounded like *courtier*, but was
> spelt differently. Also, he loved a brand of car that was popular

over here in the 'seventies called the Ford *Cortina*. On the first
page of *The Scholar*, I spoke of the car, thinking someone would
pick up on the similarity, but no one ever did.[6]

The comment is typical of Newland's spare and understated style:
provocatively multivalent in alluding to Britain's deep-rooted
aristocracy while gamely positing a family claim to equally lofty
status and referring to the materialism or fetishism of the newly
immigrated from the Caribbean Isles, dryly humorous in its self-
reference, and no doubt reliable as family chronicle – all at the same
time.

Like most of the young Black women in Newland's fiction and
drama, Courttia's young mother took her role as caregiver very
seriously and reportedly went to all the parent-teacher meetings at
Courttia's schools (see Moore interview). The boy began his
schooling at Whitehall Primary School in Uxbridge, Sussex. His
parents had married and moved out of London when Courttia was
three; and when they split up, about six years later, his mother
moved back to London with the two children because, as Newland
explains, "I was around nine by then. We were one of only two
Black families in the [Sussex] area, and the constant racism [there]
had led me to view my Blackness very negatively." Back in London,
Courttia attended Bentworth Primary in Shepherd's Bush until age
eleven and Burlington Danes Secondary School, also in Shepherd's
Bush, until age fifteen.[7] He spent one year there doing A-levels in
English literature and Sociology but dropped out, declaring the
program's course of study "boring!" He was not, however, averse to
reading and read constantly and voraciously throughout his
childhood and adolescence – and still does. While his favorite
subjects in school had always been English and drama, he thinks he
"would've liked history, too, if it hadn't been so Colonia".
Newland's creative writings combine these ongoing interests as he
undertakes to describe a new social reality in Britain and to rewrite
contemporary British history in genres that will appeal directly to
the country's newest citizenry, Black British youth, as well as to
seasoned readers of world literatures.

Newland lists as his "childhood favourites" the following: Roald
Dahl,[8] J. R.R. Tolkien, Rosa Guy,[9] Maya Angelou, and Chester
Himes,[10] The list is significant in alluding to a rich mixture of
influences clearly still present in his novels. Dahl's dark humor and
world of crime, Tolkien's epic struggles among groups with starkly

contrasting moral alignments, Guy's straightforward novels for young people, Angelou's unembarrassed and even lyrical representation of a sometimes gritty personal reality, and Himes' fast-paced narration of stories about crime, corruption, and institutional racism – all resonate in various ways in Newland's writing. As a 'grown-up' ("so far," Newland cautions), his favourites are Paul Auster,[11] Rupert Thompson,[12] Stephen King,[13] Richard Price,[14] Colson Whitehead,[15] Dashiell Hammett,[16] Banana Yoshimoto,[17] Iain Banks, Junot Diaz,[18] Langston Hughes,[19] and Walter Mosely.[20] These rosters of Newland's dearly loved writers are highly significant, comprising, as they do, some of the most innovative and distinguished practitioners of the genres of detective fiction, crime thriller, cultural jest, family narrative, and Black folk parable. While serious critical study of correspondences between each of the writers Newland openly admires and his own work has not yet begun, when it does begin to appear, it will richly increase the world's understanding of contemporary British writing.

Fascinated as Newland was by narratives of various sorts, his earliest career objective was to be *not* a writer, but a musician: "I really wanted to be a rapper or involved in the music industry in a production capacity." Besides fiction, he confesses,

> the other art form I admire the most is hip hop. True, real un-commercial hip hop is the closest thing to musical literature and poetry that you can get. For 'lyrical skill' I admire Jay Z, Mos Def, Talib Kweli, Masta Ace, Don Blaq, Black Thought, Big L, Big Pun, Common Scarface, Eminem, Biggie and hundreds of other hot MC's.[21]

Here, certainly, is another lead for Newland's future critics and biographers. Newland exploits the Black urban experience and the street language rhythms so evident in authentic British hip hop in the narrative style of his novels and in the dialogue of his plays. In *The Scholar, Society Within*, and *Snakeskin*, the action frequently takes place to the accompaniment of specifically named musical recordings. The final scene of Snakeskin, for instance, occurs against a backdrop of "some mournful indie song" played on the radio by a group that Mason identifies as Radiohead ('Great band they are,' Mason says) just before he pulls the trigger and shoots himself. That aural imagery – described so differently by the narrator and by Mason – adds piquancy to the hardboiled realism of the scene and provides psychosocial insight into both the detective and his quarry. According to Newland, who listens to popular music while composing his stories, the world of hip hop is still vital as inspiration.

The world of commerce, likewise, has provided experiences that Newland has been drawing upon to enrich his art. Like Charles Dickens, Courttia Newland garnered first-hand experience in childhood and early youth of the urban workplaces that he later described in his fiction and drama. Before completing his first novel, Newland had worked as a paperboy, sales assistant, stock room attendant and door-to-door salesman. Meanwhile, some of his closest acquaintances fell prey to the various seductions of illegal substances and to the lure of quick, illicit money from drug trafficking and robbery. While he never gave in to the temptation to engage in crime, despite poverty and opportunity and never tried cocaine or any of the other dangerous drugs so openly available in the neighborhoods where he lived (and still lives) in London.[22][23] Newland paid thoughtful attention to that underground economy as well. Dramatic, close-up, intelligent – Newland's fiction imparts insights into young Black British lives; and that real-world knowledge, present like a pulse throughout the narrative, is the heartbeat of Newland's fictional world.

As the young Newland was developing his literary talents, two individuals took particular interest in his creativity and served as mentors: film director and screenwriter Barney Platts-Mills and Post Office Theatre Company director Riggs O'Hara. They had already garnered considerable success themselves in the business of dramatising stories for film and stage. Besides earning wide critical acclaim in Britain for his cinematic directing, Platts-Mills had won international recognition, including a Cannes Film Festival Award, and O'Hara, a New Yorker now based in London, had "worked with some of the very best actors in England" before collaborating in the production of Newland's theatrical works: *Estate of Mind, Women of Troy 2099, The Far Side, Mother's Day*, and *B is for Black*.[24] Both men, Newland says, helped him hone his writing skills.

After the critical success of his first novel, *The Scholar* (1997), Newland began to travel widely and he continues to do so. By the summer of 2001, he had visited The Hague, Amsterdam, Prague, Berlin, Frankfurt, Miami, Washington, D.C., New York City, Dublin, Iceland, Cuba, Scotland, and Wales – for readings and other professional appearances. In addition, he toured Barbados,

Thailand, and Egypt, purely for holiday recreation. About his travels in Egypt, Newland exclaimed, "Talk about life changing!" While most of his writings to date – fiction and drama – are set in England (present or future), Newland's range of characters has expanded in each successive work to reflect his growing awareness of the ethnic intricacies in England's multicultural towns and of their inhabitants' global connections. Like the greatest European novels of the nineteenth-century, Newland's more recent fiction achieves its *gravitas* from mature consideration of the play of moral values in the day-to-day lives of people living in dynamic multi-ethnic societies.

Newland's reviewers have extolled his "powerful" talents as a storyteller: his "classic" construction of plots, their social relevance, the vividness of his imagery, and his "savage aplomb" as a narrator (Royce, Wolff, etc.). Not much critical attention has been paid, however, to the psychological and philosophical aspects of Newland's artistic endeavors. Could it be that his characters' realistically crude language[25] has drowned out, for so many reviewers, Newland's more sophisticated artistic accomplishments?

NEWLAND'S PSYCHOLOGICAL REALISM

The world of Newland's fiction is contemporary London, a post-colonial metropolis inhabited by Britons who are young, non-religious, segregated from middle-class Anglo-English communities, at least partly Black and conscious of the impact of racial bias on their psyches and economic prospects. Newland's youthful protagonists are searching for love, material wealth, freedom from various forms of oppressive cultural domination and the power to determine for themselves lives of possibility, satisfaction and joy. His antagonists are either older, greedy, armed and ruthless or else mentally unstable. From the perspective of plot, these are probably the oldest tales of all. What gives Newland's fiction current pertinence and imbues it with originality is not so much Newland's ability to plot a thrilling saga as his meticulous attention to his characters' fluctuating emotions and mixed motivations. Newland told Paul Sullivan: "The whole reason I chose my subject matter was because everyone was getting it wrong, man."[26]

Newland's fiction posits as its principal and overarching subject matter the life-cycles of certain cultural formations: the shifting generational differences that emerge and wane as biological clocks tick away (regarding, for example, sexuality, recreation, work, civil society), the psychosocial fallout from certain sorts of civic decisionmaking (*e.g.*, segregating the 'unemployable' into high-crime 'welfare' zones, tearing down a youth centre), the contagiousness of activist enthusiasms (*e.g.*, of organisations including the Black Muslims and Neo-Nazis, but also of trendy raves, sporting matches, emergent community-operated radio stations), and so on. Newland's emphasis, though, is not on colliding social forces delineated *grosso modo* (not merely, for instance, on the fire-powered contest between drug warlords and ambitious, cocksure, upwardly motivated Black youngsters, as so many reviewers have duly noted), but on the daily psychological pressures of hard choices on individuals of differing personality types (for instance, alert and suspicious Cory Bradley; trusting and conscientious Sean Bradley; their loyal pal Garvey; pathologically co-dependent but recovering Valerie Parker, vulnerable and remorseful Arthur Lynes, optimistic and enterprising Nathan Walters, truth-seeking Ervine James, and so on) and diverse alignments (the basically good, the misguided, the degenerate and the outright pitiless) who populate Newland's fictional world. While the narrative provides to outsiders a window on little-known populations of Britain, to others it offers a mirror. Collectively, the individual stories of Newland's enormous cast of characters combine to form a broad picture of Newland's busy (mostly West London) urban neighbourhoods, whose separate identities are ultimately distinguishable and recognisable by their real-world topography and typical social mores and practices. Were it not so, readers would not be so quick to spot their verisimilitude to the real-world locales of Ladbroke Grove, Shepherd's Bush, and Notting Hill, of Soho, Eltham, Central London, Leicester, and so on. Like all realistic fiction, Newland's relies to a certain extent on the predictable, on probable if not exactly recognisable environments and credible details: the appearance of estate courtyards, Caribbean fast-food places, youth centres, a crack house, and a variety of flats, stores, pubs, streets, parks and vehicles.

What is *not* predictable in Newland's fictional neighborhoods is *why* events unfold as they do. To grasp that Newland highlights life (see Cobham interview), *emotional* life, not merely knifing and shooting, a reader must be able to recognise just how the narrative invites insight into what Raymond Williams somewhere famously called "the whole way of living of a people." Providing psychological insight into his characters' motivations as well as reactions is Newland's *forte.*

When *The Scholar* was being reviewed initially, despite the abundant praise heaped upon this first novel, critics were quick to react to what they saw as its 'noir' setting: it was, according to Stephen Morrissey, recognisably "the seedy West London familiar to anyone who's read Martin Amis"; it was, as Sean Coughlan put it, "a dangerous place, exploited by violent drug pushers, patrolled by a corrupt police force and fought over by warring teenage gangs." Morrissey wrote: "Newland's characters are doomed"; and, like most early reviewers, Coughlan underscored the idea that Newland's characters were hopelessly trapped in their ghetto, "unable to escape". These early reviewers were blindsided to major features of the novel – perhaps by racial or class bias – and did not register where, in the action, characters had made clearly wrong choices at signal moments in the plot, choices that would have averted their catastrophes. Concerned that reviewers might go on missing the point, Newland disclosed to Nicholas Royle that *The Scholar* is to be read as 'a warning': "It's *about escaping*", Newland explained, "from the traps in your head" (my emphasis).

In his interview with Royle, Newland was drawing attention to his major artistic objectives, only part of which had been to render the harshest realities of the street, its well-oiled mechanisms of evil. Newland's larger aim is to confront readers with the challenge "How may these be avoided?" In *The Scholar*, evil is incarnate in the person of Lawrence Peterson, whose nickname 'Levi' is an anagram for his sort of power. He is also known as 'the Dredd.' He is a living nightmare: "one of the most feared men in Greenside",[27] a drug lord and crime kingpin, someone who could always be counted on to have 'a nasty little surprise up his sleeve, a sting in his tail that he would unleash with no regrets and even less sympathy'.[28] He is, nevertheless, no flat allegorical figure, but a figure carefully portrayed in the round. We note his self-consciously emphasised Jamaican accent, his calculated modulations from affable to volatile speech rhythms, his heavy jewelry, his unconscious gestures (like brushing a dreadlock away from his face), his menacing body language, and his intimidating rhetoric. Levi feels no remorse, readers learn, about drawing the "vibrant" twelve-year-old Mo into a lethal robbery and reducing him to a "pathetic looking person" by doling out crack to counteract the boy's budding consciousness of the wickedness he has just been a party to.[29] Levi entangles young people in his webs by flattering the susceptible and goading the recalcitrant, just as he ensnares Sean and Cory, the protagonists of *The Scholar*, by inviting the upstanding teenager Sean (whom he calls a "brainy lickle fucker") to "go fe a drink" and by pretending to pay no attention to Sean's badboy cousin Cory, who then falls into Levi's trap by defiantly tagging along.[30] Once in Levi's clutches, the teenagers are both slowly transformed morally by Levi's inexorable reasoning, his pointed threats of violence, and the gut-wrenching horror of what they eventually experience in his world. But they were hardly doomed.

Newland's narrative does not lose sight of his characters' consciousness of free will and their psychological struggle to hold on to whatever freedoms they manage to possess. For instance, immediately after Levi (who had long been planning a serious robbery) coerces Cory into promising to stand in for one of Levi's subordinates whom Cory has incapacitated in a knife fight, Cory realises, "Levi's got me where he wants me, f'real." The cousins, once out of Levi's earshot, review their options while waiting for the lift to their family's flat.

> 'So how you gonna get out of it? Sean wondered aloud.'
> 'I dunno man, I'm stuck on dat one.'
> The bell for the lift chimed pleasantly and the two boys stepped in and pressed their floor, both trapped inside their own thoughts.[31]

By the end of the novel, Cory, who will not touch cocaine, has managed to out-manouvre and to kill Levi, to help himself to Levi's ill-gotten money and – most important of all – to escape from Greenside with his life. Sean, on the other hand – book-smart but not so street-smart as his cousin and with his judgment at a crucial moment distorted by crack – makes a number of stupid moves and ends up in police custody for his part in an armed robbery that he had never wanted to participate in, in the first place.[32] Newland's Greenside neighborhood is not a modern locus for the enactment of inexorable, Greek-style tragedy, where characters are doomed from the start, as so many reviewers have maintained, but a place where the complicated negotiations of life are carried out by individuals learning, one way or another, how to live safely and happily in a difficult world. In writing to warn, Newland is undertaking a revolutionary role.

To succeed in suggesting to his readership how to "escape the traps in your head", an author must first attend to the convincing representation of characters as thinking and feeling beings. Angela Carter's declaration along these lines is apposite: "I personally feel much more in common with certain Third World writers, both male and female, who are transforming actual fictional forms to both reflect and to precipitate changes in the way people feel about themselves."[33] While Newland is certainly not a 'Third World writer', his fiction is confluent with the artistic aims that Carter describes – towards psychological realism in the service of an avant-garde dedication to transforming how "people feel about themselves." P. D. James, in describing her own means towards similar ends, has said: "You need to free the form to be truthful about sexual and other matters."[34] Newland's writing is truthful and purposeful in *those* ways – *and* about suffering, guilt, self-delusion, and the pleasures of power as well. David Simpson – in his review of *Terry Eagleton's Sweet Violence: The Idea of the Tragic* – noted that while "many critics have claimed that modern life has no place for exemplary transgression or suffering", some contemporary writers, on the other hand, "are entirely persuasive about the moral dignity and social significance of suffering and death in ordinary lives"[35] Newland, in choosing to emphasise ethical concerns, strives to be among the latter.

Newland's integration of recognisable topographical details, his evident delight in noteworthy details of dress, gesture, facial expression and so forth are not by themselves what makes Newland's writing so down-to-earth and so persuasive about sexuality, transgression, suffering, redemption and the rest. The experiences of sex, crimes and misdemeanours, sorrow and guilt, pride and joy are the daily matters that trouble or delight his characters: they talk about them constantly. Newland's dramatic use of dialogue, in an array of accurately rendered contemporary Black British Englishes, is convincingly lifelike – and Newland's dialogues, noted for their sparkle and hard-hitting realism, are the feature of his work most abundantly praised by his reviewers. But, well and beyond the dialogues themselves, it is Newland's smart use of figurative language for the concise representation of mental states, his psychological realism,[36] that sounds the persuasive (and potentially transformative) chord of truth. The chief instruments Newland employs to provide tangible clues as to the characters' foci of attention and states of mind are simile, metonym and synecdoche.

Newland acknowledged these devices in his interview with Paul

Sullivan, where he credited his past as a rap artist as excellent preparation for writing dialogue: "Rap is a wicked form of writing. It's close to prose," he explained, "because it uses similes and metaphors in a really tight way."[37] Right after Levi bears down on Cory with "if yuh 'ad a programme...an' someone fuck wid yuh programme...what would yuh do, hmm? What would yuh do?" the narrator uses a simile: "The question hung in the air like a dust particle, riding the thermals and dancing around the confines of the car."[38] The figure of speech (*hung . . .like a dust particle*) refers to Levi's question, but indirectly it indicates what is *really* happening as a response. The simile concisely suggests bewilderment and the passage of some time before anyone responds to the question; at the same time, it traces the captive teenagers' vague consciousness of *their own confinement* – and even, perhaps, of their own aimlessness (*riding*, for no good reason of their own, in Levi's car) and of their insignificance to Levi (about as important as a bit of *dust*). Newland's fiction is rich in similes; but, like this one, their terms do not often break out of a character's actual field of vision: both Levi's badgering question and the sunlit motes are registered in Cory's mind. The integral (isotopic) nature of the simile not only adds to the realistic texture of the scene, it also brings into sharp focus exactly what the characters are conscious of in their own mental worlds. Similarly, in *Society Within*, when white youth-worker Trish inadvertently causes four Black masks to fall from a former colleague's bag into her lap, she "grabbed at one to confirm what she saw. Three empty holes forming two eyes and a mouth punctuated her find like a trio of full stops. She wondered what Lacey could want with balaclavas, besides the obvious."[39] The simile (*like a trio of full stops*) registers Trish's reaction as a brisk sequence of sharp shocks, of terminations, presaging as they do the stuttering finish to Trish's idealistic and amorous illusions about Lacey.

Newland's synecdoches and metonyms occur throughout his fiction to guide his readers in following precisely how the characters are feeling about the events they are undergoing. Down-hearted youths, for example, do not see their streets or neighborhoods; they see only the under part, "the pavement"[40] Instead of the corridors of his building, Cory close-focuses on the defaced parts, the "blood on the walls...faded into a dry brown...flaked in places" before inwardly exclaiming, "Damn...what's happenin' to my life, man?"[41] When Sonia slams out of Sean's life after hearing that Sean will join the arch-criminal Levi in an armed robbery, "In a flash she was gone, leaving the letterbox shuddering in her wake."[42] Sean, we know, has only consented to participate because going along with Levi's deal seems to him the only way to keep Levi's thugs from killing Cory in retribution for Cory's assault on one of them. The rattling letterbox is a metonym for the whole house shaking (in itself a potent symbol), but it is through Sean's brave new consciousness of the dreadful duties of love that the sound is heard as a shudder, an anthropomorphic psychological projection, implying Sean's own chilling fear and disgust at what he is about to do. Newland's subtle figures of speech – as in these few examples – are not in the least ornamental, but judicious clues about the characters' attitudes and emotions. By helping us to see through the eyes and minds of his characters, they add a dimension of psychological realism to Newland's stories and give an authenticity of feeling to his whole *oeuvre*.

NEWLAND'S MORAL PHILOSPHY

Authenticity and persuasiveness – these are important to an author set on depicting what Dostoevsky scholar Joseph Frank has termed the equally 'morally repugnant consequences'[43] of antisocial behaviour and of social engineering. In Newland's works, antisocial behaviour (at its worst) means rampantly preying on others for personal gain and social engineering (at its worst) means institutionalising systems for holding back whole categories of people culturally and economically from leading fulfilling and meaningful existences. Both forms of oppression can condition people psychologically to live lesser lives than they would otherwise be capable of enjoying. Like other realist British writers of the post-World War II period, Newland would almost certainly "contend not only that veridical accounts of the world are possible but also that they are *necessary* if various forms of oppression are to be opposed by rational critique and if the transformation of society is not to recede from view as a political desideratum."[44] Newland's fiction posits a starting place for reform. After the 1999 publication of his second novel, *Society Within*, Newland told *Pride* magazine's Diana Evans, "In the two books that I've written, I've dealt with what Black people can do about themselves. I think, in a sense, it's pretty useless to talk about what White people do to you because you can't control that. We as Black people, we can control what we do to each other"[45]. It's a bit of an over-generalisation, I think, but its core message is clear: morality and moral responsibility begin at home with rational assessments of the behaviour of one's closest kin. *Society Within*, in particular, abounds with no-holds-barred critiques like Trisha's of her former charges' belligerence[46] and Carolyn's of her mother's bigotry.[47] Realistically the conditions surrounding young people growing up in Britain's urban projects – offers no panaceas, but instead traces out, in memorable sequences of dramatic episodes, the results of delusional thinking and reckless choices. His stories are thrilling on the plot level, but their deeper implications demand close reading and thoughtful philosophical analyses.

Newland's good characters are not angelic; neither are they particularly heroic in the classical sense. But they are, like Lynette in *Society Within*, aware of the difference between transgressive and virtuous behaviours.[48] They frequently cuss each other out and smoke marijuana (like Lewis, who is otherwise "a straightforward, decent and law-abiding soul"[49]), indulge in premarital or extramarital sex, even steal (like Sissy[50]); but they can see through most foolish and untrue talk. And they do not approve of gratuitous cruelty or violence. Newland's fictional protagonists are drawn into vortical trajectories by the practical (let's call them *ethical*) choices existing between the two extremities. Newland's depraved characters are their antagonists: devious and corrupt, selfish, pitiless, and lethal.

In Newland's stories, readers can see how individuals develop admirable traits and despicable ones. For instance, conscientious Sean Bradley, the exemplary student in *The Scholar* – accustomed as he is to gratifying teachers, coaches, and other authority figures – is highly susceptible to praise and censure, even when it comes from the decidedly psychopathic Levi. "Sean beamed brightly"[51] when Levi approved of Sean's quick verbal responses and invited him to share equally in the spoils of the robbery the dealer was planning. After the robbery is over, Sean worries that Levi's gang does not admire him and might be "laughing at him even now, over their Chinese dinner and glasses of Moët."[52] Recalling Levi's wise-seeming advice ("try it before you decide that you don't like it"), Sean, in a pique, foolishly lights up Levi's gift, the spliff of crack that gets Sean hooked on cocaine and derails his future. Levi's advice is unethical and logically absurd when applied to an addictive and destructive substance, but Sean's disturbed psyche (after his having participated in what he knew was wrong) hears only the fatherly tone and clichéd benefit in Levi's fiendish platitude. Sean – unaware of the *conscientiousness trap* in his own head – has become one of those "benighted creatures" whom Iris Murdoch described as "sunk in a reality whose nature we are constantly and overwhelmingly tempted to deform by fantasy". Cory's questionable motivations, on the other hand, are quite different. Knowing that he does not have time to appeal to the civic authorities, which are probably too corrupt to help him anyway, he feels compelled (deontologically, as the ethicists would say)[53] to take matters into his own gun-toting hands.

> Cory hit the darkening streets like a vengeful spirit, his mind fully focused on the task that lay ahead of him. . . . His plan was to force Levi not to testify in court against Sean by putting the Dredd in hospital. He wholeheartedly believed Sean that it had been the dealer who shot the courageous yet foolish black man in the jewelers, and he didn't see any reason why his cousin should take the blame for something he didn't do.
>
> Cory knew that he was taking a big risk and he also knew if any of his friends had any inkling of what he had in store for Levi, they'd think he'd lost his mind. Maybe he had. At the end of the day it didn't matter, because Cory was prepared to go to almost any lengths to make amends for the way that things had turned out. He thought of all the people who had been upset, indirectly perhaps, through him.[54]

In *Society Within*, Newland again presents his readers with an array of characters "locked in the complexities of their own lives"[55] and here, too, he is assiduous in detailing how they go about extricating themselves from problems, especially "the traps" in their heads, so as to obtain the objects of their diverse desires. They are not, as one reader put it, lacking in "the skill... and the will to get out of their ghetto" (King). Quite the opposite. Here, Newland's moral philosophy comes into even sharper focus. Let us put it into some sort of context. In her article titled 'Ethical Narrative in Dickens and Thackeray', Judith L. Fisher distinguishes Dickens' melodramatic deployment of his own philosophical certainties and his characters' "innate moral natures" from Thackeray's ironic use of deliberate ambiguities and his narrator's distrust of his characters' subjective judgements – judgements that Thackeray shows to be relativistic anyway, culturally constructed, and "self-deluding".[56] While

Dickens' moral universe is ultimately assessable in penological terms, by what punishments Dickens (or God) metes out and while Thackeray demonstrates that absolute moral certainty has all but disappeared from Europe in the nineteenth century, Newland's ethical world more closely resembles that of philosopher Martha Nussbaum, where emotions play a substantial part in establishing moral understanding and promoting civil ethics.[57] In philosophical terms, Newland's moral universe is consequentialist rather than deontologist: it resembles the world of the ancient Greek philosophers, who posited a general human desire for happiness, much more than it resembles that of, say, post World War II rights revolutionists, whose fundamental arguments concern setting up legal systems to engender and protect egalitarian civil justice.[58]

Society Within is about the ethical pursuit of happiness. It contains twelve chapters, four of which centre on the day-to-day life of Elisha, an eighteen-year-old newcomer to Greenside Estate who is not thrilled at first to have to settle there but stifles expressing her disappointment in her new surroundings with the thought: "*Mum's happy though, I mustn't stop her from being happy ...*"[59] By the end of the book Elisha has found employment ("a regular wage"), a circle of friends, and a male admirer: "She couldn't help being enthusiastic about how good she was feeling."[60] Orin, the book's handsome young hero, gets into a series of dangerous predicaments after finding a kilo of hashish in the estate park but, with the help of his trickster-figure mate Malcolm, narrowly escapes danger and discovery. Even though the chapter ends with Orin and Malcolm hugging and laughing, "the joy at coming out on top taking over."[61] Orin is already vowing to himself that, despite Malcolm's confidence and evident ability to outsmart the brutal thugs to whom the hashish had belonged, for "himself there would never be a "nex" time"[62] because the whole lawless episode had been far too frightening. Another chapter centres on Trisha, a white youth worker whose starry-eyed illusions about her community role and personal relationships in Greenside shatter when she realises that much of her happiness had been on built upon false impressions and dodgy municipal policies and fiscal resources. Valerie Parker's problem is so complex that it takes a whole page to define its ramifications in summary terms[63]: she has been molested by her stepfather, raped by her crack-addicted boyfriend Ray and one of his pals and derailed from a life she had envisioned for herself: "She was intelligent, good-looking, and sick to death of having to watch over Ray and his fucked-up habit. It wasn't fair on her...It was *his* fault she wasn't following a career in art, or design and tech, or any other field in which she was talented."[64] Her rationalisation that she needs to "watch over Ray" is unconvincing; but when Ray and Johnny rape her, she reasons more convincingly that she cannot report the assault without subjecting herself to humiliation by local authorities, personal mortification, even graver danger, and character assassination by "everyone in the area."[65] After Valerie vengefully exacts her own precise justice and punishes Ray by shooting his offending hand, she is able to redirect her life happily, get psychiatric help and acknowledge to a friend, "I feel good dat's all. I was thinkin' about my DTP [desktop publishing] course."[66] The rest of the chapters of *Society Within* explore ways that young people living in the estates free themselves from unhappy hang-ups: about sexual inexperience ('A Little Bump an' Grind'), drug dependency ('The Art of Long Games with Short Sharp Knives'), family bigotry ('Small-Island Mindedness'), insecurities about long-term commitments ('Rejection'), and others' expectations of failure ('Midnight on Greenside'). The chapters all bring in the compass of happiness, one way or another. Here is a typical instance: Stacey "was happy for his mother because Lewis [her man-friend]...was a straightforward, decent, and law-abiding soul. He was less happy for himself, as he was none of those things, and the two elements were bound to come into conflict at some stage."[67]

Readers can sense the moral compass swinging between 'right' and 'wrong' polarities, for the characters are themselves aware of these valences while sometimes acting defiantly against their better judgment, sometimes caving to temptations and self-delusions, sometimes doing the decent thing. Jean-Paul Sartre, in defending his own portrayal of "characters that are base, weak, cowardly and sometimes frankly evil", explained the enormous philosophical difference between showing "that the behaviour of these characters [is] caused by heredity or by the action of their environment upon them, or by determining factors, psychic or organic" (as Émile Zola did, for instance) and showing such characters as *responsible* for their behaviour, for making themselves base, weak, cowardly, or evil by their own actions.[68] Like Sartre and Newland, the existential ethicist portrays his characters facing dilemmas and shows them resolving what to do with their time, their brains and their energy. Newland makes Ervine James, the detective narrator of *Snakeskin*, a prime example of this sort of modern manhood. Ervine is himself a warm-hearted but open-eyed existentialist who believes that "without some sense of discipline in a man's life he becomes weak, unable to function, left to the whim of emotions and desires with no control over either."[69] As it turns out, *Snakeskin* is more than a murder mystery and "inner-city whodunit"[70]; it is a *bildungsroman* that dances Ervine James into enlightening contact with a whole spectrum of characters, many of whom live deplorable and unhappy lives at the mercy of unchecked emotions and undisciplined desires. In fact, once their elaborate covers are removed, the murderer and his victim both turn out to have been miserable, roleplaying sociopaths.

Newland reframes the challenge concerning 'traps in [our] heads' in his plays. Near the end of Act II of *The Far Side*[71], the town councillor who has assembled a community jury to re-try a white boy who was acquitted of the murder of a Black youth is frustrated in his effort:

> There's not one of you in here that can do that simple, decent, human thing and give in to the greater good of your fellow man or woman. And that doesn't just make me sad. It frustrates me. And when I'm frustrated it clogs up inside me like . . . like . . . fat, clogged in an old man's arteries.

A few minutes later he adds:

> Someone chucks you a lifeline . . . and you push them away. . . . See, in your confused state of mind, you believe that that's the English way. You know, stiff upper lip, never let the enemy see your pain, all that shit. The murdered Black Youth, an unseen ghost, comments on the ensuing brouhaha: Boy, oh boy, oh boy. Listen to all dis man . . . Madness innit? Who woulda believe it would come to dis? People shoutin' an' screamin', everyone sayin' they're right, no one believin' they're wrong, even for a second. Dat's the trouble wiv all dis man. Justice I mean, dat's the trouble wiv justice. Cos no matter the way the law looks at tings, there's always someone who's gonna be unhappy about the decision the law makes.

The law sets down rules for the conscientious to follow, but laws are not always applied fairly to conduct and certainly do not guarantee happiness or justice. Newland's ethics are consequentialist, not deontological.[72] As Newland implies even more emphatically in his play *B is for Black* – sound societies call for ethical behaviour on the part of their members, and ethical behaviour entails caring for the true happiness of others, over and above racial, class, ethnic or gender differences. Not too deeply embedded in Newland's works, as I hope to have demonstrated, is the suggestion that a viable code of ethics for our day and age may well be to make happiness – personal *and* community-wide – the goal. Newland's ostensibly apolitical brand of morality is not too bitter a pill to swallow, which may account for the fact that Newland has a strong following among young, smart, optimistic Black Britons.

NOTES AND REFERENCES

[1] Luke Jennings, 'Courttia Newland,' *The Evening Standard* (28 May 1999), p.20

[2] See www.mynottinghill.co.uk/nottinghilltv/faces-moviesandbooks.htm

[3] Andrew Sanders, 'High Victorian Literature' in *An Outline of English Literature*, edited by Pat Rogers (Oxford University Press, 1992), p.315

[4] Newland e-mail response to Arana (4 January 2002)

[5] Newland e-mail response to Arana (4 January 2002). Here also, Newland comments: "I think people should call themselves what they or their immediate people feel suits, just like street names. When you call some *Bigga*, or *Eazy* or *Black Thought*, it means something deep…"

[6] Newland's response here (4 January 2002) is to my earlier e-mail interview question: "I know that your dad made up the name *Courttia* (you told us this in Philadelphia—and that you had wanted to change it to something short and common and your publisher was speechless with disbelief!!). However, *Courttia* sounds like *courtier*; and I was wondering if your dad was signifyin' (as we say here in the States). Lots of people are called *Duke* and *Earl* and stuff like that. Does your name have any resonances like this for you?"

[7] Newland-Arana e-mail interview (22 October 2001).

[8] A British postwar author of crime short stories (praised also for his television dramas), Dahl exhibited 'a unique flair for combining shock and humor' in his writing (Robert C. S. Adey in *The Oxford Companion to Crime and Mystery Writing*, p.412

[9] Guy is a Caribbean novelist whose rites of passage novels written for younger readers have attained high visibility for featuring frank treatments of young lesbian love and sexual awakening, among them *My Love, My Love* (or *The Peasant Girl*), Holt, 1985. See the following web pages for further information and more links: http://members.aol.com/harambeeco/guy.htm & http://www.shef.ac.uk/english/modules/lit306/site/N_Millns.htm

[10] Himes is famous for 'his darkly comic tales of criminal life in Harlem' that feature African American detectives plying their trade against a background of racism, overwhelming corruption, and cruelty (Robert E. Skinner in *The Oxford Companion to Crime and Mystery Writing*, pp.206-207)

[11] According to T. R. Steiner, Auster highlighted the uncertainty of reality by creating narrators as well as hardboiled detectives who are often uncertain 'that what their gazes fixate on may be read as clues' (see 'Point of View, Narrative' in *The Oxford Companion to Crime and Mystery Writing*, p.335)

[12] Ervine James, the narrator and detective hero of *Snakeskin*, is reading Rupert Thompson's crime novel, The Insult just as the real action of *Snakeskin* begins. Ervine comments: "Whenever I had free time, I lost myself in his darkened world."p.39

[13] Stephen King is widely known as one of the most successful writers of horror fiction, a genre that has been defined as 'not necessarily concerned with the supernatural but rather with forces, psychological, material, spiritual, or scientific, that can be 'supernaturalised' and made into a force that threatens the living with annihilation' (Clive Bloom in *The Oxford Companion to Crime and Mystery Writing*, pp.225-226)

[14] Price is the author of screenplays, for example: *Mad Dog and Glory* (Perf. Robert De Niro, Uma Thurman and Bill Murray. Dir. John McNaughton), Universal Pictures and Mad Dog Productions, 1993; *Sea of Love* (Perf. Al Pacino, Ellen Barkin and John Goodman. Dir. Harold Becker), Universal Pictures, 1989; 'Life Lessons' (short film from *New York Stories*) (Dir. Martin Scorsese), Touchstone Pictures, 1989; 'Bad.'(music video) (Perf. Michael Jackson and Wesley Snipes. Dir. Martin Scorsese), 1987. His publications include: *Ladies' Man* (novel), Boston, MA: Houghton Mifflin, 1999; *Freedomland* (novel), New York, NY: Broadway Books, 1998; *3 Screenplays: The Color of Money, Sea of Love, Night and the City* (screenplays), Boston, MA: Houghton Mifflin, 1993; *Clockers* (novel), Boston, MA: Houghton Mifflin, 1992 & Paperback edition, New York: Avon Books, 1993; *The Breaks* (novel), New York, NY : Simon and Schuster. 1983; *Bloodbrothers* (novel), Boston, MA: Houghton Mifflin, 1976; *The Wanderers* (novel), Boston, MA: Houghton Mifflin, 1974. For further information, please see http://www.writers.cornell.edu/price.html

[15] 'Whitehead's *John Henry Days* (2001), his follow-up to the critically acclaimed *The Intuitionist* [1999], has made him the first young Black male novelist in years (maybe decades) to be treated like a major new American writer. The reviews of the new book have either been celebratory or, at least, thoughtful, including a serious essay on Whitehead by John Updike in the *New Yorker*.' See http://www.africana.com/Column/bl_125street_29.htm

[16] According to Julian Symons, Hammett 'created a specifically American kind of crime story, loosely called the tough-guy or hard-boiled tale, and made it respectable' (see *The Oxford Companion to Crime and Mystery Writing*, 198-199)

[17] 'Yoshimoto Banana was born Yoshimoto Maiko on July 24th, 1964. It is said that she changed her name to Banana because it sounded 'cute,' but a Japanese professor I know has suggested that the name is a homage to the Japanese poet Basho, whose name is an old word for the English 'banana.'* (Yoshimoto's father was also a writer, and was quite influential in Japan during the fifties and sixties). Banana graduated from Nihon University in 1986, where she won the Izumi Kyoka prize for her short story *Moonlight Shadow*. She also won the Kaien Magazine New Writer Prize in 1987 for *Kitchen*. She lives with her husband in a luxurious apartment in Tokyo, and says that her life's dream is to win the Nobel Prize for Literature. Her works include *Kitchen, N.P., Lizard, Fruit Basket, Songs from Banana*, and *Moonlight Shadow*. Her novella *Kitchen* has been made into a movie by a Chinese director.'** *Kaneda Tomoko, former Assistant Professor of Japanese Language at Earlham College. **Information on Yoshimoto Banana comes from a web page on Yasunari Kawabata and Banana Yoshimoto by Rebecca D. Larson at http://www.earlham.edu/~japanink/banana.html

[18] 'Junot Diaz is a fiction writer and the author of Drown, a critically-acclaimed collection of short stories. His stories have appeared four times in The Best American Short Stories anthologies, as well as in *The New Yorker, African Voices*, and on the radio show 'This American Life.' He is the recipient of a Guggenheim Fellowship and a Lila Wallace Readers Digest Award.' See http://www.nypl.org/press/pepfall2001.html

[19] Langston Hughes (1902-1967) was a major writer of fiction, drama, and poetry of the Harlem Renaissance. He incorporated elements of jazz and blues into his poems about Black urban life in New York and rural life in the post-Civil War American South

[20] Combining 'the hard-boiled first-person style of narration' with 'African American oral and protest traditions,' Mosley's detective novels 'are the first major works in the crime genre to induce a large biracial audience to cross over the line that typically separates

the Black and white mainstreams of popular literature' (Robert E. Skinner and John M. Reilly in *The Oxford Companion to Crime and Mystery Writing*, p.295)

[21] Newland-Arana e-mail interview (31 December 2001)

[22] Judah, Hettie. 'Word on the Street.' Interview with Courttia Newland. *The Guardian*. July 1, 1999:6

[23] Carty, Peter. 'Society Within.' Rev. of *Society Within*. *Time Out*. September [?]1999:202

[24] Newland e-mail (31 December 2001)

[25] Rustin, Susanna. 'Spirited Stories that Stay in the Memory'. Rev of *The Scholar*. *Financial Times* (18 December 1999)

[26] Sullivan, Paul. Feature and rev. of *Society Within*. *Touch*. July 1999 p.85

[27] Newland, Courttia, *The Scholar*, London: Abacus, (1997) p.330

[28] Ibid. p.322

[29] Ibid. p.242

[30] Ibid. p.74

[31] Ibid. p.79

[32] Ibid. Ch.s 19, p.21

[33] Werlock, Abby H.P. *British Women Writing Fiction*. Tuscaloosa and London: U. Of Alabama p.2000. Cartep.7

[34] Ibid. p.9

[35] *London Review of Book*, [3 April 2003] p.7

[36] See R. Victoria Arana, 'Metonymy and Psychological Realism in Autobiography,' in *Apocalyptic Visions Past and Present*, ed. J. James and W. J. Cloonan (Tallahassee: Florida State U P, 1988), pp. 99-110. This essay methodically explains how the various effects of psychological realism are produced by narrative reliance on the close focus of metonymy and synecdoche.

[37] Sullivan, Paul. Feature and rev. of *Society Within*. *Touch*. July1999 p.85

[38] Newland, Courttia. *The Scholar*, London: Abacus, 1997 p.75

[39] Newland, Courttia, *Society Within*, London: Abacus, 1999 p.82

[40] Newland, Courttia. *The Scholar*, London: Abacus, 1997 p.78

[41] Ibid. p.80

[42] Ibid. p.149

[43] See Joseph Frank's *Through the Russian Prism* p.182

[44] G_siorek, Andrzej. *Post-War British Fiction: Realism and After*. London: Edward Arnold, 1995

[45] Evans, Diana. 'The GreenSide' *Pride* Magazine, July (1999) p.16

[46] Newland, Courttia, *Society Within*, 1999, London: Abacus, pp.70-72

[47] Ibid. p.234

[48] Ibid. pp243-244

[49] Ibid. p.178

[50] Ibid. pp.162-163

[51] Newland, Courttia, *The Scholar*, London: Abacus, 1977, p.144

[52] Ibid. p.179

[53] Philosophers today distinguish at least two broad approaches to ethics. Deontologists 'think that ethics is a system of rules' or 'a set of prohibitions' and argue that the moral content of an action is not wholly dependent on its consequences. Consequentialists, on the other hand, 'start not with moral rules but with goals. They assess actions by the extent to which they further these goals. The best-known, though not the only, consequentialist theory is utilitarianism' (Peter Singer, *Practical Ethics*, 2-3). Singer's

discussion also (indirectly) illuminates the ethical dimensions of Newland's treatment of social insiders and outsiders (252-253, 255) and of Newland's depiction of the contests within his main characters between their altruistic impulses and self-interest (322-330)

[54] Newland, Courttia, *The Scholar*, 1997, London: Abacus, p.320

[55] Newland, Courttia, *Society Within*, 1999, London: Abacus, p.89

[56] Fisher, Judith L. *'Ethical Narrative in Dickens and Thackeray.'* Studies in the Novel 29,1 (Spring 1997), 108-118 (p.110)

[57] Nussbaum, Martha C. *Love's Knowledge : Essays on Philosophy and Literature.* New York, :Oxford UP, 1990, pp.218-313

[58] Mathewes, Charles T. 'Agency, Nature, 'Transendence and Moralism' *Journal of Religious Ethics* 28, 2 (June 2000), pp.287-300

[59] Newland, Courttia, *Society Within*, London: Abacus, 1999 p.5

[60] Ibid. p.82

[61] Ibid. p.53

[62] Ibid. p.53

[63] Ibid. p113

[64] Ibid. p.105

[65] Ibid. p.113

[66] Ibid. p.66

[67] Ibid. p.178

[68] Sartre, Jean-Paul. *Existentialism and Humanism.* Trans., Philip Mairet. 1946. References are to the selection quoted in *The Norton Anthology of Literary Criticism*, ed..Vincent Leitch et al. New York, Norton, 2002. p.855

[69] Newland, Courttia, *Snakeski'*, London: Abacus, 2002, p.21

[70] Clark, Alex. 'Mean Streets' Rev. of Snakeskin. *The Guardian*, 27 April 2002

[71] Newland, Courttia, 'The Far Side' First staged at The Tricycle Theatre, London, summer 2001

[72] See note 53

The Language of Madness in Leone Ross' *Orange Laughter*

Susan Yearwood

> Human thought becomes genuine thought, that is, an idea, only
> under conditions of living contact with another and alien thought,
> a thought embodied in someone else's voice, that is, in someone
> else's consciousness expressed in discourse. At that point of
> contact between voice-consciousnesses the idea is born and lives.
> - M M Bakhtin (1994)[1]

Trauma, and its contested psychoanalytical definition, Post
Traumatic Stress Disorder, is described as a response to an event,
which can be catastrophic and the recurrent dreams and
hallucinations that occur as a result of this episode. These
hallucinations appear *real* to the sufferer, as if the event is being
replayed in the mind. In *Orange Laughter*,[2] Tony's hallucinations
occur as a pathological response to an event that happened in his
childhood and it is its repetition and distortion, as well as any
biochemical reaction, which induces madness. This madness is
secured within the strict confines of the underground world that he
inhabits and it is its articulation as monologue that provides the
narrative's focus on disaffection.

This chapter will look at Tony's role as an unreliable narrator of
his own disaffection and trauma. This will facilitate a discussion on
the mad interlocutor or disordered dialogue within the narrative.
How is the protagonist's disorder linked to a wider discussion on
witnessing and implosion? Is the mad interlocutor dialogically sound
or an example of inverted inner speech that has no social or moral
function? Does the addressee (the implied reader), who becomes the
other to Tony's inverted self, facilitate dialogue within the text and
how is the "idea" of madness constructed in the text? Bakhtin's ideas
on the subject appear to be relevant and succinct; it becomes clear
that he is able to articulate the notion of voice-consciousness in a
manner that facilitates a discussion of the text. Bakhtin's
summations seem to me to be the best example of a theorists ideas
on the unutterable being unspoken and best illustrate the ideas made

clear in this essay. I believe that the subject of madness deserves indepth discussion and throughout the works of the many theorists presented in this essay such a discussion becomes possible.

Madness in its ontological sense deals with what Richard Bernheimer calls the "persistent psychological urge [for] impulses of reckless physical self-assertion which are hidden in all of us, but which are normally kept under control."[3] In his discussion on wild men in the Middle Ages, he asserts that such men had abnormal qualities that differentiated them from the norm and they suffered moments of madness that propelled them into a netherworld of fury and abandonment.

That the wild man was a creature of his own habits and habitat was essential to the mythology that persisted about him, as was the distinction between civilised approaches to societal problems and the aberrant thought patterns of the socially excluded. The habitat was a confounding place in which the wild man's search for origins took place, both metaphorically and mentally. This search was not always manifested physically, but had the potential for reasserting itself according to prevailing circumstances.

In *Orange Laughter*, Tony's self-absorbed reflections on the darker side of what was a traumatised childhood re-admit themselves as aspects of repetition compulsion, a condition that is seen in "schizoid" individuals who have suffered childhood trauma that has affected their sensibilities and encouraged them to look inwards.[4] In fact, the protagonist suggests that he doesn't believe in childhood at all[5] which possibly alludes to the physical break from his biological mother when quite young and the witnessing of and involvement in the murder of his surrogate mother, Agatha. This physical break from a "personal continuity of existence"[6] which Donald Kalsched proposes to be the continued relationship with the mother, induces months of muteness in Tony and is relational to a reading of madness. For in his inward strike for an existence that carries order in his muteness, Tony shows signs of the "archetypal defense"[7] – that of the drive to keep the personal spirit "safe" but detached from body, mind and time/space reality.

THE UNRELIABLE NARRATOR

The chronology of the chapters, that alternates between Tony's narrative denouement in the 90s and his childhood in the 60s, suggest a truncated linearity, in keeping with Tony's loss of focus and reason. The detachment of spirit from any time/space continuity is evident in the character's displacement from Topside and his detachment from his own sense of reality. Topside is the name given to life above ground and is the place from which Tony posts his letters to Mikey, his former (white) friend from the South who also witnessed Agatha's murder. What appears to be an act of sufferance on the character's part as he copes with his existence underground could be construed as a mental aberration, a breakdown of societal values and ethics within the individual. This suggests a fixed break in the dialogue of the mad interlocutor as the language structure becomes marred by narrative play. This is apparent in the monologic chapters dedicated to Tony's inner speech:

> "it wasn't hard to find Mikey when I was Topside I followed his career found out he's married to a famous poet ha Mikey always was a creative whore and he's been at Princeton for years…I came down here with blankets chump change and Mikey's address…so I wrote the letter…to see if he'll just tell me the story because there's so much I don't remember just tell me the story of how we came to be pals."[8]

Here, dialogue is deconstructed to the point where, in Lacan's words, speech leads us ultimately to the mind.[9] As the one truly human, subjective process, speech can confound or instruct, construct ideas and mediate between them through what Lacan calls the "Symbolic Order". Speech reveals itself as part of the Symbolic Order here and constructs meaning only on a symbolic level. However, if the psychotic is relevant to the subject rather than a representation of anything else, Tony's psychosis is revealed in speech as more than a mere symbolism but as language that reveals its cultural, social and political speech genres. This could be described as speech performed under the auspices of objective psychology[10] as it contends with the supposition that the social has something to do with the spoken and is not merely a psychic function. Tony's scatological monologue suggests the culture of the speaker and his displacement; one is able to picture an urban socialite that was, with a penchant for words on paper and a psychological disorder that affects memory. His language is capable of dysfunction and re-interpretability. As Daniel Ferrer points out, language exists through the exclusion of madness due to the necessity of making sense.[11] If subjectivity is the aspect that detects the unreliability of the social, mental and physical manifestations around the subject, then is it not clear that language can be uttered with this historicity in mind and given the postmodernist "incomprehensibility" of historical fact? In Tony's case, this historicity comes to the fore as madlanguage and with regards to Lacan's idea of a structure-less unconscious[12] and in the sense that language ultimately cannot be represented, there is the possibility that this unreliability remains to be stated and cannot be heard. This becomes clearer when one takes into consideration the subjectivity of the hysteric and how this relates to a self- image, in its Symbolic form, and final reflection.

The self-image of the hysteric is unreliable and conflicting, the final reflection a mere mimicking of the body and true self. Doubling, or another way of seeing double-consciousness in African American theoretical history, is a process that disengages the subject from a single self, reiterating points of erudition in another aspect with whom to reflect her/himself on to the world. This 'hysterical response' is reflected in Tony's (in)articulation of the self and his disembodied reaction to his trauma; he becomes another self to his true image and tells his story through this other persona. This lends the text its dialogic referent as the polyphonic voices of the protagonist and other characters converge on what appears to be chapters of monologue but are in fact dialogue as they reflect the relationships *within* the individual voice as well as outside of it.[13]

Dostoevsky's 'underground man' from *Notes from the Underground*[14] represents the obsession with the state of being; the knowledge of existence below the surface of life. Nina Allan describes his state as that of being "frozen" – being unable to relate to anything outside of himself and reassert his state of being.[15] Ross' protagonist relates to the 'underground man' in the fundamental aspect of his sense of self; his self-analysis and self-absorption becomes obsessive and alters aspects of compulsion. While Dostoevsky's protagonist holds on to any semblance of memory by becoming fixated, Tony's obsession is clearly to regain what memory has been lost, to remember what happened to him in his past with Agatha and Mikey. His state of being is lost to him as he struggles with auditory and visual hallucinations about Agatha and the legitimacy of existence underground. The loss of memory makes it clear that Tony's dialogues can only be referential in terms of aspects of his present predicament and other less volatile times of his life (particularly his childhood relationship with Marcus). His subjectivity is marked by absence and this in turn demonstrates the flawed nature of his utterances. For instance, when he has auditory or visual hallucinations about Agatha, she is depicted thus,

> "... her voice burst through my orgasm and I'm pushing Chaz
> off it's the bitch she's in the beams and she's grinning as
> big as a bus shaking that hair down...Agatha is caressing
> the walls with her long fingers and velvet hair she's smiling
> at me SHE'S IN THE ROOM she's talking to the walls like
> they're new...and her fingernails are chalk on the walls...
> the bitch will take my soul I am convinced of that she will
> watch me and torture me and then when I am sleeping
> she will come to me and peel me..."[16]

That Tony had a loving relationship with Agatha during his childhood is clear from the alternating third person chapters in the text. What occurs in the "mad" chapters is the distortion of reality that sets Tony's utterances into the realm of unreliability. He cannot know the whole story because his memory has been impeded by trauma and self-implosion that necessitates the self-questioning and search for truth in his conscious state. Tony's role as mad interlocutor suggests the problematic nature of truth here, as it is unutterable.

In a post-structuralist sense there is no differentiation between the external and internal function of the author image. In terms of narration, one cannot distinguish between "... the narrative 'I' (and) the object of narration (as this may be a) constant within one narrative text"[17] Therefore there is room for certain displacements within the text that alter continuity and inform discontinuity. These displacements form ellipses set against real time and in the form of a fabula, primarily a product of the imagination,[18] inset into the narrative. This becomes most evident when, looking at the previous quotation from *Orange Laughter*, one is drawn to the loving description of Agatha – long fingers, velvet hair – seared by the livid language of trauma and the absence of a characterisation of Agatha. This characterisation or build up of notions about the character occurs in the alternate third person chapters of the novel yet each of these are read as a story within a story, as text discontinued from the trauma-laden narrative. Therefore, Agatha's character can only be a product of the ellipses or the anachrony in the text – "when I am sleeping she will come to me and peel me..." is a break in chronology and disturbs the order and marks the point where Tony's memory does not allow for erudition and where the author-image functions on binary planes, inclusive of the narrator.

Ross writes Tony's disaffection in a number of ways: a) through what Gérard Genette calls the implied author image's appropriation of the text,[19] b) through the narrator's unreliable dialogue as questionable and possibly obtrusive, and c) as the utterance as acceptable dialogue. The first point has the advantage of the implied author image's omnipresence and precipitates the trauma and the reaction to it by predisposing the implied reader to reliable plot, narrative and schema. This takes place in the third person chapters that contain the story of Tony's early childhood in the southern states of America during the turbulent 1960s. The author is implied simply because her articulation is a direct evocation of the diegesis yet goes beyond the form of the work; Genette is uncomfortable with this poststructuralist reading of the author yet is given to quoting Shlomith Rimmon-Kennan who in turn details the efficacy of a position that deems what is voicelessly implied far more intelligent than the silent real thing[20]. The unreliable narrative is unreliable because it details the narrator's questionable value system[21]; in the above quotation and in the rest of the internal dialogue, Tony's narration is pitted against the voiceless implied author as we can assume that they do not show the same predilection for violence and self-censure. The unreliable narrator informs the implied reader of Tony's adult disaffection in terms of the socialising determinants that define his existence through the functioning mad interlocutor and those external factors, such as the social and cultural make-up of the contemporaneous narrative, that make his voice convincing. Utterance is acceptable here as it is implied that the mad interlocutor is rearing between lucidity and madness due to his own self aggrandisement:

> "It was me who pressed the cushion across her face, past that
> skin, those scars, that tale. It was me who saw the alarm in her
> eyes and I know now that her fear was not for herself but for us.
> The price we would pay and the smell of our inevitable nightmares.
> I was thirteen years old. I leaned forward and I took the last of her
> life, and it is my guilt that has made her a monster in my mind."[22]

The unreliability of the narrator in the alternating first person chapters and the ambiguous nature of the narrative as a whole meets a juncture in the final passage from the novel, as Tony comes to a realisation that stops his oscillating thoughts and re-positions the narrator's place in the text. The end passage in the novel is told in the first person but it is a reliable narrator who takes over. His role as subjective narrator is sublimated by the implied author image, that which is the result of an exploration of the meaning of the text, not the source of that meaning and can only be inferred as a result of that interpretation.[23] This takes into account the efficacy of telling and the systematic function of re-telling – its intradiegetic function. However, before the implied reader gets to this passage, the implied author image, or role, as it has a function, continues to render the narrator unreliable.

Like Ralph Ellison's *Invisible Man*, whose basement sojourn furnishes him with a way to selfenlightenment, Tony's self-imposed incarceration takes him through a subliminal, darkened world that leads him to a point of self-knowledge that is revealing and answers his own questions about his past relationship with Mikey and Agatha. The role of unreliable narrator becomes that of storyteller as Tony relinquishes his position to that of conscious, subjective narrator of his own life and the part he played in Agatha's death – "It was me who pushed the cushion across her face..."[24] The mantle is taken away from the subjective or overt narrator as all-seeing interlocutor and given over to the mad man made coherent by his own self-confinement and obsessive thoughts. This revision of the unreliable tenet re-writes the protagonist's errant narrative to that of safe, reliable narrator, now equal to the implied author's omnipresence and authority in the intervening chapters. The memory lapse is rendered conditional to any sense of sanity and is relied upon, as well as the seemingly ersatz relationship with meaningful dialogue, to enable Tony to eventually function as interpreter of his own fate. A radical break away from conformity, with little punctuation and false commentary in the dialogues, would apparently re-appropriate the text in question to that of re-constituted narrative. Tony's narrative approximates the distancing of the social pariah from enigmatic conversation and drives the witness of social and political dysfunction into a defined morass. From this position one can see Tony's dilemma quite clearly as the alternating chapters unravel most of the answers. Yet it is the narrator as unmitigated tool of suppression and antithesis of the implied author image, that reveals much about the idea of the witness of repression and trauma.

WITNESSING AND IMPLOSION

When the dialogue is disordered the protagonist displays much of his own witnessing and the implosion thereafter. The witness does not necessarily utter testimony itself or become part of an act of bearing witness as it can be beyond their knowledge at any particular time.

Tony becomes lucid again and remembers the nightriders shooting Agatha and the decision he and Mikey made to take "the last of her life" before they do. As a witness and active participant in her murder, Tony's narrative is part confession and his final realisation, just before the novel ends, that it is his guilt that has pre-empted the torrid hallucinations about Agatha, suggests a "confession" of a stubborn illness. This clinical evaluation, as Felman notes in assessing *Dostoevsky's Notes from the Underground*[25] can preclude a larger perspective on wider issues other than the illness. Yet in *Orange Laughter*, Ross provides a testimony that takes into consideration the trauma, including the trauma of survival, madness and political oppression that anticipate the clinical response.

The level of implosion implicit in the clinical response is important here. It creates the need for the evaluation of madness as a response to trauma and its use as an "idea" of madness. In *Madness and Civilization*, Michel Foucault points out that the mad who were confined in the seventeenth and eighteenth centuries in Europe took part in an act of silencing.[26] Their circumstances mitigated the need for fortresses of suppression that told of the fear of their unconventionality, their *unreason*. This act of imprisonment, mirrored by Tony in his own physical confinement, is a process external to any self determination yet is replicated in the phantastical detention within the perimeters of the mind.

These moments are marked by Tony's hallucinations concerning Agatha. His self-mockery and great fear create moments open to the reconstruction of self-image and counter-implosion; his external reality is challenged but not refuted by his self-loathing and mental degeneration. Thus, self-implosion and the limitations of a harsh self-development have recourse in the emotional environment that the madman finds himself in. In Tony's case, he finds resolution and meets the external head on, placing the role of storyteller at the mercy of the newly lucid mad character.

INNER SPEECH AND THE ADDRESSEE

"Gather around as I become the storyteller.
In the end I told it all. It had to be me. In this hell.
In this heaven, kicking the needles aside."[27]

Before we realise that Tony is in fact a representation of the omniscient narrator of the third person narrative of the alternating chapters in the persona of the implied author, he is assigned the role of the madman as interpreter of events. This, as stated earlier in the chapter, provokes notions of unreliability and the unsafe, yet there are certain aspects of his life that the madman shows real clarity in remembering and representing. The character's bisexuality is celebrated by his mad persona and remains a metaphor for the freedom of his Topside existence before delusions took over his psyche. Despite reports on malfunctioning in positive sexual identity in bisexual people due to society's rebuttal of difference,[28] Ross presents her protagonist without this dilemma forming an integral part of his mental breakdown. In fact, aspects of his sexual orientation are articulated in a scatological, confident style that is part of Tony's re-invention of himself underground. Ideas about sexuality do not change from Topside to underground whereas ideas about madness become complicated by an increase in hallucinations and disorder. As Stephen Angelides notes, much queer theory postulates that the role of identity is an exclusive and prohibiting position that does little to posit a realistic notion of individuality within a given context.[29] His reasoning supports the notion that Tony's self-acceptance of his sexuality is a direct result of his non-polarising attitude towards it and its function, while Eli Coleman and B. R. Rosser would argue that this has little to do with a positive attitude but relates to his mad persona as prescribed by societal indifference.[30] What is clear is that Tony's role as a transgendered individual can be associated with what Dallas Denny and Jamison Green note is outside of the binary fields of sexual orientation and facilitates discussion on the profundity of identity.[31] In this instance, Tony's clarity of remembrance can be associated with surety of identity in all of its manifest forms. Yet, it is telling that during a lovemaking session with Chaz that Tony suffers with a hallucination that makes him attack his girlfriend. This shakes his sense of reality, as he has not associated mental dysfunction with his sexuality before this occurrence. His sexuality had remained sacrosanct and enabled by his sense of positivism and self-acceptance in that context. This further accentuates the notion that Tony's disruptive thoughts are linked to his own repression of the past and libido or forgotten material, forcing its place in the consciousness.[32]

Tony eventually comes to realise thoughts of love for Agatha when he reaches a kind of catharsis about his feelings of guilt at the end of the novel. As we gather around the storyteller, we learn that Agatha comes to bring him warmth and power, strength and resilience. She loved him and he loved her. What isn't clear is the efficacy of using inner speech to enunciate his disaffection and its function in the text. Bakhtin refers to inner speech as that which "enters into dialogue with the outside world", but it does so at the level of consciousness, in the reality of "concrete historical human exchange."[33] Tony's references to his sexuality are uttered to himself in exchanges that do not always define themselves as real, concrete exchangeable aspects of fictional speech. The inner speech is uttered without the direct recourse to an altercating Other, implying that mad discourse has no social referent apart from the implied addressee. This implication takes the act of original thought and constructs a barrier around its intimated confessions so that reported conversation can only be related in a distinctly detached and removed way. Therefore, when Tony speaks of his discussions with Chaz or past encounters with Marcus, one is aware of the chronology of events and their distancing through free indirect discourse. The conversation that Tony has with himself, free direct discourse, is less indirect and passive and is certainly more bombastic. Yet, in retrospect, the suggestive mad motif that the narrator encounters renders his conversation with the implied reader untenable. This is partly to do with the unreliability of the narrator, as discussed earlier in the chapter and partly due to the significance of the language of madness itself.

This language is mediated by aspects of censure and is critically symbolic of dysfunction. For example, Tony states:

> "... I only hit her three times because she begged me
> and I told her that I wouldn't do it again and then I lay
> down and thought about this new secret and I guess I
> am an animal now and I understand why the Creeping
> Man did it no big psychological theory the Creeping Man
> is mad and he could yeah you know he boiled that boy's
> hands because he could do it and the whole town killed
> those boys because they could do it"[34]

Here the character ruminates on his increasing violence while relating ideas concerning a phantom that supposedly resides underground. The discussion of a phantasm suggests the forbidden and unanswerable coming to the fore but more than that proposes a fantastical premise to notions of madness. This conjugates ideas around reality and transcendence but ultimately is unnamed by any one discourse outside of madness. Within the discourse of madness it can only be unreliable and an act of dysfunction – the dialogue itself is a sign of madness that goes beyond the particularity of the dialogue itself. If, as Foucault states, language is defined by its infinite possibilities and extends even the moment of death to an instance of repetition,[35] mad-language must find trauma in its repetition and its longevity. Therefore, the idea of madness as a creeping wild man who resorts to violence against children is replete in its supposition that mad-language omits barriers to inclusion and readmits areas of social exclusivity into its boundaries. This readmission is an afterthought, a creative rebuttal of all things normal and exclusive. The wild man has metaphysical properties that negate any false reasoning that this is a mere phantasm; the wild man is Tony's own reflection reduced in language to the metabolics of an animal yet recharged as an aspect of social representation. The idea of him is his madness and this extends to an understanding of belated, latent repetition within unreason; Tony's story to himself is a retelling of himself, an opening to a censured sense of his condition. In this state of hebetude, the external world is rendered obsolete and as Freud notes, can be a point of reconstruction.[36] In his 1924 essays on neurosis and psychosis, Freud goes further to identify the nonfulfilment of childhood wishes that make up the inception of psychosis and the subsequent loss of reality, as opposed to the dependence on reality of neurotic conditions. As fresh circumstances precipitate new forms of delusion and reconstructed reality, Tony becomes subject to the redefinition of an ultimate wish – that Agatha was not shot by the Klansmen. This reconstruction of his own self as a killer of children merely replicates his own participation in her death and extends the phantasm to a point of erudition. This part-recovery of fact and reality in delusion readmits the frustrated childhood wish to the mad-language of orchestrated exclusion and pre-empts the question of Tony's social and moral function; with dialogic interaction between the self and the other as a site of maturation for self-consciousness, can Tony be located in the social world?

If, as Bakhtin asserts at the epigrammatic beginning of this chapter, an idea comes to fruition only at a point of contact with at least two forces of living thought, the expression of discourse is unutterable to Tony within the dominion of the text. His monologues/internal dialogues are symbols of the intractability of human thought to articulate itself into a nameless, unanswerable entity, the implied addressee, yet suggests that the language of madness in this instance has a limited moral and social function. Tony articulates himself to himself and it is only the intervention of the implied reader that marks the dialogic moment (a moment of reciprocity in dialogue) as potentially answerable. What is emblematic here is the suspected answerability of the utterance. Tony exists within a space that is marked by historical and experiential time. This leads the implied reader to other parts of the text to gain an insight into the historical inferences, thus relying on the duality of the compromised and nondelusional aspects of the narrator's voice. This underlying binarism allows for the essential answerability within the text. Therefore, in the context of *Orange Laughter*, the madman can be heard and understood because of the novel's construction and the parallel stories answering the mad dialogue.

Although, on the one hand, Bakhtin contends that "... the 'other' already exist(s) in the inner speech of the self"[37] he also states that being, knowledge and expression belong to the conscious dialogue with another – that outside of the self.[38] This determines that there is a place for conversation with the self at the level of discourse but that this is in itself an anomaly. What is clear is that inner speech is not acknowledgeable – it resides outside the confines of society and social morality. If, then, the individual is socially and morally reprehensible yet relates information about the self through thought only, does he have a social or moral function? Bakhtin would argue that he does as his accountability stems from his otherness and this otherness relates to his state of being-in-the-world. There is nothing but shared states – even the "I" of exclusivity has a condition that is not unique[39] therefore the sociality of that state is determinable. Tony's social function is thus answerable if ultimately unutterable in the form of discourse. Morally, he inhabits the confines of the wild man and thus exists external to a religious morality or a social one. In *Orange Laughter* the "I" takes on the duality of a bruised humanity accessing the implied reader through acts of sensationalism, as was common with populist slave narratives and is apparent in postmodernists' narrative of "selective memory", acts of forgetting as a driving narrative force; see Toni Morrison's slave saga *Beloved*.

Jeanne Phoenix Laurel's discussion on slave retentions in African American women's writing on madness suggests that contemporary African American fiction permits a pre-modernist view of tragedy to access its evocation of madness.[40] In *Orange Laughter*, the implied author challenges this by accepting the idea of regeneration within a postmodernist framework of discontinuities and fragmentation. Therefore, although slave narratives and witness testimonies perhaps share the nomenclature of protest literature, contemporary fictional appraisals of historical events take on a postmodernist vacuity and symbolism as opposed to literalism. In the slave narrative, inner speech recounted the ideological concerns of the ex-slave and abolitionist, rendering what was personal to the level of social implication by way of political agency.[41] Through thematic and social appropriation, *Orange Laughter* inherits the African American literary mantle yet revises it to allow a certain flexibility.

Therefore, inner speech plays the role of the inquisitor of the human psyche yet is confounded by its social and moral function. As stated before, however, there is some contestation as to the role of the addressee as Agatha becomes the receiver of information elicited from the text. What was contextually unutterable becomes open to the addressee's interpretation and conveyance; the text is answerable but only through an intermediary on the part of the addressee, the implied reader. In this context, utterances may be spoken or written but, as Holquist notes, the dialogic utterance does not assume the notion of free will on the part of the addresser as is apparent in the context of the written form.[42] Therefore, Tony's utterances are displayed with a prerequisite of active aspects of restraint. These restraints are complicated further by the conditions under which the addresser represents his subject; addressing the subject of madness confines the protagonist to a representation of disorder that will have certain connotations for the implied reader. This aspect of polyphony, that determines the differences inherent within the individual voice, locates the presumed addressee as the other, as both object and subject, and engages the unutterable utterance in interplay. The language of madness is the definitive representation that the implied author wishes to display, but it is its subjective other that facilitates dialogue within the text and emboldens the sometimes difficult to read text to a point of recovery.[43]

Tony's deliverance of his "social purview", that which is directed in a culturally specific way, informs the language and pretext of the piece and emphasises its social context. As Feder notes, the mad persona is capable of representing aspects of dysfunction in things cultural, personal and psychological to the point of fragmentation or survival.[44] At the end of *Orange Laughter*, Tony is proposing a visit Topside to visit Mikey. His suggested survival comes with the drawn-together fragments of his memory making a place for them to reiterate the past in lucid form. His act of forgetting redefines itself as a point of recovery and articulates itself in real time without the run-on cadence of mad-language. In this way, Tony finds redemption in remembrance and perhaps, salvation from crisis in Topside. Resolution is by no means final, as it is merely a re-evaluation of events.

NOTES AND REFERENCES

[1] Morris, P. (ed.) *The Bakhtin Reader: Selected Writings of Bakhtin, Medvedev, Voloshinov*. London: Edward Arnold, 1994. p.98

[2] Ross, L. *Orange Laughter*. Kent: Angela Royal Publishing Ltd, 1999

[3] Bernheimer, R. *Wild Men in the Middle Ages: A Study in Art, Sentiment, and Demonology*. Cambridge: Harvard University Press, 1952. p.3

[4] Kalsched, D. E. *The Inner World of Trauma: Archetypal Defenses of the Personal Spirit*. London: Routledge, 1996. p.11

[5] Ross, L. *Orange Laughter*. Kent: Angela Royal Publishing Ltd, 1999. p.62

[6] Kalsched, D. E. *The Inner World of Trauma: Archetypal Defenses of the Personal Spirit*. London: Routledge, 1996. p.33

[7] Ibid. p.38

[8] Ross, L. *Orange Laughter*. Kent: Angela Royal Publishing Ltd, 1999. p.18

[9] Hogan, P. C. et al (eds.) *Criticism and Lacan: Essays and Dialogue on Language, Structure and the Unconscious*. Georgia: The University of Georgia Press, 1990. p.14

[10] Holquist, M. *Dialogism: Bakhtin and his World*. London: Routledge, 1990. p.51

[11] Ferrer, D. *Virginia Woolf and the Madness of Language*. London: Routledge, 1990. p.5

[12] Lechte, J. *Julia Kristeva*. London: Routledge, 1990. p.32

[13] Pearce, L. *Reading Dialogics*. London: Edward Arnold, 1994. p.50

[14] Dostoevsky, F. *Notes from the Underground*. Oxford: Oxford University Press, 1864/1999.

[15] Allan, N. Madness, *Death and Disease in the Fiction of Vladimir Nabokov*. Birmingham: University of Birmingham, 1994. p.17

[16] Ross, L. *Orange Laughter*. Kent: Angela Royal Publishing Ltd, 1999. pp.73-74

[17] Bal, M. *Narratology*. Toronto: University of Toronto, 1985. p.126

[18] Ibid. p.49

[19] Genette, G. *Narrative Discourse Revisited*. New York: Cornell University Press, 1988. p.140

[20] Rimmon-Kennan, S. *Narrative Fiction: Contemporary Poetics.* London: Methuen, 1983. p.87

[21] Ibid. p.101

[22] Ross, L. *Orange Laughter.* Kent: Angela Royal Publishing Ltd, 1999. p.225

[23] Bal, M. *Narratology.* Toronto: University of Toronto, 1985. p.120

[24] Ross, L. *Orange Laughter.* Kent: Angela Royal Publishing Ltd, 1999. p.225

[25] Felman, S. et al *Testimony: Crises of Witnessing in Literature, Psychoanalysis, and History.* London: Routledge, 1992. p.11

[26] Foucault, M. *Madness and Civilization: A History of Insanity in the Age of Reason.* London: Tavistock Publications, 1967. p.250

[27] Ross, L. *Orange Laughter.* Kent: Angela Royal Publishing Ltd, 1999. pp.224

[28] Cabaj, R. P et al (eds.) *Textbook of Homosexuality and Mental Health.* Washington DC: American Psychiatric Press Inc., 1996. p.715

[29] Angelides, S. *A History of Bisexuality.* Chicago: The University of Chicago Press, 2001. p.14

[30] Ibid. p.715

[31] Firestein, B. A. (ed.) *Bisexuality: The Psychology and Politics of an Invisible Minority.* California: Sage Publications, 1996. p.84

[32] Feder, L. *Madness in Literature.* New Jersey: Princeton University Press, 1980. p.26

[33] Hohne, K. et al (eds.) *A Dialogue of Voices: Feminist Literary Theory and Bakhtin.* Minneapolis: University of Minnesota Press, 1994, p.7

[34] Ross, L. *Orange Laughter.* Kent: Angela Royal Publishing Ltd, 1999, p.118

[35] Bouchard, D. F. (ed.) Michel Foucault: *Language, Counter-Memory, Practice: Selected Essays and Interviews.* Oxford: Basil Blackwell, 1977, p.61

[36] Freud, A. (ed.) Sigmund Freud: *The Essentials of Psycho-Analysis.* UK: Pelican Books, 1986, p.565

[37] Adlam, C. et al *Face to Face: Bakhtin in Russia and the West.* Sheffield: Sheffield Academic Press, 1997, p.34

[38] Hohne, K. et al (eds.) *A Dialogue of Voices: Feminist Literary Theory and Bakhtin.* Minneapolis: University of Minnesota Press, 1994, p.7

[39] Ibid. p.24

[40] Laurel, J. P. 'Slave Narrative Retentions in African-American Women's Writings about Madness' in *Womanist Theory and Research,* Vol 2.1/2.2 at www.uga.edu/~womanist/laurel2.1.html

[41] Gates, H. L. *Figures in Black: Words, Signs, and the "Racial" Self.* New York: Oxford University Press, 1987, p.104

[42] Pearce, L. *Reading Dialogics.* London: Edward Arnold, 1994, p.39

[43] Ibid. p.40

[44] Feder, L. *Madness in Literature.* New Jersey: Princeton University Press, 1980. xiii

"Happy Multicultural Land"?[1] The Implications of an "excess of belonging" in Zadie Smith's *White Teeth*

Molly Thompson

> And underneath it all, there remained an ever-present anger and hurt, the feeling of belonging nowhere that comes to people who belong everywhere.[2]

Zadie Smith's first novel, *White Teeth*, published at the dawn of a new millennium, marks a significant moment in Black British writing and its unprecedented success and excessive media coverage heralds a new era in the literary history of Great Britain.

Born and brought up in London, to English and Jamaican parents, Smith belongs to a generation of writers who are articulating what Kwame Dawes has described as "a new invention: the Black British voice."[3] Previous generations of migrants, because their roots and history were firmly locatable in the Caribbean or Africa, were able to maintain a strong identification and connection with 'home'.

However, for their progeny who have been born in Britain, definitions of 'home' have become less distinct. As a result, subsequent generations have arguably had to navigate a more problematic relationship with their racial identities, often having to straddle two different, conflicting cultures. Notions of 'belonging' have therefore become more complex, as temporal and geographical distance from Africa or the Caribbean has increased. When comparing the writings of different generations of Black British migrants, one critic concludes that for the earlier writers, "living in London was felt as part of a wider experience of travel and adventure; for a later generation, England is felt as a place of oppression and restriction."[4]

The narrative of *White Teeth* at first might seem to contradict this idea that the more recent texts of Black writers are likely to depict England in a less positive light than their forebears. Set in Willesden, North West London, between 1975 and 1999, *White Teeth* traces the inter-relationships between three families, one from Bangladesh (The Iqbals); one with maternal roots in Jamaica (The Jones); and the other, a 'white' English family (the Chalfens). Because the narrative is predominantly written in a humorous, buoyant tone, referring several times to a "Happy Multicultural Land", it could be mistaken as a representation of a world of inter-racial equanimity. Indeed one reviewer believes it recounts an "optimistic vision of racial easiness ... which celebrates differences as well as acknowledging them", and another that it is a novel that "wears its cultural pluralism lightly."[5] However, these claims are clearly reductive as they overlook the fact that *White Teeth* also tells a story of intergenerational tensions and cultural conflicts within and between its protagonists. Indeed, the text suggests that, as a result of belonging to different generations and holding a diversity of cultural beliefs, the possibility of feeling at 'home' in this multicultural world is unlikely. The experience of many in the text is of "an ever present anger and hurt, the feeling of belonging nowhere that comes to people who belong everywhere"[6] and the novel ends in fragmentation and uncertainty.

Smith's use of the words "Happy Multicultural Land" in the novel must, therefore, be ironic. I intend to argue that all is not necessarily well in the world of *White Teeth* and that the novel attempts to highlight the ambiguity such a phrase contains. By problematising the notion of 'multiculturalism', as Smith undoubtedly does, she is in accordance with many postcolonial critics and theorists who have contested the term and who believe it may obscure a different reality – one with more sinister connotations. According to Salman Rushdie 'multiculturalism' is a fake panacea, a new 'catchword', and "the latest token gesture towards Britain's Blacks." He says, the term "ought to be exposed, like 'integration' and 'racial harmony', for the sham it is".[7] For those second and third generation children of migrants in this country, who possess what Alison Donnell and Sarah Lawson Welsh have called "multiple belongings", 'multiculturalism' may indeed carry negative associations.[8] Ontological uncertainty, coupled with conflicting societal influences, paradoxically results in experiencing both a lack of belonging as well as what one critic has defined as an "excess of belonging".[9] This so called 'excess', that is a consequence of belonging to "too many places at once", has been interpreted by theorists and cultural critics in a myriad of ways. Kwame Dawes calls this hybridity an "in-between identity";[10] Ali Rattansi uses the term "hyphenated identity";[11] and Homi Bhabha posits the notion that the offspring of migrants must inhabit the "third space".[12] Whether "in-between", "hyphenated", or in the "third space", all of these identities challenge the existence of a "happy multicultural land" as they connote transience, indeterminacy and 'homelessness'.

As one cannot talk about 'multiculturalism', 'belonging' or 'home' without thinking about familial origins and historical genealogies, finding the location and definition of ones 'roots' has been an important quest for many Black people who have at times had their personal and cultural identities eroded. Thus many Black writers, past and present, have focused on themes relating to their ancestral heritage.[13] Because history, family backgrounds and cultural legacies are all major preoccupations of *White Teeth*, Zadie Smith could be seen as part of this Black literary tradition. However, she sometimes uses a methodology that has more in common with medical or biology textbooks than with genealogy, focusing, for example, on the subjects of genetics and horticulture, as well as teeth and hair, all of which are, of course, associated with 'roots' in one way or another. I intend to argue that through the theme of roots, whether biological, historical, familial or societal, the text can offer us alternative ways of thinking about belonging and unbelonging in our multicultural, global world. It is hoped that, as a result of this exegesis, a clearer idea of just what the text might be saying – about the negotiation of diverse racial identities within contemporary Britain – will be gained.

GETTING BACK TO THE ROOTS

Because teeth have roots, Smith's utilisation of this imagery in the book's title is significant and immediately indicates that teeth are to be a major preoccupation of the text.[14] Indeed many chapter headings are associated with this theme (for example, "Teething Trouble";[15] "Canines: The Ripping Teeth";[16] "Molars"),[17] and there are references to teeth in several vignette scenes. The trope of *white* teeth, however, ironically signals a semantic paradox. Although all racial types have white (ish!) teeth, racist discourse has stereotyped – people of African and Caribbean descent using the image as a potent essentialist marker of Blackness as well as an identifier of difference. The text of *White Teeth* displays an awareness of this damaging essentialist mythology that has 'othered' Black people and caused them to feel alienated from hegemonic culture and society.

For example, on visiting an elderly gentleman, Mr Hamilton, as part of Harvest Festival activities, Irie Jones (daughter of Archie and Clara née Bowden), and Magid and Millat Iqbal (twin sons of Samad and Alsana) are confronted with an example of this prejudicial, imperialist thinking. Of his time in the Congo, Mr Hamilton says:

> Clean white teeth are not always wise, now are they? Par exemplum: ... the only way I could identify a nigger was by the whiteness of his teeth ... Dark as buggery, it was. And they died because of it, you see? Poor bastards.[18]

White teeth act as a kind of synecdoche here as, for Mr Hamilton, the Congo native was characterised purely and simply by this one attribute. By implying that such a conspicuous and visible 'difference' endangered the "niggers", negatively places the idea of essentialism. If it is true that the natives innately and "naturally" had "clean white teeth" and that this attribute led to their undoing, as Mr Hamilton believes, the suggestion is that the possession of essentialist characteristics can be perilous. This mythology, however, is juxtaposed with the fact that Mr Hamilton is unable to eat the youngsters' Harvest offerings as the food given is too hard for his false teeth. Because of this paradox, and the notion that artificial teeth are usually both clean and white, just like the "niggers" he describes, the folly of his beliefs is highlighted, and the essentialist argument is challenged. This idea is further explored in the depiction of Archie's white boss, Mr Hero, who has a "double row of pearly whites that owed more to expensive dentistry than to regular brushing."[19] The suggestion is that the aesthetic appearance of one's teeth is not always a clear indicator of ethnic allegiance, but rather something that can be bought, modified and reconstructed.

Essentialist physiognomical assumptions about teeth exemplified in the (pseudo)-scientific subject of anthropometrics, are deconstructed when we learn that Clara's upper set of teeth are prosthetic, having lost them in a motorbike accident.[20] The very precarious concept on which to base racial identity is exposed in the incongruity of a white man (Mr Hamilton) having artificial "white teeth", a Black woman (Clara) without the stereotypically expected perfect "white teeth", and a white man (Mr Hero) who has the kind of teeth Mr Hamilton believes only a "nigger" might have. The fact that all three have acquired "white teeth" in one way or another challenges essentialist physiological notions of 'difference' on which many (pseudo)-scientific arguments have been based. The notion of *white teeth* in the book's title is therefore a novelistic absent centre that satirically subverts its own signification by suggesting that these attributes are not innate but are artificially constructed. By drawing attention to Clara's prosthetic teeth that are 'incomplete' in a sense, and which represent both the notion of rootedness and rootlessness (real teeth are embedded in the gums whereas artificial ones are not), the text metaphorically refers to the impermanence and uncertainty that characterise multicultural society.

IRIE JONES AND THE FIGHTING OF GENES

Teeth are not the only part of the body to have roots however. Indeed, the narrative also features another with a similar physical attribute – namely hair. As well as having 'roots', an individual's hair texture and type is determined by its genetic composition that is 'rooted' in one's ancestral heritage. In addition, hair, for many Black people, is not purely an aesthetic issue, but is one that also has cultural and political applications.[21] Given that 'Afro's' have been used as a statement of rebellion against 'white' ideological values by many,[22] and that Rastafarian dreadlocks symbolise a challenge to "the prevalent white-dominated view of beauty,"[23] Irie's desire to change her 'Afro' hairstyle enters this political arena.[24]

As the only child of an English father and a Jamaican mother, Irie has inherited dual racial characteristics of mixed physiological allegiances. The resulting "contradictions" of her body have culminated in a belief in "her ugliness, her *wrongness* ... She was all *wrong*"[25] (Smith's emphasis). One of the consequences of this conviction in her "wrongness" is the decision to change her hairstyle. Despite the opposing forces outlined in the novel that state, "[S]trange as it sounds there are plenty of people who refuse to meet the Lord with an Afro"[26] and "[S]ome of us are happy with our African hair",[27] wishes to beat the "curved African follicle(s)" of "each curly hair into submission"[28] in order to gain "[S]traight hair. Straight straight long black sleek flickable tossable shakeable touchable finger-through-able wind-blowable hair. With a fringe,"[29] In his essay 'Black Hair/Style Politics', Kobena Mercer highlights the semantics of the terminology associated with black hair that suggests "white" hairstyles have been privileged over "black". For example "good" hair is used to describe hair that "looks European, straight not too curly, not that kinky".[30] In a contemporary magazine aimed at the young Black (largely female) market, products are advertised that will "smooth down *unruly* hair" (emphasis added) to 'relax' and 'stretch' it, implying that anything other than long and straight is undesirable.[31] Clearly affected by this kind of ideology and wishing to eradicate her "African-influenced" attributes, Irie endures the masochistic hair straightening process. As well as her dissatisfaction with her African-influenced hair, Irie is also "intent on fighting her genes" that she believes have given her a particular body shape and size.[32] As with the aesthetic qualities of her hair, the external messages she receives conflict with either or both of the English and Jamaican physical attributes she has inherited. On the one hand her mother is saying "you're fine – you're just built like an honest-to-God Bowden – don't you know you're fine?"[33] and on the other, she is confronted with advertisements urging her to "Lose Weight to Earn Money."[34] Although her mother, Clara, had a figure of "European proportions", this we are told, "had skipped a generation, and she (Irie) was landed instead with Hortense's (Irie's grandmother's) "substantial Jamaican frame, loaded with pineapples, mangoes and guavas; the girl had weight ..."[35] Irie once again decides it is those characteristics inherited from her "African" side that need changing in order to "diminish that swollen enormity, the Jamaican posterior".[36] To this end she attempts to alter her body shape by wearing concealing clothes and elaborate corsetry. This dissatisfaction with her body also extends to skin colour, reinforced by the classical literature she is taught at school. Shakespeare's ironic sonnet (Number 127) seems to speak directly to Irie:

> In the old age Black was not counted fair ...
> Or if it were, it bore not beauty's name.[37]

This desire to minimise her African characteristics could be seen as a crisis of racial identity for Irie.

Inhabiting a body that is physiologically rooted in two places, 'belonging' to both England and Jamaica in a sense, she experiences a kind of corporeal nomadism or a not-at-homeness in her own skin. Lauretta Ngcobo believes that the process of self-definition, whether via the location of one's roots or otherwise, is more difficult for those of mixed racial heritage. She states that: "Instead of being drawn to identifying with either half of themselves, they (those of mixed race) are often pushed one way or another or else repelled both ways.[38] Desire for a body that denies its African-ness could be symptomatic of this clash of roots which challenges Irie's social and cultural location. Whilst it could be said that bodily self-consciousness and self-disdain are prevalent in most Western teenagers (particularly girls), Irie's body 'problems' are specific to her Jamaican heritage and living in a country that offers few images with which to identify and where 'white' ideals of beauty dominate. This results in a feeling of alienation both from her body and from the wider community: "There was England, a gigantic mirror, and there was Irie, without reflection. A stranger in a strange land."[39]

The texts implies this lack of positive imagery is a destructive force, evidenced by the fact that Irie's desire to have straight, "flickable" hair, as well as a European silhouette, results in bodily damage. For example, her mother questions whether or not Irie can actually breathe inside the "breast-reducing bra" and "belly-reducing knickers" that form part of her "lycra corseting – the much lauded nineties answer to whalebone."[40] Similarly, her hair is irrevocably damaged as a result of the long ordeal at the salon, and she has to have someone else's hair woven into her own.[41] Whilst the straightening process 'works' for most of the clients of PK's salon, "[T]hey all came out straight or straight enough", it seems that, "they also came out dead. Dry. Splintered. Stiff. All the spring gone. Like the hair of a cadaver as the moisture seeps away."[42] The hair follicles (in other words the roots) are destroyed. So Irie's wish to change her Afro hairstyle, as well as minimise her "Jamaican proportions" could be read as a metaphorical denial of part of her cultural origins. In this way, the novel emphasises the 'problem' of roots in a multicultural society where an "excess of belonging" can adversely affect an individual's bodily self-image. As Irie attempts to negotiate culturally opposing standards of beauty, the effect this has on her identity and her roots (both symbolic and figurative) is shown to be potentially destructive.

"MULTIPLE IDENTITIY RE-NEGOTIATION"[43]:
ROUTES AND ROOTS

It is interesting that Irie's contemporaries, Magid and Millat, do not appear to suffer from a poor self-image in the same way. This could be of course because they are male and arguably not under the same kind of aesthetic pressures. It could also be that, unlike Irie who comes from mixed racial parentage, Magid and Millat share the *same* physiological and racial origins with their parents, (both from Bangladesh). They would, therefore, presumably at least 'look' Bengali, and have physical identities that are less racially ambiguous. Whilst this might help them to feel at home in their bodies by having a sense of physically belonging to their family, (compounded by the fact that they are identical twins with the same genetic makeup), it does not prevent them, however, from experiencing problems with roots. For Magid and Millat, rather than being preoccupied with changing their bodies in the way that Irie is, questions of roots for them relate more to their sociological and geographical positioning. Because of a dual cultural and national heritage – their birthplace is England and their parents' original 'home' is Bengal – they have had to adopt hybridised identities that incorporate both Bengali ideology and Western values. Without their father's interference however, it seems they would negotiate these dual identities with fewer problems. Samad's decision to send one of his sons 'home' to Bengal because he believes "a month back home would sort each and every one of them out",[44] exacerbates the situation and what Paul White calls "multiple identity re-negotiation" becomes more problematic for both twins as a result.

Whilst he is determined that his sons should have "deep roots" created for them "that no storm or gale could displace", Samad's own roots are clearly being scrutinised and disturbed. Although he believes "[R]oots were what saved", he is tempted away from his own ancient religious traditions by a teacher at his sons' school, "a siren named Poppy Burt-Jones".[45] What he calls the "corrupting" influences of English culture ("I have been corrupted by England, I see that now – my children, my wife, they too have been corrupted"),[46] have resulted in an attitude towards roots that is duplicitous, intertwined as it is with notions of tradition. He believes "tradition was culture and culture led to roots, and these were good, these were untainted principles."[47] Samad's wife Alsana, however, realises that this conflation of roots and tradition is both problematic and yet inevitable even before the birth of her sons. She predicts that this second generation she is spawning will "always have daddylong-legs for fathers. One leg in the present, one in the past ... [T]heir roots will always be tangled."[48]

Perhaps not surprisingly Samad's actions backfire and contrary to what he had hoped for Magid returns from Bengal more 'English' than Millat, who remained. He arrives back in England wearing a white linen suit, speaking the "Queen's fucking English and no mistake"[49] and openly rejecting his religious background by ordering a bacon sandwich when out with his father.[50] Samad describes Magid as "Mr white-trousered Englishman with his stiff upper-lip"[51] and being with him he says is like "sitting down to breakfast with David Niven."[52] Despite, or perhaps because of, staying in England, Millat has similarly confused cultural influences. The text recounts how he "stood schizophrenic, one foot in Bengal and one in Willesden"[53] and that, as a result, he is "neither one thing nor the other, this or that, Muslim or Christian, Englishman or Bengali"[54] Because of this irony, the text shows that the definition of roots within a multicultural environment is conceptually ambiguous, and that living within a culture of conflicting ideals , whether relating to tradition, standards of beauty or some other issue, is problematic.

This is particularly so if the external environment privileges one culture over another, as would seem to be the case in *White Teeth*. Whether visiting 'home' as in the case of Magid, or remaining in their birthplaces, all are heavily influenced by the hegemony of Western culture. Despite the fact that societies are "open, porous formations" with many "overlaps, borrowings and two-way influences", the novel implies that the osmotic process of transculturation in Britain is not – evenly balanced.[55] Homi Bhabha concurs with this, suggesting that there is an unequal relationship between different groups in Britain. Because host societies or dominant cultures set up what he terms a "transparent norm" that implies "these other cultures are fine, but we must be able to locate them within our own grid", an oppression of certain values will occur.[56] As a result, cultural diversity is *permitted*, but cultural difference is always *contained* within the 'grid' of the dominant (host) society.[57] Thus, even within societies where multiculturalism appears to be encouraged, certain "roots" are privileged over others.[58] As Irie "fights her genes" by minimising her Black – physical attributes, and Magid and Millat rebel against their Bengali past, *White Teeth* could be read as an attempt to expose the fact that, both in terms of beauty as well as cultural values and practices, 'white' ideals are still dominant. The persistence of stereotypes arguably reinforces the fact that the dominant belief systems remain firmly in place in England and that society is often unwilling to be open to alternatives, at the same time as negating any ideas of multicultural 'tolerance'. Millat, clearly aware of the stereotypes constructed about him simply because he looks 'Asian', realises:

... that he, Millat, was a Paki no matter where he came from; that he smelt of curry; had no sexual identity; took other people's jobs; or had no job and bummed off the state; or gave all the jobs to his relatives; that he could be a dentist or a shop-owner or a curry-shifter, but not a footballer or a film-maker; ... that he worshipped elephants and wore turbans ...[59]

Those with 'hyphenated identities', then, as well as having to encounter such racist beliefs, may find themselves having to choose between colluding with dominant social and cultural practices, thereby possibly weakening their own sense of rootedness, or rejecting the idea of assimilation or integration altogether and remaining 'rootless' on society's margins. Or they may have little choice but to inhabit the 'in-between' which – according to *White Teeth* – is not always an easy place to be.

THE END OF HISTORY

The difficulties of inhabiting the in-between are further suggested in the novel's dialogical explication of the importance of history on multicultural subjectivities. By applying the notion of roots via a conflation of the subjects of genealogy and history, the text questions the importance, verisimilitude and accuracy of discursively documented information. Of course the challenge and deconstruction of hegemonic history is not new, but when applied to multicultural heritages, the emphasis shifts. Although some postmodern theory has advocated the end of history, many do not find this to be a useful concept, indeed for some it is possibly a hazardous one.[60] According to Stuart Hall, "the powerful", that is hegemonic authorities that have policed ideology, culture and signification, "want to bring history to an end. They want one set of meanings to last forever."[61] In other words, the suggestion is that if one belongs to the "powerful" group, the belief that history is at an end may be beneficial as the "meanings" have arguably been created with a self-serving bias. Whereas for those with less power, univocal signs and interpretations can potentially be harmful as the dominant significations may occlude the specificity of individual experience.

In accordance with these debates, the novel reveals the frequent slippages that can occur between history and truth, indicated by Archie's awareness of the possibility of discursive falsifications. In recollecting his school days, he recalls that history was taught "with one eye on narrative, the other on drama, no matter how unlikely or chronologically inaccurate."[62] He experiences this inaccuracy at first hand when his achievement in the 1948 Olympics (he came joint 13th in track cycling) is accidentally omitted from the record books due to an error in transcription.[63] The novel also tells of the contradictory records concerning Samad's great grandfather's exploits in the Great Indian Mutiny of 1857 which disagree as to whether he (Mangal Pande) was a hero or a coward.[64] In one of the records, Pande is described as "half drunk with bhang, and wholly drunk with religious fanaticism.[65] in another it claims: "[H]is self-sacrifice gave the siren to the nation to take up arms against an alien ruler."[66] Similarly, Archie and Samad's recollections of their shared military experiences, having both fought as British subjects in the Second World War reveals that their part took place on a "day that History has not remembered", indicating that the personal testimonies of these two war veterans were clearly not recorded in history books.[67] By problematising assumptions about the documented accuracy of such "grand narratives" and the effects this can have on individuals (whether migrants or not), the text thus highlights the chimerical and untrustworthy aspects of history by challenging its discursive representations. The text suggests that rather than history being at its end, its univocal stories need to be re-imagined and rewritten in order that fewer omissions and asymmetries will occur, because, according to Norman Davies, we need to "argue" with history and that "[R]e-evaluating the past ... is a basic civic duty."[68]

For Irie, "historical truth" is a similarly elusive concept and her ambivalence towards the past is evidenced by her reference to "historical shit"[69] and the "ball and chain" of history.[70] Conversely, however, she also realises the importance of finding her own personal history. On running away to her grandmother in North London she undergoes a metaphorical journey to her – original – homeland of Jamaica. Through photographs and written accounts, she finds the truths of her family's past. Whilst this enables a slightly better understanding of where she comes from, her own personal certainties are contrasted with the obfuscatory quality of historical narratives as her family tree remains incomplete. The roots of the tree, if you like, are obscured. Its inadequacies and scanty details are graphically illustrated by the many gaps and abstractions annotated by phrases such as "Lord knows", "unknown issue" and "paternity unsure."[71] This lack of a firm foundation is further compounded by the fact that her grandmother's birth took place during a Kingston earthquake in 1907, literally being born "while Jamaica crumbled".[72] Irie's roots, therefore, are both literally and metaphorically based on a "shaky" and disintegrating, foundation.

Even the quintessentially English Chalfens, whose family tree is "an elaborate illustrated oak that stretched back into the 1600s and forward into the present day",[73] have an uncertain history with Jewish immigrant roots that are "third generation, by way of Germany and Poland, née Chalfenovsky."[74] The notion of home as having a fixed and singular origin for anyone in a multicultural world is therefore shown to be illusory. Indeed, Irie, although dreaming of a utopian – home – where, according to her, there would be "no fictions, no myths, no lies, no tangled webs", also realises that this can remain only as a dream. She knows that "*homeland* is one of those magical fantasy words, like *unicorn* and *soul* and *infinity*."[75] It is because of this that Irie's search for origins, roots, or historical certainties, will inevitably be futile, ending always in what the text defines as "the perfect blankness of the past"[76] Judith Butler has referred to the futility of such a quest, claiming that there is an impossibility in the notion of return to historical origins and that this creates "a desire for history that is never quite satisfiable."[77] Irie's response to this impossibility is perhaps hinted at in her wish for roots to be meaningless:

> Irie has seen a time, a time not far from now, when roots won't matter any more because they can't because they mustn't because they're too long and they're too tortuous and they're just buried too damn deep. She looks forward to it.[78]

By complicating notions of truth and history the novel highlights the tenuous and insubstantive nature of the quest for 'roots' or 'home' in a plural society where nothing seems to be dependable or definable, and where fiction and 'truth' have become indistinguishable. This lack of surety would appear to be a necessary element in multicultural societies if Stuart Hall's claim is applicable. He contends we should perceive our ethnic identities as being connected with the notion of movement, multiple origins and hybridity and advocates a replacement of "roots" with "routes". Because we have "no single origin ... no routes which are unified", Hall believes "we are all *becoming* diasporic".[79] This is undoubtedly a concept that many in Britain wish to reject, preferring to perceive themselves as belonging to a country that is culturally cohesive. Yet, according to an article in *The Political Quarterly*, the belief in a national identity of single origin is based on myth and that, "[T]he British have long been distinguished by having no clear idea about who they are, where they are, or what they are."[80] Despite this, however, many stubbornly hold on to the belief that we do share a common ancestry, in other words that we in Britain 'stem' from the same 'roots'. *White Teeth* reveals the anxieties inherent in the notion of racial diversity, both for migrants and their children, as well as for those, like the Chalfens and Archie, who might normally be considered quintessentially 'English'.

It seems that all of this uncertainty about historical and familial roots leads to a fragile present and an unpredictable future. For example, Archie and Samad's friendship, a cornerstone of the narrative and around which much of the plot is structured, is shown to be based on a lie, "made of nothing more firm than marshmallow and soap bubbles."[81] Similarly, Hortense's existence, which we are told is like "living in the eternal instant, ceaselessly teetering on the precipice of total annihilation"[82] as well as the novel's apocalyptic preoccupations, indicate that nothing can be relied upon. Such unreliability is exemplified by the arbitrary nature of genetic selection and is clearly demonstrated when Irie becomes pregnant. Having had sexual intercourse with both Magid and Millat in quick succession (approximately 30 minutes apart), she is consequently unsure of who the father of her expected child is, because:

> She could not know her body's decision, what choice it had made, in the race to the gamete … She could not know if the choice would make any difference. Because whichever brother it was, it was the other one too. She would never know.[83]

As even a DNA test will not reveal the identity of the father.[84] Irie's offspring will always have a feeling of rootlessness, and, like Irie, he/she will never be totally sure of the past.

Contrasted with such ceaseless uncertainties however, is the idea of *certainty*. It is in Marcus Chalfen's experimental research that the text suggests it *may* be possible to have certitude. His genetically modified mouse (FutureMouse©) is ironically the only character in *White Teeth* that seems to have a completely reliable ontology and teleology. Under the omniscient control of the God-like Marcus who is able to mastermind every detail of its life, the mouse will give birth, grow tumours, harbour infections and even die at his command.[85] Because of this ability to manufacture a being for whom past, present and future are predictable, rootedness and rootlessness become meaningless concepts. FutureMouse's© roots are not in question as they have been genetically engineered and "un-naturally" selected, thereby preventing the incorporation of any arbitrary or contingent elements. The genetically certain roots that are part of FutureMouse's© existence are thus starkly contrasted with the contingent and at times, precarious lives of the human protagonists in *White Teeth*. However, the certainties of Marcus' experimental mouse are challenged in the novel's dénouement, when, despite its seemingly reliable and predictable trajectory, even the researcher cannot account for all possibilities. Indeed, as FutureMouse© breaks free and disappears through an air vent, its future is cast into doubt. This paradox highlights many of the complex interactions that exist between certainty and uncertainty, essentialism and constructivism, genetic reliability and unreliability, all of which are inherent in the complicated notion of roots.

By interrogating roots via the inter-related subjects of familial, genetic, societal and historical belongings, Smith's novel, rather than painting a picture of a "Happy Multicultural Land", reveals an ironic ambivalence towards such a possibility and I believe infers a general unease or discomfort with the *status quo*. Whether in terms of genetic construction or cultural allegiances, the idea that anyone can have definitive roots is thrown into doubt within the world of the text. Because an inevitable consequence of multiculturalism is a fusion of culturally and biologically derived -roots-, the negotiation of 'routes', is shown to be anything but straightforward. Via the recurring metaphor of teeth, which the text demonstrates can be both permanent and impermanent, real and artificial, the tension between rootedness and rootlessness that exists for migrants as well as non-migrants, can be clearly seen. This tension that incorporates essentialist debates, according to Paul Gilroy is created "not from the ruthless enforcement of stable racial categories but from a disturbing inability to maintain them" and has resulted in what he defines as "an anxious setting."[86] This "anxious setting" is evidenced in *White Teeth* by the exaggerated compulsion to preserve some sense of certainty with regard to identity and origins. For example, Marcus' obsession with creating a mouse that is genetically determinate, Irie's identity crisis and consequent search for family history, as well as Samad's attempts to maintain stable and isolated racial categories for himself and his sons, could be read as indicative of this need.

Although some members of the white community think Britain should metaphorically pat itself on the back for its "tolerance" and ability to integrate with a diversity of peoples, some Black theorists and critics would dispute whether or not such praise is deserved. According to Salman Rushdie, "Britain is now two entirely different worlds, and the one you inhabit is determined by the colour of your skin."[87] Ali Rattansi reinforces this when he writes of the Windrush celebrations of 1998, that:

> Although punctuated with references to urban riots and the nasty faces of British racism, the overall note was one of complacency, even celebration, of narratives of integration, multiculturalism and notable cases of immigrant success.[88]

So whilst the white community celebrates its 'success' in embracing multiculturalism, some of the Black community, it seems, see the situation differently. This is epitomised in the text by Irie's desire to alter her Afro hair. By signifying dissatisfaction with her African/Caribbean heritage in this way intimates an uncomfortableness with her Blackness. It may be inferred that living in multicultural Willesden (and by implication the wider environment of Britain), where 'white' ideals clearly predominate, causes a cultural and racial dis-ease for those who feel they are outside of the dominant system.

The text suggests, however, that it is not only due to racial differences that cause corporeal unease. It also demonstrates that inhabiting a multicultural society is not easy for *anyone*, and that we are all implicated by an "excess of belonging" due to the fact that (whether we want to believe it or not) our history, corporeality and nationality are constantly in flux. This is reflected in the fact that the very definition of 'multiculturalism' is still "being determined in a wide-ranging, conflictual, and, at present, open process."[89] Coming to terms with an "excess of belonging" is shown to be intractable in *White Teeth*, thus indicating that there are no easy answers to the universal and trans-historical questions of being and belonging. Indeed, it suggests that such existential problems are magnified when applied to a multicultural society. This is evidenced by the narrative voice that points out:

The sheer quantity of shit that must be wiped off the slate if we are to start again as new. Race. Land. Ownership. Faith. Theft. Blood. And more blood. And more.[90]

The phrase "Happy Multicultural Land" is thus clearly oxymoronic, and the possibility of achieving it is shown to be a remote one. The Britain depicted in *White Teeth* is one that is reluctant to accept that in this era of globalisation we are *all* migrants, or that: "The migrant's sense of being rootless, of living between worlds, between a lost past and a non-integrated present, is perhaps the most fitting metaphor of this (post) modern condition."[91] Instead, the outcome of what Zadie Smith calls the "great immigrant experiment"[92] does not seem to have been successfully resolved or completed, to whichever generation or ethnicity one belongs.

The multicultural world of the novel, then, exists within an "anxious setting". By interrogating the effects of assimilation and syncretism, rather than depicting a utopian, integrated society, *White Teeth* offers a *critique* of multiculturalism. As well as a polyvocal and dialectic text resistant to the hegemonic narratives of racism, nationalism and essentialism, Smith speaks with a "Black British voice", that negotiates a route between genealogical history, the history of colonisation as well as the present cultural moment. It is this negotiation, or "multiple identity re-negotiation", that is narrated in *White Teeth* and which I believe threatens the perhaps complacent hope that we inhabit a "Happy Multicultural Land".

And then you begin to give up the very *idea* of belonging. Suddenly this thing, this *belonging*, it seems like some long, dirty lie ... and I begin to believe that birthplaces are accidents, that everything is an *accident*.[93]

NOTES AND REFERENCES

[1] Term used by Zadie Smith in *White Teeth*, (London: Hamish Hamilton, 2000), p.398, and elsewhere in the novel

[2] Smith, Zadie, *White Teeth*, (London: Hamish Hamilton, 2000) p.233

[3] Kwame Dawes, 'Negotiating the Ship on the Head: Black British Fiction', *Wasafiri*, Number 29 (Spring 1999), pp.18-24 (p19). An updated version of this paper appears as Chapter 14 in this book

[4] A. Robert Lee (ed.), *Other Britain, Other British*: Contemporary Multicultural Fiction,

(London: Pluto Press, 1995), p.29

5   John Smith, *The New York Review of Books*, Vol. 48, No. 2, 09/02/01, pp29-30. Mick Brown, "Precocious? Moi?", *The Daily Telegraph*. This cutting was provided in a Publicity Pack received from Penguin Books in 2002 and was undated

6   Smith, Z, *White Teeth*, (London: Hamish Hamilton, 2000) p.233

7   Salman Rushdie, *Imaginary Homelands*, (London: Granta, 1991), p137

8   Alison Donnell & Sarah Lawson Welsh (eds.), *The Routledge Reader in Caribbean Literature*, (London: Routledge, 1996), p264

9   Ahmad (1992) quoted in Minoli Salgado, "Migration and Mutability", in *British Culture of the Postwar*, ed. By A. Davies & A. Sinfield, (London: Routledge, 2000), pp31-49 (p39)

10 Dawes, "Negotiating the Ship", p19. An updated version of this paper appears as Chapter 14 in this book

11 Ali Rattansi, "On Being and Not Being Brown/Black-British: Racism, Class, Sexuality and Ethnicity in Post-imperial Britain", *Interventions: International Journal of Postcolonial Studies*, Vol. 2 (i) 2000, pp.118-134

12 Jonathan Rutherford, "The Third Space" Interview with Homi Bhabha, *Identity, Community, Culture, Difference*, ed. by Jonathan Rutherford, (London: Lawrence & Wishart, 1990), pp.207-221

13 Black writers of all nationalities have been preoccupied with these issues, Alex Haley's *Roots* perhaps being one of the most well known. Toni Morrison's *Beloved*, the poetry of Grace Nichols and Joan Anim-Addo, amongst numerous others, have also interrogated notions of roots and these debates similarly preoccupy many postcolonial critics

14 Not only are teeth a recurring theme within Smith's novel, this trope also featured as the subject matter in a plethora of texts (particularly poems) written by Black women. Jackie Kay, for example, has written many poems concerning teeth and dentistry. See particularly "Teeth", "The Black Chair", and "Pride", all published in *Off Colour*, (Newcastle upon Tyne: Bloodaxe, 1998)

15 Smith, Z. *White Teeth*, (London: Hamish Hamilton, 2000) p.23

16 Ibid. p.267

17 Ibid. p.140

18 Ibid. p.149

19 Ibid. p.61

20 Anthropometrics is the study of racial "differences" in terms of measurement. These "scientific" researchers would base their ideas on measurements of, for example, number and size of teeth, size of skull or genitalia. See Sander L. Gilman, "Black Bodies, White Bodies: Toward an Iconography of Female Sexuality in Late Nineteenth-Century Art, Medicine and Literature" in *'Race', Writing and Difference*, ed. H. L. Gates Jr. (London: University of Chicago Press, 1986), pp.223-261 for more information about the study of anthropometrics

21 Of course it is not only the Black community for whom hair has political associations. For example, the "punks" of the 1980s used their hair to symbolise an anarchic rebellion against society

22 According to Beverley Bryan et. al. in *The Heart of the Race*, (London: Virago, 1985), by not straightening their hair, Black women could demonstrate that "we had succeeded in resisting the social, cultural and commercial pressures to strive to imitate the white ideal of womanhood ... We started to emphasise, rather than minimise, the physical characteristics which set us apart from white women", pp.222 & 223

23 Hiro, *Black British, White British*, p72

24 The symbolic value of dreadlocks has arguably lessened in strength as now many white people also wear their hair in dreadlocks, and many Black people who are not

Rastafarian similarly wear this style

25 Smith, Z. *White Teeth*, (London: Hamish Hamilton, 2000) p.232

26 Ibid. p.236

27 Ibid. p.242-3

28 Ibid. p.237

29 Ibid. p.239

30 Kobena Mercer, 'Black Hair/Style Politics', in *Black British Culture and Society: A Text Reader* edited by Kwesi Owusu, (London: Routledge, 2000) pp111-121 (p113)

31 *Woman2Woman*, October 2001, p20, (published by Woman2Woman Ltd, London)

32 Ibid. p.236

33 Ibid. p.230

34 Ibid. p.229

35 Ibid. p.229

36 Ibid. p.229

37 Ibid. p.231

38 Ngcobo, Lauretta (ed.), *Let it be Told: Black Women Writers in Britain*, (London: Virago, 1987). See introduction by Ngcobo, p.33

39 Smith, Z. *White Teeth*, (London: Hamish Hamilton, 2000) p.230

40 Ibid. p.229

41 Ibid. p.242 & 243

42 Ibid. p.238

43 Paul White's terminology in 'Geography, Literature and Migration', *Writing Across Worlds: Literature and Migration*, (London: Routledge, 1995), p.15

44 Smith. Z, *White Teeth*, (London: Hamish Hamilton, 2000) p. 190

45 Ibid. p.168

46 Ibid. p.125

47 Ibid. p.168

48 Ibid. p.69-70

49 Ibid. p.384

50 Ibid. p.385

51 Ibid. p.389

52 Ibid. p.386

53 Ibid. p.190

54 Ibid. p.302

55 *The Future of Multi-Ethnic Britain – The Parekh Report*, The Runnymede Trust, (London: Profile Books, 2000), p37 and pxv respectively

56 Bhabha, 'The Third Space', p208

57 Paraphrase of Bhabha's statement. Ibid, p208

58 Past and previous British Governments claiming that they wish to engender the ideology of "one nation" evidence such encouragement. See *The Parekh Report*, pxv

59 Smith. Z, *White Teeth*, (London: Hamish Hamilton, 2000) p.102

60 Some feminists, for example, have been engaged in a battle with historical narratives, claiming that "herstories" have been obliterated in dominant discourse.

61 Interview with Stuart Hall, 'Culture and Power', in *Radical Philosophy*, No. 86, Nov/Dec 1997, pp.24-41 (p.30).

62 Smith. Z, *White Teeth*, (London: Hamish Hamilton, 2000) p.219

[63] Ibid. p.219

[64] Ibid. pp.219-224

[65] Ibid. p.220

[66] Ibid. p.224

[67] Ibid. p.78

[68] Davies, Norman. Quoted (1999) in *The Future of Multi-Ethnic Britain*, p4

[69] Smith. Z, *White Teeth*, (London: Hamish Hamilton, 2000) p.440

[70] Ibid. p.281

[71] Ibid. p.291

[72] Ibid. p.29

[73] Ibid. p.290

[74] Ibid. p290

[75] Ibid. p.345

[76] Ibid. p.345

[77] Said during an interview with Judith Butler in *Performativity and Belonging*, ed. Vikki Bell, (London: Sage, 1999), p.1

[78] Smith. Z, *White Teeth*, (London: Hamish Hamilton, 2000) p.450

[79] Hall, 'Culture and Power', p.34. Paul Gilroy also uses these terms in his challenge to replace the certainty of *roots* with the contingency of routes.

[80] Quoted from *The Political Quarterly*, in *The Parekh Report*, p.4

[81] Smith. Z, *White Teeth*, (London: Hamish Hamilton, 2000) p.454-455

[82] Ibid. p.339

[83] Ibid. p.441

[84] Ibid. p.440

[85] Ibid. p.369-70

[86] Gilroy, Paul *Between Camps*, (London: Penguin, 2000), p.22

[87] Rushdie, Salman. *Imaginary Homelands*, p.134

[88] Rattansi, Ali. 'On Being and Not Being Brown/Black-British' Ibid. pp.119-120

[89] Gilroy, Paul *Between Camps*, (Harmondsworth: Penguin, 2000), p.243

[90] Smith. Z, *White Teeth*, (London: Hamish Hamilton, 2000) p.391

[91] Robin Cohen quotes I. Chambers in *Global Diasporas: An Introduction*, (London:UCL, 1997), p.133.

[92] Smith. Z, *White Teeth*, (London: Hamish Hamilton, 2000) p.281

[93] Ibid. p.349

Part Two: Writers in Verse

Biography of Patience Agbabi

Patience Agbabi is a poet, performer and workshop facilitator. She was born in London in 1965 to Nigerian parents and spent her teenage years living in North Wales. She was educated at Oxford University and has appeared at numerous diverse venues in the UK and abroad during the last twelve years.

R.A.W., her groundbreaking debut collection of poetry, was published in 1995 and won the 1997 Excelle Literary Award. Her poetry has been published in numerous journals and anthologies, including *Bittersweet: Contemporary Black Women's Poetry* and *IC3: The Penguin Book of New Black Writing in Britain*. Her latest collection, *Transformatrix*, a commentary on late twentieth-century Britain and a celebration of poetic form, was published in 2000. It received excellent reviews in publications including the *Daily Telegraph, the Independent on Sunday* and *Poetry Review*.

A poet who tours extensively, Patience Agbabi collaborated with Adeola Agbebiyi and Dorothea Smartt to create FO(U)R WOMEN, a polyvocal performance piece that premiered at the ICA in 1996. She was a member of Atomic Lip, poetry's first pop group, from 1995 to 1998 whose final tour, Quadrophonix, 1998, incorporated video with live performance. She has also taken part in Modern Love, a UK tour featuring a number of Spoken Word poets exploring the themes of love and modern relationships. In March 2002, she toured Modern Love in Switzerland with poet and playwright Malika Booker.

Primarily a solo performer, Patience Agbabi has read repeatedly at key literature festivals in the UK including the Edinburgh Book Festival and Ledbury Poetry Festival; and music festivals including Glastonbury Festival and Soho Jazz Festival. She has also worked extensively for The British Council, delivering her work in a range of venues from university lecture theatres to a metro station, in countries including Namibia (1999), the Czech Republic (2000), Zimbabwe and Germany (2001) and Switzerland (2002). Her work has also appeared on television and radio. In 1998 her work was featured on Channel 4's Litpop series and she was commissioned by the BBC to write a poem for the Blue Peter National Children's Poetry Competition in 1999.

An experienced workshop facilitator, Patience Agbabi has completed a number of successful residencies. After being selected for the Poetry Places scheme run by the Poetry Society, she was in-house poet at The Poetry Café in 1999, and Flamin' Eight, a London-based tatoo and piercing studio, from 1999 to 2000. From January to June 2001, she was Poet-in-Residence at Oxford Brookes University, where she devised, taught and graded a Poetry Writing module for English Literature undergraduates; and delivered a wide range of workshops for trainee nurses and teaching staff in the School of Healthcare.

She is currently studying for an MA in Creative Writing, the Arts and Education at the University of Sussex at Brighton and was an Associate Creative Writing Lecturer at the University of Wales, Cardiff.

In 2004 she was named as one of twenty, New Generation Poets by The Poetry Society. During 2005 she takes up a writer in residence post at Eton College.

An Interview with Patience Agbabi

Molly Thompson

PERSONAL AND GENERAL

MT: This is a quote from Alice Walker. She says, "from whence do I, as a writer, come?" Can you tell me what your response to this question would be?

PA: Well, I wrote from a very early age, ever since I could write at about the age of four. I have written. Stories, poems. It's really hard to say when it began – it's just always been there and I think some of that has been from being fed lots of stories and being read to as a kid – a lot of fairy tales, the whole range of nursery rhymes which I could recite from a very early age. I do think that that has a very profound effect on young people if they hear these from a very young age. It's much more natural and I think they are less likely to lose it when they hit their 'teens and it suddenly becomes very unfashionable to say they're into poetry. I see it as a doubleedged thing. I think the poetry was inspired by the rhythms of the nursery rhymes – by a real love for rhyme – and that is something I have not lost. And of course the prose is just more of a sense of loving a good story and all kids love good stories. When I say that I mean people are much more open to novels than they are to poetry.

MT: Yeah I agree with that. Some people claim they don't like poetry! I'm not sure how they can say that.

PA: Yes, whereas most people wouldn't claim they don't like a good story.

MT: Although you have already touched on it, perhaps you could say a bit more about when you began to write.

PA: There have been intermittent periods of intense creativity. For example, when I was about seven or eight, I wrote a lot of very, very long "short" stories – well long by those standards – about 26 pages of an exercise book. I got really interested in stories. I liked magic realism – I didn't know what that was then – I'm still not sure I know what it is now! When I hit my teens, that is when I started writing poetry. So the two are distinct. I mean when I started with a vengeance, when I was writing loads and loads of it. I was inspired by punk lyrics and two-tone lyrics where for the first time in history really you could get on a microphone and sing, and if you couldn't sing, you could speak the words – and that appealed to me so I started writing what I called lyrics and then got interested in more poetic forms.

MT: So what or who have been your major influences?

PA: Certainly in my teenage years it was punk and two-tone lyrics initially and then after university I got into rap – I'm talking about the mid-80s. I listened to lots of rap.

MT: Anyone in particular?

PA: Public Enemy, Public Enemy and Public Enemy! The lyrics were so good and they published them on the record sleeves so you could actually read them. I just think that Chuck D is a fantastic lyricist and poet – there is a crossover going on there. That doesn't apply to all rappers, but I think the best ones do – you can read it on the page and think, "wow that's really clever." I did listen to other rap artists as well but Public Enemy really stood out. I was reading an anthology at the time too – *Watchers and Seekers* published by the Women's Press in 1987[1]. I remember thinking I want to write stuff that I can't seem to find anywhere. There was this huge gap between what I was reading which was mainly dead white poets and what I wanted to write which was coming from a Black female perspective. So I found this anthology and I could relate to it on so many levels, some had very different experiences to me, but it was just fantastic to read Black women's poetry and prose. That was another green light. There were a lot of influences – so it is difficult to pin this question down. I started going to groups like Apples and Snakes, watching poetry performances; watching groups like African Dawn[2] and poets like Merle Collins and Ahmed Sheikh from Senegal. I was inspired by them; made friends with them and hung out with them. I met Lemn Sissay, Jackie Kay and many more.

More recently, I have been very inspired in an interesting way by Kwame Dawes who ran a course called Afro Style School[3] for young Black writers. So it is not so much from reading his work, but more from having his support. He reads my manuscripts, he's my mentor. He gives me fantastic instant feedback, and he doesn't just do this for me, he does it for many other Black poets too. I don't know where he finds the time! I get the best feedback from Kwame.

I have also been influenced by Carol Ann Duffy's work. I think it really inspired the second book, because I had just read virtually all her books. She is my favourite poet. I can't remember a bad poem of hers! I think it's because she is really into form and she uses rhyme very cleverly. I think rhyme has come back into fashion actually.

PUBLISHING ISSUES

MT: When was your first piece published?

PA: In *Feminist Review* in1988, issue 30 or 29, I can't remember. Two poems – 'The Sign of the Times' and 'Getting Dressed for Love'.

MT: So how difficult was it to get that recognition and get them published?

PA: It was very easy actually. The background to it was that I had sent a short manuscript to the Women's Press very naively. They wrote back saying usually people get published in anthologies first! They gave me a list and *Feminist Review* was on it. I just sent two poems off and they published them. It was easy in a sense. Obviously I had tried another route, but then I was determined. Then after that I think I must have sent some poems out to various publishers but not with a vengeance. Then about two years later in 1990 I started performing and because I was performing a lot, I was getting instant feedback from the performances which you don't get from publishers who take a long time to give feedback. Because publishers were slow to respond, I actually stopped sending things out because it wasn't very good for my mental health. But then I was very lucky because I was out there – I started getting recognised. So for example my contribution in *The Virago Book of Wicked Verse* which came out in 1992 was as a result of someone seeing me perform. Interestingly most of the magazines that published my work were not "literary" as such. Some were more political magazines or cultural such as *Wasafiri*. By the time *R.A.W.* came out, I had actually had quite a few poems published, but not in *Ambit* for example. So, yeah, I've been really lucky, an easy ride. I don't believe in banging my head against a brick wall, although, sadly, at times in my career I have felt like I was banging my head against a brick wall, but that's been for different reasons – that's usually been about performance stuff rather than about writing. I think I have been incredibly lucky.

MT: Have you noticed a difference in publisher reception to your work over the last decade. Has it been easier or more difficult or has it just always been that they wanted your stuff, no questions?

PA: That's interesting, because when Payback Press[4] met me in Edinburgh a couple of years ago when *R.A.W.* came out, (*R.A.W.* was with a different press, Gecko[5], which no longer exists) Payback said "yes, if your new book is *R.A.W.* we'll be interested in it. I have always known about form and loved it. But I chose in *R.A.W.* to use more modern, seemingly more free, form. But nothing is free because I use rhyme schemes and things. I think the publishers were a little bit surprised in *Transformatrix*. They weren't sure about whether they wanted to publish it or not, although, to be fair to them, they didn't have a full manuscript at that stage. I sent them about five of "The Seven Sisters", a series of seven linked sestinas and some other poems and I remember thinking at the time, well if they're not interested in what I'm trying to do, then I'll go somewhere else!

MT: That seems a bit stultifying for the publishers to say if you can produce something like you've done before, then we'll publish it ...

PA: The bottom line is they think "will it sell and will it fit"? That's the big issue for publishers. Until fairly recently Payback published only novels by mainly dead, Black authors – the stuff they published was really quite raw, and hard-edged and very male. Now they're publishing Lemn Sissay, Gill Scott Heron and so on. They're publishing British poetry too. The problem is that they wanted me to be hip and happening – that was the unsaid thing and I actually think at one stage they were worried that the book wouldn't be hip enough. This is me reading between the lines. I know they love the book now.

MT: Has it sold well?

PA: Yeah. I haven't had any recent figures. It sold very well in the first three months. They did a print run of just over 1000, and it virtually sold out, which for a poetry book is very good. It's not a bestseller or anything or making them large amounts of money! They're not that excited about it.

MT: Although you have already broached this next subject, there might still be more to say. Do you ever feel you have to consider what a publisher may be looking for and collude with that?

PA: No. No, I know it sounds really arrogant. But because I have very, very strong views on what my books are going to be and what they should be and where I'm at aesthetically and politically and spiritually. No, I'm confident enough that I feel what I am writing people will want to publish. I feel competent enough as a writer so I don't see any reason why people won't publish me.

MT: A few years ago would this have been the same for you? Were you less confident and perhaps felt you should write what publishers want?

PA: Although less confident than I am now, I always thought my work would get published. Remember though that the first book was published by a very, very small company and the people knew me, so it was a case of knowing the right people. I think I would have struggled more had Gecko not been around. And with Payback I was put in the very fortunate position of them wanting first refusal on my next manuscript – that's a very good position to be in as a writer.

MT: What do you think the current status of Black women's writing in Britain is, in terms of production, appreciation, magnitude, etc?

PA: That's quite a difficult question.

MT: For instance, is it appreciated enough – does it have enough profile?

PA: One of the issues is whether people are published – that makes a hell of a difference. If you don't have a book, you don't get invited to do a lot of specific kinds of readings anyway. Certain types of book festivals don't invite you unless you are published so that already means that you're not going to get exposure. It's frustrating for the audience also if there is nothing in print if they have enjoyed the reading. The *Bittersweet* anthology was good for raising the profile (that came out in 1998). The Women's Press⁶ published it – which everyone has heard of. The tour accompanying the anthology also was very helpful to raise awareness. Of course it contained American writers as well as British. I think if you ask most people, even Black people in this country who they read, they will probably say African-American authors over British – they still dominate. But let's face it, there's more of them, they've been around longer etc. Alice Walker, Maya Angelou, Toni Morrison – the heavyweights – of course people are going to read them – people who win huge prizes and have blockbuster films – of course they're going to have a lot of impact. We're really behind here, although the last 12 months have been very positive – my second book got a lot of profile. Bernadine Evaristo's *Lara* got a lot of attention and some very good reviews.

MT: And, of course, Zadie Smith.

PA: Yes, obviously. *White Teeth* has had the most profile of any Black British woman, without question. I've heard a lot of criticism of it, interestingly, from the Black community. It seems that now publishers are only interested in that kind of book from Black writers. That's another problem. It's as if all Black writers are supposed to be the same, whereas white writers, of course, they're allowed to write lots of different styles and genres. But because that 'Black thing' is still seen as a separate market by a lot of publishers. I think that's why people have been less than generous about Smith's book. I think they feel not that she's done us a disservice, but the publishers have leapt on that and it's very racist to make the assumption that the only books publishable by Black authors have to be like *White Teeth*. So they have to be quite hip, quite humorous, very current. What if you want to write a historical novel as a Black person – does that mean no-one would be interested? I do think that's definitely an issue. So, it's been a good period recently for Black women writers. Even a few years ago people were debating "why aren't there enough Black people published?" People said it was just me and Bernadine – this is just about poetry, by the way. It's harder to get published anyway as a poet I think. But at the moment, things are the healthiest they've ever been. For young writers there are more role models; there are more published Black women from Britain out there. It is possible now, whereas, certainly when I was coming through people like Merle Collins and Jean 'Binta' Breeze were around, but I'm not sure that they would define themselves as British – they were born in the Caribbean.

MT: Where would you place your work within, let's say, the Black British genre?

PA: I was just thinking about the Afro-Style School (a series of poetry workshops for up-andcoming Black writers led by Kwame Dawes) which was mostly women – but the styles we wrote in were just so different. So, yes, we were all Black, but actually at times I think there is a danger about the idea of a Black aesthetic – that we all fit into that. It's a really difficult thing for me to say where I fit in. In terms of actual style, I generally write in Standard English (apart from say "The Wife of Bafa" which is in Nigerian-English). I suspect that with a lot of poems in both books, people wouldn't necessarily know I was Black. From the style – but the content – I'm making a distinction between the form and the content here …

MT: Right, so from the form, you think they wouldn't know, or from the content?

PA: From the form they wouldn't know. But from the content, they quite often would know, if I'm talking about hair for instance. All Black women talk about hair![7] It's a subject we all write about! In terms of subject matter, there's a lot of unity amongst us, but in terms of the forms we use, we are all very different.

MT: I wasn't suggesting that all Black women's writing is homogenous …

PA: I think in terms of content, there are obvious similarities, but in terms of form, I probably am more influenced by the classics, by dead white people or poets like Carol Ann Duffy or Michael Donaghy or Roddy Lumsdon, people who are really into form. That's what inspires me in terms of the mechanics. In terms of the subject matter, the Black identity and the woman identity comes through very strongly.

MT: Are you happy to define yourself as a Black British writer, or is there another way you would prefer to describe yourself?

PA: I would be if I was on a panel of Black British writing! But I used to just call myself a performance poet, although I know that "performance" can be both a pejorative and a celebratory term – that's another huge issue.[8] So it depends on who's saying it. And now I'm branching out into prose as well I would probably just call myself a writer. White writers don't have to say I'm a white writer, or I'm a straight man or I'm a this or that. I just say I'm a writer – that's the only thing you can say. But I have no problem with something like the *IC3* anthology. Obviously I am a Black writer, of course I'm a Black writer – I'm not in denial about it, but I think there is a danger and I don't like it when promoters bill you or label you in a certain way. Sometimes it's a pure marketing thing. If you're trying to sell *Bittersweet*, it wouldn't make sense to not say it was a 'Black woman's anthology' – it's a celebration of Black women's writing and all the contributors are Black. There's a danger in being colour blind. I hate it when people pussy-foot around the race issue, and I almost prefer it if they say something racist than just come up with something bland that isn't saying anything at all or clouds the issue.

AUDIENCE

MT: Do you see your work as Black-woman-centred?

PA: That's an interesting question. No, not really. It is in that I'm a Black woman and I write for myself primarily, but I don't have this sense that my reading audience are only Black women. So, no.

MT: Are you writing with a particular audience in mind?

PA: No! Not at all. Although occasionally, like for *R.A.W.*, although nothing was commissioned as such, when I wrote "Sentences" which is about domestic violence, I wrote it for Justice for Women. I was asked to do a benefit specifically for that so sometimes I specifically know what my audience will consist of, like I knew that would be a woman-only event, but I do that piece all over the place – to mixed groups. So even though some pieces might be initially written for a particular purpose, I would hope that the words speak beyond that particular audience. And, yes, whilst women who have experienced domestic violence will perhaps relate on a deeper level than those who haven't, I write for the world, for want of a better term, men and women. But initially I write for me, and I am a woman. I can't get away from that. I am my audience in a sense, but luckily other people are interested! Otherwise I'd be a very lonely person!

MT: Would you say generally your audience is largely Black or white at performances that you give for example? What sort of ratio is it?

PA: Because recently I've done a lot more Literature Festivals, the audience has been predominantly white. If you think about the demographics of the UK, there are far more white than Black people, so inevitably this is going to be the case. When you start up perhaps, if you perform in groups like Chocolate Art[9], the audience would be about 95% Black, whereas once you branch out and start doing Literary Festivals as well, you find audiences are more likely to be white, especially outside London. Within London I'd say it was more racially mixed, but there is still a white majority generally.

If it's an all Black line-up like the 'Bittersweet' tour there will be more Blacks than whites in the audience. In the early days there used to be more women-only or Black-women-only events, and obviously more Black women would go to them, even the women-only events would be supported by Black women. They're not happening any more. I don't know of any womenonly or Black- women-only events now – not at all. Because of the sort of venues I appear at now, the audience is much more mixed. Although obviously if I'm performing in Zimbabwe, my audience is predominantly Black!

MT: Do you get a good reception from an audience that has lots of white faces in it? Do you feel your work is appreciated?

PA: Yes, I do. White audiences are quieter! Apart from London – white audiences in London know they can misbehave; they can shout. But even then sometimes they can be very polite. But if you get a virtually all-Black audience, they are always much louder. Everyone, white and Black alike, will respond and join in. But some poems relate directly to Black experience. For example, I was performing in Nottingham a few days ago to a predominantly white audience, although there were a few Black people there. I performed "The Wife of Bafa" which is in Nigerian-English and with a Nigerian accent as well. There was a lady there I suspected was Nigerian and certain phrases made her burst out laughing whilst the rest of the audience was dead quiet. She really roared at the word "oyinbo" which is a Yoruba word meaning white. The white audience laughed at other bits. Interestingly though, I don't know if that Nigerian woman knew about "The Wife of Bath" – she may have done, I don't want to make assumptions here. Whereas some of the white audience obviously had read Chaucer and were familiar with the references. So on one level they wouldn't get the joke about the oyinbo, but they might get the bits relating to Chaucer's "Wife of Bath". So it can work on lots of different levels.

MT: You said in an interview published in *Feminist Review* that a Black audience is always going to respond more to your work. Do you feel therefore that there are elements in your writing and performance that always elude a white person's understanding? In other words, do you believe there are intersubjective limitations?

PA: I think some people relate who have lived through an experience. For example in "Ufo Woman" where the question "Why's it white on the inside of your hand?" appears. As a child, you get asked those kind of stupid questions. Personally though I prefer it if people come right out with it rather than pretend they haven't noticed. Pure shared experience which is sometimes a Black thing, sometimes a woman thing, sometimes a living in North London thing. There are so many different levels to my work and any Black woman's work, it's dangerous to just see that side of it – although that is a very powerful side of it obviously. As you know, the number of interpretations is endless. I don't feel that being Black is a prerequisite to understanding my work or getting all the nuances. They might get half the Black nuances and a white person might get the other half!

That statement I made in the interview you're referring to should really have been challenged, but the primary thrust was women and how it is possible to make a living as writers. So we only touched on issues like audience, we didn't discuss or delve deeper. If we had, it would have gone on forever! We had to keep the focus.

MT: What prompted the question was an event I went to at the Kuumba Project in Bristol where the audience was largely Black. They were laughing in all sorts of places where I didn't understand what was going on! It made me feel excluded in a way.

PA: That's interesting. Was it in patois?

MT: Some of it, but not all.

PA: Sometimes I've been in all Black audiences where Jamaican patois was used by the performers and at times I couldn't get everything that was said and at other times I could understand what was being said but did not get the humour. But when I'm in Nigerian audiences, at certain words and phrases, I'm usually rolling round on the floor because I understand better. So I do know what you're saying – that can happen and is an issue. But sometimes I have noticed that white people get stuff that I don't get from a Black performance. Sometimes you think it's just a humour thing, or a sense of humour thing. It might just be the intonation, or a personal association, or an obscure word play that only if you're from one particular region would you understand – it could be all sorts of things.

MT: Perhaps it was saying something about me and the fact that I felt uncomfortable in that situation. I was unfamiliar with the vocality of the audience; the call and response type of thing going on – it wasn't something I was used to! Although I liked that actually, like in Black Pentecostal churches where people just say what they want to say. It's better than quietness!

In the same interview you claimed that your audience was predominantly women – have you any comments to make on why this might be?

PA: Yes, that's still the case. Even though there aren't women-only spaces now, it's a fact that more women go to poetry readings than men anyway. More women read poetry – I think it's in the Arts Council report. It's interesting – all about poetry. Women tend to support the arts in general. That certainly is my perception too. Let's face it, two of my most popular poems from *R.A.W.* – "It's Better Post-than Pre-" which is the obvious one because it's funny, and "Sentences"– I perform those a lot so I am very much seen as writing about women's issues. Although my work is appreciated by men as well, far more women can relate to these. So in a way I'm setting myself up as being quite militantly feminist even by modern standards. And in *Transformatrix*, even though it's less overtly political, it's about women. Almost every single poem. And the men that are in there are gay or their girlfriend is sleeping with a dog! So the men don't have a very good time! Then there is a drag queen which is a parody of womanhood in a way. It is called *Transformatrix* after all and it's about women: 'matrix' which originally meant womb, so it's not surprising really that women respond more to my work.

FORM

MT: Much of your poetry both looks and sounds interesting. It is obvious that form is a vital component of your work. Do you think there is the possibility of what Toni Morrison has called "an indisputably Black form", or a "Black aesthetic" in Kwame Dawes' terminology?

PA: Could you clarify what Toni Morrison meant by that?

MT: I think that she is suggesting that Black writing can have a form that is clearly identifiable as Black – that a form could be described as Black by looking at it. It's an abstract concept. It's akin to Cixous' theory of écriture féminine[10] – the idea that female writing might contain no punctuation because of the freeness or fluidity of women's bodies, for example. In other words the form of the body is somehow seen in the writing.

PA: In terms of form, what I see written on the page, I can't imagine that I would know that something is written by a Black person necessarily. I mean if it's written in patois then you might assume it's written by a Black person. Although two years ago a white woman wrote a patois poem and won first prize in the National Poetry Competition. They were really shocked when she came to the prize-giving! In terms of hearing Black poets (like on the 'Modern Love' tour) and prose writers, I think they're really, really, really into imagery – simile and metaphor seems to be quite a common strand – especially those writers brought up in the Caribbean. That's not so much about form as content really.

MT: Yes, but the two are intertwined, aren't they?

PA: That's right. But I'm thinking of say the sonnet which is clearly a European form. So is there a Black form? I can't think of one. Except that Black poets are very into rhyme which comes from the rap culture – feminine rhymes, clever rhymes ... they really go with it. Some of the rap rhymes I think some people critiquing might say are cheesy. And with feminine rhymes, people think they're more humorous or more frivolous, and Black poets and rappers do cross the line and use feminine rhymes. Perhaps that's something to be explored...it's just a general observation.

MT: I think rappers' use of rhyme is so clever and original. They take a word and then gradually change it until it turns into something else – like you do in some of your poems. It's a technique that white poets don't seem to be able to replicate, or maybe not that they can't, but they don't.

PA: There's a rapping track ('Sound of da Police' by KRS One) which repeats the word "overseer" until it gets to "officer" – it's brilliant. I was inspired by that in *R.A.W.* In my poem "Cain", for example, "white powder" changed into "white power". Then in "E (Manic Dance Mix A)" "made man" turns into "man-made", and the last line is "fruit of the factory tory tree tree."

There are respected white rappers on the underground scene – as good as the Black ones. They've lived the life and practised and are really good. But for a white person coming into rap later in life, I think it would be harder for them and they probably would feel self-conscious. Even if they had the intellect and the love of words, they probably just wouldn't do it in public. It's hypothetical though.

MT: But doesn't rap come out of a more oral culture that white people are perhaps less familiar with?

PA: Yes. That's right. But if you think of today – most modern rappers didn't stand on street corners and rap – it just isn't like that. Albums were talked about at school and that was their influence as much as anything. Even though rap has come out of that vibrant Black culture; in the old days it consisted of clubs and dens of iniquity where men would get together; this would be a way of sparring. It still has that element and it is still male dominated, but a lot of rappers didn't come from the ghetto – they don't even know what a ghetto looks like! Chuck D was from a middle class family. There is a difference now. Some literally were from the ghetto and did stand on street corners, but a lot of them didn't – so it's a bit more mixed now. I still think there is an element to rap that necessitates having lived the life. I haven't lived the life properly – I've lived the life enough perhaps. I have this one rap friend who I spend two or three days at a time with just listening to rap the entire time. So it is something that has really influenced me but I am not immersed in it.

I think saying there's a Black aesthetic is a bit dangerous – it's too universalising. And as for Toni Morrison – is she talking specifically about poetics and poetic form? I suppose there's someone like Ntozake Shange (an African-American, I know) – she writes in a particular style using slashes instead of a line break. As soon as I see that I know that's a Black writer, so in that sense there is a Black aesthetic. That's the only specific thing that I could point to.

MT: Do you think that Black/white identities are essentialist?

PA: What do you mean by that?

MT: I mean that there might be something essentially specific to a particular racial identity.

PA: I had to look that one up. I remember being at a lesbian event and someone mentioned lesbian essentialism, saying that there was some innate goodness in being a lesbian woman. Is there a value judgement on it?

MT: No. It is abstract and eternally open to debate. It is the opposite of constructivism – like in the case of sex and gender; sex is what we are and gender is what we become. It could be described as a racist issue in a way, but at the same time, I have read many things by Black writers who want to be thought of as having an essential difference. It's a two-edged thing – it can be used against or for.

PA: Is this implying that if you are born Black, there are certain characteristics that nothing can change?

MT: Yes, I suppose – just the same as if you are a white person. In a way it is the same question as I've asked you in other ways.

PA: I think it's so much more a question of nurture and nature.

MT: Right, yes, it's part of that debate. It's again going back to that écriture féminine idea, which is also an essentialist argument – that you're essentially female and therefore you are going to write in a certain way. And if you're essentially male, you're going to write in another way, both in terms of form and content. I won't labour that one as we have already sort of covered it!

PA: I think it's such a difficult one because there are certain expectations … I used to be more that way inclined, doing workshops where I talked about the fact that possessing a female body meant that we would write in a certain way. I don't agree with that anymore, but I think I had been influenced by that specific strand of feminist thinking. So, no. I think there is a danger in making those kind of arguments.

MT: Many of your poems, I'm thinking particularly of some in *R.A.W.* ("London's Burning", "The Black The White and The Blue") are overtly political. Do you wish your poetry to be seen as a political tool or are you an advocate of 'art for art's sake'? Or are the two mutable as suggested in the title poem of *R.A.W.* in which you use the portmanteau word 'edutain'?

PA: I've really swung round on this issue and I think the main difference between *R.A.W.* and *Transformatrix* for me is evidence of this. I used to hate art for art's sake – I used to think it was completely self-indulgent. I thought art had to *do* something. Whereas now I'm more open to the fact that you can do art – and in the process you can offload, by drawing a water lily, for example and that's alright. I think there's a danger if you put it in a gallery and start making people think it's a work of genius. There is something to be said for a piece of work that is very finely wrought but that isn't political in any way. Having said that, I don't particularly warm to that kind of work, although I do think there is a place for it. I still prefer work that has some kind of an edge or is saying something – it doesn't have to be political but it can be telling a story. For me, it has to *do* something.

MT: I think a lot of people expect "Black expression", if I can call it that, to be political, that it *should* be political.

PA: I don't think that's the case any more. I turned around and I think the times turned around as well. For example, about five years ago, I went to a few events, there were young Black poets doing love poetry and I thought, "wow, that's wonderful." We don't have to do poems about racism all the time! Or class oppression, or neo-colonialism or whatever "ism". It was good to see other young Black poets being supportive of that. I do think within the older generation there is more of a sense of duty, that as Black poets we have to talk about this or that. Like we all have to do a Stephen Lawrence poem – I haven't done a Stephen Lawrence poem!

If that had happened ten years ago, I would have done a Stephen Lawrence poem, but because …

MT: You would have felt a pressure on you to do that?

PA: I would have been more driven to do it, but there could definitely have been a pressure. I've heard about five good Stephen Lawrence poems, so why would I bother? Whereas "The Black The White and The Blue" covers issues that had not been covered before. Yeah, so I think I've come round on that. The primary drive is poetic for me. Obviously if the content is controversial then of course it's going to be a political poem. I think in *R.A.W.*, I did spell out much more what the political message was in some poems. For instance in "The Black The White and The Blue", "Nigger Paki Queer/ when will we walk the streets without fear?" were the last two lines which is spelling out the message of that poem. If I were to re-write it I would probably change those last two lines. I think I've become more covert.

MT: So do you feel comfortable with separating the personal from the political? Do you feel you always could? As you say, you feel the climate has changed in terms of what people now expect – they don't necessarily expect a political stance?

PA: Yes. Although there is clearly pressure. One Black poet came up to me in the late 1980s and said "I really want to know where you're at politically, because I'm not sure". It was quite full on.

MT: Was it like a challenge? Was it saying "Why aren't you writing more political stuff?"

PA: They didn't say exactly that, just the feeling that they weren't sure where I was coming from. I hadn't been brought up with a strong Black community like they had. I hadn't been brought up in London or gone to school there. I spent time in Sussex and North Wales and then went to Oxford, so I was quite removed. When I came to London, I didn't have friends here. I just came as a kid for holidays to see my family. In a weird way though I think it was good for me because I had a more unique voice. Whereas sadly I think about 50% of the poems in that era sounded the same. I think now young Black writers realise that they are allowed to write about Greek myth, rap or whatever – there's much more freedom now – and that's very positive for Black literature and culture. Of course there are publishers who come up with rubbish like "well if you write another *White Teeth* we'll publish it." But there are enough young Black writers around now, like Courttia Newland, Diran Adebayo etc, writers with different styles, some of it political, some not. But of course if they want to write another *White Teeth*, they should be able to! There certainly seems to be more freedom within the poetry scene.

MT: At the recent 'Write Black, Write British'[11] conference held in the Barbican, this debate seemed to form a large part of the discussions, at least on the first day anyway. So it seems the issue of art versus politics is still current.

Could you tell me more about the word chosen for the title of your second collection – *Transformatrix*? To me the word suggests change, adaptation. Is this about the ability or need for Black women to be able to adapt, or is it something else?

PA: There were three elements in the book – women (of course); women going through change/metamorphosis; and travel. So I wanted a word that could encompass and encapsulate those three things. The word matrix has loads of meanings- it's an incredible word. It originally meant womb; and it is the place in which ideas are engendered. It was also a celebration of my own creativity and coming through the block after *R.A.W.* – this is all stuff that no-one reading the book would know about. It was a title for *me* and what I had come through to get to the book. Really it's not about Black women specifically, but looking at women going through some form of transformation, either a physical one, like having your first period, or more about a change like a shift in the head. In "Ufo Woman", for instance, I move physically to different places and each time I have different insights which build into who I become.

Then of course there is the word 'form' in "transformatrix" – and the book is a celebration of form, so it says completely what I want it to say on so many different levels. Yeah, the form was a really big thing – constantly re-working existing forms – the sestina mainly and the sonnet. I have still got ideas up my sleeve – so it's continuing. It's not like I can say, "right I've done form – that's it." I love form, I want to work more with form.

MT: Many poems, particularly in *Transformatrix*, are about words, language and the process of writing (for example "Prologue", "The Excoriation"). Would you like to comment on why this theme might be so important for you?

PA: Probably again just completely personal stuff. I could barely read for two years because I wasn't able to concentrate and I wasn't writing. So when I did start writing again it was as if I was a born-again writer, a born-again poet. So it's a celebration of that, and a celebration of performance and having your own voice as well. "The Prologue" (known as 'Word' outside the book) is very performable, it's very rappy, it's very in your face in a way, but it starts off almost like it's on the page and then it leaps off and goes into the air. It sort of celebrates the act of performing, the act of communicating. For me the whole book is a celebration of that. Then there's "69 bpm" – again about communication and also about double entendre. There are misunderstandings too like in "The Change" – so yes, there are really quite a lot of poems in *Transformatrix* about words. Much more than I consciously realised at the time. If you think about it *R.A.W.* is an acronym – although it could mean lots of things – it is an acronym for Rhythm And Word – so that in itself is celebrating the word. My next book will be 'Body Language' .../

Interview - November 2001

NOTES AND REFERENCES

[1] Cobham, Rhonda and Collins, Merle, *Watchers and Seekers: Creative Writing by Black Women in Britain* (London:Virago 1997)

[2] African Dawn were a spoken word collective combine poetry, mime and African music in the mid 80s. It's members were, Merle Collins, Ahmed Sheikh, Kwesi Owusu and DJ Wala.

[3] A series of 3 day courses organised by Spread the Word and included poets such as Karen McCarthy, Dorothea Smartt and Bernardine Evaristo, Roger Robinson, Chris Abani, Malika Booker and Delroi Williams.

[4] Payback Press was started by Jamie Bynge as an imprint for Canongate Books. The list has now been incorporated into Canongate Books with Jamie Bynge as publisher.

[5] Gecko Press was a new innovative poetry press started by poet Jade Reidy. She published *R.A.W.* by Patience Agbabi and her own collection, *LUST* before deciding to return to New Zealand.

[6] The Women's Press wound down its operations in 2004 as the longest surviving independent women's press in Britain.

[7] See Chapter 9 on Dorothea Smartt.

[8] See Chapter 15, Black British Poetry:Some Considerations.

[9] The Chocolate Art Project was a collective of young performance poets in the mid 90s formed by Roger Robinson.

[10] In 'The Laugh of the Medusa,' leading French feminist, Hélène Cixous proposes *l'ecriture feminine* as a model that allows feminine desire, the language of the body, to reconstitute expression as a revolutionary movement against the masculine rhetorical structure that has defined language over time. Cixous, Hélène. 'The Laugh of the Medusa.' *The Routledge Language and Cultural Theory Reader*. Ed. Burke, Crowley and Girvin. (London & NY: 2000) 161-6.

[11] Write Black, Write British:From Post Colonial to Black British Literature Conference held at The Barbican Art Centre, 27-28 Sep 2001. See Introduction.

Cosmopolitanism and Marginalisation in Bernardine Evaristo's *The Emperor's Babe*

Dave Gunning

The epigram to Bernardine Evaristo's *The Emperor's Babe* is taken from Oscar Wilde: "The one duty we owe to history is to rewrite it".[1] Wilde's aphorism takes the form of a pun that plays on the two meanings of 'history' used most commonly. History as the objective past, 'the way it really was' that has the causal and emotional power to direct both our present and futures, is undermined by the recognition of the constructed nature of history and the interventions of the recorder in creating the physical historical archive. It is precisely this dual character of historical knowledge that Evaristo seeks to both point out and capitalise upon. E. H. Carr famously defined history as "a continuous process of interaction between the historian and his facts, an unending dialogue between the present and the past."[2] Evaristo is able to reclaim the agency invoked in this notion of interaction and assert a vision of history tuned to the political requirements of her age. She is also able crucially to challenge the legitimacy of other narratives of the British national past that have been called upon to mould opinions on race within recent political thought in Britain.

In *The Emperor's Babe*, the idea of a homogeneous white Britain existing before the era of multiracial immigration is challenged through the creation of a Roman Britain that is emphatically multicultural in its codes and enunciations. Ideas of the purity of cultures across history are dispelled not only through the depiction of this cosmopolitan metropolis but also through the challenge made to the easy separation of the present and past enacted through Evaristo's deliberate anachronisms. However, in contradistinction to more utopian theorists of the fate of race in the (post)modern city environment, she demonstrates how the cultural plurality of the contemporary urban habitas is not sufficient on its own to annihilate racial oppression. Evaristo's engagement with the idea of history takes place through a conscious interrogation of the cosmopolitan. In this way she is able to claim the telling of Black British histories as at least partly the job of the imaginative writer, and to challenge any vision of the nation that relies on historical 'truths' to elucidate a philosophy of exclusion.

The Londinium of *The Emperor's Babe* is emphatically a space defined by the expression of cosmopolitan identities. Evaristo's use of English, Latin, Italian, Scots and Cockney slang helps to suggest an arena where cultures are intermixed and where any single fixed register will prove insufficient to the task of categorising the social transactions that take place within the city. Her description of the tattoos displayed by the sailors in the Fishermen's Tavern demonstrates this plurality:

> *I Luv Mei Ling*
> > *Zindiwe IV Me*
> > > *Yasmin, Mi Numero Uno Futuo*
> > > > *Doris: Mi & Tu: IV Ever II Gether*[3]

The names of the sweethearts are drawn together from all corners of the Roman Empire and beyond and are linked in a playful register that appears to reject absolutist models of cultural diversity in favour of a portrayal of hybrid space where the different origins of these women are made unimportant in the present moment of proclaimed sexual desire.

The use of a textual sign as the image that Evaristo employs here is significant. The tattoos are clearly on display, publicly spelling out the force of their message. Iain Sinclair has written of how graffiti can signpost the unconscious of the modern city[4] and it seems that Evaristo intends her inscribed words to have the same effect. There is a concentration on the text of the popular urban experience; a form of writing that is perhaps the polar opposite of historiographical or high literary forms. The tattoos write out the cultural circumstance of their own conception in an explicit, visual way that is as permanent (and as transient) as the human body. This message connects to Homi Bhabha's writing on the work of cultural production in the cosmopolitan environment. For Bhabha, cosmopolitan culture cannot be read as performing any kind of "authenticating/identity bestowing function" for individuals or ethnic/national groups but rather is concerned with "the activity of negotiating, regulating and authorising competing, often conflicting demands for collective self-representation."[5] This process then translates the very public space in which contact between all members of a society takes place. The script on the sailors' arms pays material witness to this unsanctioned revision of the shared public environment.

Several reviewers of the novel have commented on Evaristo's intervention into the traditional narratives of white British history and how she is able to disrupt the conventional formulation of these accounts and challenge the supposed justifications they may provide for contemporary racism. In doing so, it is argued, she is also able to "imagine a usable past for black Britons of today."[6] However, other commentators on the novel have observed the way in which it can serve as a reflection of contemporary London and illuminate the workings of hybrid, cosmopolitan identities. In this way, critics claim, she is able to undermine right-wing pleas for preserving the purity of cultures and demonstrate that "multiplicity is a source of strength."[7]

I wish to argue that the city depicted by Evaristo is eminently able to present the cosmopolitan reality of the modern metropolis, but that it is certainly possible to maintain that the model given is less than positive. Evaristo apparently dislikes the word 'oppressed',[8] but it seems an exceptionally accurate epithet for Zuleika, the heroine of *The Emperor's Babe*. Her verse-novel demonstrates the varying pressures that are exerted upon her and, through to its tragic ending, shows how the hybridity of the city may not be sufficient to liberate the individual from extant constructions of domination.

The Emperor's Babe is the story of Zuleika, whose Sudanese parents migrated to Londinium and raised her in this outpost of the Roman Empire. As a child she roams through the streets of this lively city with her "rag doll" friend Alba, who, together with the transvestite Venus, provides Zuleika with a source of strength and friendship in a world where she is dispossessed of most of her agency. Aged eleven, she is forced by her father into a marriage with the Roman senator, Lucius Aurelius Felix. Trapped in this loveless union, she feels frustrated until, encouraged by Alba and Venus, she embarks on an affair with the Roman Emperor, Septimus Severus. Their passionate few months are cut short when he is killed in his campaign to capture the northern reaches of the British Isles. Zuleika's tryst is then revealed to Felix by her Caledonian slaves, Valeria and Aemilia. The novel ends with Zuleika suffering a slow death as her husband punishes her by a gradual poisoning of her food.

The novel appears to present a wealth of identities that Zuleika and her friends are free to choose from. When her parents managed to complete their journey from sub-Saharan Africa to Londinium, it would seem that their offspring were granted the opportunity to invent themselves as they saw fit. The experiences of the migrant parents are obscure to their children, who are unable to imagine "that country a lifetime away that Mum // called home and Dad called prison."[9] The experience of the generational gap is so vivid that Zuleika and her mother often seem to be experiencing a different city. Their perceptions are so distinct so as to give the impression of taking place in discreet geographical locations: "I looked up at the sky // Mum had been studying / It was not one and the same" (86-87). Here, Evaristo also echoes the situation and experience of *Lara*, the protagonist of her previous versenovel, Lara, set in recent London.[10] As Lara becomes older, she realises her own perception of the world is different as a Black Briton from that of her one Irish, one Nigerian parent, to the extent that she has to leave Britain and travel to their homelands in order to return and realise that they do in fact live in the same city. The young thus initially map themselves onto the city in a way that seems exclusively tuned to the immediacy of the present, without concern for what has passed before. Venus sums up the way in which identities are formed in this absence of historical consideration:

> 'The thing is,' she'd say, 'a life without a past
> is a life without roots. As there's no one
>
> holding on to me ankles I can fly anywhere,
> I became the woman you see before you.' [11]

This concentration on *becoming* at the expense of *roots* seems to free Zuleika and her friends from the burden of having to conform to pre-fabricated identities and enable them to write their own destinies. (Again, this parallels Lara's leaving Britain to search for her roots, in order to discover her personal identity).

However, the limitations imposed on this self-assertion soon become evident. Britain is staged as a far-flung outpost of the Roman Empire – "the wild west"[12] – where the imperial codes might seem lax and the counter-narratives of cosmopolitanism can blossom, but it becomes apparent that the hybridity of the city must be contrasted to the world outside. The Britain that lies without the boundaries of Londinium is feared and unknown to Zuleika. The city-space which seems to open up so many opportunities for Zuleika is translated into a place where a different order of restrictions prevails and is imposed upon her. It is significant that she resigns herself to her marriage to Felix while regarding the city. Having swum out to the middle of the River Fleet, she looks back at the panorama of Londinium before announcing, "I knew I had to accept my fate."[13] The inevitability seems generated by the force of the city itself that constrains the options which may have been open to her. In one section of the novel Zuleika prays for her menstruation. She suspects that she has been made infertile by Felix's premature taking of her virginity. Her infertility, which can seem linked to her inability to express herself within the stifling terms of her marriage, is brought to mind in this passage when she states, "My womb is stuffed / with shifting cumulus."[14] However, this meditation on the storm that rages inside her with no outlet is twinned to a query about the world outside London:

> [...] This empty roof
> this sleeping town, this great stone wall
> which circummures us.
> I have never left its gates. What is out there?[15]

In this way, Evaristo indicates Zuleika's awareness of the threefold bond imposed upon her liberty by her body, her home, and the city itself.[16]

Within her home, which becomes symbolic of the confines imposed upon by Felix, even in his absences, Zuleika seems even less able to articulate freely. She longs, by contrast, for the freedom offered by the open city streets. A telling example of this is in her reaction to the grand "Templum of Excrementum" which Felix has built in the house.[17] Uncomfortably alone, she pines for the "camaraderie of the public latrinae"[18] where the boundaries between the intimate and the communal are less able to alienate her. If the city is shown as denying the unlimited potential for self-realisation that she craves, then within her villa her options are even fewer.

As a child, Zuleika pictures herself and Alba as "the wild girls of Londinium,"[19] able to roam freely in the city and openly to satisfy their desires. She is confident that this autonomy will persist as she matures and that she will be the master of her adult life as much as of her childhood. Felix, of course, has very different ideas. It is instructive to examine exactly why he chooses her as his bride. Her black skin certainly plays a part in his decision, "She reminds me of the girls back in Ægyptus, / where I spent most of my teenage years,"[20] but he is also influenced by her social position. He regrets the independence and self-assertion of the women of Rome and regards their sophistication as decidedly unfeminine. He confides to Zuleika's father that the wife he seeks will be expected to be subservient and conscious of her inferior position. It is these qualities he detects in Zuleika rather than the freedom she feels.

Zuleika is controlled by a discourse imposed by Felix that dictates how a senator's wife should behave. It is revealed that his power has a greater ability to shape events than was offered by the cosmopolitan city-space. The Londinium she conjures is not purely a place of untrammelled personal freedoms, but also a place in which the plethora of cultural identities on offer are ultimately unable to mask the alienating power relations of a inegalitarian society. Rather than there being an infinite scope for self-fashioning in Evaristo's imagined world, the workings of power always circumscribe the amount of ways in which agents may invent themselves. The city may appear to be the site of open cultural transactions and therefore appear as a liberating arena, but it is also the embodiment of the law, where the logic of power acts as social cement and an individual's role is determined by their place in a larger structure.

However strict Felix's injunctions may be, it is not the case that he (and, by extension, society as a whole) can fully contain the entirety of Zuleika's individuality. Her transgressions (such as the unspoken deal she makes with the head servant, Tranio) are, in the main, minor, yet are significant in that they illuminate the faultlines inherent in the system to which she is interpellated. The dictates of power are always open to a degree of negotiation, if only she can ascertain how. The frustrations of this subordinated position, in which resistance is possible but difficult to formulate, are central to the novel. This is demonstrated in the Prologue, 'Amo Amas Amat'. The moment of stasis depicted in this section encapsulates the derailment of Zuleika's life prior to her meeting with Severus and can be read as condensing much of her experience in the largely unnarrated years between her marriage aged eleven and her infidelity with the emperor when eighteen. The opening line "Who do you love? Who *do* you love[?]"[21] demonstrates both the seeming hopelessness of her position and her urgent desire for redress. The repetition helps to convey the sense of frozen process while the inflection on the second time of asking hints at a questioning of the finality of the situation and suggests the possibility of a resolution that may exist beyond the terms of her incarceration.

The characters that populate Evaristo's Londinium all seem able to assume identities that help to frustrate attempts to impose a totalising narrative of cultural homogeneity onto the place. However, it is not obvious that this is always a positive process. Zuleika reinvents herself throughout the novel but not necessarily for the better. In fact, her fashionings seem more imposed upon her than freely chosen. Bhabha has written of how migrants are "compelled to make a tryst with cultural translation as an act of survival" in the cosmopolitan metropolis.[22] Zuleika is certainly forced to fit in with the cultural currents that sweep across her city, but the duration of her survival is tragically short. The lack of cultural absolutes does little to overcome the fact of her marginalisation and the fatal consequences that it brings about.

Like Zuleika, Alba and Venus adopt shifting cultural identities to cope with life in the fractured city. However, they are never left quite as adrift as she. They are able to claim some space as their own and, in their own ways, participate in the life of the community. Despite her efforts, Zuleika can only ever be in, and never of, the city in which she dwells. The narratives that dictate the boundaries of the operations of power seem carefully assembled always to exclude her. Her blending of registers in the performance of her cultural identity has little impact on the persistent fact of her marginalisation. Power is revealed to be as fluid as the urge for self-reinvention and is constantly able to re-define the parameters that determine inclusion within the ranks of the privileged.[23]

Evaristo has argued that, in *The Emperor's Babe*, Zuleika "is noticed because of her colour but she is not discriminated against because of it."[24] In fact, the situation appears more complex than this. Within the margins of the synchronic presentation of the city as an alternative vision of Britain, there certainly does not appear to be the systematic anti-black prejudice that has actually existed throughout centuries of British history. Yet, as long as it is possible for Zuleika to be defined by her skin colour, then it is evident that this attribute can be used as a tool to justify her oppression. This is well demonstrated when Felix's sister Antistia reveals to Zuleika the truth that "You will never be one of us":

A real Roman is born and bred,
I don't care what anyone says,
and that goes for the emperor too,
jumped-up Leeebyan. Felix will never

take you to Rome, Little Miss Nooobia[25]

Those who hold power are able to define the criteria for inclusion within the circle of influence. Even Severus's achievement does not necessarily allow him the right to participate within this group. Membership is always granted or withdrawn by the existing elite and, although the limits of their jurisdiction are subject to revision and can be intruded upon by those from outside, they always remain the bearers of the deciding authority.

I have given the impression that *The Emperor's Babe* is a bleak story, which offers a vision of the city as an alienating locale where Zuleika is stifled and put upon. My reading would seem therefore to be at odds with the more usual interpretations, which argue that it revels in its positive depictions of London. A typical example of this kind of reading is that of Sukhdev Sandhu:

> [T]he novel is best read as a romping, highly enjoyable,
> and surprisingly affecting piece of silliness, the literary equivalent
> of a seven-inch bootleg that slathers dance beats on to an old
> 78 rpm tune.[26]

Sandhu's somewhat patronising remarks are interesting in that they demonstrate the way in which Evaristo's novel has been commonly perceived as light in tone, but also because of his choice of comparison. The splicing together of disparate elements evoked in his example is reminiscent of the use of *bricolage* in postmodernist cultural production. He suggests that *The Emperor's Babe* can be read in this way, as playful rather than political, and ultimately displaying a lack of concern with 'serious' issues of human freedom and racism.

It is easy to understand why this impression of the novel might be obtained. Certainly the preeminent mood of the novel is light-hearted and the repetitions of certain key jokes (such as the inscription of modern life onto Roman Britain – Armani and Versace togas, for instance) remind the reader that the text is, at least partly, comic. The form of the novel also helps to reinforce the notion of a fast-moving, fluid textual space. Each event of the story enjoys its own section and can almost be read as a complete poem in its own right. The predominant use of the couplet as the mode of expression also quickens the pace and gives the impression of easily digestible information. Evaristo's choice of style seems to have been freed from constraints of prose that would have slowed the frenetic tempo of the novel. *The Emperor's Babe* is as lively as it is playful and these two aspects together help to contribute to the positive atmosphere that most critics seem to find in the work.

However, I wish to contend that *The Emperor's Babe* is as concerned with exploring the limits of the playful as it is with capitalising upon it for the sake of humour and pace. As I have observed above, the ability of the characters (and especially of Zuleika) to traverse cultural boundaries and invent new ways of being is eventually revealed to be severely restricted. In a largely negative review of the novel, Bruce King observes that the characters fail to assert individual voices and that the repeated jokes begin to pall and dull narrative progression.[27] However, Evaristo seems aware of this. When Alba attacks Venus in one of their many disputes, she affects the same voice that Evaristo has been putting into the transvestite's mouth: "Venus, you're fake, every*fink*, my *dee-yah* // about you is fake."[28] Evaristo notes the artificiality of the personas adopted by her characters. Venus's reply – "Wrong! I'm true to what's inside me / I allow the real Venus to float to the surface"[29] – seems unable to overturn Alba's accusation that the artificial is always recognisable as such.

In writing fiction, Evaristo is of course required to manipulate the artificial to provide a reflection of any real world. We can see her writing as an articulation of the desire she shares with Zuleika: "*to remake my town / with bright stones and glass*".[30] The phrase suggests a rendering of the real world in a way that lenifies it and makes it attractive to view. This tallies with the prevalent reading of *The Emperor's Babe* that sees Evaristo creating a comedic and liberating space. The privations of Roman Britain (and indeed of black life from then until the present day) are seen to be subsumed into Evaristo's celebration of the cosmopolis that reverberates in each of her lively, joking couplets. That I would resist such a reading of the novel is evident from my arguments above, but I now wish to examine Chapter VII of the novel. This chapter details Zuleika's trip to the amphitheatre and I examine it to begin to provide an explanation for the apparent disjunction between Evaristo's upbeat tone, which has led so many critics to identify the novel as celebratory, and the often bleak content which I have highlighted in bringing the positive view into question.

The chapter begins with one of Zuleika's poems. It conjures a vision of the river trip that is about to take place. The sentimental imagery of this poem conforms to the reader's expectations of the "first hot date" between Severus and Zuleika, as we have been primed by Severus's invitation[31] to expect a continuation of the joyful and passionate affair that has been delineated in the previous two chapters. However, the poem is followed by twelve lines from which Zuleika is absent and we are instead presented with an image of the imperial flotilla, majestic yet impersonal. Zuleika is then allowed to appear as a voice and recognise that "I would be nowhere near him."[32] The trip, which promised initially to be a continuation of the Emperor's and her tryst, instead regresses into a further bout of introspection. The jocose tone is not absent from this section (particularly as the disembodied voices of Venus and Alba are present to undermine the more elevated of her musings) but a darker tone is also observable. The amphitheatre, "a gargantuan spherical monument" to be found at Greenwich,[33] is clearly a comedic riff upon the perceived ridiculousness of New Labour's Millennium Dome project, but it also serves another purpose: its sheer size displays an imperial arrogance "embodying // the very ethos of empire: to conquer."[34] The Conqueror, then, is a concrete example of the imperial urge toward violence and brutality and, as such, can begin to provide a counterpoint to the positive mixing that the Roman Empire seems to have engendered within the cosmopolitan space of the city.

The next section of the chapter can seem to be a return to the style that has characterised many of the earlier parts of the novel. As the action moves inside the building, Evaristo describes an eclectic scene. The accounts of the amphitheatre, the crowds, and the entertainments are fast-moving and punctuated with the slang and cod-Latin that help to convey the multicultural bazaar that Londinium appears to be. Her description of the 'star' gladiators shows Evaristo at the zenith of her witty turn of phrase – the couplets revel in flowing enjambment, carried by traces of an iambic rhythm and a preponderance of half-rhymes. The joke at the expense of contemporary professional footballers is drawn out, but inventively played upon (for example, in the reference to "the news tablet *Ave!*"[35] However, Evaristo brings this flow of verse to an abrupt halt with the line "But it was not to be.")[36] The following lines are inflected with an irregular rhythm and scan more like prose than verse. This slowing of the pace fits well with the change in mood. The frailty and infirmity of the gladiators and slaves who are to die is highlighted by the careful pace and short sentences. As the scene becomes increasingly dreadful, as pregnant women are fed to lions, the wisecracking heroine of the novel is so affected that she is largely robbed of her ability to articulate. Instead she is only able to scream "so hard my stomach hurt."[37] Evaristo does not allow the repercussions of this violence to stay solely within the arena. Zuleika is stirred by the horrific spectacle to face all the violence in her own life and to perhaps begin to recognise how the harshness of the world she inhabits might conspire to silence any affirmation of her individuality. For Zuleika,

> The Grand Opening of The Conqueror
> had turned into the Grand Opening
>
> of my fucking Pandora's box –
> and not since my wedding night
>
> had I cried.[38]

In this detail we can read a magnified representation of the violence done to cosmopolitan liberty by the barbarity of a society. Evaristo artfully plots the limits to which her free-flowing prose can depict a situation of oppression. The playfulness, which is so applauded in reviews of *The Emperor's Babe*, comes to a sudden close when dealing with the full awfulness of human conduct. Of course, while Zuleika is struck dumb by the horrors of the gladiatorial scene, Evaristo is still able to narrate. It is later in the novel that the author's voice stops shy of narrating Zuleika's death and this elision perhaps echoes the inarticulacy to which the cosmopolitan subject is reduced in the face of great wrongs. Yet, despite the inevitable gloominess that ends the tale, Evaristo's novel repeatedly revisits the lively style that characterised the description of the first scenes in the amphitheatre. I would contest any reading which held this pleasure taken in language to be indicative of a wholly positive celebration of the possibilities on offer within metropolitan life but I would accept that it does offer a challenge to a reading that sees Zuleika's story as absolutely bleak. I wish to suggest that Evaristo's blending of tones shows her to be aware of some of the aspects of representation confronted by Adorno in his discussion of the politically committed work of art. Adorno argues that art that presents a realist view of the horrific things that people can do could actually work against the moral and political imperatives that inspired its inception. As all art translates the world it depicts, "[t]he aesthetic principle of stylisation [...] make[s] an unthinkable fate appear to have had some meaning, it is transfigured, something of its horror is removed."[39] He goes on to recommend work that abandons verisimilitude to the experienced world in favour of the autonomous and complete-in-itself artwork.

Evaristo navigates the bind in a slightly different way. The marginalisation of Black women in contemporary Britain is reflected onto an imaginary landscape of two thousand years past. However, to avoid this creation becoming something leaden and strained, or allowing the processes of narrativisation to deaden the political impetus of the work, Evaristo has chosen an eclectic style. The pace of the work, the unusual form, and, above all, the wit allow Zuleika's world to be presented in a way that entices the reader to accept the whole of the conceit as legitimate in the context of the novel. Through relating back to contemporary practices and artefacts explicitly in the comedic tropes of the novel, Evaristo allows an implicit understanding of the negative events in her text to be read as reflecting an existing social world.

The emphasis on the links that are made between the lighter elements of the story and the real world (rather than on the darker parallels) serves to fix these aspects in the modern reader's mind as the more central to the novel. This may go some way to explaining the critical consensus that sees *The Emperor's Babe* as a light novel despite its moments of bleakness. However, it also serves another function in that it can nullify some of the danger that an expressly political novel must necessarily cheapen its subject through the very act of representation. Zuleika is clearly victimised by the harsh world she inhabits, but she is never reduced to *just* being a victim. The joy of her humanity as rendered by the stylistic novelty of the text enables her story to avoid becoming a simple account of a brutal structural oppression that offers no opportunity for the enunciation of human resistance. Zuleika may ultimately perish but her ability to have flared (however briefly) within the confines of restrictive social position enables the novel finally to retain the seeds of hope that are essential for any kind of political renewal.

A common lament in racist discourse of recent years bemoans the passing of a notion of cultural integrity bequeathed by an unbroken national history. Examinations of the reality of the British past have helped to shatter this ideal of continuity while the fact of cultural translation disconcerts any attempts to establish a stable and unchanging national identity. However, it is not the case that this destabilisation necessarily strips power from the dominant classes who have previously justified their right to rule by reference to these unchanging forms. James Clifford has observed that, with the dissolution of the idea of homogenous, unsullied cultures, "the notion that certain classes of people are cosmopolitan (travel[l]ers) while the rest are local (natives) appears as the ideology of one (very powerful) travel[l]ing culture."[40] However, it is not evident that the increasing prevalence of this idea necessarily must do much to improve the lot of those classes who were made subaltern under the previously extant knowledge. *The Emperor's Babe* offers a portrayal of the way in which dominance can still be enacted within the cosmopolitan space and demonstrates that, in fact, the crumbling of the distinctions so precious to the preservation of a racially-exclusive national history need not entail the end of the practices of racial dominance which are forever open to reformulation. Evaristo's has cleverly engineered *The Emperor's Babe* to depict this continuing structural imbalance whilst not allowing resistance to be seen as wholly unachievable. Her literary innovation develops Zuleika into a character whose defiant humanity may not be enough to preserve her own life, but remains as a supplement at the end of the novel, tracing out a way of being that rejects total victimhood.

NOTES AND REFERENCES

[1] Bernardine Evaristo, *The Emperor's Babe: a novel* (London: Hamish Hamilton, 2001), p.vii

[2] E. H. Carr, *What is History?* [1961] (Basingstoke: Palgrave, 2001), p.24

[3] Evaristo, Bernardine, p.104

[4] Iain Sinclair, *Lights Out for the Territory: 9 Excursions in the Secret History of London* (London: Granta Books, 1997), pp.1-54

[5] Homi K. Bhabha, 'The Manifesto' in 'Reinventing Britain – a Forum', *Wasafiri* 29 (1999), pp.38-39

[6] Bruce King 'Review of Bernardine Evaristo's *The Emperor's Babe*', *World Literature Today* 76:1 (2002), p.147

[7] Diana Evans, 'Bernardine Evaristo: Welcome to Swinging Londinium', *The Independent*, 1 June 2001, p.25

[8] See Erica Wagner, 'Ancient and Modern', *Times* 2, 6 June 2001, p.8

[9] Evaristo p.12

[10] Bernardine Evaristo, *Lara* (Tunbridge Wells: Angela Royal, 1997)

[11] Evaristo p.48

[12] Ibid. p.26

[13] Ibid. p.18

[14] Ibid. p.109

[15] Ibid. p.109

[16] Zuleika's infertility can also be read as reminiscent of Robert Young's writing on hybridity. Questioning certain postcolonial championings of the hybrid condition as reflecting the ideal intermingling of cultural differences in the cosmopolitan state, Young is concerned to point out the roots of the term and to emphasise the viewpoint of nineteenth-century racial science in exploring hybrid offspring of different races. Infertility would be taken as proof of polygenesis and of distinct human species, ultimately incapable of amalgamation and more suited to relations of domination. See Robert Young, *Colonial Desire: Hybridity in Theory, Culture and Race* (London and New York: Routledge, 1995), pp.6-19. Zuleika's childlessness is then perhaps metonymic of the wider exclusion she faces from the Roman world

[17] Ibid. p.63

[18] Ibid. p.64

[19] Ibid. p.9

[20] Ibid. p15

[21] Ibid. p.3

[22] Homi Bhabha, 'The Vernacular Cosmopolitan' in *Voices of the Crossing: The Impact of Britain on Writers from Asia, the Caribbean and Africa* ed. by Ferdinand Dennis and Naseem Khan, pp. 133-142 (p. 139)

[23] This seems to tie in with Timothy Brennan's argument that the current popularity of cosmopolitanism consists of little more than imperially-minded globalism that celebrates the exotic as long as the reins of power remain comfortably in the same hands. See Timothy Brennan, *At Home in the World: Cosmopolitanism Now* (Cambridge, MA: Harvard University Press, 1997)

[24] 'Alastair Niven in Conversation with Bernardine Evaristo' *Wasafiri* 34 (2001), 15-20 (p.18)

[25] Evaristo p.53

[26] Sukhdev Sandhu, *London Calling: How Black and Asian Writers Imagined a City* (London: HarperCollins, 2003), p.286

[27] Bruce King 'Review of Bernardine Evaristo's *The Emperor's Babe*', p.147

[28] Evaristo p.189

[29] Evaristo p.189

[30] The choice of words here is reminiscent of the title given to George Lamming's anthology of black writing *Cannon Shot and Glass Beads: Modern Black Writing* (London: Picador, 1974) which invoked the idea of black writers returning the gifts that European colonisers took to the rest of the world: violence and (possibly ersatz) culture. Interestingly, it is only the second image that is echoed in Evaristo's phrase.

[31] Evaristo p.158

[32] Evaristo p.164

[33] Evaristo p.168

[34] Ibid. p.168

[35] Ibid. p.175

[36] Ibid. p.176

[37] Ibid. p.179

[38] Ibid. p.180

[39] Theodor Adorno, 'Commitment' [1957] in Dennis Walder ed. *Literature in the Modern World: Critical Essays and Documents* (Oxford and New York: Oxford University Press, 1990), pp.89-98 (p.95)

[40] James Clifford, 'Traveling Cultures' in *Cultural Studies* ed. by Lawrence Grossberg, Cary Nelson and Paula Triechler (London and New York: Routledge, 1997), pp.96-112 (p.108)

Medusa? Medusa Black! Revisionist Mythology in the Poetry of Dorothea Smartt

Laura Griggs

"At first thought, mythology seems an inhospitable terrain for a woman writer." So admits Alicia Ostriker in *Thieves of Language: Women Poets and Revisionist Mythology*.[1] This much is true; those myths and legends which pervade our culture, inherited from the patriarchal societies from which our own originates, conspire to perpetuate the idea that woman must be either 'angel' or 'monster' and that those who deviate from the prescribed role of femininity must and will be demonised and ultimately punished. Nowhere is this lesson more aptly demonstrated than in the traditional Greek mythology surrounding that instantly recognisable symbol of all that is grotesquely, monstrously female: the Medusa. With her head of writhing snakes and basilisk eyes, Medusa is the epitome of feminine power, a combination of sexuality and danger that poses a serious threat to the male order. As such, her role in Greek myth is something of a cautionary tale; raped, betrayed and made monstrous, the power she possesses is symbolically seized and reappropriated by Perseus, the 'hero' of the myth. She who rejoiced and found solace in her punishment, this awesome ability to inflict terror, is simultaneously slain and enslaved and her feminine power stolen and harnessed.

Yet, Perseus is not the only thief here. In a defiant reversal of roles, the women writers Ostriker speaks of in *Thieves of Language: Women Poets and Revisionist Mythology*[2] take these patriarchal myths and make them their own, subverting the cultural and literary authority of the ancient stories to give voice to their suppressed female selves. For the characters that inhabit these myths are both ancient and contemporary. Representative of more than just mythological figures and mythological struggles, Medusa and her sisters – Philomele, Penelope and Euridyce – are the instruments through which women writers write themselves.

Ostriker was writing in 1986. Since then, a new, defiant voice has emerged which also seeks to reclaim and reinterpret myth, that of

British-born Barbadian performance artist and poet, Dorothea Smartt.[3] By using the reconstructed image of Medusa as a point of reference for both her gender and her race, Smartt creates a mirror image in which Medusa reflects us all, allowing us to identify with her ambiguity, her indefinability and project our own female image onto hers. Medusa is monster, mother, lover. She is both powerful and vulnerable, life-giving and lifedestroying, she is woman. Patricia Klindienst, in 'The Voice of the Shuttle is Ours',[4] explains the fascination Medusa holds when she says, "If Medusa has become a central figure for the woman artist to struggle with, it is because, herself a silenced woman, she has been used to silence other women." Here then, through what Ostriker defines as revisionist myth-making, this enforced silence is being shattered, and at the same time that Perseus, with his phallic sword, strikes Medusa dumb, her voice is restored by the subversive power of language and imagination.

In order to fully appreciate the nuances of Smartt's revisionism, it is necessary to understand more about Medusa's origins. The gruesome tale of her defeat at the hands of Perseus, whilst the most enduring myth surrounding her figure, is far from an accurate representation of her beginnings. Derived from the Greek 'medein', meaning 'to protect, to rule over', Medusa's name denotes her as a queen of the ancient world, a great and powerful ruler. Her roots date back to a forgotten matriarchal dreamtime when the female was celebrated and worshipped as the creator of life and the feminine respected above all things – when god was a woman. Evidence of this matriarchal dreamtime, marginalised by the history books, dates back to 25,000 B.C. in the form of rotund fertility figures and statues with exaggerated feminine features. Over a period of several millennia, these female deities developed into a complex mythological goddess figure, around the worship of which entire cultures were based.[5] It is from this goddess that Medusa is derived.

Medusa's mythical ancestry is believed to stem specifically from the Libyan Amazons' serpent goddess, Neith, also known as Athene, and from whom the Greek goddess of justice and warfare is similarly derived. Like many representations of the goddess, Neith was manifested in three aspects, each denoting a stage in female development: the maiden, the mother; and the crone or destroyer. While Athena finds her roots in the maiden aspect of this triple goddess and the Greek figure Hera is derived from the mother,

Medusa signifies the destroyer and, as such, is patron of the cycles of nature, with the ability to both create and annihilate life.

Furthermore, far from being a hideous disfigurement, Medusa's serpentine tresses were originally intended to indicate her life-giving properties. With its seemingly miraculous ability to shed its skin, the snake was seen by ancient people as being synonymous with birth and rebirth, and was revered as a symbol of both wisdom and fertility. Prior to the dissolution of the matriarchal religions, images of powerful snake-goddesses were in abundance, adorning temples and places of worship throughout the ancient world. This aspect of Medusa has survived into the Greek version of the myth – Ovid's 'Metamorphoses' tells of the healing properties of Medusa's blood – yet many other aspects of her ancient origins have disappeared, deemed inappropriate or dangerous to the purposes of patriarchal Greece.

Many critics support the view put forward by Robert Graves: that the destruction of Medusa, in whom he sees "the goddess of the matriarchy [which] ...existed before the Greeks established their society" is, in effect, an "historic memorial of her cult's eclipse," commemorating both Medusa's decline and the triumph of the male order.[6] This idea is particularly well supported when looking at further details of the Greek legend; consider the glorious birth of Pegasus, who, writes critic Grant F. Scott, "leaps from the Gorgon's spilled blood like a kind of jubilant phallic trophy," the ultimate "image of masculine resurrection and reassurance."[7] Consider further the episode immediately following, in which the reader is presented with a sinister, erotic vision of feminine passivity in the naked Andromeda, chained to a rock as an intended sacrifice and utterly at Perseus' mercy. A heavy-handed metaphor for female bondage and submission, Andromeda is presented as Medusa's successor, the 'girl who gets the boy' by conforming to gender stereotypes and allowing him to fulfil his masculine role. So far, so good for ancient Greece's patriarchal propagandist machine.

This reshaping and manipulation of Medusa's image, then, has drastically sidelined her original mythical status as patron of the cycles of nature, with the ability to both create and annihilate life. The embodiment of female potency and wisdom, Medusa's ancient persona was clearly counterproductive to the functioning of patriarchal Greece; as such, these aspects have long been buried and suffocated by an all-encompassing culture of masculinity, leaving Medusa's once awesome and positive figure to erode into the one-dimensional monster of popular culture with which modern audiences are now familiar.

Undeterred, or rather, fuelled by this injustice, contemporary female writers are reaching back through mythic history, beyond the reconstructed façade of Medusa's story and using her origins to inspire their own stories, weaving together legend and truth, myth and autobiography, into a Sophoclean tapestry of female experience. Smartt has gone further than any other contemporary writer in exploring and rewriting the Medusa myth, producing several live art pieces and a complex cycle of poems centred around the gorgon. By conflating her own experiences as a modern Black woman with those of the ancient mythological figure, Smartt has created an entirely new and transcendent persona that seeks to engage the reader on both personal and universal levels.

Smartt's fascination with the gorgon originally developed as a reaction to the negative labels she was forced to endure while growing up. She explains: "Medusa was a name that was given to me by the kids next door when I started to locks-up my hair in the 1980s. That together with the general reactions of people, both Black and white, to the changing nature of my hair started me thinking about the possibilities." Instead of allowing this label 'Medusa' to constrict her, Smartt re-appropriated it as an empowering force, researching Medusa's ancient roots and rewriting her as a strong, beautiful, Black woman. Medusa's African origins make this link all the more appropriate; Smartt's traditional locks may hold more than a mere coincidental resemblance to Medusa's cascading serpentine tresses – it is, in fact, quite possible that they were the very inspiration behind the myth. Smartt came to this conclusion herself as she delved deeper into Medusa's mythological past, writing: "I thought to myself: Medusa was probably some Black woman with nappy hair, and some white man saw her and cried: a monster! and feared her, and so told stories about her dangerous potential." By making this identification, Smartt humanises Medusa, transcribing her from a supernatural creature into a real that we can all recognise. This is Smartt's central aim: to create a Medusa that is human, that is woman, that is real.

Taking as a starting point this visual, historical and personal parallel between Medusa's head of snakes and her own hair, Smartt uses the ancient myth and persona of Medusa to express modern, individual concerns. As the poet herself explains, exploration of Medusa's mythic figure enables her to discuss "the politics of hair and beauty, seeing and not seeing, misinterpretation and reinterpretation," with specific reference to the position in society occupied by contemporary Black women, their responses to one another and their own selfimage. For Smartt, hair is an integral part of our identity, and the label once directed at her in the form of an insult is now reassigned as an empowering image in her poetry. Instead of associating her head of snakes with all that is monstrous and grotesque, Smartt chooses to celebrate it and, as Lizbeth Goodman writes in a critique of Smartt's work, "reclaims Medusa's hair as...a source of power and symbol of strength."[8]

In the first of her seven Medusa poems, 'Medusa? Medusa Black!', Smartt confronts the denial of identity that occurs when Black women, told that their natural African hair does not conform to the modern ideal of what is beautiful and acceptable, attempt to alter the structure of their hair. The violence of the language articulates this masochistic desire to punish the self in a misplaced quest for conformity:

> Scrub it, step smiling into baths of acid
> and bleach it red raw
> peel skin of life-sustaining melanin
> Fuck it, wild-haired woman,
> straighten it fry it, desperately burn scalps[9]

Similarly, the poet's use of the refrain, "Make it go away, the nappiheaded nastiness / too tuff too unruly too ugly too black'",[10] conveys with disturbing accuracy and honesty the self-loathing of women who have been coerced into becoming their own enemies, hating their own bodies and, therefore, themselves. When Smartt refers to this struggle, this "ancient war" enacted on "the landscapes of our bodies", she exposes the irony inherent in the fact that women and particularly for Smartt, Black women, are now, through the insidious manipulation of their body image by a white, male society, potential victims of their own violence.

This aspect of Smartt's work echoes the writings of French feminist theorist Hélène Cixous, who, in her seminal essay 'The Laugh of the Medusa', laments these same women for whom the enemy is within.[11] Cixous uses the figure of the gorgon to demonstrate the way in which masculine culture has suffocated female creativity and caused us to fear and loathe our female mirror-images. She urges us to reject this masculine culture and instead, write ourselves into history using our own female language, *écriture féminine*. This ideal of a feminine practice of writing looks to rupture the male systems of sense imposed by society to create new uninhibited worlds of meaning in which the female can be explored without constraint. Here is where the links with Smartt are developed further, for it is out of this desire to shake off the constraints of male, white language and history that Smartt's own work originates.

Cixous' theories use as their basis the idea that language is composed of binary oppositions in which the first term is privileged over the second: male/female; light/dark; mind/body; speech/silence. The various primary terms in each pairing are aligned with one another, as are all secondary terms, so that speech, that most active and powerful of communicative tools, is consequently identified as a masculine domain. As a result, the female is instantly pushed to the sidelines while the male is imbued with the greatest power and cultural significance.

Women, then, are marginalised by language, and all our myths, stories and literature are inherently masculine because they are related to us through this system. Cixous writes that culture has "riveted us between two horrifying myths, between the Medusa and the abyss," arguing that the language of myth and patriarchy forces women to see themselves as either the castrating, monstrous female or the submissive receptacle of the phallus, the empty space waiting to be filled by the proactive male. The female, as it really exists, in all its multitudinous possibilities, is inexpressible; the traditional myths and fictions of our culture are inadequate to communicate the quintessence of female experience. In order to reclaim language as our own and shatter these insidious myths, Cixous urges us to write as women, to explore new and unstructured forms, to write in the white ink of our mother's milk.[12]

This is exactly what Smartt, through her re-creation of Medusa, has done. For both writers, Medusa represents the misunderstood woman, the muted figure on the peripheries of language whose voice has been stolen and suppressed by the forces of patriarchy. Medusa is Everywoman, she exists in all women but has been hidden away, as though she holds the key to a shameful secret. Through her Medusa poems, Smartt is asking us to stop hiding our inner Medusa, to bring her out of the shadows. Smartt's Medusa is the very antithesis of the modern women she writes of in 'Medusa? Medusa Black', women who are themselves burdened under the weight of yet another patriarchal myth – the beauty myth, which tells them that irrespective of intellect, success or happiness, they are still too ugly, too old, too overweight, "too nappy". Using Medusa as an inspirational force, an emblem of the reclamation of female history and language, Smartt is asking her fellow Black women to stand up to this pressure to "banish the snake woman", to set aside these constructed notions of beauty which work as a form of ideological control and, instead, equate beauty with all that is natural and individual in themselves.

When asked to explain what she hoped to achieve through her poems, Smartt tells us, "I wanted Medusa to say "Black is Beautiful", and put to rest the need to wipe out so much of our (physical and spiritual) African self."[13] Cixous also explores this idea, albeit on a semiotic level. Returning to the binary oppositions that are at the centre of our language, where the first term is valued over the second, Cixous equates femaleness with blackness, writing metaphorically, "You are Africa, you are black. Your continent is dark. Dark is dangerous...we have internalised this horror of the dark." Like Smartt, Cixous goes on to demand that women recognise and reject this distorted self-image, asserting defiantly, "we are black and we are beautiful."[14]

In the second of her Medusa poems, 'Medusa: Cuts Both Ways', Smartt shifts her focus away from the self-loathing, self-harming women of the previous piece and directly onto Medusa, creating a proud, awesome figure of beauty:

Medusa
dread anger
welling up in her stare
natural roots Blackwoman
loving Blackwomen
serious[15]

The polysemous nature of the word 'dread' allows Smartt's ideas about the importance of her locks in relation to her self-image to be read against the feelings that they, and her persona as a whole, inspire in others; 'dread' can of course mean both fear and awe, therefore representing in a single syllable a number of reactions to Smartt / Medusa's physical presence. This equivocal word is used to further effect later in the poem, when Smartt writes, "Medusa is... / ...my battle dress armour / of serious dread."[16]

Smartt also brings into play other aspects of Medusa's image. Introducing the associations with menstruation and childbirth that date back to Medusa's pre-Grecian roots, she writes: "He'd be frighten fuh dat / mark wid d'living blood / that bleeds and never dies."[17] Here, Smartt articulates the male fear of female reproductive power and all its mystery, using the menstruating woman's once inexplicable bleeding in synchronisation with the tides and the moon as yet another empowering image, one that inspires fear but also indicates unknown power. The poet continues to develop this idea of Medusa as maternal goddess, restoring her to her former glory and reinvesting Medusa with those powers attributed to her before her desecration at the hands of the Greek mythmakers:

> Medusa...
> is godmother
> our mother
> Medusa is our mother's mothers
> myself all coiled into one...
> Medusa in you is you in me
> is me in you[18]

Here, as Smartt celebrates the matriarchal line at which Medusa is the head, the gorgon's ancient origins as patron of the cycles of nature, of life, death and rebirth are revisited and revived.

Smartt goes on to ally Medusa with other proud, tragic women of history and myth, constructing a many faceted character that reflects a multitude of female faces and making clear the equation, the identification, between Medusa and the battling, oppressed, Black female self:

> Medusa is Assata Shakur
> Medusa is Cherry Groce
> is Eleanor Bumpers is Audre Lorde
> is Queen Nzinga Sarraounia[19]

This list of names reads like a litany of feminine resistance: Shakur, the wrongly incarcerated revolutionary; Groce, whose accidental shooting at the hands of the police initiated the 1985 Brixton riots; Bumpers, a mentally ill, elderly, Black woman who was shot dead by NYPD as they evicted her from her home; Audre Lorde, inspirational poet, feminist and liberator; Nzinga and Sarraounia,

African Queens who fiercely led their nations against European invaders and Medusa, another African Queen, murdered at the hands of another overzealous male attacker. Smartt's message here is clear: Medusa stands for the pain, cruelty and injustices all women – our mothers, daughters, sisters – have suffered. Every woman who has ever been hit by her husband, every woman who has been raped, every woman who has been made to feel inferior, every woman who has been verbally abused because of her gender, her sexuality or the colour of her skin...they are all Medusas. However, as Smartt writes, these women must convert their pain to anger and strength and invoke Medusa's fabled protection. "Medusa", she writes, "is my shield."

Throughout the cycle of poems, Medusa is presented in a number of guises, not only as a strong Black woman or omnipotent mother figure, but also as the psychologically scarred victim of Perseus. 'Medusa Dream,' the fourth poem in the sequence, tells us how, 'Perseus comes. Full of intent / to carve out a name for himself in blood.'[20] Here, the onus is upon Perseus as the aggressor, whilst Medusa is victim. Instead of viewing the myth as it is traditionally told, via the male gaze of Perseus, 'Medusa Dream', tells it differently, expressing Smartt's own suspicions: "I began to wonder if what we are told [Perseus] saw was actually who she was." As a mythical figure, Medusa by definition is, of course, fictitious – any discussion of her 'real' persona, or 'who she was' is futile if we don't believe in the stories themselves. Yet, in a way, we do believe in them, in the sense that what they symbolise becomes ingrained into society's consciousness like a kind of shorthand, instigating chains of semiotic meaning which are impossible to control once set in motion. As Virginia Woolf writes, "It is far more difficult to murder a phantom than a reality."[21] Thus, although we may recognise the fictitious nature of the Medusa myth and her character, the archetype of lascivious female predator which she traditionally represents is nevertheless seen as authentic. In an inversion of logic, the archetype constructed through the one-sided telling of the myth is seen to confirm the reality that does not widely exist. Here, instead of demonstrating the innocent mimesis of art mirroring life or the reverse, art is insidiously manipulating how we perceive life, embedding itself so deeply into our culture that its authority or 'truth' is rarely questioned and subconsciously presumed.

It is here, with Medusa Dream, that the structure of Smartt's cycle of Medusa poems begins to take on greater significance. We have just passed the halfway point of the entire sequence and this coincides with the first overt references to the Greek version of the myth. While Smartt's earlier poems portray Medusa in her most ancient guise, the powerful earth mother of the matriarchal world, as the cycle progresses, it reveals itself to be almost a chronological record of the changing nature of Medusa's image through the ages. More than that, it chronicles all female history: from those first female-worshipping cultures, their decline and subsequent degradation at the hands of aggressive male invaders through to the modern day, where women are finally learning to love their inner gorgon and use her as a source of strength, not shame.

This next poem in the sequence, 'Medusaspeak', describes exactly that: the difficult process of recognition that must be undertaken in order to reconcile the female self with the gorgon inside. The first instinct when confronted with Medusa is to flee: 'You turn / run afraid. / You refuse to be alone / with her'. Once this fear is mastered, however, then we can face Medusa head on and find out who she really is:

> Who's 'she'?
> Honey,
> sweet honey,
> you are.
>
> Here she is
> standing ready
> to rip to claw to beat
> you to your monster self.[22]

The reader is again reminded of Cixous, who asks us to confess to our own monstrous selfaccusations and in admitting, destigmatise them: "Who, surprised and horrified by the fantastic tumult of her drives...hasn't accused herself of being a monster?" Instead of being ashamed of this identification, however, we should embrace and explore it, we should be proud of our bodies and our desires. Women must ignore the patriarchal warnings to avert our eyes from the gorgon and, implores Cixous, "look at the Medusa straight on." Only then will we realise that, far from being deadly, "she's beautiful and she's laughing."

Smartt is equally willing to acknowledge the monster within, explaining wryly, "Every monster has her place." Yet, the poet is asking for more than mere acknowledgment or token recognition. She wants us to be that monster, to let it take over our passive, sanitised feminine bodies and revel in the return to instinctual, unchecked primitive desires:

> crouch quiver whimper.
> Let your hair grow long. Rage
> down to skin and bone. Rage
> red-hot-blue-cold
> tearing you.[23]

The power of Smartt's poetry is most apparent in moments like this, moments which ignite the page with swirling mixtures of words and vivid, startling images. The isolation of certain words, the repetition and combination of others, all serve to rework language and redefine meaning. The phrase "red-hot-blue-cold" mixes ostensibly opposing adjectives to form a new all-encompassing phrase which disregards linguistic convention and ignores the masculine concept of binary oppositions. Smartt's poetry rewrites the female, exploring the subversive possibilities of *écriture féminine*, and creating a disruptive, semiotic mess of language which defies sense and unity and escapes the confines of phallogocentric discourse.

The next poem in her Medusa sequence, 'Let Her Monsters Write', again echoes Cixous by exploring the possibility of a feminine practice of writing and challenging the female artist to break free from the chains of the patriarchal mythmakers to write from the dark side. The opening lines, "Medusa squeezes herself into / irregular-sized compartments, / wooden and fortress-like,/...too small",[24] suggest the inhibitive nature of her ancient Greek incarnation. Transformed from an awe-inspiring goddess of infinite power into a hideous monster, Medusa, in all her glory, cannot fit, will not fit, neatly into the masculine mythical discourse. Smartt continues: "Surrounding her is / an older I, her centre cave". Here, we are reminded of the ancient Medusa, patron of the cycles of nature, too huge to be contained within the hard, wooden boxes of the male mythmakers, too complex to be articulated within the limited, blinkered forms of their language. "Under hair", Smartt urges, "let her monsters write / from all sides – ceiling walls floor. / Make a deep welcome / for this singsong body".[25] If, as Cixous believes, there lies within us all a little of that good mother's milk, then white ink is what these monsters must write in. Our monsters are our primal female selves – displaced, ignored, suppressed – and they will write themselves, sing themselves, scream themselves through our female bodies.[26]

For Smartt, then, Medusa is a potent icon of resistance, the means through which contemporary women can positively redefine their own identity. Like many other female poets, artists and theorists, Smartt recognises the power of naming and ownership; therefore, by reclaiming Medusa and proudly identifying herself with the moniker of gorgon, she has redirected the myth's power, reinvesting Medusa with the respect and dignity she once possessed. Reacting against the tyranny of the male gaze, which forces women to see themselves indirectly, through the distorted reflections of a man-made mirror, Smartt presents us with a direct, deeply personal yet at the same time universal, female perspective. Speaking of her desire to write Medusa's story, she explains simply: "Perseus talked about what he saw, but what about what she saw and what about what I would see?"[27]

Smartt's subject matter reinforces this harmony with Cixous' ideas – the reclamation of women's bodies and body-images through the subversive medium of writing is as central to Smartt's poetry as it is to Cixous' feminist theorising, both writers stressing the impossibility of women's spiritual and mental liberation without them first learning to love and be satisfied with their female bodies. Smartt's exploration of Medusa represents this mental journey; she works her way through the variety of responses Medusa inspires in women, from fear and shame to pride and identification, considering, throughout, the dynamics of language and silence, of seeing and not being seen, of self-love and self-hate.

Through these varying characterisations, Smartt moulds Medusa into a multitude of female shapes, demonstrating her inexhaustible potential and proving that acceptance of Medusa equals acceptance of the female self. As Cixous explains, modern culture demands we choose between the Medusa and the abyss.[28] The choice, as it stands, is not a particularly appealing one. Unless, that is, women redefine Medusa, discover her real origins and prise off the lid of centuries of silence.

Reinterpret, revive, revise: this is the subversive process Dorothea Smartt and her contemporaries are now engaging in. To write their own stories, to weave their own words into the sturdy fabric of male discourse, is a daunting prospect; yet, it is one which is being undertaken with confidence, eloquence and most importantly, success, undermining from the inside the presumptions of those revered patriarchal myths and insidiously imploding their timehonoured authority. This increasing distrust of the male tradition is essential to the growth of women's writing: "with women poets,'" says Ostriker,[29] "we look at or into, but not up at, sacred things; we unlearn submission." In this sense, Dorothea Smartt's examination and questioning of the Medusa myth, searching for meaning in her matrilineal origins and destroying the negative connotations that cling to her, are all forms of rebellion, assertions of female independence: rewriting Medusa is unlearning submission.

NOTES AND REFERENCES

[1] Ostriker, Alicia Suskin. 'Thieves of Language: Women Poets and Revisionist Mythology. *Stealing the Language: The Emergence of Women's Poetry in America.* Boston: Beacon Press, 1986, pp.210-38

[2] Ibid.

[3] Biographical information and bibliography of Dorothea Smartt can be found on http://www.sablelitmag.org

[4] Klindienst, Patricia. 'The Voice of the Shuttle Is Ours.' *Literary Theory: An Anthology.* ed. by Julie Rivkin and Michael Ryan Oxford: Blackwell, 1998. pp.613-29

[5] For more information on the proliferation of goddess workshop in ancient cultures, see Merlin Stone, *Ancient Mirrors of Womanhood* (Beacon Press, Boston: 1990) and Merlin Stone, *The Paradise Papers* (London: Virago, 1976)

[6] Graves, Robert, The Greek Myths, (London: Penguin, 1984)

[7] Scott, Grant F. 'Shelley, Medusa and the Perils of Ekphrasis.' *The Romantic Imagination: Literature and Art in England and Germany.* Ed. Burwick and Klein. (Amsterdam: 1996. Editions Rodophi B. V., Amsterdam/Atlanta, GA 1996)

[8] Goodman, Lizbeth. Introduction. *Mythic Women/Real Women; Plays and Performances* by Women, (London: Faber & Faber, 2000)

[9] Smartt, Dorothea. *Connecting Medium,* (Leeds: Peepal Tree Press, 2001) 'Medusa? Medusa Black!' pp.57-58

[10] Ibid. pp.57-58

[11] Cixous, Hélène. 'The Laugh of the Medusa.' *The Routledge Language and Cultural Theory Reader.* Ed. Burke, Crowley and Girvin. (London & NY: 2000) pp.161-6

[12] Ibid.

[13] Smartt, Dorothea, 'Knowing You Like I Do...' Email to the author. 7 June 2001

[14] Cixous, Hélène. 'The Laugh of the Medusa.' *The Routledge Language and Cultural Theory Reader.* Ed. Burke, Crowley and Girvin. (London & NY: 2000) pp.161-6

[15] Smartt, Dorothea, 'Medusa Cuts Both Ways'. pp.59-60

[16] Ibid.

[17] Ibid.

[18] Ibid.

[19] Ibid.

[20] Smartt, Dorothea, 'Medusa' Dream pp.62

[21] Woolf, Virginia. *Professions for Women*. Ed. Nathan, Monique (New York: Grove Press, 1961) p.170

[22] Cixous, Hélène. 'The Laugh of the Medusa.' *The Routledge Language and Cultural Theory Reader*. Ed. Burke, Crowley and Girvin. (London & NY: 2000) pp.161-6

[23] Smartt, Dorothea, Medusa Cuts Both Ways, pp.59-60

[24] Smartt, Dorothea,'Let Her Monsters Write'. p.66

[25] Ibid. p.66

[26] Cixous, Hélène. 'The Laugh of the Medusa.' *The Routledge Language and Cultural Theory Reader*. Ed. Burke, Crowley and Girvin. (London & NY: 2000) pp.161-6

[27] Ibid.

[28] Ibid.

[29] Ostriker, Alicia Suskin. 'Thieves of Language: Women Poets and Revisionist Mythology.' *Stealing the Language: The Emergence of Women's Poetry in America*. (Boston: Beacon Press, 1986) pp.210-38

Benjamin Zephaniah, the Black British griot

Eric Doumerc

WHO IS BENJAMIN ZEPHANIAH?

Benjamin Zephaniah was born in Birmingham, England in 1958. His father, a Barbadian immigrant, worked as a postman and his mother, of Jamaican origin, was a nurse. Benjamin's parents separated when he was 11 years old, and he chose to stay with his mother. Mother and son had to move house frequently in order to run away from Benjamin's father, and as a consequence, the young Benjamin did not do very well at school, and by the age of 14, he had become a street-wise tough. Following an attempt at shop-lifting, he was sent to an approved school near Shrewsbury and stayed there for about 18 months. A few months after leaving that school, he was involved in a scuffle in Birmingham and was accused of causing an affray. This time he was sentenced to two years imprisonment and sent to Winson Green prison.

Following health problems, he was moved to Borstal[1] (a remand centre for young men) but released a few months later on account of his deteriorating health. This combined spell of detention and ill health led to Benjamin's decision to adopt a more constructive attitude once he left hospital and became a DJ on the local 'sound system'[2] scene. He became really popular as he never failed to lace his 'toasts' with biting social commentary and sarcasm. This immersion into the sound system culture led Benjamin to write short poems, although this time with no musical backing. His friends provided much encouragement and in 1980 at the age of 22, Zephaniah published his first collection of poems with Page One Books, an underground publishing house that Zephaniah had founded with some of his friends in Stratford, in the East End of London. The young poet then started performing at various venues, pubs and cafes, and became very successful on the New Variety circuit that was then developing thanks to publishing houses like Page One Books, Akira Press, Apples and Snakes (an organisation that promotes and produces live poetry events). The music press soon recognised Zephaniah's talent and as early as November 1982 the *New Musical Express* featured an interview with him.[3] In January 1983, *Soundmaker* reviewed one of Zephaniah's readings at the Institute of Contemporary Arts in glowing terms : " Benjamin Zephaniah has over the past year, and countless gigs, built up a massive following amongst the Alternative Cabaret scene […] and is gradually being accepted as one of the most important and inspired artists in his field."[4]

In 1985 the 'Bard of Stratford's second collection came out. Entitled *The Dread Affair*, causing quite a stir on account of its violent rhetoric and its use of the English language.

Zephaniah's popularity reached its peak in the 1980s when he was shortlisted in 1987/1988 for the post of Creative Artist in Residence at Cambridge University, and then for the Chair of Professor of Poetry at Oxford. This recognition of the poet's talent triggered a debate over the value of Zephaniah's poetry and its relationship with high culture. The Sun, a tabloid newspaper, carried an editorial entitled, "Would you let this man near your daughter". The left-wing broadsheet press (*The Guardian* and *The Independent*) took Zephaniah's defence. Even *The Times* felt compelled to devote some of its space to the poet. In spite of this controversy, Zephaniah's star kept rising and he wrote several plays including 'Job Rocking', 'Hurricane Dub' and 'Streetwise' which received high critical acclaim.

Benjamin Zephaniah is also noted for his numerous television appearances including the popular soap opera 'Eastenders', and appearances on the radio during which the poet reads/performs his poems or gives his views on various topics.

More recently, in November 2003, Zephaniah was at the centre of a new controversy when he turned down an O.B.E offered to him by Tony Blair's government. In an article published in *The Guardian* on November 27th, 2003, the poet explained that the concept of empire "reminds me of slavery, it reminds me of thousands of years of brutality, it reminds me of how my foremothers were raped and my forefathers were brutalized."[5] This anti-Establishment stance is reminiscent of the position adopted by Zephaniah in the 1980s and shows that, to him, the poet is also a public figure.

Zephaniah's phenomenal success is all the more surprising as the poet had great difficulty in reading and writing when his first book of poems was published and had been written off by his teachers as a "born failure". Surely the controversy over the value of Zephaniah's poetry is linked with the inherently oral nature of his art, which can be partly explained by his late development as a reader and writer.

Whether we like his poetry or not, it has to be admitted that Benjamin Zephaniah is a major player on the British literary and cultural scene and has made his mark in a significant way. It could be said that his poetry is characterised by its stereoscopic nature and presents us with a double vision of British society. This 'double consciousness' appears in both the thematic concerns and forms that Zephaniah uses in his poetry and which make his art truly 'Black British'. His poetry transcends racial and cultural boundaries as it is steeped in the very British tradition of doggerel and nonsense while paying homage to the Caribbean oral tradition in its various forms and guises. His poetry is a hybrid, creolised product of the meeting of two cultures and is characterised by the coexistence of several voices which correspond to various roles or functions assumed by the poet : the wordsmith, the broadcaster/griot, and the satirist.

BENJAMIN ZEPHANIAH AS WORDSMITH

When reading a Benjamin Zephaniah poem for the first time, one is immediately struck by the rhythmic potency of the piece. Indeed Zephaniah's poetry is first of all defined by its rhythm, and rhythm takes us back to the roots of poetry.

This rhythmic power is clearly heard in the poem entitled 'Overstanding', a poem that should be read aloud if its power is to be fully appreciated as it relies on a four-beat rhythm or tetrametre to carry its message:

> Open up yu mind mek some riddim cum in
> Open up yu brain do some reasoning
> Open up yu thoughts so we can connect
> Open up fe knowledge an intellect[6]

The other characteristic of this poem is its use of rhyming couplets. The use of the tetrametre and rhyming couplets places this poem in the tradition of popular poetry or light verse, but also goes back to the roots of Old English poems like 'Beowulf'- traditional ballads and nursery all characterised by the use of the tetrametre. 'Overstanding' exemplifies Zephaniah's approach to language and poetry, and this primarily has to do with the pleasure of reading and listening to poetry. In fact, Zephaniah has repeatedly insisted on this aspect of his work: "I got interested in poetry before I knew it was poetry. I just thought it was words that ... sounded the same, words that meant something, words that... I didn't particularly know what the words meant, but... I knew the kind of emotions they were trying to express... and I love rhyme! So, there was a particular time when I would just say, "I play with words", I have fun with words. Ever since I came across words I started playing with words."[7]

So Zephaniah has always liked to "play with words" , but also to play on words. In 'Overstanding' Zephaniah uses wordplay and plays on the literal and figurative meanings of the verb 'to open up'. Indeed "open up yu mind", "open up yu thoughts", "open yu heart" and "open up yu self" are examples of the figurative meaning of this verb, while "open up de speaker", "open up yu house", "open up yu bank account", and "open up de books" refer to its literal meaning. This literary device, the syllepsis, consists of juxtaposing literal and figurative or abstract and concrete uses of a phrase.

This enables the poet to insist on the poem's main theme, in this case 'openness'. Indeed every stanza starts with the verb 'open up' and ends with the exhortation 'open wide', and thus the notion of openness is a kind of framing device. In 'Overstanding', Zephaniah also resorts to Rastafarian talk as the very title of the poem is a well-known example of the kind of surgery Rastafarians practise on the English language. Indeed the Rastafarians claim that the verb 'to understand' carries negative connotations as it conveys the idea that man lacks a proper understanding of reality. Thus they came up with a new word, "overstanding".

The overall message in 'Overstanding' is one of hope and tolerance: the poet urges us to open our minds to other cultures in order to broaden our horizons , "open up yu brain do some reasoning" and "open up yu thoughts so we can connect" and thus stands as Zephaniah's personal manifesto. 'Overstanding' is also a good example of the oral nature of Zephaniah's art as the poem is reminiscent of English nursery rhymes with their tetrametric metre. The galloping rhythm carries the message successfully and the reader/listener finds himself or herself chanting the poem, which is as it should be. In fact Zephaniah's art as a wordsmith takes us back to the oral roots of poetry as described by P.D. Roberts in his *How Poetry Works*: "The sound of the poem has always been its primary magic. During the earlier centuries of English, the written or printed page was altogether beyond the reach of the average person, and to most people poetry was sound and sound alone. The old English bard declaimed his ringing alliterations to the rhythmic sweep of the harp. Chaucer and other medieval poets read their work aloud, often to a courtly audience. The habit of reading poetry silently to oneself developed relatively recently."[8]

Zephaniah's poetry is about the magical power of the word and the pleasure principle associated with the rhythm of nursery rhymes. This appears clearly in the rant entitled 'Money' which is one of the most popular Zephaniah pieces and receives enormous applause whenever he poet performs it.

Zephaniah first performed 'Money' in 1992 on a Tyne Tees Television programme entitled 'Wordworks' in which well-known poets were asked to present a visual interpretation of some of their pieces. In other words the idea was solely to perform these poems, not to read them. Zephaniah chose to perform, 'Money' whilst taking a walk in the streets. The poet, Brendan Kennelly found this performance very convincing:

"Another good example of image working with image occurs in the poem 'Money' by Benjamin Zephaniah. Here, the poet advances down a city street, his body in rhythm with his words, his words a mesmeric music evoking the power, character, influence and presence of money. His face, his hands, his body, the entire street he's passing through, become utterly at one with the poem itself, which is inexorable and hypnotic, a spellbinding evocation of the moneyed universe."[9]

Just like 'Overstanding', 'Money' relies on a tetrametric rhythm and rhyming couplets for its percussive effect:

Money mek a rich man feel like a big man
It mek a poor man feel like a hooligan
A one parent family feel like some ruffians
An dose who hav it don't seem to care a damn,
Money meks yu friend become yu enemy
Yu start see things very superficially[10]

Zephaniah's use of a number of literary devices in 'Money' marks him out as a consummate wordsmith. These devices include, continuous rhyming, alliteration, anaphora ("Money meks marriages / Money meks divorce/ Money meks a student think about the course") and chiasmus or parallelism ("Money meks commercials / Commercials meks money"). Their employment emphasises the omnipresence of money in our society and its inescapable nature: the listener feels trapped by the power of Mammon.

Zephaniah uses the devices of wordplay and irony to denounce the power of money, as is shown by the lines, "Some people never see it yet dem work hard / Other people never see it because dem carry cards" and "Nobody really understands the interest rate / When dere is interest den it is too late."

Zephaniah resorts to accumulation, repetition, alliteration and continuous rhyming to insist on the power of money, and this appears clearly in the following excerpt, with its rolling rhythm:

> And de Bredda feels betta dan dis Bredda next door
> Cause dis Bredda's got money, but de Bredda's got more
> An de Bredda thinks dis Bredda's not a Bredda cause
> He's poor
> So dis bredda kills de oder
> Dat is economic war[11]

In fact, the devices used by the poet reflect the oral nature of his art and the fact that oral cultures operate in primarily mnemonic terms: "In a primary oral culture, to solve effectively the problem of retaining and retrieving carefully articulated thought, you have to do your thinking in mnemonic patterns, shaped for ready oral recurrence. Your thought must come into being in heavily rhythmic, balanced patterns, in repetitions or antitheses, in alliterations and assonances, in epithetic and other formulary expressions […], in proverbs which are constantly heard by everyone so that they come to mind readily and which themselves are patterned for retention and ready recall, or in other mnemonic form."[12]

Many poems by Zephaniah use such mnemonic devices and formulary expressions, which are reminiscent of those found in Rastafarian and reggae cultures, but also in British culture. Zephaniah considers himself a modern-day griot, bard or wordsmith, as is shown by the following lines from 'Rapid Rapping':

> Long time before the book existed
> Poetry was oral an not playing music
> Poetry was something that people understood
> Poetry was living in every neighbourhood

[...]
Found in many forms it was de oral tradition
When governments said quiet, poets said no
Submission[13]

This radical stance led the poet to adopt other voices such as that of the broadcaster.

BENJAMIN ZEPHANIAH AS A BROADCASTER

Benjamin Zephaniah once defined himself as an "alternative newscaster", that is a kind of social commentator and observer. This role is reminiscent of the DJ's function in the reggae community – although the DJ's rhymes often amuse the listener, his social commentary bears upon important issues or derides or mocks a figure of authority. Zephaniah's poetry has an undeniable journalistic quality as, over the last twenty years, the poet has covered many topics, from race relations and Britain's royal family to the environment and politics. Several of these raps/rants were published in *The Guardian* in the late 1980s. 'Rapping Up the Year' appeared in *The Guardian* on 30 December 1988, containing the poet's thoughts on the main events that made 1988 a year memorable, Gorbachev's glasnost policy in the USSR, American troops' departure from Afghanistan, and closer to home, the popularity of Australian soap operas in Britain:

Aussie soaps went big in
Britain, Neighbours cap
tured masses
Fame hit them so fast dey had
No time for acting classes
Young Doctors had Sons and
Daughters all at Cell
Block H
Kylie Minogue came to
England, she had to escape[14]

The rumours concerning the fragile nature of Prince Charles' and Lady Diana's marriage also got a mention ("Some believe Charles has gone / off Lady Di"), but the poet did not forget his own community and dealt with the problem of negative stereotyping in the press and police harassment:

> De press and police said de
> "Yardies are here"
> Blacks seh it's those Scotland
> Yardies we fear
> [...]
> Clinton Mc Curbin's case was
> Out of order
> Reverse de roles and it would
> Have been murder
> From now on must Black always
> Look over their shoulders ?
> Through fear of a case of death
> By misadventure[15]

It must be remembered that in the late 1980s the Yardies were very much in the news and that the word 'yardie', originally referring to a Jamaican-born person, had come to designate Jamaican gangs' members. The media's coverage of the Yardies' activities led to British people stereotyping all West Indians as violent people. Zephaniah focused on the Clinton McCurbin case as a sad example of negative stereotyping : in 1988 McCurbin went into a Next shop and tried to pay for purchases with his credit card. The shop assistant panicked, the police were called and a scuffle ensued during which McCurbin died.

The end of the rap humorously points to the poet's role as a griot reporting on current events:

> Dats my quick review of 1988
> I couldn't cover everything
> You must appreciate
> De rhyme might be quite simple
> But de riddim you must feel
> Yes, I expressed some personal
> Views
> But dat was in de deal
> Thank you for your attention[16]

In this passage, the poet uses well-known journalistic catchphrases such as, "Thank you for your attention" in a parody of TV newscasters' style in order to let the reader/listener know the kind of poet he is.

The reportage nature of Zephaniah's poetry also appears in raps he has written on the Royal Family ('The Day I Met Lady Di' and 'Royals Do it Too'), the environment ('Me Green Poem') and the 'troubles' in Northern Ireland ('Troops Out'). His poems often deal with serious issues like animal rights or the situation in Palestine in a humorous way, but they always raise the reader/listener's consciousness. Humour is also evident in another voice the poet uses, the satirist's voice.

BENJAMIN ZEPHANIAH'S AS SATIRIST:

In some of his poems, Zephaniah uses a dry, acerbic tone to denounce well-known evils like the exploitation of underdeveloped countries by the 'first world', negative stereotyping and the power of the 'gutter press'.

The poem entitled 'A Bomb Pusher Writes' is a good example of this approach. The persona created in this poem is that of a weapons manufacturers who sells arms to 'third world' countries, thus growing rich on these countries' backs:

> Our people can eat, drink, and make babies
> In the comfort of their own homes
> Watching our bombs bomb your people[17]

The last four lines of the poem illustrate the poet's terse and concise satirical style as they denounce the exploitation of the 'third world' by the 'first one':

> We love our country
> We love your climate
> We love our bombs
> We made your bombs[18]

These hard-hitting lines actually contain the main accusations levelled at first-world weapons manufacturers: their patriotism, pride in their technological superiority and their view of the third world as a tropical paradise for rich tourists.

The problem of negative stereotyping is tackled in a well-known Zephaniah poem, 'How's Dat' which takes the form of a confrontation between a teacher and a West Indian pupil. The teacher thinks that a West Indian child must be good at cricket and sports more generally, as Black people are commonly said to be no good at academic subjects.

As for the power of the tabloids, it is admirably dealt with in 'The SUN' in which the poet uses irony, wordplay and sarcasm to denounce some tabloids' biases:

> Every hippie carries nits
> And every Englishman love tits
> I love Page Three and other bits
> I stare into the SUN[19]

The fierce nationalism which characterises these tabloids is also denounced ("I believe Britain is great/ And other countries imitate", and the last line of the poem, the punch line, "I am blinded by the SUN", insists on the biased reporting associated with the tabloid press.

Zephaniah's talent as a satirist also comes through in his treatment of the publishing industry and the 'marketing' of Black poets. Indeed, Zephaniah is aware that he has been 'promoted' as the voice of Black Britain, the 'angry Black poet' as the title of one of his poems goes:

> Next on stage
> We have the angry Black poet,
> So angry
> He won't allow himself to fall in luv,
> So militant
> You will want to see him again[20]

These lines immediately bring to mind the piece entitled 'Revolutionary Poets'[21] by the Jamaican dub poet Mutabaruka in which the poet laments the demise of the protest tradition in dub poetry and its commodification or commercialisation. Zephaniah knows that his art can be seen as an act or a 'performance', and in a more recent poem entitled 'Knowing Me', he addresses those who would like him to play the part of the radical Black poet in the throes of an identity crisis:

> According to de experts

I'm letting my side down,
Not playing the alienation game.
It seems I am too unfrustrated.
I have refused all counselling
I refuse to appear on day time television
On night-time documentaries,
I'm not longing and yearning.
I don't have an identity crisis[22]

So the poet seems to shy away from the commodification of his art and to adopt an independent stance.

Thus, the many voices used by Benjamin Zephaniah testify to the complexity and stylistic variety that have come to characterise his poetry. Zephaniah's poetry is a living entity that reflects the ethnically diverse nature of Britain today. His latest collection, *Too Black, Too Strong*, celebrates this new Britain. Indeed, many poems in *Too Black, Too Strong* are celebratory and joyous. For instance, 'Carnival Days' is a wonderful celebration of Caribbean culture in Britain and sets the Notting Hill Carnival[23] in the context of a multicultural Britain: the empire has become a centre for Carnival/Caribbean culture:

On days like these the elders say
Astronauts can see us dance
Glittering like precious stones
On dis rocking British cultural crown[24]

The theme of celebration is also present in poems like 'The London Breed' and 'The Big Bang' which deal with the poet's Black British identity. Zephaniah's use of humour and wordplay is again apparent in this poem entitled 'The London Breed', a poem about the pull of the big city and its ability to produce a new culture:

It's so cool when the heat is on
And when it's cool it's so wicked
We just keep melting into one
Just like the tribes before us did[25]

The entire collection is a potent assertion of Zephaniah's Black Britishness. The poems are preceded by an essay entitled, 'What Am I Going On About?' in which the poet candidly informs the reader of his Black British identity: he is not a Rastafarian who yearns to go back to Zion/ Ethiopia, but a British person who happens to be Black. He makes it clear that Britain is now 'home' to him and that he sees it as his duty to tour the world and let it know what today's Britain is all about. Thus, the poet has made it clear with his close association with the British Council that he is not "the voice of Black Britain," but an ambassador for Britain and its increasingly diverse nature.

NOTES AND REFERENCES

[1] A British reform school, like a prison for youths boys who were too young to be sent to an ordinary prison

[2] For further information about sound systems see the talk by Michael la Rose recorded in Roxy Harris & Sarah White, *Changing Britannia* (London: New Beacon, 1999) pp. 120-148.

[3] Habekost, Christian. *Verbal Riddim – The Politics and Aesthetics of Afro-Caribbean Dub Poetry*. Amsterdam: (Rodopi, 1993) p.29

[4] Ibid. p.29

[5] Name, *The Guardian* 27 November 2003

[6] Zephaniah, B., 'Overstanding' in *City Psalms*. (Newcastle upon Tyne: Bloodaxe Books, 1993) p.17

[7] Personal Interview, February 1996

[8] Roberts, Philip Davies. *How Poetry Works*. (London: Penguin) 1986. p.55

[9] Astley, N. and Lavender, M., eds. *Wordworks – Poetry on Television*. (Newcastle upon Tyne: Bloodaxe Books, 1992) p.9

[10] Zephaniah, B., 'Overstanding' in *City Psalms*. (Newcastle upon Tyne: Bloodaxe Books, 1993) p. 20-23

[11] Ibid. p.20-23

[12] Ong, Walter. *Orality and Literacy – The Technologizing of the Word*. (London and New York: Methuen, 1982) p.34

[13] Zephaniah, B., 'Rapid Rapping', in *City Psalms* (Newcastle upon Tyne: Bloodaxe Books, 1993) p.38-40

[14] Rapping up the Year, *The Guardian*, 30 December 1988)

[15] Ibid

[16] Ibid

[17] Zephaniah, B., 'A Bomb Pusher' Writes in *City Psalms* (Newcastle upon Tyne: Bloodaxe Books, 1993) p.15

[18] Ibid. p.15

[19] Zephaniah, B., 'The SUN' in *City Psalms* (Newcastle upon Tyne: Bloodaxe Books, 1993) p.58

[20] Zephaniah, B., 'Propa Propganda' in *Propa Propoganda* (Newcastle upon Tyne: Bloodaxe Books, 1996) p.29

[21] Mataburaka, 'Revolutionary Poets' in Burnett, Paula. *The Penguin Book of Caribbean Verse in English*. (London: Penguin, 1986.) p.80

[22] Zephaniah, B., 'Knowing Me' in *Too Black, Too Strong*, (Newcastle upon Tyne:

Bloodaxe Books, 2001) p.62

[23] Notting Hill Carnival takes place in Notting Hill, London, England. An annual event held each August, it's led by the British African Caribbean community who moved to Notting Hill after World War II. The carnival generally attracts up to 1.5 million people from Britain and around the world, making it one of the largest street festivals in Europe.

[24] Zephaniah, B., 'Knowing Me' in *Too Black, Too Strong,* (Newcastle upon Tyne: Bloodaxe Books, 2001) p.46

[25] Ibid. p.84

Part Three: Locating Writers in History, Culture and Society

'Blacks in Ivory Towers Can't Write About Ghettos'[1]: West Indian Worker Writers in 1970s Britain

Sandra Courtman

OLD FATHER

Old Father to England in Winter '59
Cold bite him hard,
Make him bawl in his small basement room
By the Grove.
Every day he cry out:
"Man, a tekkin' de nex' boat back home."
But come Spring,
Old Father still here.

Time passed.
Old Father feet begin to shift.
His roots have no meaning now.
He straighten his hair,
Press it smooth.
Coloured girls no good for he -
Day after day you see him
Bouncing down the road with a blonde
Never brunette,
And his suit, cream or beige,
Never anything dark.

[...]

Boy,
Old father don't want to know we now,
In his white Rover,
With his slicked back hair.
And them white people saying
"He's an example to his people!"[2]

Hugh Boatswain

Hugh Boatswain is one of a number of talented young Black poets who met in London in the 1970s under the auspices of a radical publishing project called 'Centerprise'. Based in Hackney, Centerprise was a focal point for a British organisation collectively known as 'The Federation of Worker Writers and Community Publishers' (FWWCP). They published their inaugural collection in 1978, entitled *Writing*, to showcase contributions from its 15 creative writing groups, whose members lived in London, Manchester, Liverpool, Bristol and elsewhere. Its foreword claimed:

> This book brings together some new writing by working men and women round the country. It also brings out some of the creative powers a class society tends to kill, or bury alive.
>
> Most of the writers represented live and work in the poorer parts of towns and cities. The schools and jobs they've been through have not encouraged them to write.[3]

This chapter traces the origins of this working class organisation, exploring the historical conditions that led to its formation and will argue that its little-known role in promoting an emerging Black British cultural identity should be recognised. The examples of writing which follow evidence 'ordinary' people claiming a public space for their work, and it is work which often sells many copies and occasions reprints. The writing which is the focus of this chapter makes no claims for inclusion in the high culture of a literary 'canon'. 'Very little of the prose and poetry here would have seen the light of day had it been left to the individual "genius" of commercial publishers.'[4] However, the agency it demonstrates is concerned with a broader questions about culture (whose culture is validated?) and its relation to Black British history and politics.

The FWWCP was (and still is) a unique organisation, which premised its activities on a left-wing grass-roots solidarity and created opportunities for Black people to articulate their feelings *constructively*. By the mid-1970s, when the organisation was formed, areas of British cities were destroyed by racial tension and civil unrest. But looking back at the violent events of 1976, Caryl Phillips tells Maya Jaggi in an interview: "although there were riots in Toxeth, Brixton, Handsworth and Moss side, our lives were not determined by them".[5] Phillips reminds us that we might look to alternative forms of resistance from West Indian migrants and their children. The act of writing, in various forms from literacy acquisition to performance poetry, emerges as a survival strategy for the deracinated.

Hugh Boatswain's 'Old Father' is one of the poems in *Writing* and it speaks to those conditions of the 1970s and engages, in an unequivocal and sparsely poetic form, in cultural analysis. His poems suggest that in the historicising of West Indian migration and settlement, we should recognise that community publishing played a role. It is interesting that 'Old Father' describes a movement towards a Black British autonomy, which was fully formed by the late nineties. Stuart Hall describes the transformation as follows:

> There is no sense that Britishness is an ideal to which we might
> want to subscribe or assimilate. We are fully confident in our own
> difference, no longer caught in the trap of aspiration which was
> sprung on so many of us who are older, as part of a colonial
> legacy described in Fanon's famous phrase Black skin, White
> mask. Black identity today is autonomous and not tradable.[6]

'Old Father' is dialogic in that it dramatises the world-view of two generations of people: a first-wave West Indian settler and a Caribbean-British poet who berates his elder for 'selling out'. They are both agents in the ideological and generational shift that Hall describes above.

It is little known that the so-called 'ordinary' and often silent majority of post-war West Indian migrants, and a generation of children born to them in Britain, chose to redefine and reaffirm themselves through the cultural transaction of *creative writing*. Few scholars of the Caribbean diaspora have attended to the safe space created by the FWWCP for this activity. The FWWCP archives contain examples of prose writing and poetry from subaltern agents of history who published for, and through, their politicised constituency. They illustrate that, as Raymond Williams wrote in 1958, 'culture is ordinary' and that the need to create, record and share experience is a common impulse:

> Culture is ordinary: that is the first fact. Every human society has
> is own shape, its own purposes, its own meanings. Every human
> society expresses these, in institutions, and in arts and learning.
> The making of a society is the finding of common meanings and
> directions, and its growth is an active debate and amendment

under the pressures of experience, contact, and discovery, writing themselves into the land.[7]

The FWWCP offers cultural historians a unique record of society's growth and this is a much more dangerous process for its Black working class activists than the quote from Williams would suggest. Community publications demonstrate that migrant labourers, under the pressure of experience, do choose to write themselves 'into [their new] land'. This chapter is interested in how an alliance between Black and white working class writers contributes to society's growth towards a – multi-ethnic -shape for British culture.

It is fair to say that the alliance of Black and white working class people is not usually emphasised in histories of the period. Ron Ramdin's study, *The Making of the Black Working Class in Britain,* writes of the division between Black and white, between state and Black youth in the consciousness raising years of the 1970s.[8] In Britain, we became familiar with media images of Black youth running from police, followed by the violent flare-ups which signalled that they, and their parents, refused to be beaten and harassed anymore. Boatswain's poem 'Cut Up Dub' tells of the turning point:

> A goin bounce up Stokey tonight,
> But a h'aint goin' run through the night.
> You see Babylon got a thing:
> (Nigger running in the dark) = CRIME.[9]

If the British police force's institutional racism validated such behaviour to young Black people in the 1970s (and was still the subject of debate in 1993 when Stephen Lawrence was murdered) what hope was there for a future equable multiracial citizenship?[10] An emerging 'structure of feeling' is captured in the *Writing* anthology in a photograph depicting the 60,000 British citizens, carrying 'Anti-Nazi League' shields, demonstrating their political support for the victims of racial harassment at an anti-fascist rally in Victoria Park in 1978. The photograph reminds us that there are significant moments in the history of race relations when large numbers of British people have sought a public means to express their fear of racism. The photograph also frames the writing within a discourse of anti-racism.

In the 1970s, it was this race and class alliance which reclaimed poetry from its high-art status. Writing poetry was not considered 'ordinary' in cultural terms because it had become separated from its origins in an oral tradition. This phenomenon has a famous historical precedent in the First World War: Catherine Reilly's *English Poetry of the First World War: A Bibliography*, lists 2,225 poets. What was shocking was that a large number of these poets were 'common' soldiers writing about their trauma. In 1916, the army's *Wipers Times* reported:

> We regret to announce an insidious disease is affecting Division, and the result is a hurricane of poetry. Subalterns have been seen with a notebook in one hand, and bombs in the other, absently walking nearing the wire in deep communion with the muse.[11]

It the 1970s, angry Black youth might also be seen with a brick in one hand and a note book in the other. Linton Kwesi Johnson tells of the importance of carrying a notebook on the streets of London. This might be used for scribbling verse or, as instructed by the Black Panther Movement, for noting the name and number of the arresting police officer during the days of the 'Sus Law'.[12]

The case of the acclaimed poet Linton Kwesi Johnson demonstrates that whilst many FWWCP poets would remain unknown, it would be seriously misleading to suggest that is the case for all Black working class writers of the 1970s. We know that exceptionally determined, talented and charismatic writers from British 'ghettos' did eventually break through into the literary mainstream. Inspired by his own 'muse of anger', Johnson bore poetic witness to the consequences of the 'Sus Law'and The New Cross Fire.[13] Growing up Black in a working class community in London or Leeds also created the ferment for the esteemed work of Fred D'Aguiar, David Dabydeen and Caryl Phillips. These are award-winning writers who succeeded against considerable odds to go to university to be finally claimed and, in part supported, by the academy. Dabydeen acknowledges how important D'Aguiar and Phillips were in terms of his own ambitions; they provided a cohort for inspiration and competition. Dabydeen remembers that as they grew into their roles as postcolonial writers they were: "constantly looking over their shoulder saying – he's got another novel out!"[14]

Linton Kwesi Johnson's interview for BBC Radio 4's 'Desert Island Discs' suggests that British culture is happy to appropriate his line of protest. In her interview, Sue Lawley is amused that he, an ex-Black Panther, has become one of only two living poets to be published in 2002 in the Penguin Modern Classics Series.

Johnson responds with characteristic charm: "I've made a small contribution to bring poetry back to the people".[15] Johnson also contributed to 'The South Bank Show', dedicated to Caryl Phillips.[16] By 2003, regular appearances on mainstream radio and television programmes suggest that these writers have successfully moved from the margin to the centre and challenged a white cultural norm. They have come far, but they, like other children of working class migrants growing up in the turbulent conditions of 1970s, found it difficult to identify with any Black British writer.

THE FRAGILE ALLIANCE OF THE POOR

For West Indian migrant workers, initially an experience of racial exclusion compounded by class alienation led them to seek empathy with some members of the white working class. As Selvon wrote in the 1950s: "It have a kind of communal feeling with the Working Class and the spades, because when you poor things does level out, it don't have much up and down".[17] The Black and white 'poor' that Selvon refers to might have recognised each other's immediate poverty, they were not always aware of some of their explicit historical connections. They both made sacrifices in two world wars (largely unrecognised in the case of Black service people) but the poor also played their part in a much longer history of the production and processing of cotton. Their labours, picking cotton in the plantations of the Americas and in the spinning of that same cotton in the industrial factories of Britain were important to the foundation of Britain's expansion and prosperity. During the height of the industrial revolution and prior to the emancipation of slavery, child apprentice mill workers, many of them orphans taken from the workhouses of London, suffered terrible cruelty at the hands of mill owners. Their suffering suggests that mill owners and plantation owners shared the same awful tendency to maim and degrade. By way of example, the following account of Ellice Needham of Litton Mill in Derbyshire describes a discourse of cruelty which we would also find in the narratives of slavery:

> Mr Needham stands accused of having been in the habit of
> knocking down the apprentices with his clenched fists; kicking
> them about when down, beating them to excess with sticks, or
> flogging them with horsewhips – of seizing them by the ears,
> lifting them to the ground and forcibly dashing them down on the

floor, or pinching them till his nails met. To the boys he was a tyrant and oppressor. To the girls the same, with the additional odium of treating them with an indecency as disgusting as his cruelty was terrific. [Those unhappy creatures were at once the victims of his ferocity and lust][18]

Runaways were as likely to be treated to leg irons in Derbyshire as in they were in the Americas. At Litton Mill: 'Palfrey, the Smith, had the task of riveting irons upon any of the apprentices, whom the masters ordered'.[19] However, accounts of cruelties on both sides of the Atlantic that might have united social reformers divided them in a competition to persuade legislators to end the appalling conditions at home before attending to those of slavery. In 1828, Richard Carlile wrote:

> [...] it might have afforded a sort of sorry consolation to the Negro slaves of America, had they been informed, that their condition, in having agriculturally to raise the cotton, was not half so bad, as that of the white infant-slaves, who had to assist in the spinning of it. The religion and Black humanity of Mr Wilberforce seem to have been entirely of a foreign nature. Pardon is begged, if an error is about to be wrongfully imputed – but the publisher has no knowledge, that Mr Wilberforce's humane advocacy for slaves, was ever of that homely kind, as to embrace the region of the home-cotton-slave trade.[20]

In the 1830s, the political rhetoric of liberal humanism constructed plantation slaves as 'the other', instead of representing their labour and suffering as part of a continuum of cotton production. 130 years of this shared working class history had been erased by the time large numbers of West Indian migrants arrived in Britain after the Second World War. Historical amnesia disconnected the people it should have united and working class fraternity proved fragile. A decade after Selvon's *The Lonely Londoners*, London dockers and Smithfield meat-packers openly demonstrated their support for Enoch Powell's anti-immigration lobby.

THE FEDERATION OF WORKER WRITERS AND COMMUNITY PUBLISHERS IS FORMED

The compound of this historical legacy manifested itself, along with other movements, in the FWWCP's challenge to a white, male, middle-class hegemony. 1976, the year of FWWCP's formation was, according to Patricia Waugh, a watershed year.[21] Waugh describes a move towards postmodernity and a breaking down of the process of society's will to find the 'common meanings and directions' which Raymond Williams wrote of in 'Culture is Ordinary'.[22] A challenge to 'cultural assumptions', inherent in the formation of the FWWCP, created an environment to promote the expression of 'ordinary' West Indian writers in a quite unique way. A brief explanation of the political ethos of the organisation is necessary in order to understand the conditions under which some of the writing came to be generated.

Nine groups of writers formed the initial membership of the FWWCP, orchestrated by Chris Searle and Ken Worpole in 1976. Initially, the groups thrived on an alliance between activists, creative writers and alienated migrant workers. Founding member group Centerprise was initially set up by the radical Black publisher Glenn Thompson who saw books as a way of opening the minds of the oppressed.[23] As another example, Liverpool's politicised 'Scottie Road group' (which included such talent as the young Jimmy McGovern) also joined the Federation. In 1970, this group of white working class writers, Liverpool's Irish immigrants of 150 years before, founded a group encouraging West Indians and an exiled South African to join them. The workshop was held in a staunchly white catholic area of Liverpool – Scotland Road. The group gave readings, taking Black writers and performers into pubs where they would almost certainly not have been accepted as individuals.[24]

The formation of the FWWCP was sparked by progressive educational, as well as political, concerns. Searle and Worpole demanded a curriculum for English teaching that would relate to the lives of working class children and which would validate forms originating from that culture.[25] In a sense, their efforts mirrored those of teachers engaged in the process of 'Caribbeanising' the syllabi in newly independent ex-colonies. In Britain, at the same time, Beryl Gilroy and Petronella Breinburg, amongst others, were producing what was then considered radical writing for children.

Centerprise's Glenn Thompson was inspired, as were all the FWWCP literacy projects, by the pedagogy of Paolo Freire; liberation of the oppressed must involve literacy acquisition, and a move toward reconceptualisation based on agency. Freire's doctrine teaches that the process begins with the oppressed first speaking then writing his or her own words.[26] There was a general movement, both by radical schoolteachers and those committed to new adult-literacy schemes, to empower through creative expression. Diverse voices – regional, foreign and ungrammatical – became the subjects of development rather than eradication. The state system had failed an alarming number of adults who were leaving school with poor reading skills. National research into literacy needs revealed the extent of a problem which meant, importantly, that the funds suddenly became available for projects specifically targeted at adults.[27] Some FWWCP groups were funded as Adult Literacy projects to standardise written English but ironically, these were to provide West Indians with a rare opportunity for expression, including for some, their first attempts at writing in Creole.

Arts Council funding was sought to enable the FWWCP to have a full-time paid national coordinator (the Arts Council insisted on calling the post 'Literature Development Officer') and to fund the publication of *Writing*, in 1978.[28] However, the 1979 Literature Finance Committee did not welcome the emphasis on working class participation, and the Federation's application was hotly debated as the product of a 'politically partisan and socially exclusive' organisation.[29] FWWCP groups went on to publish short stories and poems in small-scale community anthologies and poetry journals, and it was rare for a FWWCP writer to cross over into mainstream publishing.[30] The workshops were organised to enable all members to read something short and receive comments on it and this practice was not conducive to novel writing.[31] It was this democratic forum that typically provided a safe cultural space for a second generation of Caribbean-descended adolescents who, by the 1970s, had gone through a British education system which misdiagnosed cultural difference for poor intelligence. Some of these adolescent writers made an important connection with The Caribbean Artists Movement (CAM), formed in London in 1966 by John La Rose, Edward Kamau Brathwaite and Andrew Salkey.[32] James Berry had been secretary of CAM and he forged a productive link between the organisation and the London group Centerprise. This connection enabled him, as an established West Indian poet, to encourage Centerprise Black poets and to include their work in his *Bluefoot* collections.[33]

Unlike the commercial publishing houses, FWWCP groups were free to publish their anthologies with no regard for received notions of what constituted 'poetry' or 'fiction'. Consequently some of the written forms that follow are difficult to categorise in conventional literary terms. Their significance lies in the fact that these are publications from first- and second-generation West Indians, in some cases writing for the first time in Britain, evidencing an important shift from oral to written expression.

POETS OF THE FWWCP TRANSFER
THE ORAL TRADITION INTO WRITING

There is little doubt that a desperate sense of homesickness is the key to the release and production of much of the writing by migrants. Living in a foreign country created an urgent need to acquire standard English and literacy, but they also sought comfort in the sharing of their feelings with other West Indian writers in the group. Their homesickness is a theme that Louise Bennett parodies in the vernacular language of 'the immigrant'. In the following extract from her poem, 'Homesickness', she employs a double-edged satire, which is characteristic of the author, both to acknowledge and ridicule the suffering of the West Indian migrant:

> Go back to me Jamaica,
> To me fambly! To me wha?
> Lawd-amassi, me figat -
> All a me fambly over yah![34]

But for many West Indians in Britain, homesickness – the actual severance from loved ones, familiar objects and rituals – was a very real problem that might be partially eased by reminiscence work. The differences between British and Caribbean food and the difficulties of obtaining simple ingredients, such as long-grain rice, would often serve as a locus for their alienation.[35] Ironically, it was under the auspices of an 'English class', which nevertheless insisted on maintaining the authenticity of West Indian language and expression, that *Captain Blackbeard's Beef Creole and other Caribbean Recipes* came to be published. The introduction explains: 'As far as possible we have written Captain Blackbeard as we spoke it, each recipe in the voice of its author'.[36] And those authors, all thirty-four women and six men, are named. The book is ostensibly a recipe collection, but it also includes stories of events attached to certain meals, poems and songs, and as such it represents a particular response to change brought about by migration and the reconstitution of rituals and identities under threat. The publication affirms the importance of knowledge and skills which would have previously been passed on as an everyday part of an oral culture.

The book is an unlikely treasure-trove of recipes, instructions on cooking and preserving methods, and age-old fishing techniques; some of these survival strategies may well have developed out of the contingencies of an enslaved society taken from Africa. Significantly, some of this material may have been written down for the first time in order to ensure its further survival by people who travelled on 'the final passage' from the West Indies to England. It is not surprising that the group commonly shared reminiscences which were to do with food and the rituals associated with meals. We should understand how socially and historically significant food rituals are for people who become separated from their homelands and culture. The recipes, and the instructions concerned with social occasions, carry with them the coded messages of a 'people without history', just as the descriptions of material artefacts, such as cooking tools and utensils, also carry historical information. These are the hitherto unrecorded links that Christine Craig described as her 'silent legacy'. In her poem she uses the image of 'The Chain' to articulate the continuation of women's silence and to explore the effect of breaking the chain of that silence:

> such a closed linked chain
> to hold us until we could speak out
> loud enough to hear ourselves
> loud enough to hear ourselves
> and believe our own words.[37]

Craig celebrates the women who would manage to hold all the unrecorded links – of history, of family, of story-telling – in place until such time as they were free to speak out. In Britain, some of these links between a vernacular culture, tradition and creative expression were in fact recorded under the direction of FWWCP projects like *Captain Blackbeard*, and it is in these projects that the blurring of the boundaries between song, market-cry, poetry and story-telling is most evident.

A written record is unnecessary in a closely-knit community with a shared heritage and culture. In a small African-Caribbean village it is possible to maintain a shared history within the repository of its people's memories and stories. In a sense, the Peckham group of Caribbean writers, separated from that community, represent the need to find new ways of recording material that would not normally be written down. The rituals, processes, cooking implements, recipes, songs and poems that are collected in *Captain Blackbeard* record a culture with a long history of deracination brought about by slavery, exile, tourism and global capitalism. The anthropological nature of the information reveals aspects of life that may well have remained part of an important but 'silent legacy'. An example here is the recipe for 'Simon's Strong Rum Punch', which is set alongside the following information on how to obtain the main ingredient:

'The Rum Factory'

I know these men
who work at the sugar cane factory
They make rum there
The men usually take rum home
by soaking their coat in the rum in the vat
when they get there in the morning.
When they are ready
to come home in the evening,
they take their coat out and put it in a plastic bag
and take it home with them.

When they get home
they wring the coat out,
and leave the rum to settle.
Then they put it in a bottle
and keep it for drink
and give their friend some.
This was the strong rum.
You can't buy it in the bar.[38]

'The Rum Factory' is, like much of the writing in the collection, set out in the quasipoetic format above and is intent on giving detailed instructions to the novice on quite specialised practices. For example, skills such as 'killing a Chicken', 'Salting, Smoking and Pickling' might be supposed to be redundant in urban Peckham, but their preservation reaffirms the survival of a distinct Caribbean identity. The following passage is typical, and suggests that what is conveyed has been of importance in the past and is worth recording:

'How to fish with a piece of pipe'

You take a piece of pipe of any length
put it in the river -
by the bush on the side of the river
or near the rock.
Leave it over night.
Next day, you go with a friend.
Each of you put your hand
over the ends of the pipe.
Take it on shore, tip it over one side,
then the fish comes out.[39]

Much of the *Captain Blackbeard* collection is concerned with the transmission of skills, but equally important is the record of rituals and celebrations such as those depicted in 'Christmas in St Lucia':

Most of the people keep a pig
And fatten them to kill on Christmas Eve
Everywhere you pass on the morning of Christmas Eve
You will hear the crying of the poor pigs. [...]
Christmas Eve night we go to midnight mass.
When we get home
We have pig's liver
and special butter bread
we bake ourselves.[40]

Also recorded are practices which have proved essential to people who have, through a combination of tradition and historical necessity, relied on herbal medicine. Some writers interject an 'extra' medicinal tip into the recipes, such as 'White Chocho is very good for blood pressure', while many of the contributors recognise the appropriate selection and application of herbs as a valued skill – as in the following traditional cure for colds:

'A Cure for Colds'

In the West Indies, when you get a cold,
you don't go to a doctor.
We boil our own herb medicine -
We grow up on it.

Our parents do it, so we do it the same way.
And I think that is the best.

Some people use marijuana
Boil it is the best
and if you put rum on it and drink
it's good.
But the one for smoke, no good.

If you got a chest cold
and you break it up in little bits
and put some white rum in it,
people say it is good.[41]

The 'people say it is good' validates it as part of an oral tradition and suggests that the benefits of this remedy, with all its local variations, have been matters for transmission and debate.

People who are seldom recorded in 'official' historical documents are honoured in the names of the recipes: 'George's Pumpkin and Chocho Soup with Dumplings'; 'Vilma's Roast Chicken' and 'Eualia's Okra, Shrimps and Saltfish'. The giving of names may also be a method for distinguishing and remembering variations in the recipes, such as 'Lynneth's Fish Tea' and its alternative 'Muriel's Fish Tea'. For an oral society, such lyrical memory-aids were shorthand methods of conveying important information, as also were ring-games and work-songs. For people outside the knowledge of such a community, these are difficult to interpret, but it seems likely that they had a function which would be passed on to children in the pleasure of their repetition.

To be fully understood, ideally these poems and songs need to be studied from within the community that continues to carry them. The very existence of community publications (by definition) reflects their supposed significance and validity for their immediate constituents (in this case Peckham). As they become written down to ensure their survival, their wider availability poses a problem of interpretation. In *Nice Tastin: Life and Food in the Caribbean*, a much later example of a similar project to *Captain Blackbeard*, songs are recorded that must have survived through countless generations. For example:

'Song From Tobago'

Me mama gone,
Me papa come in,
We go cook rice an' peas to eat,
We go cook rice an' peas an pile up some,
And wait till me mama come.[42]

The significance of the song is not explained, leaving the reader to guess at a meaning (in which the 'mama' appears to be the absent but most important character). To understand the 'secret' significance of the Tobagan song we will need to access both the knowledge it carries and the conditions which maintain its continuation. That may become possible through scholarship and the circulation and discussion of such songs. The problem is that some of these songs are hidden away in little-valued community publications and are difficult to access. Occasionally they are made available in mainstream collections of Caribbean poetry. Paula Burnett's *Penguin Book of Caribbean Verse in English* devotes a large section which emphasises the importance of traditional songs and calypsos and their relationship to a developing literary tradition. We must attend to the record of preliterate societies who employed the folk-song as the carrier of news and comment with topical variations that were extemporised with great skill. As part of an oral tradition which was, as Burnett reminds us, 'typified by the sung word long before it adapted itself to spoken poetry', they continue in the performance and commentary of contemporary poets.[43] The Tobagan example, which tells its story through song, is part of a tradition which travelled from Africa and Asia to the Caribbean and which would eventually produce a sophisticated hybrid in the performance poetry of Linton Kwesi Johnson, Benjamin Zephaniah, John Agard, Grace Nichols, Valerie Bloom and many others. Regardless of Linton Kwesi Johnson's successful Jamaican import (a blending of reggae and spoken verse), as a new aesthetic, it is still regarded with ambivalence. Whilst some Black poets have embraced the descriptor, as Kwame Dawes writes "Many Black British poets, even those who began as performance poets, have begun to seek ways of avoiding the label."[44] We can look to a history of cultural colonisation to this explain this ambivalence. In the early 1970s,when many Black poets were developing their art in these quite distinct forms, there was recognition that cultural forms arising from non-scribal traditions had long been devalued. In 1967, at one of the first public meetings of The Caribbean Artists Movement in London, Edward Brathwaite began to talk about the future for West Indian poetry, but he was forced to consider that "... Our problem is that we have been trained over 300 years to despise these indigenous forms".[45] Wilson Harris spoke to same meeting and he too stressed 'the importance of critical scholars examining not only the structure and language of West Indian literary work, but also the kinds of tradition which informed it."[46] Unlike the highly literate Brathwaite and Harris, the migrant writers who joined the groups of FWWCP in the 1970s, had little choice but to work with those oral traditions which they carried with them from the indigenous culture.

Returning to Boatswain's poetry, we see that it demonstrates an alternative type of 'survival' writing. It was not concerned with recipes and reminiscence, neither did it exist solely to combat homesickness and to record traditional Caribbean rituals and practices. It is clear from the archives that young Caribbean poets joined the FWWCP because they were highly politicised and their writing spoke to the hostile conditions of the 1970s. A much less well-known 'anti-sus' poem was published in a 1987 anthology, *Not All Roses*.[47] 'Watch It!' by Thandiwe Benjamin relates the 'sus' law to a history of migration in the context of its various stages: of the failed assimilation of the 1960s and the disassociation and resistance of the '70s. In so doing, it anticipates the reactions which would provoke the riots of the '80s:

'YOU BETTER WATCH IT'

We build up de street
And we clean up de street,
A drive a bus in de street
But you won't leave us in peace.
Now we a go a rioting in de street.
Me seh fe watch it
Black people a go mash it.
When blood a running
Know that we're not funnin'.
No bother hide cos
We a go get you
You better watch it![48]

Benjamin's work is a barometer of the changed consciousness of a second-generation of Caribbeans who would have no experience of the agrarian lifestyle recorded in *Captain Blackbeard*. However, both types of poetry – the reminiscence work and the politicised commentary – were made possible because of important shifts. By the late 1970s, events in Britain which had stimulated the formation of the FWWCP were to provide a unique set of conditions for poets whose work had never 'fitted' European models and whose opportunities for expression had been hitherto confined to the private domain.

The unique atmosphere of the politicised workshops provided for a disaffected second generation of Caribbean-British adolescents who, by the 1970s, were seriously under-achieving in a British education system. The gifted twelve-year-old poet Vivian Usherwood had spent much of his time in the remedial department of Hackney Downs School. During our interview, Ken Worpole recalled that Vivian Usherwood, Sandra Agard and Hugh Boatswain were part of a group of 'very talented young Black writers around Centreprise' in the mid-1970s.[49]

As time passed, the nature of the FWWCP changed. Initially membership of FWWCP groups was not determined by race or gender, since the notion of separate groups 'hadn't become an issue at the time'; but this was to change when a supposed unifying working class alliance fragmented once again on gender and race issues.[50] In addition to The Arts Council and adult literacy schemes, financial support for publications could also be attracted from organisations like the Southwark Race Equality Unit. By 1984, the diasporic experience began to be represented in separatist anthologies such as *So This is England*, which was funded by Southwark and produced by a 'Black Studies Group'.

In the course of my gathering material from community publishers, it became clear that deracinated migrants and their children sought the means to develop their creative writing. However, it is pointless to attempt, as the Arts Council's funding committee did, to judge its merits by Eurocentric literary standards with its exclusive notion of tradition and taste. The real achievement of the FWWCP was its ability to create the conditions to release denied expression, in the form of oral history projects from groups marginalised by society and by projects which enabled adults to acquire help with expression and literacy. By facilitating the publication of the outcomes, the FWWCP validated a lived

experience of 'difference', and provided an environment for writers
to explore that difference. Many West Indian women writers were
particularly isolated and suffered a triple oppression – by class, race
and gender. Black women found it difficult to imagine themselves as
writers but were helped by the encouragement and mentoring
provided by FWWCP groups. A recuperation of denied experience,
coupled with practical and critical skills, enabled the workshops to
develop the emerging voices of a new generation of West Indians
who became unlikely writers in exile. The success of this movement
led Stuart Hall to express his 'amazement' in an interview with Anne
Walmsley:

> Europe has shunted culture off to one side. It's the higher arts.
> [...] And so what has happened since then, I think, has certainly
> amazed me and would have amazed, I think, anybody in that
> [first CAM] conference at the time: the notion of Black school
> kids writing about their experience in poetry and so on.[51]

As one of the most grounded and influential 'Blacks in an ivory
tower', Hall recognises the significance of a working class writing
movement, and its accomplice community publishing, as part of a
new type of ownership of a different, non-European, notion of
culture.

People in the poorest parts of Britain are much less easily defined
along race lines than in the American ghetto. But what is clear from
the FWWCP archives, is that working people in some of the most
deprived areas of Britain engage in their *own* cultural analysis. We
cannot know whether Hugh Boatswain had read Frantz Fanon
before he wrote his poem 'Old Father'. But it is clear that he
communicates the idea of 'Black Skins and White Masks' in a
language and form that his immediate constituency can respond to.
We can learn from these under-researched archives that the people
more usually written about, will write about themselves, for
themselves, and for each other.

ACKNOWLEDGEMENTS

This chapter is reprinted from Sandra Courtman, ed. *Beyond the Blood, the Beach and the Banana: New Perspectives in Caribbean Studies* (Jamaica: Ian Randle, 2004). I am indebted to the people who gave generously of their time in interviews and who allowed me access to rare textual materials to enable this research: With thanks in particular to Tim Diggles, Nick Pollard, Barbara Blanche, Barbara Shane, Dorothy Blake, Roger Mills, Ken Worpole, Rebecca O'Rourke, David Dabydeen, and Anne Walmsley. I thank Eva Lewin at The Centerprise Trust for permission to cite 'WATCH IT' by Thandiwe Benjamin and Hugh Boatwain's 'Old Father' and 'Cut Up Dub'. Every effort has been made to contact the Peckham Publishing Project and the authors of *Captain Blackbeard's Beef Creole* and anyone claiming copyright of their material should contact me via the publisher.

NOTES AND REFERENCES

[1] From a review of William Banks, *Black Intellectuals: Race and Responsibility in American Life* (London: W.W. Norton, 1997): Robin Blackburn, 'Blacks in ivory towers can't write about ghettos', *The Observer Review*, 2 March, 1997, p.16

[2] Hugh Boatswain, 'Old Father, in *Writing*, by the Federation of Worker Writers and Community Publishers (London: Centerprise, 1978), p.45

[3] Greg Wilkinson, 'Foreword', in *Writing*, by the Federation of Worker Writers and Community Publishers (London: Centerprise, 1978), p.3

[4] Wilkinson, *Writing*, p.3

[5] Maya Jaggi, 'The Final Passage: An interview with writer Caryl Phillips' in *Black British Culture and Society,* ed. by Kwesi Owusu (London: Routledge, 2000), p.159

[6] Stuart Hall, 'Frontlines and Backyards: The Terms of Change', in *Black British Culture and Society*, ed. by Kwesi Owusu (London: Routledge, 2000), p.127

[7] Raymond Williams, *Resources of Hope* (London: Verso, 1958), p.4

[8] Ron Ramdin, *The Making of the Black Working Class in Britain* (Aldershot: Wildwood, 1987)

[9] Hugh Boatswain, 'Cut Up Dub', in *Writing*, p.46-47

[10] See Chapter 6, 'Racism' in *The Stephen Lawrence Inquiry: Report of an Inquiry by Sir William Macpherson of Cluny presented to Parliament by the Secretary of State*, February 1999, available online http://www.archive.officialdocuments. co.uk/document /cm42/4262/4262.htm [accessed 5 August]

[11] Cited in Dominic Hibbert and John Oinions, eds., *Poetry of the Great War: An Anthology* (Basingstoke: Macmillan, 1986), p.1

[12] Sue Lawley, interview with Linton Kwesi Johnson, BBC Radio 4, *Desert Island Discs,* 25 July 2003

[13] Linton Kwesi Johnson, *Tings and Times* (Newcastle on Tyne: Bloodaxe Books, 1991)

[14] David Dabydeen, personal interview. July 25, 1995

[15] Sue Lawley, interview with Linton Kwesi Johnson, BBC Radio 4, *Desert Island Discs*, July, 25, 2003

[16] 'Caryl Phillips', *The South Bank Show*, April 13, 2003

[17] Samuel Selvon, The Lonely Londoners (London: Longman, 1985), p.75

[18] John Brown, *A Memoir of Robert Blincoe* (Firle, Sussex: Caliban Books, 1977), p.61. First published in Richard Carlile's radical paper *The Lion*, in five weekly episodes from 25th January to the 22nd February 1828

[19] Brown, *A Memoir of Robert Blincoe*, p.71

[20] Brown, *A Memoir of Robert Blincoe*, p.3

[22] Patricia Waugh, *Harvest of the Sixties: English Literature and its Background 1960 to 1990* (Oxford: Oxford University Press), p.13

[22] Williams, *Resources of Hope*, p.4

[23] John Berger and Margaret Busby, 'Obituraries: Glenn Thompson', *The Guardian*, September 12, 2001

[24] Barbara Blanche and Barbara Shane, personal interview with founding members of 'Scottie Road' writers' group, June 28, 2000

[25] In 1971, Chris Searle was dismissed from his teaching job as a result of a dispute concerning his publication of school-children's writing. Searle had not gained official permission to publish *Stepney Words* (London: Centreprise, 1973; First published in two editions by Reality Press in 1971). The back cover validates the project: '15,000 copies of these poems have been printed and sold, giving these young working-class children a readership far larger than many established poets'

[26] Paolo Freire, *Pedagogy of the Oppressed*, trans. by Myra Bergman Ramos (London: Penguin, 1996)

[27] A.H. Charnley and H.A. Jones, *The Concept of Success in Adult Literacy*, 3rd. edn (London: Adult Literacy and Basic Skills Unit, 1986; first published, Huntinton, 1979), p.2

[28] See Jim McGuigan, 'The State and Serious Writing: Arts Council Intervention in the English Literary Field', Doctoral thesis, University of Leicester, 1984

[29] McGuigan, 'The State and Serious Writing: Arts Council Intervention in the English Literary Field' , p.242

[30] Rebecca O'Rourke, personal interview, July 17, 1995. As Rebecca O'Rourke states: 'Within the Federation, there have been two novelists in twenty-one years – myself and Roger Mills' Rebecca O'Rourke was a founder member of Centreprise and published short stories with Virago and a detective novel, *Jumping The Cracks* (London: Virago, 1987). Jimmy McGovern is perhaps one of the most commercially successful writers to have their beginnings in the FWWCP. McGovern was a member of Liverpool's Scottie Road group. He contributed prose pieces to the first anthology, *Writing*, and to the 1979 and 1983 editions of *Voices*. McGovern writes for television, including *Brookside, Go Now, Priest,* and *Hillsborough*. He is probably best known for his award winning writing for the Granada Television series, *Cracker*

[31] During a discussion with Roger Mills, he explained how he has attempted to address this restriction by setting up a separate group for novelists, which he convenes in Tower Hamlets. Roger Mills, personal interview, April 5, 1997

[32] Anne Walmsley, *The Caribbean Artists Movement 1966-1972* (London: New Beacon Books, 1992)

[33] James Berry, ed., *Bluefoot Traveller* (London: Limestone, 1976), and *Bluefoot Traveller*, rev. edn (London: Harrap, 1981)

[34] Stewart Brown and Ian McDonald, eds., *The Heinemann Book of Caribbean Poetry* (London: Heinemann, 1992), p.11-12

[35] First-wave migrants from the Caribbean tell how they were forced to use a type of pudding rice in their recipes. This would transform one of their favourite recipes, rice and peas, into a mush

[36] Written and collected by a group of Caribbean writers attending a 'Peckham Bookplace' English class, *Captain Blackbeard's Beef Creole and other Caribbean Recipes* (London: Peckham Publishing Project, 1981), 64-65. The introduction states that the writing originates from work in 1979

[37] Christine Craig, 'The Chain', from *Quadrille For Tigers* (London: Mina Press, 1984), is cited in *Daughters of Africa*, ed. by Margaret Busby (London: Vintage, 1993), p.555

[38] *Captain Blackbeard*, p.64-65

[39] *Captain Blackbeard*, p.52

[40] *Captain Blackbeard*, p.55. The Christmas pig-fattening and killing is reminiscent of a similar practice described by Flora Thompson in *Lark Rise to Candleford*, rev.edn (London: Penguin, 1995)

[41] *Captain Blackbeard,* p.67

[42] Geneva Thomas, 'Song From Tobago', in *Nice Tastin': Life and Food in the Caribbean* ed. by Liz Bartlett (London: Kensington and Chelsea Community History Group, 1991), p.44

[43] Paula Burnett, ed,, *The Penguin Book of Caribbean Verse in English* (London: Penguin, 1986), p.xxix

[44] Kwame Dawes, 'Black British Poetry, Some Considerations', *Wasafiri,* 38 (Spring, 2003), p.44-48, (44)

[45] Walmsley, *The Caribbean Artists Movement,* p.67

[46] Walmsley, *The Caribbean Artists Movement,* p.66

[47] 'According to a report published in 1978, 44% of the 'sus' arrests in London in 1977 were Black youths; but Black youths made up only 2.8% of the total population', in 'Racism and the Law', *Racism in the Workplace and Community* (Milton Keynes: The Open University, 1984), p.3

[48] Thandiwe Benjamin, 'Watch it', in *Not All Roses: Poetry and Prose* by the Black Anthology Group (London: Centreprise, 1987), p.49

[49] Ken Worpole, personal interview. 28 November 1995

[50] Ken Worpole, personal interview. 28 November 1995

[51] Anne Walmsley's personal interview transcript with Stuart Hall, London, 8.10.87

The 1980s: Retheorising and Refashioning British Identity

R. Victoria Arana

Alex Wheatle's novel *East of Acre Lane* (2001) transports its readers into the daily life of the 1980s, into 'Black'[1] Brixton, that region of south London where in 1981 some of the most violent race riots exploded in response to racist police brutality and were captured on television screens and the front pages of newspapers around the world. Wheatle's story may be fiction, but it is interwoven with clearly recognisable historical details of the riots and accurate representations of the 1980s Black British youth culture to which Wheatle himself belonged. *East of Acre Lane* is a direct product, albeit delayed, of that decade's countrywide cultural upheaval. In prison "shortly after the 1981 Brixton riots" Wheatle determined to improve his life and his eighteen-year-old mind – and, as soon as he was released, began to read his way through the Brixton town library[2]. The generation of writers to which Alex Wheatle belongs and which includes Diran Adebayo, Bernardine Evaristo, Jackie Kay, Andrea Levy, Kadija George Sesay, and Dorothea Smartt, to name just a handful – were all impressionable children or teenagers during the explosive 1980s. Each has responded in one way or another to the cultural legacy of the 1980s and participated in the radical retheorising of British identity that has overtaken the British Isles ever since the countrywide race riots of 1981. Nevertheless, their writings *do not* reflect the same sort of bitterness and anger evident in the works of the 1980s' generation itself. Even their differences from earlier trends of feeling have sprung, as we shall see, from that same fertile soil: the political, cultural and intellectual activities of the Black activists and artists of the 1980s. This essay explores the important part played by that elder generation of writers of African and Caribbean parentage – specifically during the decade of the 1980s – in refashioning public conceptions of British identity.

The civil uprisings throughout Britain during the spring and summer of 1981 prompted Parliament to enact the revisionary British Nationality Act of 1981, which stipulated that only those "whose parents had been born in the United Kingdom, or had been legally 'settled' there, would henceforth qualify for the newly created British citizenship."[3] Everyone else would be subject to new laws entitling the police to arrest them on mere suspicion, might be subject to losing their former legal and civil rights, and could be vulnerable to deportation. In protest, Salman Rushdie began a series of periodical essays[4] in which he excoriated the Thatcher establishment and its bigotry. Others joined the intellectual fray. The Centre for Contemporary Cultural Studies, led by Stuart Hall, edited *The Empire Strikes Back: Race and Racism in 70s Britain* (1982). In 1984, Peter Fryer published his groundbreaking book *Staying Power: The History of Black People in Britain*, a historical account of the Black presence that begins with the earliest days of the Roman Empire. In the following year (1985), Ivan Van Sertima published his study *African Presence in Early Europe,* and David Dabydeen brought out a collection of scholarly essays by an array of illustrious academics: *The Black Presence in English Literature*. The scholars he featured were uncovering and deconstructing the racist signifying systems that had supported colonialist and imperialist ideological state apparatuses and were still operational.[5] In an essay included in Dabydeen's collection, Kenneth Parker wrote, he said, for the express purpose of "contribu[ting] to the project of destroying racism in contemporary Britain."[6]

The importance of the 1980s to the development of the current boom in (non-'white') British culture and art cannot be overestimated. A sudden concatenation of extraordinary events – cultural, literary, and political – imparted an embattled tone to the era, and many of the new voices in fiction, poetry, and theatre immediately sounded the topic of radical insurgency. The chronic troubles between the English, Scots, and Irish – violent as they might have seemed earlier – began quite literally to pale in contrast to the threats felt when race riots erupted across high density Black populated cities in Britain beginning in 1981. Highly asymmetrical economic conditions played an important part in destabilising the body politic. During the 1980s (later dubbed the 'Greedy Decade') monied classes profited from huge hikes in interest rates and a spiraling inflation while others suffered work layoffs, social insult, and demoralising indigence. Among the poor – 'Black' as well as 'white' – tempers flared, Black markets flourished, and blood flowed. The Conservative establishment's infamous tolerance and even encouragement of flagrant police brutality evoked a counterblast of street violence. Africans, West

Indians, Asians, and bi- or multi-racial artists and intellectuals flocked under one political banner as 'Blacks' to strengthen their voices and redress their social and economic grievances. They did not band together for the purpose of internationalising England, but instead to assert their Englishness, their demands for equal and just treatment as English citizens despite their skin colours.

While generally offering scant literary criticism – little more than a reworking of first reviewers' pronouncements (and even though his 'Grand Narrative'-style conclusion distorts somewhat the larger picture it seeks to project), Bruce King's *The Oxford English Literary History, Volume 13. 1948-2000. The Internationalization of English Literature* is, nevertheless, a handy introduction to the breadth of non-'white' literary productivity in Britain after World War II because it catalogues post-World War II authors, titles, historical events, and cultural developments with an unprecedented degree of detail.[7] It is likely, however, that Black British citizens will strongly contest the broad claim that King makes, including the insinuation that the efforts of migrant populations to make England a bit more theirs are "morally wrong."[8] Contrary to King's thesis, the new, post-1980s English literature takes possession of the definition of Englishness to include diversity *within* Englishness; it is decidedly not a faction that attempts to internationalise and, thus, to disintegrate the country's culture and discourse. Its objectives are quite the opposite of 'globalisation', 'internationalisation', and 'universalism' (King's terms). Post-1980s British literature in general portrays the new England, the new Scotland, and the new Wales as *still* English, Scottish, and Welsh, respectively, though culturally *modified* and updated.

At the very beginning of the decade, Jamaican-born Linton Kwesi Johnson sounded the discontent of a whole generation of immigrants in defiant tones and Caribbean cadences:

> mi know dem have work, work in abundant
> yet still, dem mek mi redundant
> now, at fifty-five me getting' quite ol'
> yet still, dem sen' me fi goh draw dole
>
> Inglan is a bitch
> dere's no escapin' it
> Inglan is bitch fi true
> is whey wi a goh dhu 'bout it?[9]

His poem. 'It Dread Inna Inglan' drums the theme that Blacks were in England 'to stay':

> African
> Asian
> West Indian
> an' Black British
> stan firm inna Inglan
> inna disya time yah
>
> far noh mattah wat dey say,
> come wat may,
> we are here to stay
> inna Inglan . . . . [10]

According to Johnson's triumphalist mythos, even the police could not stem the currents of change, for England's Black migrants knew their power and were determined to prevail:

> we're di forces af vict'ry
> an' we comin' rite through
> we're di forces of vict'ry
> now wat y'u gonna do[11]

Grace Nichols (who moved to England from Guyana in 1977, when she was twenty seven) writes succinctly of acculturation and artistic adaptation in her 'Epilogue' to *The Fat Black Woman's Poems* (Virago 1984):

> I have crossed the ocean
> I have lost my tongue
> from the root of the old one
> a new one has sprung[12]

T-Bone Wilson's *Counterblast* (1980), Benjamin's Zephaniah's *Pen Rhythms* (1980), Roy Heath's *Kwaku – Or the Man Who Could Not Keep His Mouth Shut* (1982), Grace Nichols' *I Is a Long Memoried Woman* (1983), Tariq Mehmood's *Hand on the Sun* (1983), Valerie Bloom's *Touch Mi! Tell Mi!* (1983), Hanif Kureishi's *My Beautiful Laundrette* (1984), Maud Sulter's *As a Black Woman: Poems* (1985), and many other works published in the first half of the 1980s were passionately critical of racist English mindsets, politically motivated, and aggressively Black. Turning English stereotypes upside-down, Grace Nichols begins her poetic critique of European aesthetics with the lines "Beauty/ is a fat Black woman".[13] Valerie Bloom's poems oscillate between delight in the trickster who bests his English oppressors and disgust with the racist status quo in England. The speaker of the last poem, 'Yuh Hear About?' in *Touch Mi! Tell Mi!*[14] asks if anyone has heard whether any of the racist killers in Britain and their government accomplices have been arrested and brought to justice, or not, but ends admitting "me neida". Like Linton Kwesi Johnson's, Grace Nichols's and Valerie Bloom's speakers, the Black characters in the literary works of the first half of the 1980s either grumbled or railed about Anglo-English frostiness and provincial meanness; but they did not mount a frontal attack. Although Johnson himself has always been what Kwame Dawes refers to as a "very public poet" and was often seen and involved in campaigns on the street.

Compared with his immediate precursors, Caryl Phillips in his trenchant *The European Tribe*[15] took the criticism up a few notches as he crafted a young Black intellectual's coming-of-age (travel) narrative. Phillips there briefly laid out a long and revisionary history of Britain and the European continent, in terms of savage 'white' ethnocentrisms and resultant global plunder and exploitation. By the end of the 1980s a new confidence was being felt.

While Black writers were laying out contestatory visions of their new homelands, Black-run institutions also played a role in promoting critical awareness of and new perspectives on British literature and the other arts. The Centre for Contemporary Cultural Studies at the University of Birmingham, under the direction of Stuart Hall, was instrumental in developing approaches for the study of postcolonial cultures, their social formations and signifying systems. The CCCS's 1982 publication *The Empire Strikes Back: Race and Racism in 70s Britain* offered keen insights into the politics of representation and of resistance within the postcolonial context of then-contemporary Britain. Other institutions followed suit. Founded by Eddie Chambers in 1981, the Black Art Group arranged exhibitions by Black artists, one of which – the 'Pan-Afrikan Connection' – elucidated Chambers' confrontational manifesto for an ambitious postimperialist Black aesthetic. The Minorities' Arts Advisory Service (MAAS) founded the outstanding arts periodical *Artrage* in 1983, a magazine that introduced first-rate Black writers, including poet-editor-anthologist James Berry, poet-scholar Fred D'Aguiar, producer-writer-editor-anthologist Kwesi Owusu, poet-editor-critic E. A. Markham, and dozens of others. The Black Arts Alliance, founded in 1985 by poet and live artist, SuAndi, the longest surviving network of Black artists in Britain, was conceived as a cultural change-agency dedicated to coordinating Black arts activities of all sorts – including exhibitions, performances, workshops, symposia, conferences, and publications; and it is still going strong. Headed by Labour radical Ken Livingstone, (currently the Mayor of London) the Greater London Council "massively increased arts spending for ethnic arts programmes from £10,000 in 1981 to £2.5 million by 1985", the year before Parliament abolished it.[16] Media enterprises got into the act. For example, Channel 4, a public interest television station was established in 1981 with a mandate to cover ethnically diverse topics of multicultural interest. Many new publications (of all sorts) sprouted – including *Chic* (a slick women's magazine first published in 1984), *Wasafiri* (a journal of literature and literary criticism also founded in 1984), and Rasheed Araeen's *Third Text* (an art journal founded in 1987). New newspapers appeared, including the *Asian Times* and *African Times* (established in the early- and mid-1980s, respectively) and *The Voice* (first published in 1982 – and today the Black newspaper with the largest circulation in Britain). By the 1990s, the Arts Council of England, the British Council, the Barings Foundation, the Barbican Library, PEN International, the Museum of London, the British Museum – all had supported Black arts and literary events, often in collaboration with smaller, enterprising Black organisations or businesses. To gain a fuller awareness of the extent of this sort of burgeoning cultural activity during the 1980s, one needs only to page through Alison Donnell's 2002 *Companion to Contemporary Black British Culture*, a 356-page resource for quick information on recent developments in fashion and design, film and cinema, intellectual life, music, cultural organisations, performance works and artists, print-based media, television and broadcasting groups and individuals, visual and plastic artists and venues and curators, not to mention novelists, poets, essayists, scholars, publishers, editors, and teachers.

By the decade's end, a fragmentation or analytical partitioning of that Blackness had already begun, accompanied by the cultural and intellectual activities now famously retheorising British ethnicity.[17]

Interested in the dynamics of various kinds of centrednesses, marginalities, hybridities, and subject positions, a generation of cultural critics – including Stuart Hall, Paul Gilroy, Caryl Phillips, Kobena Mercer, and Homi Bhabha – began in the late 1980s to point out the absurdity of 'Black' (by itself) and similar essentialising signifiers, terms that mask the 'constructedness' of much more complex racial and ethnic identities. Stuart Hall, in his 1988 essay on 'New Ethnicities', makes the point explicit:

> What is at issue here is the recognition of the extraordinary diversity of subjective positions, social experiences and cultural identities which compose the category 'Black'; that is, the recognition that 'Black' is essentially a politically and culturally *constructed* category, which cannot be grounded on a set of fixed trans-cultural or transcendental racial categories and which therefore has no guarantees in Nature.[18]

In two books published in 1987 (*Problems in Anti-racist Strategy* and *There Ain't no Black in the Union Jack: the Cultural Poetics of Race and Nation*), Paul Gilroy began the exploration of hybridity that culminated in *Against Race: Imagining Political Culture beyond the Color Line*, where he reaffirmed the point that "whether the process of mixture is presented as fatal or redemptive, we must be prepared to give up the illusion that cultural and ethnic purity has ever existed, let alone provided a foundation for civil society."[19]

A decade later, Onyekachi Wambu, in writing about the younger generation of Black British writers, in his edited anthology about Black British Literature since Windrush, takes the 'constructedness' of identity for granted and traces the cultural and literary shifts this way:

> By the 1980s there was no going back. At least not in the old romantic sense. In order to make sense of the present, the British-born generation began to find their voice in novels. Looking back to their own childhood, they began, like Caryl Phillips in *The Final Passage* [1985], to rewrite the story of the arrival of their parents. They also began, uniquely, to map out the contours of their own identity as Black British people, not as rejected outsiders, but critical insiders. We moved from post-colonialism to multicultural Britain.

By the middle of the 1990s the contours of that identity were now
more blurred and less Black and white. The new generation of
writers are increasingly bound to move away from the limitations
of the biographical narrative [. . . and] into the varieties of genre
fiction in order to capture this new complexity. Now the grasp of
Britain is surer.[20]

In this new spirit, Wambu's unit on 'The New Britain' in that same
volume is sharply prefaced by an apposite Igbo proverb: "If you love
the land, nourish it / For the land provides for those who nourish
it."[21] In the essay 'At Home in England' with which Wambu's
anthology closes, Mike Phillips remarks on the common sense that
began to emerge by the end of the 1980s: that Britain was indeed a
Black homeland:

> Citizenship has slowly been decoupled from race, and the
> concept of the United Kingdom as a nation has loosened,
> almost imperceptibly at first, then in a rush of permission for a
> variety of identities to assert themselves .... In any case the
> geography of our cultures was never static and immovable.
> Both Blacks and whites have moved in and out of these worlds
> with increasing ease, carrying with them new and more
> ambiguous outlines of identity.[22]

Harking back to the 1980s, Caryl Phillips told Kadija Sesay that he
had long thought the term *Black British* "'just a label', as she put it
– just 'a convenience' for 'others'. You have to start asking yourself,
who constitutes as 'other', when Britain has for 200 years, at least,
been a culture of hybridity, a factor that too many people refuse to
acknowledge." It is the point that Raimund Schäffner made
specifically about the ideological outlooks of Mustapha Matura and
Caryl Phillips (from the late 1980s onward), but Schäffner's
observation applies more generally to the attitude of many younger
Britons of African of mixed parentage today:

> To them, identity formation is an open, dialectical and dynamic
> process of permanent renegotiation. It points to the future and is
> not merely a rediscovery of roots, the importance of which,
> however, is not underestimated. They plead for cultural diversity
> and deny the existence of rigid borders between different cultures,
> which are not self-contained but open to cross influence.[23]

In sum, the works by non-'white' English writers of the early-to mid-1980s were most often about social life *in England* and about what it meant to be a non-'white' *English* citizen living in very specific *English* towns and neighbourhoods, suddenly decidedly less 'white' than they once were. Timothy Mo's 1982 novel *Sour Sweet*, for example, describes the lives of restaurant owners in London, not China. Kazuo Ishiguru's *A Pale View of the Hills* (also published in 1982) connects the trauma of life in World War II Japan with its subtle emotional repercussions a generation later in the English countryside. Barbara Burford's short stories in *The Threshing Floor* (1986) depict the difficulties that Britons of Jamaican origins have solving personal problems within a society of 'others'. Such representations in the 1980s of a new and problematic Englishness were not so much a trend of literary fashion as they were mirrors held up to historical social realities.

Today, twenty-some years later, *English*men and women of African descent and dual heritage 'Afripeans'[24] are 'centreing' themselves more and more in the culture and, most decidedly, in the contemporary literary canon.[25] The 'new' African Scots (e.g., Jackie Kay and Maud Sulter) and African Welsh writers (e.g., Patience Agbabi) are there too (as many chapters in this volume amply demonstrate). They emphasise a positive attitude. Significantly, among British journalists and public intellectuals of African parentage, a new trend is fast developing to reclassify what only recently was 'Black British' and to re-label it 'African British' in an effort to stress cultural heritage and to undo the psychological damage caused by racial epithets and 'colour coding'.[26] The term *African British* seeks to yoke a continent of origin and a current nationality, or citizenship. The term is itself further evidence of the seductive and transformative powers of nationbuilding efforts and is yet another spin-off of the cultural ferment of the 1980s: the 'Reinventing Britain' movement, which did not take-off officially in the U.K. until 1997. It should be remembered, however, that however 'new' this retheorised and refashioned British identity may deem itself, it has been forming for well over two decades, as the cultural denouement of the endemic race riots of 1981. The newly proposed nomenclature predictably dismantles the politically constructed multicultural Blackness that police brutality and institutionalised racism inspired in the writers of the early 1980s. The term *African British* is rooted in the explosion of Black scholarship and cultural history of the 1980s, including Hazel

Carby's 'White woman listen! Black feminism and the boundaries of sisterhood' in *The Empire Strikes Back : Race and Racism in Seventies Britain* (in [Hutchinson, London, 1982]), Tom Brennan's *Salman Rushdie and the Third World: Myths of a Nation* (Macmillan, London, 1989), Fred D'Aguiar's 'Against Black British literature' (in *Tibisiri: Caribbean Writers and Critics* [Dangeroo Press, Sydney, 1989]), Stuart Hall's 'New Ethnicities' (in *Black Film/British Cinema* [ICA, London 1988]), Kwesi Owesu's *The Struggle for the Black Arts in Britain* (Comedia, London, 1986); it is rooted in the 1980s Black political activism of the Brixton Black Women's Group, the Notting Hill Carnival and other carnival organisers, of the Bogle L'Ouverture and other Black presses, of the Sankofa Film collective and other Black film collectives, and of many other similar entities; it is rooted in the transformative cultural critiques emergent throughout the 1980s from Manchester and the University of Birmingham and in the boom in creative works published all through the 1980s by Black British writers from all parts of the world, a richness that these few pages can sketch only very roughly.[27]

NOTES AND REFERENCES

[1] The word *Black* as a category for human beings has recently been labeled 'offensive' by some Britons of African parentage and may well soon become politically incorrect in the United Kingdom; according to Toyin Agbetu, progressive Britons should use the term African British instead (see www.ligali.org). As many *African British* deliberately called themselves 'Black' during the 1980s and afterwards, the word *Black* appears in quotation marks throughout this essay

[2] Wheatle, Alex. *Brixton Rock* (London: BlackAmber Books,1999) 'Afterword' p.251

[3] Baucom, Ian. *Out of Place: Englishness, Empire, and the Dislocations of Place* (New Jersey: Princeton University Press, New Jersey, 1999) p.13

[4] This collection of essay became *Imaginary Homelands: Essays and Criticism 1981-1991*, (London: Granta, 1992)

[5] See esp. R. Victoria Arana, 'Sea Change: Historicizing the Scholarly Study of Black British Writing' in R. Victoria Arana and Lauri Ramey, eds., *Black British Writing* (New York: Palgrave Macmillan, 2004), p.25-27; see also Maria Helena Lima's and Kadija George Sesay's essays in that same volume (esp. p.50 & p.99-100)

[6] Parker, Kenneth in Dabydeen, David. *The Black Presence in English Literature*, (Dover: Manchester University Press 1985) p.205

[7] King's claims that 'The internationalization of English literature is part of a liberalism which reappears in varied and unexpected shapes, whether in notions of decolonization or free trade. It aims at universalism. If the imaginative construction of a nation includes race and ethnicity, the change of "British" from white to multiracial is part of a modernization brought about by free-market economies and culture' (322). King's protracted confusion of race and nationality detracts from the value of his book. It takes a less confused eye than King brings to his focal texts to see that they are not

exemplars of an 'internationalization' of English literature so much as depictions of the new types of English people and clear-eyed evocations of aspects of Englishness overlooked in the stereotypical characterisations by 'white' colonials and provincials

[8] King, Bruce *The Oxford English Literary History, Volume 13. 1948-2000. The Internationalization of English Literature* (Oxford: OUP, 2004) p.7

[9] Johnson, Linton Kwesi *Inglan is a Bitch* (London: Race Today Publications, 1980) p.27

[10] Ibid. p.14

[11] Ibid. p.22

[12] Nichols, Grace, *The Fat Black Woman's Poems* (London: Virago 1984) p.64

[13] Ibid. p.7

[14] Bloom, Valerie. *Touch Mi! Tell Mi!* (London: Bogle-L'Ouverture Press, 1983) 'Yuh Hear A Bout'

[15] Phillips, Caryl, *The European Tribe*, (London: Faber & Faber, 1987)

[16] Enisuoh Andrea in Alsion Donnell's ed. *Companion to Contemporary British Culture*, (London and New York: Routledge, 2002) 'Greater London Council' p.130

[17] See, Arana, especially, endnotes p.4-5 & p.35-36

[18] Hall, Stuart, in Kobena Mercer, ed., *Black Film, British Cinema* (London: ICA Documents #6, 1988) 'New Ethnicities' p.28

[19] Gilroy, Paul *Against Race: Imagining Political Culture beyond the Color Line*, (Harvard University Press , Boston) 2000, p.251

[20] Wambu, Onyekachi, *Empire Windrush: Fifty Years of Writing About Black Britain*, (Phoenix, 1999), p.28

[21] Ibid. p.333

[22] Ibid. p.431

[23] Raimund Schäffner, 'Assimilation, Separatism and Multiculturalism in Mustapha Matura's *Welcome Home Jacko* and Caryl Phillips's *Strange Fruit*,' *Wasafiri* Issue 29 (Spring 1999), p.70

[24] The term is defined as 'an informal label' for a person with dual heritage or 'of African and European parentage'. For a complete glossary of *proposed* as well as *stigmatized* wording, see 'Terminology' on Toyin Agbetu's www.ligali.org webpage.

[25] Stuart Hall's term, discussed at length in Arana, Chapter 2, p.19-46

[26] As defined on the Ligali webpage, '*African British* is the name now used to describe the community previously mislabelled as Afro-Caribbean, Black British, UK Black, Negro, Nigger, Coloured and Black. It embraces all British nationals with antecedents originating directly from Africa or indirectly via African diasporic communities, such as those in the Caribbean and South America'. Joseph Harker's editorial essay in *New Nation* (July 12, 2004) 'Say It Loud: I'm African and Proud,' which explains 'Why the time has come to ditch the word "Black"', may be read online at www.ligani.org/forums as well

[27] But see, Randall Stevenson, ' Chapter 19 "The Century of Strangers": Travellers and Migrants' in *The Last of England: The Oxford English Literary History, Volume 12, 1960-2000* (Oxford University Press, 2004), 479-501; C. L. Innes, *A History of Black and Asian Writing in Britain, 1700-2000* (Cambridge University Press, 2002), esp. 200-244; Sukhdev Sandhu, *London Calling: How Black and Asian Writers Imagined a City* (London: HarperCollins, 2003); and James Procter, *Dwelling places: Postwar Black British writing* (Manchester University Press, 2003)

Concrete Vistas and Dreamtime Peoplescapes: The Rise of the Black Urban Novel in 1990s Britain

Fatimah Kelleher

AFTER decades of severe literary marginalisation, broadsheet supplements and literary reviews could be found waxing lyrical over the "compelling urban tales" that were being "written with savage aplomb" by writers whose work a decade prior would have struggled to make the lists at some of the larger publishing houses. This is not to say of course that the obligatory pigeonholing within 'ghetto writer' references no longer applied. Nonetheless, by the mid to late 1990s some respect was at last being given to those telling the stories of a major part of British life.

The 'Black Experience' and the 'urban landscape' have become increasingly integral over the last decade. Throughout Britain in general, census records today indicate that ethnic minority groups are always heavily concentrated in the urban centres, with nearly half of the total population in London alone. Within the capital the largest groups are comprised of Black Africans and Black Caribbean's and with ethnic minorities increasing by 53 percent since 1991,[1] everyday London tales are very much becoming stories that once belonged on the fringes of society. New millennium Britain has today developed an urban depiction propagated throughout the media that is hardly ever devoid of some type of Black cultural input. Arguably there has even been a symbiosis of terminology where the inner city and 'Black' have become synonymous. One need only look at the referencing of many Black music genres, from RnB to garage, within the new 'urban' categorisation to see a demonstration of this.

1990s Britain became a decade of cultural evolutions and manipulations during which the African Diaspora matured into second and third generation identities no longer prepared to remain on the boundaries. Parallel to this, 1990s Britain saw the publication of numerous novels by Black writers that depicted inner city realities, and they received the type of mainstream acceptance and critical acclaim unseen since Samuel Selvon's Lonely Londoners in 1956.[2]

The 'Black urban novel' during this decade holds a unique position as both an instigator of, and a response to this metamorphosis. The landscapes and myriad characters painted by the pens of the authors in this essay have contributed to the emergence of images, themes and complex realities that today inform our knowledge of the urban vista; incorporating styles that vary from stark concrete realism to urban dreamscape. Within each is the voice of one of many possible Black experiences in London.

AGAINST A SHADOW OF BRICKS AND CONCRETE

One of the most powerful images to emerge out of the Black urban novel in the 1990s is that of 'frontline'[3] and council estate (projects) realism. The depiction of this stark landscape of concrete right angles and dicey streets has gone a long way to awakening much of middle England to one of the realities of Black British life. Arguably as a result, the pictures painted so vividly by the pens of these authors have contributed to the gradual symbiosis of the 'Black experience' with general urban depictions in today's mainstream media.[4] Out of the last decade, we have seen a gradual permeation into the popular psyche of Black life through tower blocks and 'estate chic' whenever an urban portrayal is needed. This was a part of Britain that had existed in various evolutionary forms since the first Caribbean immigrants were shepherded into huge council estates in the 1950s, but had largely remained vague and unreal to British suburbia. Uncompromising, clear and unapologetically redolent with the patois of the era each novel chose to depict, the rise of this canon in the 1990s was in many ways the first time unheard voices of second and third generation Black migrants became noted on the larger scape.

As one of the first to tackle this experience to wider acclaim at just 18 years of age, Vanessa Walters and the publication of her debut novel *Rude Girls*[5] resonated with many young Black Londoners hitting maturity in the mid 1990s. A story of three young, female protagonists whose experiences and perspectives on life expressed a desire to find some sense of identity in the only place they had ever known, *Rude Girls* is a tale about the struggle to handle an environment that serves as the starting point of your own self-definition. Through the energy of its dialogue and youthful exuberance (soon to be curtailed by an inevitable coming of age) the reader is taken on a journey through a tableau of East London streets and housing estates that shimmer with the summer heat that serves as a backdrop. But amidst the parties and listless wanderings of its sixteen-year-old characters, lies the ever-present influence of crime, drugs, unemployment, poverty and gang violence. It is this reality, and the inescapable impact that it has on their lives, that the characters must ultimately come to terms with.

It is within Walters' second novel however, *The Best Things in Life*[6] that the estate vista as an embodiment of this harsh reality really comes into its own. In this colder, more mature narrative the two tower blocks that house each of the main characters hang like a shadow throughout the tale as indeed they have done through the entire lives of the two young girls. For one of the characters, Sian, freeing herself from the life it represents through aspirations of becoming a singer becomes her goal. For her best friend Lisa, the community – with all its faults – is not one she begrudges and sees no real reason to seek an escape route. Ultimately, the story is one about friendship, with a noted absence of some of the starker aspects of estate life as portrayed in *Rude Girls*. However, the sense of being enveloped within the landscape is in some ways greater, made potent by Sian's desire to transcend it.

This theme of two protagonists and their divergent responses to their environment is one we come across in far greater depth in Courttia Newland's first novel *The Scholar*.[7] In here, we are first introduced to the Greenside Estate in West London, a huge sprawling concrete monster that encompasses twenty-eight blocks packed with hundreds of lives interconnected through the locational lottery of inner-city housing administrations. Within this geographical mammoth, the reader is thrown into the lives of Greenside residents, Cory and Sean, two cousins who grow to young adulthood with very different behavioural patterns within Greenside. Cory – fatherless, motherless and angered by the violent circumstances of these losses – dabbles in the petty crime that lies as an economic foundation beneath much of Greenside. Sean on the other hand exhibits a steady world-view that encourages him to ignore the allure of this existence for perseverance in his studies. The tragic twist comes when, through loyalty to Cory, Sean finds himself forced to become involved in his cousin's criminal (under) world. In many ways the book is a damning indictment on the powerlessness of the individual over his environment and ultimately his destiny. Despite his endeavours to tread his own path under the overwhelming pressure of fellow Greensiders, Sean ultimately succumbs to the stranglehold the estate has on its inhabitants. Greenside – vindictive, malignant, vindictive and all pervading – is the shadowy force that looms throughout the highly personalised tale of one family in West London.

This hidden key protagonist truly comes into its own when Newland revisits Greenside in his second novel *Society Within*.[8] A varied collection of short stories with several interconnected characters and as many situational plots, Greenside becomes the continuum throughout: the witness to every tale, the voyeur of each transgression and hope-filled heist. Set in colder months, the prevailing sense of darkness has a cloak-like effect over the proceedings that, at times, become claustrophobic.

Atmospherically, *Society Within* is supremely potent – every time a character leaves the estate there is a vague feeling of breathing fresh air. What Newland depicts is a community with all the characteristics of self-containment: a thriving estate economy where "crack is worth more than gold", a cyclical pool of immersion and eventual re-surfacing where in one chapter the reader will encounter thirteen year olds being introduced eagerly to the first rungs of the drug infrastructure as part-time jugglers,[9] and in the next you're exposed to the struggle of an ex-hustler-turned-crack-head about to hit his twenties as he searches for an exit door to get out of the estate – an exit door that will provide the only salvation.[10]

In *Toy Soldiers* by Stephen Thompson,[11] we find this theme of escape being rendered in a tale that is at times too awkwardly intimate in the telling of Gabriel's story as his main character, Gabriel, launching into an autobiographical account of his rise as a drug-dealer on Hackney's frontline, and his eventual decay to a crack head despised by all. Having been cleverly introduced to Gabriel in the third person at the beginning of the book as he starts rehabilitation in the more benign streets of Hammersmith, the sudden drop into first-person narrative of his memoirs is like a veil being lifted from a wasteland only previously hinted at. Suddenly it becomes clear that the reader has been viewing him out of his true context; that the references made within the rehab hostel to his past life could never fully capture his life without the uncompromising honesty of his own voice. The telling is often unapologetic, with a narrative that moves along with a candour and pace resonant to the reminiscing of Henry Hill, the protagonist in the movie, 'Goodfellas'. The imagery is factual, lurid and smooth with a voice alternating between shame, pride and the cheeky resignation of an honest con prepared to own up to his part in a crime.

But what separates Thompson from other inner-city depictions is the way in which Gabriel's journey becomes the representation of the urban landscape. Comparatively lacking in the visual detail we find in Greenside, instead we are given a sense of both space and space and containment through Gabriel's own forays and frustrations, whose myriad experiences epitomise a fickle and harsh environment. Never having tapped into his true aspirations, his move into the dark, subterranean world of dealing crack from dimly lit pool halls is indicative of a lack of having truly looked above ground, of reaching beyond the narrow sphere of his existence. Although there are moments when he wishes to, circumstances never truly permit it. This ignorance is something the character admits to with much chagrin very early on when first introduced to a fresh world of individuals in the rehab home. His physical decay as a result of the addiction also mirrors the plague-like consistence with which the urban drug economy eventually decays every street and establishment it chooses to patronise.

As stories of struggle, the battles waged within these urban vistas are often dual: of fights within the community to overcome the agents of its nihilistic reality such as pimps, dealers and false-friends; and against a much wider system of repression embodied through institutional racism in particular, the police. Set in the run-up to the 1981 Brixton riots amidst all the social tension the era was soon to become notorious for, Alex Wheatle's *East of Acre Lane*[12] crackles with the promise of police brutality on every corner.[9] However, while the central culmination of this novel is the inevitable violent outpouring of civilian wrath upon its law enforcers, the novels' true climax really rests in the just demise of Nunchaks, whose racketeering, vice, manipulation and violence within the community was as viciously repressive as anything the police could dish out. Similarly, in Newland's work, the police role as aggressor is juxtaposed by the figure of the "fake Dred" Levi, whose centrality in most of the criminal activities taking place on Greenside places him as the true nemesis within the novel. In *Toy Soldiers*, Gabriel's journey of rehabilitation is also a discovery of the false friendship offered by his mentor in criminality, Jeff, while in Diran Adebayo's *Some Kind of Black*[13] we see a similar unveiling, as the main character confronts the double-handed manipulation of an aggressor who wore the mask of a friend.

By placing moral kudos on the ability to recognise and overcome the integral tumours that restrict the urban societies depicted in these novels, within each shadowy, brick-laden tale of grim reality, is the vestige of hope. In *Society Within*, the raiding of Levi's crack den by police symbolises a purging of its worst elements, with the consecutive start of Midnight FM by young entrepreneur's on the estate as a sign of more positive endeavours. Similarly, throughout each novel there is a sense of perseverance leading to final pages where the reader is confident that the environment has yet to fully conquer its occupant, an environment painted with such precision through the lives of characters whose stories had previously been either un-catalogued or misconstrued whenever the news did a 'Black inner-city feature'. Frontline and estate realism decided that the time had come in Black urban Britain for 'telling it like it is' and the 1990s proved the perfect decade for this to take effect as young Black Britons sought to harness the contradiction of being both "at the receiving end of systematic structures of deprivation and victimisation because of their race", but are also the dominant defining force in street-orientated British youth culture".[14]

Indeed, the publisher's The X Press, were founded on such storytelling in 1992 launching their house with author, Victor Headley's, title, *Yardie*, the rights of which were consequently licensed to Pan MacMillan.

THROUGH THE DIAPHANOUS VEIL

As a contrast to the crystal clear yet gritty drabness often associated with the brick and concrete landscapes of the inner-city vista, another strong image to permeate popular consciousness is that of the urban dreamscape. Within this particular vision lies a hot pot of bohemian aspirations, floating characters, warped realities and intrinsic wisdoms – all amidst the usual poverty and crime associated with the geographic parameters. Subject to this depiction perhaps more than any other London area is Brixton. Over the last two decades in particular, Brixton has been attributed with a persona that sometimes borders on mythology – a romanticisation of sorts that has led to some accusations of fetishising the notoriety that characterised the violence of the 1980s. While on the one hand Brixton represents (through news reels and documentaries), crime and poverty, on the other it is a pool of rich cultural immersion of 'The Black Experience'. Either way, today, Brixton is an area seen by many through a veil made cloudy by layers of historical happenings that everyone knows about, but nobody can quite remember where they heard them. Many Brixtonians themselves for example, would be hard pressed to pinpoint exactly where the frontline begins and ends, although its fabled goings-on are known by all.

Biyi Bandele's *The Street*[15] captures this gauzy, intangible reality through a mesmerising tale of 'New Brixton', where the "old mean streets had become the playgrounds and night haunts of Trustafarians and Afro-Saxon literary, media and artistic types".[16] And indeed, out of the ashes of the frontline depicted by Wheatle's work, rose a Brixton that would be viewed as a Bohemian haven. Unavoidably, future definitions of its reality would also be through Bohemian eyes. As one of Bandele's main characters, Nehushta happens to be one of these 'types'. As a stage designer turned painter, one of her missions is to paint portraits of the myriad of characters that inhabit Brixton's streets, while an ex-boyfriend stages a play based on the area's criminal underground amidst a profusion of much hammy dialogue and two-dimensional method acting. Those factors that had made the area at one time notorious, now made revered it to the Thatcher's rising aspiring middle class, entrenched in the '90s.

It is perhaps unsurprising however, that Brixton would have this kind of appeal. It would not be the first area where hard-times and multi-cultural tensions had led to a certain appeal among suburbanites and artists looking for a healthy dose of dynamism – think New York's Greenwich Village and Harlem. In the early stages of *Toy Soldiers*, one of the addicts accuses his predominantly middle class counsellors of fetishism in applauding the seedier sides of their West London local through a desire to live 'close to the edge'. And when placing Brixton within this context, it would be remiss for any to forget that Notting Hill, trendy bastion of all things cool that it is now, was once the scene of London's first racial riots. Therefore taking this social pattern into account, Wheatle's 1980s Brixton does not jar uncomfortably with Bandele's 1990s as it may seem at first, because it was the stark reality of that poverty and struggle that would provide one part of the foundations that would create the 'fabled' Brixton. The other part would be its cultural mysticism.

Despite much of the negativity attached to it, Brixton, as a kernel of Black cultural teachings and wisdom is a large part of its persona. Both *The Street* and Wheatle's works are rich with the cultural potency of the large immigrant populations that inhabit them. In *Brixton Rock*[17] and *East of Acre Lane* the reader is particularly drawn to the figure of Jah Nelson, a Rastafarian sage who acts as an educator within a community plagued by the social consequences of unemployment and racial cleavages. Educated at the proverbial 'University of Life' and well versed in the knowledge of an African history often left buried, Jah Nelson represents roots consciousness and salvation. Similarly, a decade and a half later in Bandele's Brixton, the "street clerisy" that become fixtures within the area's landscape are the many – albeit divergent – voices of righteousness within a still troubled community. Viewed with a paradoxical mixture of scorn and respect, these figures are integral to the Brixtonian dreamscape through a mysticism tinged with the hint of insanity. Bandele's greatest achievement within *The Street* is the way in which this insanity seems to permeate every crevice within the tableau, a refuge for madmen where even the sanest characters become dubious as the reader progresses.

In essence, the real and the imagined do not simply blur, but become interchangeable. In *The Street*, from the outset, we are taken on a journey into the mind of a character, Ossie Jones, who has spent fifteen years in a coma. Another principle character has a drink problem and as such the reader begins to get the impression that he/she is also witnessing the tale through alcoholic eyes. Often meandering and sluggish, the narrative's refusal to clearly crystallise the images within a more 'logical' framework is hypnotic. Bandele in fact creates the ultimate urban dreamscape, as his tongue in cheek rendering of Nehushta's father, who, on 'experiencing' Brixton for the first time in over a decade, believes he is still in a coma. Simultaneously, Bandele reflects another urban vista, that of a jazz composition, that begins and ends with the same sequence.

Ultimately, the revelation that the narrator of the book has all along been one of the colourfully dubious characters – Mr. Bill – or, "a peripatetic idiot savant" as he describes himself in the third person.[18] After which, he sneaks himself within the tale towards the end in the first person, serving to highlight a voyeuristic unease throughout while also leaving the reader with an ambiguity as to whether Mr. Bill simply made it all up. Which leads to the argument of course that Mr. Bill is no great mystery but simply Bandele himself. Either way, there is a question mark on some level as to what type of unhinged tinted lenses that we the readers have been seeing these stories through.

Which brings us to the question: how real are perceptions of Brixton within the urban landscape? As the frontline and estate realism of Alex Wheatle's 1980s Brixton moved into the shimmering surrealism of *The Street*, what part constitutes illusion? Does this mythical landscape represent how infamous inner-city sectors like Brixton appear to the rest of the country – a whorl of characters, places and circumstances that are as intangible to those outside its realms as reams of smoke that will disappear with a "poof!" when their television sets are switched-off? Perhaps more importantly, the question should be asked, are those within aware that what they are living in what may be a transient urban dreamscape with little actual substance and if so, how and where do they begin to define themselves within it – and without it?

IN SEARCH OF A BLACK BRITISH EXPERIENCE

Through seeking an understanding of what constitutes tangible reality in a landscape as seemingly endowed with Black cultural characteristics as Brixton, we are led to the question as to whether there is a definable Black Experience that runs through these British urban landscapes? After all, to speak of 'Black writing' or a 'Black urban novel' is to inevitably put one's foot into the debate over Black cultural definition. Undisputedly, similarities abound through many of the novels that emerged throughout the 1990s by Black writers seeking to portray some element of inner-city life; a commonality of existence among people of African descent. However, also prevalent within their pages are themes of fractured communities, integrated multi-cultural realities and an on-going struggle with the parameters of a contentious 'Black British' identity.

Of the latter theme, those second generation voices depicted by several authors of African descent in Britain today, are eloquently depicted and this can be seen through the use of creative mediums over the last two decades. Alex Wheatle's work attests to the fact that as early as 1980 and 1981, the earliest second-generation sounds of a creative consciousness resonated throughout Brixton's Black community. The lyricisms of DJ Yardman Irie in *East of Acre Lane* for example were indicative of a place where Caribbean roots met with British circumstance, while the poetry continued a dub tradition, (with proponents of this art form such as Linton Kwesi Johnson who has lived in South London for 42 years) already strong in its ability to caustically catalogue the experiences of a sunshine community learning to make their place in the cold. By the 1990s the homogeneity of these sounds had become dispersed, as the American hip-hop and RnB industry started to dominate urban sound systems. Arguably, this divergence away from a collective sound that all identified with, was testimony to the rise of an African immigrant population within the community that had no direct cultural links to the reggae culture of the Caribbean islands. However, out of the various sounds floating around the Black urban clubs in the 1990s emerged a phenomenon that would be hailed as Britain's first Black music genre: Jungle. Prior to this, Black British music had been far from silent, but perhaps the greatest significance of Jungle was the symbolic break it represented from following in the shadow of African American music traditions.[19] Both Adebayo's *Some Kind of Black* and Newland's *The Scholar* tell their tale to a sound track of jungle rhythms at the height of the music phenomenon's popularity. A fusion of ragga, rave and mainstream sounds, they symbolise a 'coming of age' for a generation of Black descendents born and bred within the British urban landscape. A few years later, Newland's *Society Within* had moved on to British Garage as the new wave of Black British musical identity.

As important to defining cultural 'Blackness' is the dialogue used by several authors. The issues surrounding the use of dialect by Black British authors has always been contentious and intrinsic to arguments of continued literary marginalisation. The Trinidadian playwright, Mustapha Matura put it perhaps most comprehensively by saying that writing in dialect was an important political act, with the creative benefits also being significant.[20] Samuel Selvon's *The Lonely Londoners* first stamped the need for immigrant voices to be heard within a written narrative in a form as close the rhythm and the cadence of their sound when heard. Forty years on, the West Indian patois we find in his work has evolved through stages into the hybrid of patois/cockney that the 1990s characters speak. When reading Newland for example, it is easy to spot the generational gap between a grandparent and their grandchild simply by the extent to which the grandparent retains a purer island accent. What is interesting about the growth of various stages of slang and pronunciation within a 'Black British' dialogue is the way it has permeated much of the urban landscape it encompasses, regardless of whether the speaker actually has a patois heritage. But then cultural evolution often involves cultural supplanting and hegemonies alongside 'general merging' Demographic circumstances over the past fifty years have led to a strong Caribbean influence within definitions of Black culture. For example, Dele, our main protagonist of Nigerian descent in *Some Kind of Black* makes the point that where he was living "most everybody – Africans or Small Islanders – spent at least part of the time as a kid acting Jamaican".[21]

But inevitably this move towards collectivised cultural markers is fraught with tensions. Dele and his sister Dapo both express desires to distance themselves somewhat from the Nigerian cultural restrictions their parents represent. Their only alternative thus becomes a form of Black British identity. But it is throughout Dele's sojourn within the novel that we find some of the complexities that give rise to the accusation that this identity – jungle and garage music regardless – is actually a fallacy.

As one of a very few Black students at Oxford, Dele's experiences highlight the way in which perceptions of "Blackness" are often stronger within the eyes of the Oxidant seeking an homogenous image that resonates with what popular depictions have already put forward. His position as the university's "Supernegro" demonstrated the extent to which stereotypes persist and the romanticised visions with which a large percentage of the British population – especially those outside the urban areas – have of Black life. By being out of his true urban context, we also see that Dele allows himself to fulfil these stereotypes through the need to occupy some kind of identity within an alien environment. The irony of course, is that this alienation was heightened by the presence of other Black students who Dele found it impossible to relate to having had very different up-bringings. Inevitably perhaps, the result is a character that lives a jaded and secretly bitter three-year existence while studying. What the role of the "Supernegro" also represents are separate urban and suburban realities, as the caricature went beyond mere skin colour and into a certain inner city kudos that only Dele's non-middle class London upbringing could fulfil.[22] In so doing, he embodied a broad perception of the Black British experience, as held by those outside its parameters.

But such a homogenous (not to mention two-dimensional) entity is certainly not evident within the urban landscape. Upon return to the city, Dele's Supernegro is defunct in the face of a Black community that is culturally complex and riddled with cleavages. The raw truth was, that as university educated Black man who had mixed substantially with the predominantly white reality of Oxford, he would never be considered Black enough by the standards of those who continued to live their lives within the worlds of frontline and estate realism. In fact, divisions often unseen outside of the community are so commonplace that the prejudices they incur are often taken for granted. In *Society Within* for example, Newland dedicates one tale to an exploration of the "small island mindedness" that has plagued relations within the West Indian community.[23] There, the prevalence of inter-island cultural put-downs and stereotyping expose a community that is not always united. Similarly, through the character of Jah Nelson in *East of Acre Lane* we see some of the negative perceptions held by some Jamaicans towards Rastafarians. And within almost every novel mentioned so far, some reference has been made to the often-divergent worldviews of Africans and West Indians.

An extension of this complexity is the simple fact that London is a multi-racial city and no race ever lives in seclusion within it. More to the point, there are gradations of multi-cultural integration throughout the landscape. Where Newland, Thompson and Walters have painted a frontline and estate realism populated predominantly by Black people, Bandele's dreamscape is more racially fluid. Overall, there is also a socio economic fluidity that exists within the Black community, thus complicating the dialogue for a "Black British" experience. But perhaps the most widely acclaimed vision of a multicultural urban vista is that to be found in *White Teeth* by Zadie Smith.[24] The very essence of her narrative is an exploration of some of these paradoxes within a sequence of inter-cultural relationships. Smith's Black characters are integral to a broader experience where Asian, White and Jewish cultures are also explored. On the one hand this can suggest a lack of potency within her narrative when depicting "Blackness". But on the other, the validity of a "Black experience" is highly arbitrary, as is what constitutes being Black in general. At this juncture it may be tempting to enter further into discourse on the social and biological markers of race, but that would require a discussion in a different new essay.

And this is why even within the complex reality of the urban landscape the need to define a representative Black experience is persistent. Often this is a need born out of a conflict situation like racial rioting and incidents of police brutality. For years the police relationship with Black communities has proved crucial to the desire to formulate an acceptable Black consciousness as a protectionist mechanism within a world of persecution. In line with this Dapo's brutalisation at the hands of the police in *Some Kind of Black* becomes an ideological fire-starter by various subsections of the community seeking to use the tragedy as a mechanism of unity under one banner. However, the reality remained that the banners were divergent and more fragmentation resulted. Nonetheless, what does remain constant is the fact that Dapo's ordeal was racially motivated and contemptuous of the differences (whether subtle or gaping) that separate Black people. Inner city life – as a result of its high concentration of racial minorities – has led to constant definitions among it's populace whether they are desired or not. The growth of second, third and eventually fourth generation descendents has only enhanced this as the diasporic links become more tenuous. Searching for a representative Black British identity is simply the result of this.

CONCLUSION

Without doubt, the comparative wealth of urban fiction to emerge out of the 1990s has resulted in a much stronger appreciation of the colour and complexity that constitute Black life within the inner city. Myriad in imagery and sometimes conflicting in thematic output, British society has at least been allowed an insight to a part of its life heretofore consigned primarily to media interpretations of often isolated events by writers and producers outside those realities. Perhaps the most common stories to be told from this ever increasing group of authors are those that depict the frontline and estate realism which sum-up the lives of many Black urbanites. Walters, Newland, Wheatle and Thompson have all painted vistas that have several common threads running throughout whilst allowing a broad spectrum of experience through time and place within these realities. With Bandele, we see the literary interpretation of a pseudo-imaginary visual panorama that has become slowly embedded within both internal and external perceptions of the Black experience in one of London's most famous Black communities. And finally, the ever-present debate on what it means to be Black, British, is in evidence throughout each work, perhaps most clearly found within the works of Adebayo, (whose work Dawes[25] proclaims probably heralds most clearly the future urban novel) and Smith.

However, lest one assume that the critical acclaim received by the above authors suggest an open and wide acceptance within the publishing world and society in general towards Black authors writing about various aspects of Black British life – let us review: the problem of literary marginalisation is far from redressed.[26] While the urban vistas and peoplescapes have become more visible within other creative mediums of public consumption, a few of the above authors are sometimes neglected from the 'General Fiction' aisles of bookstores and remain firmly relegated 'Black Writing', with bays that are shockingly small for the breadth and depth for such a canon. Ultimately, we must await the developments over the next decade in order to see whether the necessary outward expansion of Black writers seeking to interpret the urban experience will follow. An experience that must be continually documented through an ever-increasing profusion of culturally diverse voices, as they attempt to keep the environments as fresh and three-dimensional as possible.

NOTES AND REFERENCES

1. Census 2001, *National Statistics Online*, (www.statistics.gov.uk)

2. Selvon, S (reprinted 1979) *The Lonely Londoners* (London: Longman)

3. The frontline is a police 'no go' area, that is a central point for illegal activities such as prostitution and drug dealings. Historically, in Brixton, South London this was Railton Road; in Hackney, East London this was Sandringham Road. There has been known to be more than one 'frontline' in any one area

4. However, despite higher visibility of ethnic minorities in British film and television over the last decade, there is undeniably still much work to be done, especially if compared with the relative successes of African American input in these industries. See Etienne, T (2000) "Colouring the Face of British Film and Television" in IC3: *The Penguin Book of New Black Writing in Britain* by Newland & Sesay (eds;) (London: Hamish Hamilton, 2000)

5. Walters, Vanessa *Rude Girls*, (London: Pan, 1996)

6. Walters, Vanessa *The Best Things in Life*, (London: Pan, 1998)

7. Newland, Courttia *The Scholar*, (London: Abacus, 1997)

8. Newland, Courttia *Society Within*, (London: Abacus ,1999)

9. Newland, Courttia *Society Within*, (London: Abacus, 1999). In the chapter 'A Little Bump 'n' Grind' pp.182 –183, 2005 edition

10. Newland, Courttia *Society Within*, (London: Abacus, 1999) In the chapter 'The Art of Long Games with Short Sharp Knives' p309, 2005 edition

11. Thompson, Stephen, *Toy Soldier,* (London: Hodder and Stoughton, 2000)

12. Wheatle, Alex *East of Acre Lane* (London: Fourth Estate, 2001)

13. Adebayo, Diran *Some Kind of Black* (London: Abacus, 1996)

14. Hall, Stuart, 'Frontlines and Backyards: The Terms of Change' in *"Black British Culture and Society: A Text Reader"* by Owusu, K (ed;) (London: Routledge, 2000)

15. Bandele, Biyi *The Street,* (London Picador, 1999)

16. Ibid. p.17

17. Wheatle, *A Brixton Rock* (London: Black Amber Books, 1999)

18. Bandele, Biyi *The Street,* (London: Picador, 1999), p.181

19. For the classic treatment on the importance of music towards understanding the Black British experience and the existence of Black UK musicians throughout the 1980s, see Gilroy, Paul *The Black Atlantic: Modernity and Double Consciousness* (London: Verso 1993) Chapter 3: "Black Music and the Politics of Authenticity"

20. McMillan, Michael 'Ter Speak in Yer Mudder Tongue: An Interview with Mustapha Matura' in *"Black British Culture and Society: A Text Reader"* by Owusu, Kwesi (ed.) (London: Routledge, 2000)

21. Adebayo, Diran *Some Kind of Black* (London: Abacus, 1996), Chapter 3. p.47

22. In his 1997 article in *The New Yorker,* Henry Louis Gates Jr argues quite convincingly for the rise of "a culture that is distinctively Black and British"; one that has been facilitated by shifting dynamics over the last 25 years such as social mobility, but one where the "recent cultural ferment associated with Black London happens much closer to street level"

23. Newland, Courttia *Society Within* (London: Abacus, 1999) p.219

24. Smith, Zadie *White Teeth* (London: Hamish Hamilton, 2000)

25. Dawes, Kwame, 'Negotiating the Ship on the Head: Black British Fiction', Chapter 14

26. Getachew, Mahlete-tsige. 'Marginalia: Black Literature and the Problem of Recognition'. Chapter 18

Negotiating the Ship on the Head: Black British Fiction

Kwame Dawes

Joseph Johnson was such a famous London beggar that cartoonist John Thomas Smith featured an illustration of him in his book *Vagabondia*, published in 1815. Joseph Johnson had two distinctions. The first was his Blackness which, if we should trust Smith's craft, was quite unmistakable. Smith gave him stereotypical features; thick lips, bulging eyes and a broader nose, marking him as a splendid specimen of Black curiousity. The second distinction was his hat. Johnson was known for a hat that he wore which was topped by a fairly sizable replica of a ship complete with mast and sails with all their meticulous rigging. He carried a cane in his right hand and a crutch to support his left side which he clearly favoured because of a badly damaged leg. It is impossible to know why Johnson's fashion tastes were what they were but one cannot help recognising in this act of wearing such a hat, a profoundly symbolic gesture. On the one hand, the attire connected him to West Africa where similar headdresses were and still are quite common. On the other hand, however, Johnson's outfit seemed to reflect his intense pragmatism and his penchant for both irony and diplomacy. He literally wore the badge of his migrant status – his sense of alienation and difference – on his head. The ship was his instantaneous narrative of journey. It would mean everything to him and to those he encountered, for it was that vessel that explained his presence in England as a Black man, and that, at the same time, proclaimed his alienness, his marginalisation and migrant status.

The hat Johnson wore represented an ironic apology to white British society for his presence as a Black man in that county. Apology, not in the sense that he felt sorry for being there, or regretted being there (though considering his circumstances he might well have), but an apology in the sense of an explanation, a rationale for his presence, his existence and his condition. It is quite likely that Johnson arrived in London as one of the Black loyalists who had fought for the British during the American revolutionary war. S.I. Martin's historical novel, *Incomparable World*[1], helps us to imagine a world of existence that is different from the stereotype of the British person who talks with a washed-out West Indian accent (or the accent of some other former colony of the British), but who has, at best, a uncertain and conflicted connection to the landscape and culture of Britain.

Martin's characters seem disturbingly British and bear the stamp of Britishness that we have come to associate with whiteness. Johnson was a Britisher, at least partly determined to make it clear that he had not chosen to come to England or any other largely white society. He was brought there on the very ship of abuse, enslavement and adventure that he carried on his head. Perhaps I am reading more into Johnson's motive for carrying this symbol of enslavement and journey on his head – perhaps he wore the thing to get attention. I would like to believe that he understood the eloquent poetry and pragmatism of his act.

There is in Johnson's brand of Britishness (for he is a British figure) a peculiar poetic resonance in the manner in which Britain has evolved over the years. The extent to which Black people in Britain have worn their ships on their heads speaks to the character and nature of British Blackness and the dialogue it has had with British whiteness. For Johnson's hat does not simply reflect his own perception of himself, but certainly speaks to his understanding of the white world that was looking at him, reading him, and defining him. Black Britishness is both about the way in which identity is understood by Blacks in Britain as well as about the way in which whites in Britain have dialogued with and helped to define the meaning of 'Blackness'. Ultimately, we have to recognise that, for centuries, English society has been quite busy defining Blackness and contending with the place of Blackness in its imagination. Colonialism has ensured that Britishness shaped significantly by race and the discourse of whiteness and Blackness are central to this definition.

Nobody talked much about Black British writing until the early nineteen seventies. Prior to that period, Black people wrote in Britain but their work was not conceived as speaking to the British experience per se. These writers, sought the patronage of the British publishing system, the British media, and The Arts Council[2] while they identified themselves with another world, another home. They, therefore, were busy celebrating or grappling with their alienness. But it was not all economics. There was a sense in which many of these colonial writers, turned to Britain as to a literary Mecca.

Naturally, this relationship was contradictory and strained (read Derek Walcott, Louise Bennett, and curiously, the early Claude MacKay). Kamau Brathwaite would talk about studying at Cambridge with the hope that he would be entering a place where his instinct to write would be validated by Eliot's much vaunted sense of Tradition. He was disappointed. But the fact is that many of these writers came here as prodigals who were never quite home, they came as bastard infants seeking some sense of the familial font of good healthy milk. But central to this identification was clearly a discovery of being alien. They came when there was a movement in their home countries to extricate themselves from Britain, from empire. It is the realisation of what Frantz Fanon has described as a schizophrenia in the colonial writer.[3] It did not take writers like Samuel Selvon, Andrew Salkey, V.S. Naipaul, George Lamming and Kamau Brathwaite long to recognise that revealing their West Indianness was a useful and lucrative approach to being Black writers in Britain. Britain was not interested in how these authors saw Britain. Britain was more interested in seeing the worlds outside of Britain through these writers, even if the world was physically located in Britain as in Selvon's *Lonely Londoners*[4] or Lamming's *Water with Berries*[5]. These men understood themselves to be to be West Indian first whether because it was as a result of their blossoming nationalism or whether it was because of the way they were being defined by the British critical establishment. Even V.S. Naipaul, who in 1964 was already quite consistently caricatured as the wellknown "don't call me a 'West Indian' West Indian writer"[6] remained unquestionably unsuccessful in claiming a British identity. He has long established that his fictional landscape remains solidly locked in the Trinidad world that he grew up in. Admittedly, he sees this as something of a curse, but one that he has found remarkable ways to manipulate for his own good. The truth is that many of these writers, notwithstanding what was said about them, had somehow thrown their lot in with the anti-colonialism and nationalism of the sixties, and even when they longed to be treated as legitimate English writers, the ships on their heads were too garishly apparent. The English, it would seem found comfort in the ships for they made it quite easy for the protectors of Britishness to sustain the myth of tradition – the march from Beowulf to the moderns without the complications of these bastard – like grafts into the ancient tree. At best, the situation for Black writing in Britain at the time amounted to a compromise of history. The compromise was one that was made between the British critics and publishers and the writers themselves. The non-British writers preferred to be associated with the nationalism inherent in the shaping of a West Indian for African or Indian aesthetic and tradition, and the British had no other way of speaking of these writers but as migrant voices that belonged to that place from whence they came and not to the place to which they come. If there were exceptions, they were inevitably white Creoles who could, to use a very American phrase, pass. The fact is that colour played a significant part in the defining of race, nationalism and culture in the business of Britishness.

But times have changed and the children of the earlier generation, born in England, many to bi-racial parents, do not carry the ship comfortably on their heads. They are introducing something of a dilemma in the British literary scene because they are often either unwilling to or incapable of wearing that ship that points to a migrant identity or an identity of 'otherness'. Many of them will reject any lineage with the writers of the fifties and sixties and quite arrogantly (if understandably), and, perhaps foolishly, assert a new invention: the Black British voice.

There is something afoot. It manifests itself in several places. There is a wave of activity in the performance poetry world as well as a flurry of publication that seems to suggest that a 'movement' could be written into being by the clever ones among us. There are hints that even the 'establishment' (whatever that is) is interested in the notion of diversity in literary circles and has begun to resist the old urge to bring non-white writers from abroad to add colour to the normal literary proceedings that take place around the country. When in 1989, Benjamin Zephaniah was sent off to Jerusalem with a few other notable representative British voices to carry the cause of the Union Jack at the prestigious Jerusalem Poetry Festival. The following year, the British Council sent Diran Adebayo, a young novelist, to Australia along with five other cutting edge British writers in an exchange that brought six Australian writers to England. It is hard to see in Zephaniah's selection anything other than a strangely cynical[7] and unimaginative acquiescence to the call for diversity as I have not heard many convincing reasons offered by 'those who make the decisions' to rationalise their appreciation for his work. Even if we grant that this may be a nod to the notions of oral or performance poetry, surely there ought to be some seriously critical examination of whether in fact Zephaniah represents that kind of work in its sophistication and complexity[8]. But Adebayo makes interesting sense for there is some truth to the notion that his presence constitutes an acknowledgment that there is an element of British culture that he does speak to, an element that is asserting its Britishness in ways that are actually challenging the sometimes homogenous notions of Britishness that exists.

Typically, however, it remains unclear to many what exactly this wave of Black British writing is. And here, I am not simply referring to the easily maligned white critical establishment, but I also refer to the Black critics that exist, few though they may be. The problem is not a complex one. Critics who have emerged out of the academic milieu have cut their teeth on race as something inextricably attached to the politics of colonialism in British literature. Thus the framework used by these critics of 'minority ethnic' backgrounds in Britain has been one that holds to the notion of the ship on the head – migrant voices, colonial voices, post-colonial voices and transcultural voices. There is far less work on Black British voices as voices that actually emerge out of the British experience and the British landscape. A few attempts have been made by people like Fred D'Aguiar who has spoken of the ways in which Black British poetry is having an impact of British poetry, but his efforts have been modest[9]. Academia is thus being challenged by the assertions of some of these writers. many are claiming their Britishness and facing the implications of this. Others are unsure about what to do with the hat, but it certainly sits uncomfortably on their heads.

Of course, one of the first complications surrounding the business of Black British writing is the very meaning of the term 'Black'. In America, Black is still quite clear: it refers to people of African ancestry. The 'one drop of Black blood' rule still holds quite nicely there, and Blackness and Africanness are virtually synonymous. In Britain, however, Black is more likely to equate with 'non-white'. This would make writers like Salman Rushdie and Hanif Kureishi as much 'Black writers' as Ben Okri, John Agard and Q. There is little that is automatically common in the work of these writers listed here and attempts to draw these writers into a single grouping while tempting, could prove terribly difficult and perhaps rather futile. Nonetheless, the recent publications by a number of these writers allow us to begin to identify some patterns and trends that may help us to construct a proper critical framework for the writing that is emerging.

When a conference of African writers was held in Uganda in the early 1960s, a major effort was afoot to try and define African

Literature. Chinua Achebe advised then that such an effort was premature. There was just not enough of it to try and make any definitive or prescriptive statements about the material. He suggested that the delegates should wait until more literature was available. His was a call to the critics to hold off and let the writers define the literature from a position, not of dogma, but of the imagination. I am not absolutely certain whether the wait was especially helpful. It is true that there is far more material to work with in the defining of African literature today, but the task is certainly no easier. The central debates of the conference remain: language, nationalism, colonialism, western influence, folk culture and oral culture as defining forces in the shaping of a literary aesthetic. So, I could be cautioned that any attempt to make definitive statements about Black British writing at this point may be premature. There is not a great deal of it, some would argue, but there is quite a lot of it – a lot more than there was a few years ago 10 years ago. I venture into my discussion of the work, however, not with the hope of defining what this literature ought to be, but with a desire to chart a few directions that are apparent in the work that has appeared to date. I am also giving notice of what I perceive to be a shift in the publishing scene and in the way that these Black British writers are speaking of themselves and of their various projects. I would venture to say, for instance, that the term 'Black' is becoming increasingly influenced by the American approach of treating it as largely African centered. The reason may be a rather simple one – it is becoming politically possible to do so: the groups are now larger groups and the pragmatism of joining forces under one collective banner is gradually being eroded. There may be a greater struggle for power and position which is succumbing to the vagaries of divide and rule tactics, and in this sense, one is reading a rather diabolic and disturbing trend. But that is hardly the purpose of this discussion. Suffice it to say that I tend to be looking primarily at texts that have been produced by writers with African connections, and that the projection of this Black British voice (in its current incarnation) is quite noticeably connected to the African American literary (and business) developments of the last two decades.

I have managed to discern at least three trends in the contemporary fiction written by Blacks in Britain. The first is an expansion of the pattern of anti-colonial nationalism that rooted its sense of geography and ideology in the formerly colonised worlds that developed a complex relationship with Britain. These writers share much of the patterns established by Selvon, Salkey *et al.* They carry the ship on their heads, but their interest is to look to the place of origin as a means to make existence in the new place of living more meaningful. Most importantly, they are not as earnest about the ship on the head. The ship has become something of an icon- a fetish of universality, really, because they have somehow blurred the meaning of nation into a complex notion of exile. Exile is thus a "pleasurable construct" to coin Lamming-and proves to be a lucrative thing in a world that is shrinking. This is the internationalist writer. S/he wears the hat, but s/he is far more interested in the market value of the hat than in its symbolic value. These are writers who live in England and write of 'otherness'.

The second are the writers who are determined to reevaluate what this hat means. They have inherited the hat but are not sure they want to keep it. They write about Britain as home. They were born there or have grown up there all their life. They are uncomfortable with the notion of a home elsewhere for they have no sense of exile. Their sole exile is the exile within their own home country. Their task, naturally, is to challenge the notions that they are not home when they are in England. They are busy trying to redefine Englishness to include them. But they arrive at this place after trying to seek out a place of essence and origin. They are often disappointed people for they do not find home in that other place, so they return to 'own' England. On their heads, the hat is a spectre, a ghostly reminder of their difference, but one that represents a haunting – a disturbing haunting.

The third group is far more radical and for them tradition is far less important than the present. These are the writers who regard England as home, and therefore flee from any notions of another home. They eschew the suggestion that they come from 'somewhere else' and have a strange amnesia about that 'otherness' that results in work that may actually be working its way towards the establishment of new myths of place and identity. But the amnesia that comes with this earnestness is at once disturbing and exhilarating. The truth is that this group of writers is actually more related to the African American sensibility which emerges from a confidence in 'home', in the American soil. But it is a shallow reading of the African American sensibility. It assumes that there is a Black British populace that is interested in being consumers of Black British identity. They have discarded the hat. But their

Blackness is hard to discard. This cadre of writers is generating a fascinating brand of lively but fairly shallow fiction.

There are other trends, but these are the useful ones to work with for the time being. I suspect that it will be far too easy to show how these lines are really blurred ones and how some writers work along a continuum. So the task is not to slot writers, but to identify patterns that help us to read them. Ultimately, however, these writers are all challenging commonly held views about Blacks writing in Britain which are certainly moribund and completely inadequate for the future.

The first category has an important assertiveness that is worth looking at closely. These writers are determined to be positioned squarely in the British writing world, not as peripheral figures, but as central figures, as trend setters, as big name international writers. They are in search of a piece of the pie. They are happily cashing in on the mantra that there is nothing fresh coming out of the white European literary world these days, and that all innovation, all daring writing, all brilliance is emerging from the 'darker' parts of the world. They are cashing in, then on the myth of magical realism and the revitalisation of language by other cultures. They are therefore interested in the imprints of the major publishers and they expect to have solid advances for their work. The clever writer or agent is quick to recognise that the novel that offers a certain internationalist sensibility and that, at the same time, has enough American 'entry points' (meaning some way of proving to be relevant to a largely blinkered and self-involved American readership) to guarantee a major launch and significant sales in the USA and is therefore the kind of novel that will attract the attention of a major press. Such a novel, almost according to formulae tend to be rather flirtatious with geographical locations and decidedly multicultural in the characters that are introduced. But even beyond that, the novel must reveal a fascination with certain post modern or modernist literary styles like magical realism or a pseudo-Rock and Roll nihilism, ensuring that the work is recognised as 'cutting edge' and speaking to the much maligned moribund literary practices of the regional writers of America and England. Reviewers like to say that. 'X writer can teach us something about writing in English.' It is code for an internationalist work with 'universal' appeal, where 'universal' means relevant to mid-western white folks in America's heartland and not Punjabi intellectuals in India.

There are many examples of this kind of writer that I could use to support my rather cynical assertions-writers who, in truth, cannot be blamed totally for this whole business, but writers who, nonetheless, understand how the business works. I will settle on one for the purposes of this piece: Fred D'Aguiar. D'Aguiar is, for our purposes, a successful writer. He is published by major publishing houses in the United States and in the United Kingdom. He experienced something of a remarkable career as a poet in Britain. Recent poetic work includes *Bill of Rights*, a long narrative poem about the Jonestown massacre in Guyana in 1979, and a long narrative poem, 'novel in verse', *Bloodlines*, the story of a Black slave and her white lover, published in 2000 by Chatto and Windus. Before shifting to fiction and he seems quite committed to it these days. He has published five novels to date[10]. The first, *The Longest Memory*, is set in Virginia during the days of slavery and revolves around the inter-racial relationship between a slave and a white woman. It is a slim volume that cannot be fairly described as ground-breaking when he is competing with American novelists such as Charles Johnson, Toni Morrison, Ernest Gaines or Edward P. Jones who have written more involved studies of slavery in their various novels. *The Longest Memory* was followed by *Dear Future* which is set in Guyana and in Britain. This novel is far more intimate and amounts to an exploration of D'Aguiar's own persona narrative – the complex dialogue between the West Indies and England. *Dear Future* is effectively internationalist, but it really flirts too dangerously with becoming a classic West Indian text. So it may have been a relief to D'Aguiar's publishers when he wrote his third novel *Feeding the Ghost* which cleverly eschews geographical fixity for the most of the work, and explores briefly a rather broad range of landscapes in the latter quarter of the work: America, West Africa, Jamaica, and England. The novel takes place on the Atlantic. The Black characters in the work are African in that non-specific and anomie-weighted manner that Africans are imagined in Black America today. These are generic Blacks who speak many languages that we, the readers do not speak. But an unusual (and unlikely) accident of plot makes it possible for one African woman – the protagonist of the text – to speak to the whites in the language of the whites. She is Mintah, a captured African who apparently learns fluent English from Dutch missionaries working on the West Africa coast. Her capacity to speak English provides the book with its populist hook: a love story not unlike the story that sparkles in *The Longest Memory*. It is an interracial love relationship that develops between Mintah and the cook's aid, a blonde boy who works on the ship. Mintah is tossed overboard with other sick and not so sick captives by a diabolic captain who is seeking to ensure that he is able to get his insurers to cover his losses at sea. Mintah manages to find her way back onto the ship and creates havoc for the crew. Eventually she is shipped to the Americas, becomes a slave in Maryland and is then sold to the Caribbean where she ends her life in Jamaica. But the novel ends with a sentimental reunion with the cook's aid. D'Aguiar's penchant for these interracial relationships smacks of the kind of wishful thinking that marked his work in *The Longest Memory* and that is typical of some of the 'slave' works that have been produced in America recently, most notably the sequel to the Alex Haley series *Roots, Queen*[11] in which the pivotal articulation of racial relationships is found in the sentimentalised relationship between white men and Black women. Surely, the most memorable facet of interracial sexuality of the slavery period was not romance – this kind of misleading romance. There are far too many accounts of the standard pattern of such relationships – the exercise of power, the pragmatics of social mobility and the possibility of freedom – that render D'Aguiar's romanticism almost irresponsible. But perhaps D'Aguiar has concluded that his work is not attempting to respond to an agenda, a political ideology-what Achebe would call 'seriousness' and the propensity to teach through the novel. And in many ways, D'Aguiar is right, for what Achebe characterises as a luxury for the western world-one that is not available to writers of Africa, for example-has been grabbed by D'Aguiar for his market is one that allows him to write with a certain degree of freedom from responsibility.

Yet, D'Aguiar understands quite well that part of his rubric as a Black writer-a Black international writer-is the inclusion of politics and the inclusion of some larger ideological morality that will serve as a sign of difference. The truth is that writers like Achebe have set in stone the idea that Black writers will be at least a tad political. Overt politics will not be welcomed, but the consumer wants to be taught something about the political realities of this other world. But this is a rather light burden. The truth is that D'Aguiar, the internationalist author, while being a 'Black British writer' is not really expected to provide the 'voice' of the 'Black British experience'. Instead, such writers are expected to happily enjoy the urbane imperialist reach that is available to the white British author even while successfully colouring the landscape of British authorship at a time when multiculturalism is at least superficially in vogue. This is not a judgement on the writers themselves, for there is no question that writers like D'Aguiar, Caryl Phillips and Ben Okri are thoroughly convinced of their Blackness and their connection with Africa. What they will not accept, however, is a sensibility that ties them in reductionist ways to a small segment of the British populace that is notoriously marginalised. They are, therefore, creating an international, transcultural Blackness that is part of a grand illusion of Pan-Atlantic existence-a worldly sensibility shaped by serious ambition. They live in that twilight world of metropolitan cities around the world-wearing their rootlessness with grace and cleverness. They will not accept the limitations of nationalism and anti-colonialist rhetoric, arguing instead to be free to be who they want to be. They share something of Christopher Okigbo's oft misinterpreted mantra: "I am not an African poet, I am a poet."[12] Or his well-articulated desire (affirmed and reaffirmed by his close friend, the British poet Peter Thomas) to become a part of that tribe of poets from around the world-linked not by nationality, colour or race, but simply by the vocation of being poets. Okigbo's elitism was partly shaped by a desire to be a modern poet among modern poets. He did not like the idea of a ghetto and in many ways, he saw the world of African literature as a ghetto. Of course Okigbo died fighting for quixotic nationalism which is not quite what is in the offing for these writers.

Feeding the Ghost is really a wonderful 'poster' book for the Black British novel that is involved with an agenda that emerges out of the thinking that has guided V.S. Naipaul's struggle for decades. D'Aguiar is enjoying some of the benefits of the work of writers such as Walcott. They wore their 'Third World' labels with dignity even as they sought to enjoy the privileges of the 'First World' literary world. They won the respect of the first world through a very pained dialogue with their heritages. D'Aguiar understands himself to be Guyanese, but carries an internationalist sensibility and practice which makes the ship he wears on his head largely cosmetic-he is wearing a hat that is now a fashion statement and not quite a political or ideological statement. But this may not be entirely a question of ambition and economics. D'Aguiar is genuinely torn culturally and like his compatriot David Dabydeen, there is something of a freshness to his sense of creating a new space of identity, a new imaginative space. In *Turner*,[13] Dabydeen finds that space to be both tragically and triumphantly, the sea – that place of ultimate geographical absence. Tellingly, *Turner* too is about what happens to slaves who have been tossed overboard en-route from Africa, the symbolic act of burial at sea, and the regeneration of a new kind of humanity after this burial amounts to the quest for a new imaginative space. Dabydeen and D'Aguiar are not battling to be seen as English they are reticent about that political act, but they are constantly dialoguing with their Englishness in their fiction.

The second category, however, is fixated on 'home' – a geographical home, and in this, they are no different from the 'exile' writers of the sixties – the Brathwaites, Selvons, Salkeys, *et al*. The difference, of course, is that home is no longer the Caribbean of Africa – home is Britain. In other words, they are contending with the 'homeness' of Britain. It is an uncomfortable contention and one that does not always lead to the same conclusion, but it begins in the same fundamental place: we are citizens in this country, some of us were born here, have lived here all or most of our lives; this is home. Why does it not feel like home? Where then is home? Should we look here or elsewhere? What does it mean that this home does not feel like home?

There is, then, a serious engagement with nationalism that may be quite new for Britain. These novels are seeking to redefine the national character of Britain and to achieve this by expanding the conception of Englishness or Britishness. Their loyalties are no longer the kind of groveling Anglophillic adoration for the Mother Country that may have characterised the attitudes of colonial Blacks who were coming to live in England. No, these are English people and they are struggling to understand what this means. Such individuals have always existed in England, however, the numbers are now significant, and their colours are dark, thus introducing a curious problematic in the English literary world. I am making a somewhat slight distinction between these writers and 'migrant' writers such as James Berry, John Agard, and Grace Nichols who, while being recognised as prominent British authors, still carry with them, and in their work, a undaunted connectedness to their places of birth. They still carry their hats on their heads even as they engage in the business of interpreting England. But their work is distinct, I think, from S.I. Martin, a Bedford born novelist; Courttia Newland, a thirty-one year old novelist and playwriter from West London; Bernardine Evaristo, a London born poet and novelist; Andrea Levy also a native Londoner; Diran Adebayo, a north Londoner, and Q, an enigmatic pop figure who wears his Londoner credentials with daring and aggression.[14] What all do these writers share is the belief that they are writing British literature even as they tell the story of the Blacks who are British.

The women on this list, Evaristo and Levy, seek to chart their experience as Blacks in Britain through largely autobiographical novels that cover very similar ground. It is ground that is taken up in various ways by other British-linked novelists like Leone Ross (a Jamaican living in Britain) in her novel *All the Blood is Red*,[15] Ifeona Fulani (another Jamaican-born British raised novelist) whose first novel, *Seasons of Dust*,[16] a book that contains one of the more compelling examinations of madness among the new British minority, concludes with a rejection of Britain as home; and Pat Cumper (a Jamaican writer in England) whose first novel, *One Bright Child*,[17] explores the challenges of trying to get an education in war time England when you are a colonial. Issues of race, acceptance and place are studied by these three latter mentioned authors, but they are not impressed by the possibilities of Black Britishness-they each turn away from Britain and seek a sense of home elsewhere whenever the quest for home becomes elemental to the narrative. Evaristo and Levy are unable or unwilling to accept this. They have far more to lose.

Evaristo first published as a poet, and then published in 1997 to fairly solid critical response, a book which pretends to be a novel, but is, in many ways, a long poem with novelistic ambitions.[18] In this work, Evaristo tells the story of a mixed race British woman who seeks to reclaim her rather complicated past as a way to reconcile her sense of alienation and homelessness in British society. Her father is Nigerian, his father was a Brazilian of Nigerian heritage who returns to Lagos to make a life for himself. The result is that both Nigeria and Brazil become part of Lara's route to self discovery and she finds herself 'returning' to these places in a magical journey to rationalise the ghosts that she sees in her small town London home when she is a child. But equally compelling is the other half of Lara's life, the British half, which takes her further back to a Germanic heritage. These journeys into memory are told from a very fluid third person narrative voice, but one that shifts into the first person on occasion, and one that we can fairly comfortably associate with. Still, the narrative follows Lara's own childhood as a Black girl with unruly hair in a largely white community, living with an abusive father, a deeply dysfunctional mother and seeking to understand the meaning of her family's past.

Evaristo then takes us back to the courtship and marriage of Lara's parents in England, the difficulties of interracial relationships and marriages and the troubling business of exile that her father experiences while being so far from home. The study of this Nigerian is a complex study of alienation, pride and self deprecation. Lara's maturation comes when she realises and admits to herself her complicated sexuality, her sense of self-debasement and her desperate need to leave England to find an essential self, a place of origin. Her journey to Nigeria and then to Brazil is beautifully and evocatively written, but one always senses that haunting truth of the futility of it. And that is the heart of Evaristo's project. She finds something about the myth of self in these places, and she is able to finally understand the magicality of these 'people' who clutter her imagination as a child in London – these non-white ghosts that appear in her home and in the garden all the time, but remain outside, remain locked out by her family and the culture she exists in.[19] She meets these people and she comes to a sense of her connection with them, but she cannot settle in Brazil or Nigeria. She must return to London, to England. She must return to her now complex Englishness:

> I savour living in the world, planet of growth and decay,
> think of my island – the 'Great' Tippexed out of it -
> tiny and massive floating continents, the African one -
> an embryo within me – I will wing back to Nigeria again
> and again, excitedly swoop over a zig-zag of amber lights
> signaling the higgledy energy of Lagos.
>
> It is time to leave.
>
> Back to London, across international time zones.
> I step out of Heathrow and into my future.

These, the final lines of *Lara* articulating her ambivalence. Lagos is an embryo, a sign of an impregnation of sorts, and she will find some solace in that gene of her identity; but it is not enough. Her future is in Britain. No longer the 'Great' Britain, but just Britain. For the Britain that the Black British will embrace is not going to be 'great' as greatness is predicated on the total exploitation of the worlds of the Third World. The greatness is the greatness of Cecil Rhodes, standing in South Africa declaring Africa for Britain at whatever cost. That figure is no longer relevant to- she turns to Britain, though, for her future.

It is this that makes Evaristo such an important British author, this and her writing which is still struggling to define itself. She is influenced by Walcott, but she has clearly come to Walcott after being educated in the long British tradition. She will not celebrate that link, that lineage, but it is the presence of that lineage and the task of tackling, challenging and perhaps transforming it, that allows her to generate writing that is inventive, sometimes rugged in its tumbling metaphoric exuberance. Above all, she is quite assured about how she writes about the English landscape and how she plays with the idiolects and dialects of England. Evaristo is emblematic of a number of interesting women writers in England – that brand of bi-racial people who write in ways that offer Britain a more cosmopolitan sense of self and a fair share of good, old fashioned angst. Jackie Kay belongs to that group and so does Catherine Johnson, a bi racial writer from Wales.[20]

And yet, in these writers, as in Evaristo and Levy, we encounter a strained engagement with the question of myth and tradition. Since myth has now become a literary necessity, a manner of grounding a text racially and certainly nationally, there seems to be a strained tension in the way myth is approached by these writers, a strain that is endemic of the Black British author. The 'return' to myth (and it is almost always couched as a return), amounts to a return to an essential order, a kind of primordial sense of self that is located in the naive mythologies of the past. The myths we embrace and apply are often seen as the things that define our ideological and psychic allegiances – they literally expose our politics. The classic approach to western texts has now become a study in the retrieval of myths from the Greco-Roman tradition – the classics. In response to this powerful ordering of origin and tradition, writers from outside of the European tradition have either debunked the myths, appropriated the myths or sought their own myths.[21] The problem is that Evaristo, Levy and some of the other writers struggle with the implications of seeking mythic answers or frames to the enigma of their existence in Britain that emerge from outside Britain for the result will be a denial of their Britishness and a reinstating of the label of 'immigrant' author. There is a sense, then, in which these writers, aware of the fact that they are not grounded in the myths of the Caribbean of Africa, do not necessarily go out of their way to find a connection to those myths. It may not be as calculated as I would suggest, but there is a sense in which these works somehow avoid the myth as a framing device or casually, and without a great deal of fanfare, assume the myths of Britain even as they tell stories of a new Britain. There appears, I am saying, to be an uncertainty about how much to allow the world of their parents; the myths, the beliefs, the literary traditions and the language to inform their sense of the present, for there is a fear that it will compromise their effort to "break out of the margins and enter the mainstream":

> Where you from, La?' Susie suddenly asked one lunch break on the playing fields. 'Woolwich.'
> 'No, silly, where are you from, y'know originally?'
> 'If you really must know I was born in Eltham, actually.'
> 'My dad says you must be from Jamaica,' Susie insisted.
> 'I'm not Jamaican! I'm English!' 'Then why are you coloured?'
> Lara's heart shuddered, she felt so humiliated, so angry.
> 'Look, my father's Nigerian, my mother's English, alright!'
> 'So you're half-caste!' Lara tore at the grass in silence.
> 'Where's Nigeria then, is it near Jamaica?' 'It's in Africa.'
> 'Where's Africa exactly?' 'How should I know, I don't bloody well live there, do I?' 'Is your dad from the jungle?'
> That was it! Lara sprang up, brushed grass off her skirt, pulled up her socks, flung her satchel over her shoulder, stormed off. Susie ran after her. 'What's the matter,? 'You're bloody rude, that's the matter!'..........................
> 'Look, I didn't mean to hurt you, honest. I'm really sorry. Anyway, as far as I'm concerned you're nearly white, alright? And I adore your hair, it's like a Brillo pad. Truly!'[22]

There is something deeply emblematic about this playground scene. It haunts because the language and the setting is so familiar, so British, so much a part of the lore of the British schoolgirl narrative caught in the adolescent series like *The Naughtiest Girl in School* or the copious comics about gymnast and prankster like girls in British schools. What is different is the subject of the conversation. In many ways these writers want to fit in. They have to contend with the 'Susies' who are totally oblivious to the implication of self-confession.

Other Black British writers, however, have approached this in a somewhat different way from this strained reticence to myth that we see in Evaristo's first novel in verse. These appear to be doing something that could be termed innovative and important-they are seeking to construct new myths for the British Black world. But there is something almost artificial about what they are doing for it really entails, for the most part, a fundamentally flawed premise: that Black American experience is the same as Black British experience and that there is an interchangeablility (which is really going in one direction) in the way myth and style is approached in these two worlds. On the surface, the appeal to American jazz, hip-hop, blues, sexual politics, race politics and radical 'signifying' culture as a source for an aesthetic makes sense and seems quite reasonable. Q, Adebayo and Newland have written works that could be quite easily transplanted in urban America. Is this a triumph of universalism? Perhaps, pop culture is so thoroughly Americanised and so pervasive as a defining aesthetic force that is has constructed it own mythic order that is being tapped into by artists from all over the world. There is some truth to this, but one is inclined to be suspicious of such homogenisation when the source of it is a rather exploitative and dangerously consuming American culture. A fast-paced world of violence (gun violence), drugs, sex and hip-hop music that is the context for the novels by these three writers. They did not have to go this route, but they, like many of the performance poets working on the circuit in London today, have found their literary models in contemporary African American culture and not in the reggae washed Black British world of Linton Kwesi Johnson and Benjamin Zephaniah – an ethos that is quite coherent and quite well-realised as a Black British phenomenon. I am not sure why this has happened, but performance poets in Britain, Black performance poets, are less inclined to speak of Johnson as an influence or a model, looking instead to hip hop artists in New York, the Nuyorican poets, Paul Beatty, Sonia Sanchez, Nikki Giovanni and other 'cutting edge' Black American voices. It may have everything to do with economics, the promise of lucrative book deals and sales, or it may be that American culture is so pervasive that Blacks find their sense of belonging in the images that appear in films and on television. In itself, dialogue with this kind of influence cannot be a bad thing, but the key word here is dialogue. The novels that have appeared are not involved in a dialogue or a questioning of these patterns-they simply replicate in shallow ways a rather market driven set of novels. But what is interesting about these works is that there is a strong foregrounding of 'Blackness'.

Unfortunately, however, these works end up revealing the thinness of a significantly appropriated aesthetic. Courttia Newland's *The Scholar: A West Side Story* is described by Diran Adebayo on the cover of the book jacket in terms that offer a way to approach the novel: "An exciting, sustained and truthful novel, fine writing and firing dialogue. Courttia Newland knows his people very well". Adebayo has learnt how to write blurbs, but there is something telling about his assertion that Newland knows 'his people'. The question is who are Newland's people? The dialogue is, according to the publishers, "lifted straight off the street." The subtext and supra-text is that Newland is being 'real'- that American adjective for honesty, relevance and sincerity, in its benign form, and blatant, raw, and unrelentingly graphic in its more malevolent rendering. It implies a brutal disregard for finesse and quaint diplomacy. Being 'real' is the mandate and apology of hip hop gangsta rap. Violence and sexist language are allowable because one is being real and because one is saying it like it is on the streets: "lifting it off the streets." Those who are not 'real' are clearly being disingenuous. And all of this is implied in this wave of Black British writing. The implication is that no one is writing about Black British experience authentically, and so these new, young tykes are taking on that challenge, that grand task.

Newland's streets are the largely Black streets of West London. Drugs are everywhere, guns appear from nowhere, crime is endemic, and police brutality is *de rigeur*. The young Black male is a beleaguered soul surrounded by incredible temptations for him to compromise, to do the wrong thing. Newland then tells a story that has an uncanny resemblance to the John Singleton film, 'Boyz in the Hood'. Sean, the good, promising, intelligent brother to the wayward Cory, must turn bad to save Cory's life. Turning bad means giving up his studies at a London college and turning to a life of crime: drugs and armed robbery. He destroys a loving relationship with his girlfriend and betrays the trust that his mother, a single parent looking after three teenage children, has placed in him. Sean turns to crime because Cory life is threatened by a ganglord and drug dealer, Levi, a West London drug dealer who Cory was to have joined in a major armed robbery outside of London. Cory is hurt in a fight and the ganglord demands that he find a substitute. Sean, recognising that Cory could be killed, decides to take Cory's place and, once he does, he slowly becomes seduced by the lure of danger and the promise of fast cash. His education suddenly seems irrelevant, useless, and he is totally disillusioned about his capacity to make it out of the ghetto with an education. Sean falls deeper into crime and ends up in prison. Cory's fate is not much better. He murders Levi and becomes a fugitive. The novel ends with a rather pessimistic bit of irony:

> Sometimes the beams played on the rectangular sticker whose message had sealed Levi's fate, Nubians do it better in the dark. Now Sean and Cory were lost to the darkness.[23]

Newland's thesis is quite clear: Black British society is becoming increasingly like African American urban society and there is a warning that violence and drug use will continue to rise among the Black British. He is being real about these realities. But there is a shallowness to this realness. It lies in the absence of a critical exploration of why things are as they are. There is a temptation to read into the Black British urban world the same discourse that has shaped the African American urban blight-but that is decidedly shallow. The socio-historical context of African American experience in the urban centres of the United States are decidedly different from those facing the largely immigrant world of the Black British experience. What Newland's novel does not achieve is what I suspect is the crucial task facing the Black British writer, which is to contextualise the Black British experience within the larger British socio-political world.

At best he constructs rather Manichean approaches to race in Britain where the white figure is generally the white boogey man looming over the Black British youth. I am not questioning the presence of such a boogey man, but I am actually struggling to see more clearly what he looks like and how he works so I can know how to avoid him when I encounter him.

Still, Newland's penchant for a good story and his earnestness in his project to explore the world of inner city Blacks in Britain has produced characters who speak with a language that is uniquely arresting and that does seem to open doors to a new hybridised world of Black British experience that is inextricably connected with African American culture. The promise in Newland, however, lies in the care that he shows for his characters and the authority with which he handles the emotions and desires of his characters. In many ways, then Newland's characters seem less interested in the ship on the head. Indeed, they have abandoned it and, in process, have argued for a new paradigm of Black British experience, which, while still emerging from the margins, offers a curious vision of Britishness. Yet, having said that, it is hard not to sense in Newland, a literary affinity to the popular urban Black novel of the nineties. His work predicated on the self-justification of 'keeping it real' which amounts to an often uncritical retelling of the experience of the urban Black. Newland is a smart writer and is likely to find more sophisticated avenues for his understanding of urban Black British experience. In some ways, *The Scholar* stands in danger of establishing a 'realness' in Black British experience that is thoroughly quagmired in the troubles of urban existence; troubles that are not properly connected to the larger questions of defining home and defining the meaning of being British and Black. Of course, I could be in danger of trying to get Newland's novel to fit into my concerns in this paper the meaning of home in British life. This may be true, but I am proposing something more than that. I am arguing that Newland's work offers a vision of Black British experience that constitutes an inclination to place less weight on the question of origins and the dynamics of immigration politics in the construction of the Black British experience. It may well be that Britain has moved away from the idea of the immigrant nation, to one, closer in character to the American experience, of a native born minority culture.

Newland, then, is not wearing his hat. He has discarded the ship on the head and like Diran Adebayo in his novel *Some Kind of Black*, he skirts away from the kind of discussion that will take the reader outside of Britain for an understanding of the Black British characters. These are the British-born voices and they are voices that are at once alienated from their British society as well as from the very tethered and nostalgia-bound imaginations of their parents who are constantly repeating the mantra: "when I make enough money, I will go back and settle in Jamaica /Barbados /Nigeria /Ghana." The literature is naturally affected by this important strain. It would appear that the writers will have to contend with this reality.

In *Some Kind of Black* Diran Adebayo tells the sentimental story of Dele, an Oxford undergraduate who struggles to reconcile his experience in that institution with his connections with the street and his relationship with his Nigerian parents. Dele is a clowning Black resident in Oxford who gradually tires of the set role he is forced to play by the whites around him as a token Black face with full knowledge of all Black culture and Black music. Adebayo's treatment of this element of the novel is extremely deft and quite moving. He displays a very intelligent grasp of some of the complications surrounding the second generation Nigerians. The world of his novel is peopled by a multiracial cast of characters, and he uses this work to explore the complexities of inter-racial relationships in a manner that is never sentimental or romanticised. Dele, the main character, tells a potential white lover that he is "an educated Nigerian". She responds, "Nigerian, yeah? You can't say nothing to me about Nigerians, I know what you're like!" It typifies the troubling world of Adebayo's London. Africa, Blackness and minority status are all difficult enigmas that are constantly being pigeon holed into easy stereotypes, but Adebayo keeps trying to debunk these reductionist assumptions. The British, both Black and white, think they know what being Black in Britain is about, but they keep finding themselves unsure, in a peculiar kind of limbo of half-truths. Another lover of Dele (he has several in this work which is often as much about Black male sexual proclivities as it is a story about being an educated Black man in Britain), a religious woman of Nigerian descent becomes a vehicle through which Adebayo can display his sometimes witty and insightful commentary of Blackness in Britain:

> What she said. She said that Preston was light years behind London as regards a conscious community, like Afrocentricity hadn't happened. She said that Black folks be going around saying "Got a light, chuck?. "Ta, cock!" and "Our kid" as native as the natives. And as for romance, well Cheryl had never exactly been rushed, seeing as the brothers up there hadn't got beyond the white-girl-as-trophy trip. Dele countered that Cheryl shouldn't be so impressed with the London scene, because there was plenty of bogus brothery going down, and the fact that some proud Nubian couple named their kids Kwame and Nefertiti still didn't mean they could find Ethiopia on a map. Cheryl retorted maybe, but even if they were only paying lip-service, this would pay unforetold consequences for life, because the children would one day be intrigued at the origins of their names, and this would start them on a voyage of discovery. That Dele might be a smart guy but he shouldn't feel a way about how others tried to better themselves.[24]

Ultimately, however, Dele's cynicism is what prevails in the end, for Adebayo's task is quite often to seriously question the intentions of those activists who emerge in England with a pro-Black agenda, but who turn out to be charlatans and crooks. Dele himself is disillusioned by the entire scene and finds himself rather uncertain about loyalties of an ideological nature by the end of the work. Like the language of the novel, which is a telling patching together of 'Black talk' from the Caribbean and Africa, cockney from the East End of London and hip-hop discourse from the urban United States, its politics seems to reflect the still emerging sense of Blackness and identity of the Black British world. Unlike Evaristo, though, Adebayo's characters do not turn to a world outside of England for a sense of self and identity. In fact they reject such a proposal. Dele does not invoke his Nigerianness to resolve his dilemma – it is not sufficient and it is too rife with the complexities of his relationship with his father.

Dele recognises the seduction of being the "Black man around town", the "Number One Negro" and welcomes that attention that comes with it for a while. Gradually, however, he recognises his own sense of schizophrenia and the falseness of his sham at the university. At home in London he is moving with a crowd of drug users, and trying to 'make it' with Cheryl, the plain church-going girl while he is trying to have sex with a white fellow student of the upper class at Oxford. He betrays Cheryl (she discovers him with the white girl) and he is struck by how torn he is mentally about what he is trying to do as a Black man. At the same time he tries to keep that part of his life from his traditional and conservative father who bullies his entire family with his dated attitudes about migrant existence in Britain. The tension of the many worlds that mark the life of the Black British youngster, born into a society and yet living outside of that society are cleverly drawn by Adebayo. And yet, for some reason, to ensure a dramatic ending to his novel, Adebayo turns to violence and a somewhat unsophisticated plot about the exploitation of Black organisations that pretend to be seeking the good of the Black community while they are in fact finding ways to make money and to exploit the suffering of Blacks. Dele finds ways to defeat this group and the work ends with what can only be described as dramatic predictability. It fizzles out because Adebayo is not sure what to do with the more compelling aspect of the novel, the business of Dele's Englishness or non-Englishness, and the business of his own sense of belonging in that society. The least convincing aspects of Adebayo's novel is when he writes of the violent street world, yet it is this world that gives him the street credentials that are celebrated in the blurb on the book jacket. The pattern, though, is similar to that which I have pointed to in Newland's work – a strange uncertainty about how to locate this Black British experience in the larger British world. But Adebayo is a smarter novelist and is far less derivative than Newland. Dele's sense of uncertainty about who he is and his inability to resolve it is endemic of the literary intentions of Adebayo.

It is telling, though, that the author who seems most comfortably positioned as the quintessential Black British novelist is the crime writer Mike Phillips who is really more than a crime writer in the limited sense of the term, but whose credentials as a crime writer may best explain why he writes with the greatest sense of assurance about trying to place the Black person in the English landscape in fiction. Mike Phillips has won awards for his quick-paced and efficient narratives which are a careful study of remarkable craft. The craft is the frame and the frame is the crime novel genre. It helps Phillips because he has a basic formulae for the novel that is largely devoid of any significant ideological underpinnings – underpinnings, that is, which have to do with questions of nationalism and race. With such a basic framework, Mike Phillips then begins to colour in the plot and characters with deft skill and with a clear sense of the ideological implications of having Black characters struggle with Black issues in the genre that he has chosen. But with the narrative-the plot and its outworking-as the paramount feature of the work, he is able to restrain himself from too much distraction. The 'universality' of the 'whodunit' model guarantees that his readership remains intrigued by the work without that overweening sense that they are entering into another world – a world beyond their grasp or understanding. His characters are Black, but they are driven first by the compelling factors of the plot and only secondly by the issue of their racial identity. In his 1997 novel, *The Dancing Face*,[25] there is much that suggests that this is a book about Black people concerned about Black issues. The plot surrounds the efforts of the wealthy Nigerian Dr. Okigbo, to steal an important Nigerian mask called 'The Dancing Face', and to use this mask to make a deal with the government in Nigeria. Of course, the plausibility of this plot is deeply questionable as it is unlikely, given the political climate in Nigeria, for such an artifact to have the kind of value that Phillips places on it. But not to worry, we are really not terribly bothered by this stretch of the plot for the action is complicated by the introduction of Gus, a young university graduate-a mixed raced

Britisher, who, because of his own intensely felt desire to do the right thing in the struggle for Black identity, agrees to steal the mask for Okigbo. But when Gus begins to doubt Okigbo's intentions, he decides to take over the restoration of the mask for Africa and Africans. Okigbo has Gus killed; Gus' brother Danny along with his college friend Osman and a group of very television friendly characters come together to secure this mask. The novel hurtles along with violence and incredible intrigue, and the final scene in which the mask is actually destroyed intentionally by Osman, also a Nigerian, becomes a powerful articulation by Mike Phillips about the whole business of race, identity and heritage. It is Phillips credo that emerges in this last moment, and it speaks volumes about the way that he has reconciled his position as a Black writer in Britain. Danny is startled and extremely bothered by Osman's decision to destroy the mask. They hear the huge explosion and as they drive towards the Barbican, the argument becomes heated:

> "You wouldn't have agreed."

> "You're bloody right, I wouldn't." Danny shouted. "That was one of the most important work of art to come out of Africa. Do you know what you've done?"

> "Don't tell me what it was." Osman was angry now.
> "It mattered just as much to me." He stopped, making a conscious effort to calm down.

> "I kept trying to tell you. What we have to do is confront the past, not resurrect it. I come from the same life as the Dancing Face did. I know what it was. It was more than art. It was my history."

> "Jesus," Danny said. "You know that, so how could you do it?"

> "It wasn't a choice," Osman said. "I turned my back on history. After that it was easy."[26]

Osman's capacity to turn his back on history is a telling one for it speaks to the very meaning of what it means to be a Black British writer. Is this what Phillips has done and is this what the other writers are contending with. The act of turning one's back on history means that one does not necessarily hold on to the talismans of those literary traditions that emerge from those former colonial worlds, but one forges a new, constructed future in the new British landscape. But turning one's back on history is impossible, as Walcott well knows. (See his poem "A Far Cry from Africa", and his long, book-length narrative poem, *Omeros*).

For history is constantly defining the way in which the Black person understands him/herself in Britain. Mike Phillips realises, however, that he can no longer carry the hat with the ship of journey on his head. His novel reflects that realisation. He understands the importance of exploring the reality of the worlds that make up the new British landscape, but he is a strong advocate for the distinction of an 'indigenous' Black British voice, and he realises that his greatest struggle as a novelist has been to overcome the problems of definition when it comes to his work. It is fortunate that Phillips is a crime novelist, but that is surely a convenience. There is a slot for crime writing on the shelves of W. H. Smith (a chain of newsagents and 'airport' booksellers in Britain), there has always been one. But until recently, there has not been a 'shelf' for Black British Literature. Black British writers would have to settle for slots in the world literature shelves, or no slots at all. Phillips has spoken eloquently about the place of the Black British writer and the importance of recognising that author as a legitimate one in Britain. But Phillips, one suspects, is not necessarily advocating, as some are, that there indeed be a Black British Literature shelf. Phillips is more likely to advocate that no such ghettoisation take place and that the books should simply be placed in the shelves of British Literature.[27]

In 1997, the London Museum hosted a conference on Black British Literature.[28] It was an important gathering because of some of the questions that were raised even if they were not answered. It was clear that there was a good deal of literature being written by Blacks or non-whites in Britain. One of the and founding publishers of Bogle L'Ouverture[29], asked the question which came as a surprise to many since it was coming from a woman of impeccable radical credentials as a Black activist and from a woman who, arguably, played a major role in the coining of the phrase Black British. She asked, "is it not now time for us to do away with the term 'Black British literature', and simply demand that our writing, that is writing by Blacks in Britain, be called, simply British literature?" There were no clever answers. In fact all the Black publishers began to seriously wonder about what they were doing, and the representatives from the British funding agencies were unsure-it would completely alter the way that funding is done in that context.

She was asking a question that the presence of a growing mixture of Black writers in Britain is asking: do we discard Johnson's hat? Is it time not to turn one's back on history? From where I sit, the answer is no. Not for the writer anyway. I think the writer, the artist, has to be acutely aware of the history that has brought him or her here. The writer, I suspect, must be aware that there are significant traditions of creativity that have served to shape what they are doing now, and these writers could prevent themselves from going over old ground by recognising the history of a Black presence in Britain and the more complicated connectedness that exists between what we call British writing (read white) and colonial/post-colonial writing. That connection is not one-sided. Work that is to have a dynamic impact, work that is to respond with the weight of mythic scope and meaning must find its way towards a relatively coherent aesthetic. The search for the aesthetic still entails a sifting through history and tradition. What is done with that tradition is the test of genius, but ignoring that tradition amounts to a rather foolhardy assumption that western cultural norms are not as pervasive, dominating, and eventually insidious as they have always been to those writers who recognise in themselves a connection to something else.

NOTES AND REFERENCES

[1] Martin, S.I., *The Incomparable World*, London: Quartet 1996

[2] Renamed and reorganised Arts Council England in April 2003, they maintained the former Writer's Awards

[3] Fanon, Frantz, "Colonial War and Mental Disorders", *The Wretched of the Earth*, first published in France by Francois Maspéro éditeur, 1961

[4] Selvon, Samuel, *The Lonely Londoners*, London: Wingate 1956

[5] Lamming, George, Water with Berries, Trinidad: Longman Caribbean, 1971

[6] Dathorne, O.R., *Black Orpheus*

[7] 'Me? I thought, OBE me? Up yours, I thought' article by Benjamin Zephaniah, *The Guardian*, Thursday 27 November, 2003

[8] Ibid., Chapter 10 on Zephaniah

[9] D'Aguiar, Fred, "Building Bridges Back to the Past": An Interview with Fred D'Aguiar", *Callaloo* – The John Hopkins University Press, Volume 25, Number 2, Spring 2002, pp.418-425

[10] *The Longest Memory* (1994), *Dear Future* (1996), *Feeding the Ghosts* (1997), *Bloodlines* (2000), *Bethany Bettany* (2003)

[11] Sequel to *Roots* by the same author. *Queen: The Story of an American Family*, Pennsylvania: William Morrow Publisher, 1993

[12] Christopher Okigbo (1932-1967) was one of Nigeria's foremost poets whose life was cut short by the Biafran civil war. His poetic works include *Heavensgate* (1962), *Limits* (1964), *Silences* (1965), *Distances* (first published in Transition, 1964) and the

posthumous volumes *Labyrinths, with Path of Thunder* (1971) and *Collected Poems* (1986)

[13] Dabydeen, David, *Turner*, Leeds: Peepal Tree Press, 2002

[14] Ibid., Biographies & Bibliographies

[15] Ibid., Chapter 9 on Ross

[16] Fulani, Ifeona, *Seasons of Dust,* Harlem River Press, 1997

[17] Cumper Pat, *One Bright Child,* Black Amber, 1998

[18] Ibid., Biography/bibliography on Evaristo

[19] Ibid., Chapter 16 for a more detailed discussion on *Lara* and her search for her identity

[20] Johnson, Catherine has published seven novels to date: *Sophie's Ghost,* Pont Books, 1994 , *The Last Welsh Summer,* Pont Books, 1993 , *Other Colours,* The Womens Press, 1997, *Landlocked,* Pont Books, 1999, *In Black and White,* Oxford University, Press 2000, *Hero,* Oxford University Press, 2001, *Stella,* Oxford University Press, 2002

[21] Ibid., Chapter 1 on Adebayo. In his fourth novel that he is currently working on, Courttia Newland also deals with African mysticism.

[22] Evaristo, Bernardine, *Lara,* Kent: ARP, 1996, p.65

[23] Newland, Courttia. *The Scholar,* London: Abacus, 2001, p.343

[24] Adebayo, D, *Some Kind of Black*, London: Virago Press, 1996, p.54

[25] Phillips, Mike, *The Dancing Face*, London: Harper Collins, 1997

[26] Ibid. p.256

[27] Ibid., Chapter 18 by Getachew

[28] 'Tracing Paper: Black writing in London 1770-1997.' Conference organised in partnership with Spread the Word, the literature development project for South London. Significantly, Bernardine Evaristo was one of the Literature Development Workers for Spread the Word at this time.

[29] Since 1970s Bogle-L'Ouverture Press Ltd has been promoting an independent voice of the experiences of Black people. It is based in Ealing, West London. It followed the birth and the development of The Caribbean Arts Movement set up in 1966 by Kamau Braithwaite, Andrew Salkey, and publisher John La Rose. In this context, Bogle L'Ouverture was to be important, especially, in publishing Walter Rodney's seminal book *How Europe Underdeveloped Africa* as well as many of Andrew Salkey's explorations of the Caribbean folklore character, Anancy the Spider, Linton Kwesi Johnson's landmark second volume, *Dread Beat and Blood* and Lemn Sissay's first collection, *Tender Fingers in a Clenched Fist*

Black British Poetry: Some Considerations

Kwame Dawes

> One of the most promising of the young performance poets said to
> me once, "I want to be a poet – not a performance poet," meaning,
> I believe, "I want to write like a white poet," meaning
> subconsciously, "I would like to be a white poet"; meaning behind
> that, "I would like to be white." And I was sorry the young woman
> said that, for no great poet has ever been afraid of being herself.[1]

I apologise to Langston Hughes for this rendering of his rather
famous manifesto on race and writing, but I find it a useful way to
begin to talk about Black British poetry largely because the position
of the Black poet in Britain has become inextricably linked to the
notions of 'performance poetry' and the reductionist way in which
the co-opted use of the term has created in many Black poets a desire
to either run away from the label, or embrace it with defiance and
as a kind of statement of race and aesthetics. Many Black British
poets, even those who began as 'performance poets' have begun to
seek ways to avoid the label. Some have taken to being called
'spoken word artists' borrowing from the American scene, while
others have simply insisted on being called 'poets' not 'performance
poets'. Others, however, have, like Hughes' ideal negro, embraced
the label as a birthright, and in defiance of the marginalising efforts
of 'the establishment'.[2]

Most of the Black poets working in Britain today have emerged
through the performance medium – a medium that is seriously
aware of voice, idiom, dialogue and popular discourse.[3] They draw
upon the performance traditions of dub poets such as Linton Kwesi
Johnson (LKJ), African poets such as Ahmed Sheikh or African
American 'spoken word' writers. In both instances, the performative
is linked to the language and the language is defined by elements that
do not immediately link these poets to private, arched lyricism of
modern British poetry.

LKJ's verse grew out of struggle and the power of a voice speaking
to the larger community. He has always been a public poetic. LKJ

emerged out of reggae – a Jamaican musical form that eventually asserted its own identity and place in the UK. In drawing on reggae, Johnson was re-enacting what Langston Hughes did with the blues, what Nicholas Guillen did with *son* and what Jack Kerouac did with jazz. In his poem, 'Inglan Is a Bitch', Johnson reminds the Britain of the mid-seventies that Britishness is changing by declaring that the new migrants are now here to stay[4]. It is a bold assertion, voiced in Jamaican patois, that, too, is implied is here to stay. Johnson records his poems to music; tours (internationally) with the Dennis Bovell Band, placing him as a *bonafide* reggae recording artist. There appeared to be a *de facto* agreement that what he was doing was not 'book' poetry, so that his publications were seen by many as mere transcriptions of a performance. Johnson's insistence on publication, his own relatively low-keyed performance style, and his recent a *capella* performances and recordings demonstrate that for him, these demarcations are misguided. Perhaps the message has reached the so-called establishment as Penguin published a selection of his poetry entitled, *Mi Revalueshanary Fren* (2002), and so making him only one of two living poets in history to be published in Penguin's Classic series. The problem, of course, is that it has taken nearly thirty years for such an acknowledgment of Johnson's work.

Johnson is normally labeled a 'performance poet'. It is a problematic label only because it has come to be a restrictive one that seeks to distinguish him and others who are seen to bear his traits from 'book poets' – poets who write primarily to be published. The labels are misguided and deeply inscribed in questions of aesthetics, the politics of race and the function of poetry in society. I will not try to prove this here as I have written at some length on this matter elsewhere.[5] What I will do, is suggest that the assumptions that surround this relegating of important and remarkable poets like Johnson as 'performance poets' has become so endemic to the poetry scene in Britain that the term has now become almost synonymous with 'Black poets.' It has become an unfortunate assumption that Black poets in Britain are 'performance poets' first, – writers who are fixed in the world of performance. It is unfortunate because, like all reductionist labels, it demeans the work that is being done by these writers and encourages laziness in those who respond to the work that is produced by these writers.

But even this complaint is fraught with problems. It hints at the idea that there is something inferior about 'performance poetry'. It somehow embraces the limitations imposed on the term by those who seek to marginalise the work. The problem, of course, lies in the totalising dichotomies often created between 'book poetry' and 'performance poetry.' They are false dichotomies grounded in rather lazy acts of analysis. The poem is the thing. Its value can be tested on the page and in performance. It remains a poem regardless of how and where we choose to encounter it. If we can accept that the page is as much a performance space as is the stage, we may begin to find ways to speak about poetry without some of these prejudices. A poet ought to be able to choose her own 'performative space.'

Unfortunately, however, the Black British 'performance poet' who decides to produce work to be seen on the page is faced with a massive challenge as many publishers suspect that the work will simply not 'stand up' in print, and more than that, they think that these poets are more interested in audio recordings than book publication. At the heart of these decisions, however, is a fundamental aesthetic one. As I will argue later, most of these publishers work with a template of what constitutes 'good' poetry. The problem, of course, is that the 'template' is inscribed in a very limited understanding of poetics that is shared by most of these publishers.

Many of these editors have assumed that the poets are not aware of the different idioms that can work for the page and those that work better on the stage. They assume that these poets are not students of the very poetry that they (the publishers) publish. They do not imagine that these poets are embarked on a sophisticated encounter between the western tradition and the non-western traditions that form an elemental part of their work.

The other assumption, made by the poets, is that these publishers have absolutely no interest in the kind of work they are writing because it is work that is defined, they believe, by race and work that does not look like or sound like the kind of work these publishers are publishing. They assume that these publishers are appalled by the attention that performance poets get and regard that work as giving poetry a bad name. They assume, therefore, that it would be completely pointless sending work to these places. They even assume that if they attempt to send work that falls comfortably into the style of verse being written by many of the published poets, that they will be rejected because of the label that they carry. It is hard to say that the poets who feel this way are misguided in holding to this view. There is enough evidence to suggest that at the very least some editors hold this view.

Poets who work in the performance context face major challenges. The first is that many of them make their living entirely by performing. It is a tough living and one that requires them to do readings and workshops in schools and clubs and seek support from organisations such as ACE (Arts Council England)[6], and the National Literacy Trust, The Poetry Society, and the British Council for tours, readings with bands, and the promotion of themselves as popular artists. They must contend with the tyranny of an audience that wants the same hits to be done again and again. Often their production level is low. They need not generate a great deal of material because their work is largely consumed in the same way that a musician's work is consumed. In concert, most musicians struggle with the pressure to perform the hits at the expense of new material. The same is true of the performance poets whose shows are often not solo shows, with an average performance length of 20 minutes and so it becomes possible therefore for them to survive on five or six new poems a year.

If young Black poets hope to follow a path taken by other successful Black poets in the UK, they cannot be blamed for thinking that publication will come only when they have established themselves as marketable and popular performance poets. Apart from Archie Markham, Fred D'Aguiar, David Dabydeen, Grace Nichols, Jackie Kay and James Berry, (five of whom are still generally seen as 'migrant' writers[7]), the other published Black British poets of note are often associated with performance even when they have established quite creditable reputations as published authors. Jean 'Binta' Breeze, Benjamin Zephaniah, John Agard, Patience Agbabi, Lemn Sissay, Dorothea Smartt, Valerie Bloom, Bernardine Evaristo, have all, in some way, been directly linked with the performance scene.

There is nothing wrong with this model if it is viewed as an aesthetic exploration of poetry and its sophisticated oral traditions that date back to the earliest examples of poetry that we have. The problem comes when it is felt that the use of the label, 'performance poet' is the only way that Black authors can be successfully marketed or even accepted as valid voices. Again, as limiting as this may be, it would not be so bad were there genuinely aware and astute mechanisms for intelligent and knowledgeable criticism of this work. Often, the critical apparatus used to assess this work is either woefully lacking in understanding or decidedly patronising in its clumsy attempt to avoid being labeled racist. The fact is that performance poets are not subject to serious critical attention. Reviewers are either convinced of their inadequacy as serious poets or feel unqualified to comment on work that seems to belong to a different culture. Some argue that they are not sure whether they are reviewing poetry or theatre. Race, problematically, plays a significant part in these biases. Yet, even given a serious appreciation of these writers' complexity, it is clear that most publishing houses regard poetry by Black writers as a specialised area that is inconsistent with the kind of work that interests them. Apart from Bloodaxe, Peepal Tree Press, and in the past The Women's Press, Virago and Payback Press (which has now been incorporated into its parent, Canongate Books and seems to publish little if any poetry), none of the other established houses have published Black writers who may be said to have emerged from the 'performance' space.

The decisions that have led to this situation seem to entwine aesthetics with issues of race and culture. When editorial discussions are faced with decisions that would seem to challenge their own existence as a poetry publisher or press, editors then resort to the safe ground of 'taste.' They return to the view that they simply publish work that they *personally* find valuable as poetry. They argue in what seems a most reasonable manner that they can't be expected to represent *all* tastes in poetry. And they are right. They are *all* right. The problem is that they *all* seem to share similar tastes in poetry, a taste that ultimately excludes Black poets.

There are at least two branches of British poetry. One is the branch associated with what may be unfairly termed 'the establishment', which understands that the nation's poets are those who are published in the right journals and by the right publishing houses.

The top establishment houses are Faber and Faber, Jonathan Cape, Picador, Bloodaxe, Carcanet, Anvil and Penguin. They are the top houses, not necessarily because they sell the most titles but because they have developed the prestige and authority that comes from what is seen as quality publication and the consistent attention of the media. It is rare for any of their titles not to be reviewed in major newspapers and periodicals. But to go by the list put out by the Poetry Library, there are at least 53 other British publishing houses which publish poetry.[8] Most are small presses, some committed exclusively to reprinting classic works by major authors of the past, some to translating work, others to regional writers, a few to publishing work by international authors, and others to specialist publications – pamphlets, (chapbooks) etc.

The second branch belongs to the ad hoc performance scene. Poets who appear on stages in bars, theatres, theaters, and massive platforms to perform their work belong to this branch. Sometimes they are called, 'readings', at other times there are sessions called slams (competitive performances), but almost always they are events that draw large audiences and they are dominated by non-white performers who develop a following that is often linked to some music scene whether it be hip-hop, reggae, punk or rock and roll. Many of these artists record and sell their work on tape or cd. They have to do more than read. They have to establish a presence on the stage, they have to have some theatrical force and they have to connect directly with their audiences. Many people encounter contemporary poetry only through performance poetry. But many 'book' poets have also become regulars on the performance scene. Some do so because they resent the attention that these performance poets get, and are convinced that these performance poets lack substance. Others do so because they welcome the space to share their work with a wider audience and in a context that values the sound of poetry. And those who have clued on to the economics benefits, do so because they will often realise more income through performances than through royalties and will be booked regularly to read at major festivals (if they have a book published *and* can deliver those poems well to an audience).

Black writers usually dominate the performance scene while white writers dominate the book scene. The poetry publishing world, indeed Britain's publishing world per se, is to a large extent, a white enclave. There are few if any non-white poetry editors working in Britain today. (Although credit goes to Zimbabwean editor, Ellah Allfrey who was the publisher of Linton Kwesi Johnson's collection before she left Penguin). No poetry press exists that is devoted primarily to the work of Black British authors.[9] While a few houses can boast a number of Black poets on their list, the vast majority of the poetry houses publish no Black British poets. This is the present reality as evidenced by the 2004 New Generation Poetry announcement when only one Black poet was on the list, Patience Agbabi.

A quick trip to the Bloodaxe website will reveal (particularly when you click the area of performance poetry) twelve Black poets (although most of whom would not call themselves Black British) – yet they are the very people that we would normally regard as the established Black British poets in the country. John Agard appears there along with Linton Kwesi Johnson, Fred D'Aguiar, Jean Binta

Breeze, Benjamin Zephaniah and Jackie Kay. Beverley Braune, a Jamaican who lives in Australia has one title on the Bloodaxe list. Most of these authors have one title with them, having published with one or other small press before being published by Bloodaxe. Benjamin Zephaniah has several titles with Bloodaxe and Jackie Kay, as one of Bloodaxe's featured authors has four titles with this well respected independent publishing house. With 400 titles on their list and 250 poets listed on their online database, Bloodaxe is a massive poetry publisher that continues to do some of the best publishing of poetry in the UK. You will find poets like Kamau Brathwaite, Jack Mapanje and Aime Cesaire on their list. Nonetheless, the Black British presence is strikingly small[10]. Their boom time for publishing Black poets was in the 90s. These days Bloodaxe seem to have joined the ranks of other poetry concerns as regards to publishing Black poets. In the past few years, Peepal Tree Press, seem to have taken the helm and published Dorothea Smartt, and two Asian women poets resident in Britain, Jeanne Ellin and Raman Mundair and are scheduled to publish Rommi Smith later in 2005.

The other publishing houses that have any Black British voices tend to have one token representative. Chatto and Windus has published most of Fred D'Aguiar's collections, but he remains the sole Black British poet whom they publish. Jonathan Cape published *Turner* by David Dabydeen.[11] Since then, Dabydeen has published a number of novels with that imprint. Cape has no other Black British poet on their lists although the imprint has shown itself to be very faithful to those in its stable – producing attractive, high quality and well-designed books for such poets as Michael Longley, Sarah Maguire and Don Patterson. The Canongate imprint, Payback Press, sought to capitalise on the popularity of the performance scene when it started by publishing two of its accomplished exponents, Lemn Sissay and Patience Agbabi.[12] The announcement of the publication of dynamic and innovative performer, Michelle Reed for a new title was a welcoming one for Black British poets to hear – but since the closing of their distinctive list, both the poet herself and their innovative moves forward appear – like all innovative performance poetry – to have gone underground.

Of the other major independents, Faber, and Carcanet, and imprints such as Picador, none have recent titles by Black British poets. Carcanet published a special *Selected Poems* by Lorna Goodison, a Canada-based Jamaican poet of international standing. Picador recently published the first UK poetry publication by

Pulitzer Prize winning African American poet Yusef Komunyakaa and Payback, before they quietly dissolved published Sapphire.[13] I mention these publications to indicate that many of these publishers are not averse to publishing work by Black authors. The trend is to publish writers with well-established reputations, and, more often than not, international authors. Archie Markham has a recent title with Anvil[14]. Penguin's imprint Hamish Hamilton published the novel-in-verse, *The Emperor's Babe*,[15] of poet and fiction writer, Bernardine Evaristo, who began her career as a poet with Peepal Tree Press[16] and then moving to a fledgling Black British press, Angela Royal Publishing. After the publication of the narrative poem, *Lara*, by Evaristo, they did not publish another collection of poetry and after publishing only a few titles, subsequently decided to close its doors.[17] Evaristo's two book deal with Penguin is however as a fiction writer, despite her work to date being 'novels-in-verse'. Dorothea Smartt, a very successful performer on the performance poetry scene, published her first collection with Peepal Tree Press[18] and there joined Mark de Brito and Andrew Jefferson Miles both complex poets based in the UK. Miles, is a Guyanese poet, novelist and visual artist who graduated from the prestigious University of East Anglia with a PhD in Creative & Critical Writing. None of these would remotely be called performance poets.[19] Peepal Tree, however, has largely devoted itself to publishing Caribbean titles and only recently, began to develop its 'Black British' list. Chris Abani, also a very successful poet published his first and critically successful collection with Saqi Books in 2001.[20] James Berry, the senior Black British poet, marked his 70th birthday with the re-publication of his title, *Hot Earth, Cold Earth* with Bloodaxe Books but a new title, *Only One Me* appeared with MacMillan (a children's book in 2004).[21] Merle Collins published her collection with Peepal Tree Press as her previous publisher Virago has since been swallowed up by Time Warner and no longer publish poetry. A foundling publisher, Flipped Eye Publishing, operated by performance poet and writer Nii Ayikwei Parkes published *Suitcase*, by the popular Trinidadian born /UK performance poet Roger Robinson in October 2004; Grenadian born Maureen Roberts published her first collection, *My GrandMother Sings To Me*, with Bogle L'Ouverture Press in 2003; Grace Nichols published her last collection with Virago almost 10 years ago, and these, to a large extent, round off the Black British poets who have been published in the UK in the last decade.

Sissay, Smartt, and Agbabi, began their careers as noted performance poets in the late 1980s/early 90s. In other words they are not exactly new faces. A number of Black British poetry voices have had significant mainstream success as authors of books for children. Most notable of these is Valerie Bloom whose publisher list includes Henry Holt, Bloomsbury, Trans Atlantic Press, Macmillan, Cambridge Press and Bogle L'Ouverture. John Agard, James Berry, Benjamin Zephaniah and Grace Nichols have all published extensively with major children's publishing houses in the UK and have developed quite strong reputations as editors of a number of anthologies for children.

Despite what appears to be a quite busy listing of publications, there is little question that there is relatively little adult Black British poetry being published today. More importantly, the publishing world does not reflect the kind of activity that is going on in poetry among Black British writers. It is easy to see the activity in the performance scene where at venues like Apples and Snakes, and in clubs in and around London, and increasingly in Manchester, Black poets perform their work before receptive audiences. Less conspicuous, but equally important, are the many Black poets who attend and teach workshops and run courses by the Arvon Foundation, the Poetry School and those others run by the various literature development projects, libraries and community centres across the UK (some, with a specific remit to work with Black writers). I meet them at readings, at workshops and at performances around the country. They are writing, but they are also faced with the daunting anxiety that there is no publisher that will pay attention to their work.

The natural answer has been to encourage the establishment of a press devoted to Black British titles. At least two existed in the past. New Beacon published a number of poets for some years. They worked with the old rubric of migrant writing and to a large extent focused on Caribbean authors. By the time the new dispensation in Black British identity had become the norm, eclipsing, in the process, the migrant model, New Beacon seemed to have lost some of its relevance and energy. The press is, for all intents and purposes, no longer a viable one. The name, primarily associated with the bookstore, is publishing it's first title for many years (with funding support), a historical tome chronicling the years of the International Book Fair of Radical Black and Third World Books, that was so successful at encouraging new poets to come forward – as well as creating the rare opportunity for Black poets writers and activists globally to meet and exchange in a shared space. Bogle L'Ouverture has for nearly thirty years published some of the most important Black poetry to appear in the UK including the early work of Linton Kwesi Johnson and Lemn Sissay. The press, however, ably run by Jessica and Eric Huntley, has published only a modest number of titles each year and struggles in a publishing environment that can be quite taxing on independent houses.

The problem, of course, has everything to do with the business of poetry. Poetry is said to pay very little and to generate such minuscule revenues that for any press to survive it must turn to fiction. And this, I suspect, lies at the heart of the poetry establishment's failure to embrace the spirit of diversity that seems to want to take hold in Britain. Poetry publishing can boast of being pure, publishing not because of the financial possibilities attached to the work, but because of the editor's conviction about the work's quality. Most publishers assume that quality will do the work of selling the few copies that need to be sold for the press to stay buoyant. There is also the related fact that a significant percentage of poetry editors are also themselves poets. This means that their investment in publishing what they deem as 'good' tends to make them far more subjective in their choices about what is to be published. Most do not publish their own work, but they are not averse to making exchange 'arrangements' with other editors. This happens enough to leave one with the distinct impression that the poetry community is a small and sometimes incestuous one. At the very least we are left with the sense that editors are in the business of publishing work that is like their own work.

Perhaps this is what British poetry is suffering from; a homogenisation of poetic style. Any difference in tone, style, scope and ambition in poetic practice tends to come from translations of international writers, from the reprinting of classical (read older, canonical) texts or from the publication of non-British (primarily American) poets writing in English. The main poetry presses, and larger houses that publish poetry, perhaps with the exception of Bloodaxe, tend to reveal a sameness of taste that is now passing as the essence of good modern verse. Arch lyricism defines the style, restrained irony defines the tone, and an understated demonstration of the ability to write in meter and some western formal style defines the formal practice. It is not that we are being overwhelmed by sonnets and villanelles, but we are always being reminded that the Eliot/Yeats/

Auden devotion to form is the hallmark of British modernism and it constitutes a quality that must shape the work that is being published. Exuberance, sensationalism, a profusion of language play and a heady enjoyment of the richness of colour and texture of language are all features that we will not see in the work of the poets who are published by these houses. The poetry that dominates these houses is always terse, brief and deeply aware of the need to reveal some classical grounding. These classical groundings have to be western and must include the myths that haunted Shakespeare, Chaucer, Byron, and, of course, (Ted) Hughes. Tobias Hill, a Faber poet in an interview with reporter Michael Reckford when he visited Jamaica in December 2002, identified what he called the traditional trend in British poetry as the "popular, lyric form; the other the more private and courtly." He claimed to be more inclined to the "private" tradition in his own work.[22] Although I suspect that most people looking at the limited range of contemporary British poetry would be hard pressed to make as fine a distinction as he makes.

No doubt, many will rise up to dispute this blatant generalisation with a selection of epic book-length poems, and work that seems to enjoy excursions away from the normal fare. But I am generalising here in ways that speak to trends and inclinations. There is, clearly, nothing wrong with the style of poetry of this orthodoxy – it represents a commitment to the lyrical voice and a neo-formal quality that has produced some fine poetry in the past and continues to bring us poetry of the highest order. But the tendency represents an orthodoxy that should be worrisome. There is a sameness here that is driven not by some diabolic quest for orthodoxy, but by something more dangerous – an accepted sense of *taste*. And this idea of taste is strengthened by the conviction that these editors are making their decisions entirely on the basis of aesthetic *quality*.

We will, of course, never hear this orthodoxy spoken of in terms of culture and race – that would be too controversial. But we will hear about 'tradition' and about the need to maintain this tradition. Indeed, it becomes difficult to distinguish the devotion to tradition from a devotion to cultural identity that is rooted in issues of race. I have heard a few of these editors attempting to justify why they are not likely to publish the work of performance poets, for instance. They say that while they acknowledge that such work is interesting and has its place, it is not quite in the taste of their own publishing enterprise. Some go as far as to argue that since they are *book* publishers who publish book poets, they see performance poets as people who 'publish' on the stage and in performance and hence do not need to publish in books. Often this language cloaks a failure to appreciate the complexity of the work that is being wrongly reduced to the term 'performance poetry.' There is a failure, in other words, to make a distinction between a poet like Jean 'Binta' Breeze and Benjamin Zephaniah. The truth is that these are quite different poets with very distinctive poetic antecedents and influences.

Some publishers, as earlier noted, have published performance poets, hinting that they may be open to other styles poetry. Yet one cannot shake the impression that when socalled performance poets are actually published, they are done so largely because of the promise of their money-making potential – their popularity – and not their aesthetic strength. Much of the promotion surrounding these publications focuses on their 'performance' history even when, as is the case, for example, with Jean 'Binta' Breeze or John Agard, their collections are not distinguished only or most significantly by their connection to 'performance'.

A more troubling consequence of these trends is that they lead to a tendency to lump performance poets and Black poets as one entity. Because many Black poets find their most receptive venues to be in the so-called performance spaces they are often inextricably linked to the performance scene. Black poets (book or not) tend to read at venues where a Black audience is in attendance. And so the assumption arises that such poets are performance poets. But the problem is more complex than that. Many poets whose poetic instincts emerge out of the tradition of Caribbean poetry, African poetry, post-colonial poetry, African American poetry mixed in with a strong understanding, even if a conflicted relationship with traditional western forms, tend to regard the poem as a largely oral form – a form that ultimately finds meaning in the idea of performance. Consequently, they are strong performers of their poetry. Because of their ability to bring their poems to life, they are so easily labelled performance poets. Poets like Kamau Brathwaite, Lorna Goodison, John and Amiri Baraka, are all remarkable 'readers' of their work who regard the reading as a place of performance; yet it would be absurd to regard these people as 'performance poets' in the reductive way that the term is used in Britain, today. Those who do such labeling are actually showing a profound failure of imagination and critical discourse in trying to speak to the complexity of poetry that does not easily fall into the traditional western models. 'Performance poetry' becomes an easy way to categorise this work.

The fact, however, is that these poets are as devoted to the idea of publishing as they are to reading their work. They do not speak of performance as merely the act of stepping on stage to read or recite, but see the performance of language, sound, rhythm and rhetoric as elemental to the poem as it appears on the page. A poem's 'performability' enhances its presence on the page and it is informed by features of poetry that all poets tend to value and celebrate. For many poets, the poem is actually 'performing' on the page. The published poem is not merely a transcription of a performance. What I fear is that many editors are either not aware of this or are not convinced that there is something aesthetically profound about the work of these poets.

Thus, if we accept the idea that the current publishing establishment will not change and welcome Black voices, and if we then choose to encourage the path of establishing a press devoted to Black British poetry, will the process of ghettoisation be inevitable? This path has been taken by a number of notable presses in the United States. In 1967 Third World Press was formed by Haki Madhubuti in direct response to what was quite clearly an apparent lack of interest in African American writers by major U.S. publishers[23]. The press has continued to launch the careers of many African American poets and remains committed to its task of celebrating the work of African American authors. There are a number of such poetry houses in the United States that offer an interesting model. What is clear in the U.S. is that these houses continue to serve an important need, even as major houses are publishing African American poets. Many have argued that it is the success of presses like Third World Press that raised the profile of African American poets, winning, in the process, the respect and attention of major publishing houses.

A Black publishing house, it is assumed, will appreciate the variety of poetic work emerging from Black culture and make a concerted effort to nurture good Black poets. With Black editors and acquisitions staff, this house would be unique in the contemporary British landscape. It would make the business of publishing a part of the culture of the Black British poet. By first wooing major, established Black voices to the house, the house would be able to establish its credibility. It would sponsor poetry competitions and work with agencies to establish strong mentoring systems that seek out and nurture good Black poetry. It is, of course, a lovely vision, but it could, quite easily, become a force that perpetuates the notion of difference. Those who advocate this argue that the current publishing world is uninterested in expanding its parameters because its constituency is small and it lacks the funding to do better. They argue, therefore that such a house is simply a response to an untenable situation. They also argue that this new house would demonstrate that treated with respect and with a care for proper promotion and design values that emerge out of the culture of Black Britain, the house would provide a model of how viable Black British poetry can be.

Those who resist such a proposition fear that a house of this nature would not be taken seriously by the establishment. They also fear that a poet who is published by such a house would be seen as one who simply was not good enough for the major houses. Because of our natural reluctance to presume racism about any decisions made in larger society, few would be willing to accept the idea that something, other than aesthetic considerations, might be responsible for the failure of Black writers to make it into the major houses. Poets would be concerned that such a house would target only a Black audience – to them a disturbing prospect given the numerically small demographics of Blacks in the country and of poetry lovers in the country.[24]

For these people, the model of organisations such as Spread the Word, Cultureword and the Centreprise Literature Development Project, and other community based arts is more appealing. National literary organisations such as The Arvon Foundation, the Royal Literary Fund and a regional programme, 'Inscribe', attached to Peepal Tree Press have created mentoring arrangements that pair fledgling authors with established authors with the hope that this personal contact will lead to publication as the work of the "mentee" improves. Inscribe in fact, intends to set up an imprint of Peepal Tree Press and publish chapbooks by writers of African and Asian descent that go through it's programme of professional development. It is conceivable that a more proactive approach to nurturing the work of Black poets could be embarked upon by various publishing houses.[25]

Such a programme would require editors to attend poetry readings that feature these poets. Small, independent press already do this, and those like Nii Parkes of Flipped Eye Publishing do what others must do, and that is to be willing to explore the traditions that give shape to these writers. Publishers may have to recognise that there is a wide range of fascinating and complex poetic styles that operate in the world and that these styles are subject to the strictest and most sophisticated of aesthetic expectations. All of this would assume that these publishing houses are interested in stylistic expansion. They would certainly have to be interested in expanding their readership. This is proactive approach that has already shown can prove rewarding. Does this constitute some kind of special treatment for 'minority' writers? It does. It presumes that for the most part these writers do not have as much access to informal mentoring relationships that other writers have.

Regardless of which path is taken, it seems to me that something has to happen. Indeed, a combination of the two would be the ideal course of action. In London and around the country a significant number of Black artists are trying to make a living as poets. They are performing their work, but they are also completely devoted to the business of writing poetry. They are, as a result, finding ways to hone their skills through workshops, and through the tough and unforgiving world of performance. There is a great deal to be said about the pressure to be fresh and risky in poetic expression in the live context – a pressure that many so-called page poets do not have to contend with and whose work suffers because of that lack of a sense of audience and community. Poets like Malika Booker, Roger Robinson, Jacob Sam-la Rose, Janet Kofi Tsekpo, and Zena Edwards, among so many others are in fact charting interesting paths in the writing of poetry and all of them remain diligent students of what one would call 'traditional' poetry even as they explore ways to find their distinctive voices that have been shaped by other aesthetics. British poetry would be a far more exciting place if these poets were published. The very supportive mechanism that has operated in the nurturing of writing of poets like Lavinia Greenlaw, Selima Hill, Simon Armitage and Robin Roberston should be afforded to these poets by loyal houses like Bloodaxe, Faber and Picador.

Since there appears to be no guarantee of the kind of nurturing and support that I have spoken about above from the current main poetry publishing houses, I am coming to the gradual realisation that a great deal of work has to be done by Black British poets themselves to begin to bring about some changes. The last time that I was in London, for Poetry International, in 2002, I was lured into a surprise affair for three poets that I have come to admire a great deal in the UK. A collective of poets wanted to thank their mentors for giving them a space to work, to develop their writing and to see hope in the business of writing poetry. The collective is called Malika's Kitchen, named for Malika Booker, a poet and playwright who opened her kitchen to writers to have informal poetry workshops. Fifteen people gathered in a basement restaurant in Soho to toast Malika Booker, Jacob Sam La Rose and Roger Robinson for the leadership of the group. They were tricked into coming to a meeting with me. The surprise was wonderful and effective. As I listened to the praise being given to these poets, all of whom I knew were not only busy, but going through the frustrations of trying to make a living as poets in the UK, I was reminded of the African American project Cave Canem – an organisation established by leading Black poets in the U.S. to nurture Black writers and to offer a venue for their work to be supported by mentors, fellow poets and teachers, Cave Canem boasts the participation, support and sponsorship of ALL the top Black poets in the US. They have an annual week-long workshop, they have readings, they have developmental seminars, they establish mentoring arrangements, they establish important links with mainstream publishing and arts-driven associations, they now run a prestigious writers contest, and they have established themselves as one of the premier poetry organisations in the country because of the manner in which the have connected the young writers with the older established ones.[26] Malika's Kitchen shares the spirit of Cave Canem because it has grown out of the realisation that Black British poets will have to find mechanisms to nurture strong poetry. Yet Malika's Kitchen is still a fledgling group that has not yet expanded its vision to have the impact it can. To do so it will need funding and it will need the support of some of the more successful Black British poets and people interested in supporting the art in the UK.

As I sat in that restaurant, I began to imagine a group that created a venue for Linton Kwesi Johnson, Fred D'Aguiar, John Agard, Grace Nichols, James Berry, Archie Markham, Jean Binta Breeze, Jackie Kay, Bernardine Evaristo, to sit and dialogue with Malika Booker, Janet Kofi Tsekpo, Roger Robinson, Dorothea Smartt, Zena Edwards and the many poets who are now just beginning to give shape to their craft. The exchange of ideas about craft, about publishing, about performance, about multiple traditions would profoundly alter the position of Black British poetry today.

I realise that this is something of a dream, but I also realise that I have offered, in these three dreams a model for the future for Black British writing. It is clear that I believe that the young poet that I began this piece with will only be free to explore what it means to be a Black British poet when she works in an environment that takes seriously the variety, range and complexity that exists in Black British poetry. As with Hughes' poet, her quarrel is ultimately not with herself or her values but with the world that forces her to have to make a statement like the one that she makes. Hughes suggested self-pride, an appreciation of one's culture and a devotion to celebrating that culture, but I add to that the need to try and change the world that has made things so difficult for the Black British poet to freely create powerful art.

I have chosen to talk about systemic problems and to try and offer models of how to address these problems. I could have written a moving appreciation of ten of the leading Black poets writing in Britain today and made the case for their work to be given greater attention. I could have chosen that path, but I would not be addressing what I regard as some of the more vexing challenges that face the Black British poet today. I hope that these ideas will at least get us thinking about what can be done to give greater voice to the work of Black British poets.

NOTES AND REFERENCES

[1] Hughes, Langston, 'The Negro Artist and the Racial Mountain' in Gates, Henry L. and McKay, Nellie (eds). *Norton Anthology of African American Literature* (New York: Norton 1997) p.1267, originally appeared in *The Nation* (1926) in response to George S. Schuyler's essay "The Negro-Art Hokum", which was printed in *The Nation* the week before

[2] Examples of such can be found in, Hoyles and Hoyles, *Moving Voices: Black Performance Poetry* (London: Hansib 2002). It includes a CD of twelve performance poets such as Jean Binta Breeze, Valerie Bloom, Adisa, Cuban Redd and Patience Agbabi

[3] By Black I am referring here almost entirely to writers of African descent who live and work in the UK

[4] *Inglan is a Bitch*. London: Race Today, 1980. p.26

[5] Dawes, Kwame, "Dichotomies of Reading 'street poetry' and 'book poetry'" *Critical Quarterly* 38:4 (3-20)

[6] ACE London recently put out a tender for research into career opportunities for Black and Asian poets with the outcome expected to be announced in the autumn of 2005

[7] I make this distinction because for a long time the only commonly accepted Black presence in British writing was that of the "immigrant" author whose very presence was defined by the idea of otherness, where otherness represented alien and foreign. I explore this theme in an article, "Negotiating the Ship on The Head: Black British Fiction." *Wasafiri*, No. 29 Spring 1999

[8] URL http://www.poetrylibrary.org.uk

[9] It is readily acknowledged that this would be economically unviable, since most of Britain's poetry press receive some financial support, to run as an ongoing concern, including those mentioned such as Bloodaxe, Carcenet and Anvil. There are Black publishers though devoted exclusively to Black and Asian authors who publish some poetry, the most vibrant of all, possibly being Peepal Tree Press

[10] See the very attractive and well-designed Bloodaxe website for details about these writers at URL http://www.bloodaxebooks.com/default.asp

[11] Although Dabydeen is Indo-Caribbean, however his own work has been involved with negotiating the implications of Caribbean "creole" identity which engages Africa and Indian heritages. I include him here also because West Indian writers, whether of African or Indian descent have generally devolved into 'Black British' writers

[12] Payback Press was an imprint of Canongate that developed a strong list of general titles on hip-hop and African American culture. It was a cutting edge press that added Sissay and Agbabi largely because of their power as performers and their hip credentials. http://www.canongate.net/payback/pbp.taf

[13] *Scandalize My Name*, London, 2002

[14] Markham, E. A. *A Rough Climate*, (London: Anvil Press 2002)

[15] Evaristo, Bernardine, *Lara*, was also published by Viking, New York in 2002

[16] Evaristo, Bernardine, *Island of Abraham*, (Leeds: Peepal Tree Press, 1995)

[17] Angela Royal Publishing, Tunbridge Wells, Kent. The company was started by Angela Royal and published nine titles before she decided to take up a job at War on Want. She had previously worked in the publishing industry for about 15 years

[18] Smartt, Dorothea, *Connecting Medium*, (Leeds: Peepal Tree Press, 2002)

[19] Jefferson-Miles, Andrew, *Art of Navigation,* (Leeds: Peepal Tree Press, 2002)

[20] Abani, Chris, Kalakuta Republic, (London: Saqi, 2001)

[21] Berry, James, *Hot Earth, Cold Earth,* (Newcastle-upon-Tyne: Bloodaxe, 1995)

[22] Michael Reckord, "British writer Tobias Hill visits Jamaica," *Sunday Gleaner*, December 1, 2002

[23] Everod, Kevin Quahsie et al, (eds.) *New Bones, Contemporary Black Writers in America,* "Haki Madhubuti (1942-)" (New York: Prentice Hall, 2001) p.682

[24] According to the National statistics website http://www.statistics.gov.uk http://www.statistics.gov.uk/cci/nugget.asp?id=764 the 2001 census showed there were a total of 2.0% of Black people that made up the British population. This figure includes those who considered themselves as of Caribbean extraction, 1%; African extraction; 0.8%; Black other 0.2%

[25] Since the production of an the decibel/Arts Council/*Bookseller* report, In Full Colour which looked into the diversity issues in mainstream publishing houses in Britain, some of them, and important in this case, notably Faber, have set up 'positive action' trainee programmes. Faber were noticeably the only poetry publisher to be present at the launch of the report during the London International Bookfair in 2004. Ravi Mirchandani, the publisher of Heinemann, is the only figure of Black or Asian descent in a major firm to hold a senior editorial position

[26] "Cave Canem is committed to the discovery and cultivation of new voices in African American poetry. Beginning as an all-volunteer effort in 1996, Cave Canem has moved swiftly to become a non-profit organization with a fulltime director and an active Board, funded through individual donations and foundation and government grants. The programme has expanded from a summer retreat to include regional workshops, a first book prize, annual anthologies, and readings and events in major cities around the United States. They are a national community of emerging and established poets, a family of Black writers who create, publish, perform, teach, and study poetry, and support each others' work... In 1996 poets Toi Derricotte and Cornelius Eady began a weeklong summer workshop/retreat designed to counter the under-representation and isolation of African American poets in writers' workshops and literary programs. From the beginning, Cave Canem has offered a safe haven for Black poets – whether schooled in MFA programs or poetry slams – to come together to work on their craft and engage others in critical debate" http://www.cavecanempoets.org/

(Re)Turning to Africa: Bernardine Evaristo's *Lara* and Lucinda Roy's *Lady Moses*

Pilar Cuder-Domínguez

In a short but comprehensive account of Black British arts in the last twenty years, Gail Low makes the claim that, "'Black British' is concerned, on the one hand, with the nation-state as an imagined political and social entity, granting citizenship and residency rights, and, on the other hand, with histories of migrancy and settlement."[1] The two novels under discussion in this essay, Bernardine Evaristo's *Lara* (1997) and Lucinda Roy's *Lady Moses* (1998), fall squarely inside the limits of Low's categorisation of Black British. Their protagonists are the product of mixed-race marriages, an English mother and a West African father that came to Britain in the 1950s. In both novels there is an exploration of what it means to grow up Black in Britain in the 1960s and 1970s, which fundamentally entails coming to terms with the meaning of 'home' (geographically, racially, and culturally speaking). This is an issue that Kwame Dawes has pinpointed as central to the concerns of the younger generation of Black British writers:

> They are contending with the 'homeness' of Britain. It is an uncomfortable contention and one that does not always lead to the same conclusion, but it begins at the same fundamental place: we are citizens in this country, some of us were born here, have lived her all or most of our lives; this is home. Why does it not feel like home? Where then is home? Should we look here or elsewhere? What does it mean that this home does not feel like home?[2]

What this means for the novels of Evaristo and Roy is a turn to Africa for clues that is also, metaphorically, a *re*-turn, since the characters' physical and psychological journey of self-discovery traverses Africa as the location where they must piece together their paternal heritage.

The historical and geographical links of the stories are conveyed by means of the structure of both works. This is most evident in

Lady Moses, which is divided into three sections, named after their respective locations: London, the New World, and Lunama. The whole plot can be read as an extended flashback whose starting point is Jacinta Moses's taking stock of her life on the death of her mother Louise. Her experiences thus have to be understood in the context of these three major identity formations, British, American, and African, which in turn need to be read in the light of major events of Black history, most clearly the triangular trade.

As a novel in verse (or else a long narrative poem), *Lara*'s plot would seem to the reader to be comparatively less linear and more rambling[3]. Yet, it ultimately ties in with African slavery, since the ancestors of the protagonist's father are freed Brazilian slaves who migrated to Nigeria. The prologue is set in 1844 and the epilogue in 1995, with sections in between that roughly follow in chronological order from the 1930s to the 1990s, only to turn back again to the past (1931, 1839, 1946). This lack of linearity is meaningful in itself, for it suggests the fractures and instability of a subjectivity based on diaspora. As Roy's character asserts in *Lady Moses*: "Sometimes I think all people of colour feel like that – as if the words have already been written and the story always runs backward, to pain."[4] Ultimately however, the protagonists must always fall back on a point of origin that is less mythical and closer to them, the historical encounter of their parents in London.

In order to highlight the stages of the characters' psychological journey as well as the novels' aesthetic and political statements, I have divided this essay into three parts. First 'Interracial Transgressions', then 'A Little Coloured Girl in South London' and 'Becoming a Woman of Color.' In the first, I would like to consider the way that these writers have cast the transnational relationships that birthed them. Next, Jacinta Moses's musing on her own development, that she describes as going from a little coloured girl to a woman of colour,[5] has provided the headings for the second and third sections. They dwell on the problematics of growing up bi-racial in London and the insights to be gained from the representation of African and African American models of Black identity side by side with British mixed-race characters.

1. INTERRACIAL TRANSGRESSIONS.

Lara manages to convey a fair amount of detail concerning the boundaries of crossracial relations in post-war London, even though they are scattered throughout the different sections of this verse novel[6]. Evaristo sympathetically portrays the young Nigerian migrant Taiwo, who comes with a scholarship to "paradise," and who instead meets people who call him "sambo," "nigger," or "darkie." Most remarkably, these prejudices come not just from the white community, those who "are frightened or angry or cross the road"[7] when he greets them, but also from West Indians who want to know if Africans "still live in trees in the bush." As a result, Taiwo undergoes a process of racialisation in Britain. As he accurately concludes: "In this country I am coloured. Back home I was just me."[8]

Lara's mother Ellen, is the youngest in a working class family of Irish and German descent with middle class aspirations. Pivotal to the family's ethnic history are the two world wars. The Great War pushed the German Wilkenigs to hide behind the façade of an English surname, Wilkins. The Second also brought about a protective move, as Ellen's aunt Dora and her Jewish husband Heini seek ethnic invisibility in the quietly 'normal' middle-class suburban life of the 1950s. Interestingly, Heini and Dora are most determinedly set against the cross-racial marriage of Ellen and Taiwo. It is Heini himself who "explained the vices of racial mixing, the ostracization/ the children who'd inherit the weaknesses of both races,/ who'd bleach their skin white like the American negroes."[9]

Miscegenation is indeed represented in the white characters' voices as most abhorrent. Ellen's position is perceived by mainstream society as an extreme form of transgression, a sin against her race. Ellen's mother Edith graphically conveys the unnaturalness she perceives in the relationship with the image of "chocolate sauce on cod,"[10] though Evaristo takes good care to deflate it later by providing a rendering of Ellen and Taiwo's lovemaking where both voice their pleasure and fulfilment in each other.[11] On hearing of her son marrying a white woman, Taiwo's mother also expresses her unhappiness, but it never goes beyond a mild reminder that "There are plenty nice Nigerian girls here!"[12]

Lucinda Roy is less specific in her portrayal of the interracial couple, Louise Buttercup and Simon Moses. No relatives of either race make an appearance in the novel, and no indication of how the intermarriage was received is given. Instead, Roy delineates a very successful though short-lived relationship, so much so that Louise finds it difficult to carry on living after Simon dies. Their personal happiness drew a magic circle around their small family, that kept them safe and out of racist harm. But as the white single mother of a mixed race child, Louise must endure a much harder life, and several years later she suffers a nervous breakdown. To their child Jacinta, her parents' transracial marriage implies a double weight, that of a troubled racial identity and that of the idealised happiness she can never reproduce either for her widowed mother or, later on, for herself.

2. 'A LITTLE COLOURED GIRL' IN SOUTH LONDON.

Bernardine Evaristo's *Lara* and Lucinda Roy's *Lady Moses* display many common features in their depiction of the upbringing and coming of age of girls of mixed parentage in South London in the 1960s and 1970s. Their mixed background sets them apart in a society where there were relatively few Black people, and interracial couples were stigmatised by both Blacks and whites. Both Evaristo and Roy stress the distinctiveness of the girls by endowing them with strongly symbolic names. Evaristo's Lara is short for Omilara, meaning, 'the family is like water', while Roy's Jacinta (variously shortened to Jass, Jassie, or Cinta) is named after her rebellious aunt, a wild woman who was "the first of [her] father's family to venture out beyond the village and try to discover what was on the other side."[13] Water is indeed important in Lara, for it surfaces again in the protagonist's surname 'da Costa' as well as in the family residence, Atlantico, not far from Woolwich. Rivers, coasts, seas and oceans are alluded to here and there in people's names and locations. They point to the rituals of arrival and departure, and collectively hint at transnational passages and overseas links. Similarly, Roy's choice of the family name "Moses" can hardly be innocent, for it has become a symbol of the quintessential migrant since Sam Selvon gave it to the protagonist of his groundbreaking novel *The Lonely Londoners*[14] in 1956. Moreover, it resounds with a Christian imagery that suggests incomplete travel and, ultimately, homelessness: "Could it be a curse being named after someone who never reached the land of his dreams? My father had borne that name for more than forty years. He hadn't been able to get back home either. Every so often, the fact of my name was troubling. I didn't want it to claim me"[15].

The girls grow up in a bi-racialised environment, and receive their education in a convent school that stresses rules and devotion. Catholicism is the filter through which they view the world, as did their forebears. Lara's mother Ellen, went from dreaming of becoming a missionary, "enlightening the dark continent", to marrying a Black man. As she muses: "I wanted to help Africa but Africa was brought to me!"[16] At her convent school, the nuns entreat Lara to "think of the starving children in Africa" whilst she eats her dinner[17].

Jacinta also absorbs the Catholic missionary creed to help the disadvantaged. When the thirteen-year-old girl is invited by her friend Alison to go and visit her in Jamaica, she wants to know if there are many poor people there so that she could do good works[18]. However, while for Evaristo Catholicism implies fear and punishment, for Roy it is above all an elitist and patronising creed, as embodied by Jacinta's snobbish mother. Louise may not be prone to racial prejudice but she is certainly class prejudiced, and looks down on those poorer and less educated than herself, like the white Beadycap family, who rent two rooms from the Moses women.

Family and friends make up a colourful mosaic around the two girls, though in this respect too, the writers' approach to mixed race experiences differs. Evaristo provides a lively picture of a large family held together by strict parental control. Except for the young generation Lara belongs in, like her Black cousin Beatrice, she is closest to her white family and white friends, though these relationships are far from easy. Some of Ellen's family disowned her when she married a Nigerian, and her own mother Edith only accepted the marriage after the birth of her first grandchild Juliana. Nevertheless, Edith finds it quite impossible to overcome her prejudices, and so she warns Lara that, if she goes to Nigeria, she will

> 'come back looking like a nigger-man, dear.'
> Ellen scolded her mother when Lara reported back.
> 'What have I said wrong?' Ellen protested, injured.
> 'She will if she's not careful.' Ellen crumpled up.
> 'She doesn't mean it.' She reassured Lara. 'It's her age.'
> Lara dissented, 'Not all old people are like that.
> Age has nothing to do with it'"[19].

The situation described here is similar to that suggested by recent research on transnational mothering in Britain. In *Transracial Mothering and Antiracism: The Case of White Birth Mothers of "Black" Children in Britain"*), Twine provides data concerning the difficulties of white birth mothers of African-descent children to deal with intrafamilial racism:

> A pattern of rejection by white grandparents emerged in the narratives of women from all class backgrounds. Working-class,

middle-class, and upperclass mothers all reported that they had struggled hard to find ways to negotiate their children's relationships with one or both of their white grandparents. Mothers described how their parents expressed their racism toward their African-descent grandchildren in a range of ways including (1) not mentioning the name of their grandchildren during phone calls or in writing; (2) declining to invite their grandchildren to visit their homes; (3) withholding all physical affection such as hugs and kisses; (4) avoiding spending any time with their grandchildren in public or private settings; (5) not providing emergency, temporary, or regular childcare; and (6) employing racist language in the presence of their grandchildren.[20]

Lara is found wanting by her white friends too, who ask her where she is from, originally, and who wonder if her father is from the jungle. As she approaches puberty, the white standards of beauty also fail her. She feels ugly with her "dark skin and wiry hair,"[21] and so she spends hours before a mirror trying to imagine herself blonde or redhaired. But neither is she Black enough according to her Black family's standards, as she sadly discovers when a distant cousin from Liverpool visits. Cousin Beatrice berates Lara for her naiveté, and despises her ignorance on Black issues, particularly on Black history. To Lara's claim that she is not Black, but half-caste, Beatrice replies with a savvy, "They don't care whether/ your mother's White, green or orange with purple spots / you're a nigger to them"[22]. Neither family nor friends can provide Lara with unproblematic support against outside racism of the kind she has to face when, in going out with her grandmother, people assume she is her grandmother's nurse[23], or when boys refuse to go with her to the disco because she is "a nig nog" and mimic a monkey in front of her.[24] The girl ends up stranded in between the two races and nations, neither white nor Black, neither English nor African: "I longed for an image / a story, to speak me, describe me, birth me whole / Living in my skin, I was, but which one?"[25]

Jacinta's close family is white too, although smaller and less conventional. Nothing is known of her mother's family except for Louise's reminiscences about an aunt paying for her wedding. Two white family friends remain close after the death of Simon Moses. Alfred Russell-Smythe rents rooms from them, and Ruskin Garland can be relied upon to help out when things are dire. Alfred, who is gay, becomes a kind of surrogate parent, tempering Louise's snobbish tendencies with his tender understanding. As an alternative gender role model, Alfred provides another view in regards to being different. He is the target of homophobic attacks just as Jacinta is the object of racist remarks, and with his brave acceptance of alterity, he stands out as the most nurturing presence in the novel. As an adult, Jacinta admits in a letter to him: "You taught me about the accident of gender and Simon taught me about the profundity of race."[26]

Lacking siblings, Jacinta is a lonely girl who keeps very much to herself. Nevertheless, she has a close Black friend, Alison Bean, whose African beauty she much admires. Quite unlike Lara, Jacinta grows with an awareness that 'Black is beautiful', and never tries to imagine herself other than she is. Moreover, she feels empowered by a friendship that protects her from those that call her names like "wog." Among those the Beadycap twins, Maurice and Mary, stand out. Though both families are similarly poor and disadvantaged, class and race prejudice keep them apart. The white twins look down on the mixed race child, while the latter flaunts her better education and marginally better housing situation.

Counteracting the white environment around the girls is the always present absence of Africa, embodied by their fathers. The two girls' early childhood has a constant African component which comes to an end rather abruptly. Lara's father Taiwo keeps silent about his country of origin, and the only clear connection for the da Costa children is their Daddy's Sunday dinner of "beef pepper stew and rice with optional gooey okra."[27] Lara, though, has her very own component in the form of "the Daddy people"; from a tender age Lara sees ghost-like people watch her and sometimes talk or sing to her in soft voices. However, Taiwo interprets this as Lara's overheated imagination, and punishes her severely, so that by the time she is seven years old Lara "called the Daddy people to her,/ said farewell, willed them away forever."[28]

Jacinta's life before her father's untimely death has everyday links to Africa. Simon Moses sings to her the songs he learned from his own mother, cooks stews with palm oil when there is money, and writes stories in which Jacinta rides an elephant. On her fifth birthday, he takes her to have her ears pierced because he claims "African girls in his village always had their ears pierced."[29] Moreover, the Moses' family home in Battersea often entertains Black visitors in this period:

> Men from Nigeria and Ghana, Sierra Leone and the Congo entered
> the small rooms bringing the land with them in their flowing robes

and embroidered hats. . . . Sometimes men and women from the West Indies would show up. If the Africans brought their land in their clothes, then the Jamaicans and Bajans brought it in their voices – island voices that sang rather than spoke.[30]

When Simon dies, Jacinta is cut off from her African heritage as effectively as Lara. The latter continues to quiz her father on Nigeria, but ends up frustrated and irritated by his unresponsiveness. Africa may recede in the distance, but as they grow up into adulthood, both of them attempt to reclaim their Africanness.

3. BECOMING 'A WOMAN OF COLO(U)R'.

The following stage in the two characters' search for an integrated identity involves heterosexual love relationships. Once more, the pattern of rejection remains in place for Lara. She learns to her cost that she is not African enough for her Nigerian boyfriend Josh. He finds her too white: "You're strictly/ a fish fingers and mash girl. You'll make a sorry wife."[31] Dejected, Lara enters a period of depression that she tries to fight by travelling across Europe with her friend Trish. By going abroad and in contrast to the manifold languages and nations they visit, they get a new perspective on their Britishness, and by the time they have reached the eastern end of the continent, both feel "more British, Trish and I, darker with the Turkish sun,/ yet less aware of race for we are simply: İngiltere."[32]

Unlike Lara, who runs head on towards the African identity she would like to fit into, Jacinta's first boyfriends are so ethnically diverse that Alfred, their gay lodger, claims she is dating the United Nations, although she avoids white Englishmen because they remind her of Maurice Beadycap. Like Lara, her restlessness takes her on European travels but they fail to bring her either peace or satisfaction. She eventually meets a white American man, Emmanuel (Manny) Fox, a student and a would-be writer, who sweeps her off her feet and promises to take her to the United States. On their wedding day, Jacinta has misgivings, wondering if her marriage is only due to her need "to escape the terror of a racist island full of Beadycaps and squalor."[33]

Roy's account of Jacinta's identity search spans several years in Virginia, where she falls out of love with her husband, starts writing, and gives birth to a daughter she calls Lady. The United States emerges as a powerful backdrop to these momentous private events.

Here, Jacinta feels free and empowered, first by the sheer breadth of the country and its natural beauty, and second by the accomplishments she witnesses within the African American community. On one occasion, as she was watching the skill of a professional basketball player at a game, Jacinta experienced an insight into Black power and Black beauty, and had a vision of the potential that she could live up to: "His profile looked familiar. And then I noticed the resemblance. My father had looked like that. [Lawrence] Helios must have come from West Africa. His ancestry was mine."[34] Once more, a character's name is endowed with mythical resonances. The sun in the African American name of the player ("Helios") functions as a powerful metaphor for African success, and highlights the multifaceted ways in which the African diaspora in the "New World" has thrived.

The third and final stage in Jacinta's psychological self-discovery takes place in West Africa, in an unnamed country that is probably, Sierra Leone. There she finally learns about her father's heritage and about herself as a bi-racial African woman. After a period of adaptation in which she lives insulated from the locals, she finally comes to realise that this is wrong:

> I could see our house way up on the top of Hill Station where
> white women had lived in houses built on stilts for more than a
> century; where white men had come to get away from the
> Blackness of the city. But I didn't know the city from up there.
> It was a distant thing – something I could escape from. I didn't
> ride in crowded poda-podas or eat potato-leaf soup and foo-foo.
> I lived White.[35]

Jacinta then leaves the city and starts a journey into the provincial areas, the 'heart' of the country that is very much part of her own heart. Possibly because she has a beginning as the result of a love relationship (between her mother Louise and her father Simon) strong enough to reach beyond the grave, many of her insights into race dynamics and race identity are framed as love events. It is on African soil that Jacinta finally has to face the unexpected reappearance of a demon from her past, Maurice Beadycap, successfully confronting him and overcoming the fear he inspires in her. Here too she decides to stop trying to make her marriage work although she stopped loving her husband long before, and last but not least, it is here that she falls in love again. It is no doubt significant that Jacinta's new choice is a Black man, John Turay, an African with a European education who can therefore share with her something of her past as well as her present. Although the husband very conveniently happens to die in a car crash, the new relationship is left on hold as Jacinta steers her life and her daughter's in a new direction. This time Jacinta escapes the romantic trap she had fallen into with Manny, that of believing in a man's power to rescue her from trouble, and instead chooses her autonomy and her relationship with her daughter over a new commitment with another man.

No less importantly, it is in the provinces that Jacinta manages to recapture her own Africanness, by regaining the ability to see herself once more as Jacinta-in-the-story, the little African girl who rode an elephant. Reclaiming her roots entails reconnecting with her long-lost father, and this happens when she manages to find some villagers who, though not closely related to Simon Moses, do remember him and embrace Jacinta and her daughter as family. Moreover, her romanticised stay in the area coincides with sightings of an elephant, extraordinary because they have become extinct due to increasing urbanisation. When she sees it, she is compelled to whisper her father's name, as if Simon had for a moment taken the animal's shape, thereby allowing her to envision herself anew. Jacinta's reclamation of her Africanness is thus effected and results in her empowerment.

Lara too, eventually travels to West Africa, though she shares her journey with her parents. It is in fact the cycle of life and death as witnessed in her own interracial family, that reminds her of her cultural bridges and therefore encourages her to search for her roots. Her white mother's mother, Edith, now deceased, is metaphorically reborn in her niece Iyabo ("Mother Returns"), thus named for her Caucasian features that would have made Edith so happy. Not much later, Lara is revisited by one of the "Daddy People," the ghost of her paternal grandmother calling her/them home. Evaristo thus traces Taiwo's re-appropriation of his past in Lagos, Nigeria, simultaneously with Lara's own painstaking process of self-search.

However, unlike *Lady Moses*, Evaristo's novel does not grant a father-daughter communion unless it is through the mediation of his ancestors, probably due to the lesser idealisation of the African parent in this novel. In fact, Lara-as-adult rather resents her father's patriarchal behaviour. Lara wakes up one night to the chorus of voices she used to hear as a child. The "Daddy People" have come to tell their own stories directly to a receptive listener that has long wished for them. Their distinctive voices trace the hard lives on the Brazilian *fazenda* where they were slaves, their emancipation and subsequent journey to West Africa, and how the da Costa men settled down in Lagos where they prospered. Lara's Yoruba grandmother Zenobia, talks to her of her loveless marriage to the much older Gregorio da Costa, and of the great love she had for her twin children, Taiwo and Kehinde.

Yet, Lagos is only one step in her journey of self-discovery. In the epilogue, Lara travels to Brazil alone, hoping to be able to call it home. This is the last door to the past, and once she closes it behind her, she is able to return to Britain and welcome the future, because "the past is gone, the future is transformation".[36]

CONCLUSIONS: BLACK BRITISH VERSUS AFRICAN AMERICAN

As described above, both novels emphasise the difficulties of being mixed race by adopting the literary format of the *bildungsroman*, or novel of development. The Black/White polarisation is the main issue the protagonists have to face in all the locations they visit. As Jacinta remarks:

> I hadn't thought enough about my mother's race and my own.
> I was mixed race; Louise Buttercup was white, my father was
> African. Yet I wasn't simply a bringing together of opposites, I
> was me. Distinct. A race apart... I wanted to know other people
> like myself. It would be a luxury to be with someone who
> understood what Blackness meant from a white perspective and
> what whiteness meant inside the dark.[37]

Most of the problems for the protagonists in the two novels stem from an essentialisation of race, the implicit understanding that races are pure and stable, instead of acquiring meaning in context. Because they have been raised by white birth mothers in significantly white environments and with middle class values, the two women find it painful to live in a society that racialises them as Black even if they see themselves as "half-white", as a young Lara innocently tells her cousin. This is what anthropologist Jayne O. Ifekwunigwe refers to as "compulsory blackness" in her groundbreaking study of métisse women in Britain, *Scattered Belongings*. Ifekwunigwe then puts forward the concept of "additive Blackness" as a healing process of racial reconciliation:

> I refer to the process of coming to terms with one's Blackness as both affirmative and as a source for social discrimination as "Additive blackness." That is, an individual must start with her or his familiar social foundation and build forward without having to sever ties with her or his often White English roots.[38]

Although this kind of reconciliation relates more to Lara's situation than with that of Jacinta's, the two novels offer fascinating insights beyond such Black/white polarisation and into multifaceted 'Black' identities. Throughout the two novels, Lara and Jacinta watch themselves in other mirrors, particularly in those provided by West Africans and African Americans. In Lagos, children shout the word "Oyinbo!" after Lara meaning "whitey!" In Lunama, the women at the market laugh at Jacinta when she says she is not white, and retort: "Black American, white American, what is different?"[39] Although the protagonists can and do embrace a mythical African essence, the material and cultural practices of contemporary West Africa remain alien to them. Neither can find a permanent home there, though both assert their willingness to return. Yet, their final destinations are different: Lara goes back to Britain, an island that she describes as tiny, sandwiched between continents, but a location that she can reclaim as a home of sorts.[40] Jacinta chooses the United States because to her Britain remains a stifling and narrowminded society, where she and her daughter lack the room to grow as human beings. Instead, African Americans represent an 'imagined community'[41] that, in their fusion of Western and African, of material privilege and racial pride, she can feel more comfortable in. The fact that Jacinta chooses an African American allegiance over its Black British counterpart is not surprising if one considers the powerful influence that African American theories and practices of Black self-representation have exerted for a long time over other Black diasporan constituencies. Thus, Bronwyn T. Williams has remarked on:

> The frequent reference by Black British writers, when recalling their youth, to the significance of African-American writers as

formative and liberating voices that contrasted with the educational system's emphasis on canonical white English writers. Phillips, Kureishi, and others such as Abdulrazak Gurnah all talk of the importance of discovering the work of writers such as Richard Wright and James Baldwin.[42]

Nevertheless, whether these characters opt for the United States or for Britain as the location for a hopeful future, both novels manage to convey a complex representation of the conflicting borders of a hybrid racial identity. Neither Evaristo nor Roy settle for simple solutions. Instead, they suggest the need for strategic negotiations. As Stuart Hall stated:

> There can ... be no simple "return" or "recovery" of the ancestral past which is not reexperienced through the categories of the present: no base for creative enunciation in a simple reproduction of traditional forms which are not transformed by the technologies and the identities of the present.[43]

NOTES AND REFERENCES

[1]   Low, Gail. "The Challenge of 'Black British'". *The European English Messenger* 11.2 (2000): 17-21. p.20

[2]   Dawes, Kwame. "Negotiating the Ship on the Head: Black British Fiction." *Wasafiri* 29 (1999): 18-24. p.19. Updated as Chapter 14 in this book.

[3]   Jonathan Brennan has argued that "for the mixed race writer, identity exists in a state of liminality, a site where a mixed race narrator negotiates and transforms identity, yet often these communities in which the writer negotiates attempt to overwrite multiple identities, to maintain limitations on both form and content. This intersection of restrictions on mixed race identity leads to the creation of new literary strategies by the authors and to newly formed syncretic narratives, perhaps even new languages" (Jonathan Brennan, ed. *Mixed Race Literature*. Stanford. Stanford University Press, 2002. P. 49). Brennan's statement can enlighten our understanding of Evaristo's creative use of narrative verse to interpellate racial identity in *Lara* as well as in her second novel, *The Emperor's Babe* (London: Hamish Hamilton, 2001). For further analysis of Evaristo's work see Patricia Murray, "Stories Told and Untold: Post-Colonial London in Bernardine Evaristo's *Lara*", *Kunapipi* 21.12 (1999): 38-47; and Pilar Cuder-Domínguez, "Ethnic Cartographies of London in Bernardine Evaristo and Zadie Smith", *European Journal of English Studies* 8.2 (2004), pp.173-88

[4]   Roy, Lucinda. *Lady Moses*. London: Virago, 1998. p.351

[5]   Ibid. p.5

[6]   Another interesting rendering of the Black experience and inter-racial relations in postwar London that comes to mind is Andrea Levy's recent *Small Island* (London: Headline Review, 2004)

[7]   Evaristo, Bernardine. *Lara*. Tunbridge Wells, Kent: Angela Royal Publishing, 1997. p.5

[8]   Ibid. p.4

[9]   Ibid. p.38

[10] Ibid. p.38

[11] Ibid. p.41

[12] Ibid. p.26

[13] Roy, Lucinda. *Lady Moses*. London: Virago, 1998. p.7

[14] Selvon, Sam. *The Lonely Londoners*. Harlow, Longman, 1985. First published 1956

[15] Roy, Lucinda. *Lady Moses*. London: Virago, 1998. p.36

[16] Evaristo, Bernardine. *Lara*. Tunbridge Wells, Kent: Angela Royal Publishing, 1997. p.8 and 10

[17] Ibid. p.55

[18] Roy, Lucinda. *Lady Moses*. London: Virago, 1998. p.92

[19] Evaristo, Bernardine. *Lara*. Tunbridge Wells, Kent: Angela Royal Publishing, 1997. p.84

[20] Twine, Frances Winddance. "Transracial Mothering and Antiracism: the Case of White Birth Mothers of 'Black' Children in Britain." *Feminist Studies* 25.3 (1999): 729-46. Electronic version http://lion.chadwyck .co.uk

[21] Evaristo, Bernardine. *Lara*. Tunbridge Wells, Kent: Angela Royal Publishing, 1997. p.78

[22] Ibid. p.74

[23] Ibid. p.85

[24] Ibid. p.68

[25] Ibid. p.69

[26] Roy, Lucinda. *Lady Moses*. London: Virago, 1998. p.311

[27] Evaristo, Bernardine. *Lara*. Tunbridge Wells, Kent: Angela Royal Publishing, 1997. p.53

[28] Ibid. p.54

[29] Roy, Lucinda. *Lady Moses*. London: Virago, 1998. p.28

[30] Ibid. p.12

[31] Evaristo, Bernardine. *Lara*. Tunbridge Wells, Kent: Angela Royal Publishing, 1997. p.90

[32] Ibid. p.97

[33] Roy, Lucinda. *Lady Moses*. London: Virago, 1998. p.188

[34] Ibid. p.224

[35] Ibid. p.286

[36] Evaristo, Bernardine. *Lara*. Tunbridge Wells, Kent: Angela Royal Publishing, 1997. p.139

[37] Roy, Lucinda. *Lady Moses*. London: Virago, 1998. p.300

[38] Ifekwunigwe, Jayne O. *Scattered Belongings: Cultural Paradoxes of "Race," Nation and Gender*. London: Routledge, 1999. p.186

[39] Roy, Lucinda. Lady Moses. London: Virago, 1998. p.268

[40] Evaristo is not alone in suggesting the powerful possibilities awaiting the returning Black British subject. Andrea Levy's protagonist Faith Jackson also returns to Britain equipped with the selfknowledge stemming from a visit to her ancestors' land, Jamaica (*Fruit of the Lemon*. London: Review, 1999)

[41] By "Imagined community" I am referring to Benedict Anderson's concept of the nation as the community their members can imagine themselves as being part of. (Anderson, Benedict. *Imagined Communities: Reflections on the Origin and Spread of Nationalism*. London: Verso, 1991)

[42] Bronwyn T. Williams. "'A State of Perpetual Wandering': Diaspora and Black British Writers." *Jouvert: A Journal of Postcolonial Studies* 3.3 (1999). http://social.chass. ncsu.edu/jouvert/v3i3/con33.htm (27 January 2002)

[43] Stuart Hall, "New Ethnicities", in Houston A. Baker, jr., Manthia Diawara, and Ruth H. Lindeborg, eds. *Black British Cultural Studies. A Reader* (Chicago: U of Chicago P., 1996), p.170

"We're All English Now Mate Like It or Lump It": The Black/Britishness of Zadie Smith's *White Teeth*

Tracey L. Walters

In his 1990 essay 'Writing from Black Britain,' Tim Brennan questioned, "In a land as literary as Britain, why are its Black writers invisible – at least as *British* writers?"[1]

Black writers in Britain have been rendered invisible mainly because most of the literature they produce is ushered into a separate canon distinct from the larger body of work produced by white writers. Typically the racial ancestry of the author, the themes and subject matter of the narrative and racial and cultural markers in the text are all accounted for when placing the literature of Black authors into a separate literary canon.

Every few years though, the literary establishment recognises a Black writer as British (Salman Rushdie, Beryl Gilroy, Hanif Kureishi to name a few). Zadie Smith is the latest Black and British writer to enter the British literary mainstream. Smith earned her "British" stripes after publishing her debut novel *White Teeth*,[2] a multicultural British novel that explores Britain's colonial past and post colonial present. The "British" identification of Smith's text led me to question what makes *White Teeth* British as opposed to Black British? Like other British novels the narrative addresses a number of significant issues pursuant to the Black British experience, such as post colonialism, double consciousness, racial oppression, and cultural hybridity. Despite the obvious similarities between this novel and others by Black writers, the literary establishment has elected to define *White Teeth* as British. Smith's text is considered British because like fellow Black and British-identified writer Hanif Kureishi, Smith refuses "to represent the Black experience in Britain as monolithic [and] self-contained...."[3] Where other Black writers have focused on life in Britain from a singular ethnic Black perspective (Anglo Indian, Anglo Caribbean, Anglo African), Smith's novel focuses on the complexity of the multiethnic *English* experience, which in the context of this novel is represented in a myriad of ways: Bengali, Jamaican, Jewish, and so on. Smith's multicultural novel also reforms the British novel as we know it for she presents us with an alternative discourse to address questions of identity and nationhood. Smith reveals that in today's postmodern millennial world, notions of ethnic and racial identity cannot be defined in terms of ancestry, language, or culture because the cultural hybridisation of English society has made concepts of ethnicity and race indeterminate.

A number of authors have written about the racial transformation of British society. Smith's text differs from others though because rather than focusing primarily on how the native and immigrant populations collide she investigates how the groups adapt to each other. Smith begins by showing us that the implementation of multicultural programming (in schools, the workplace, and other social institutions) is one example of how immigration has impacted the society, sometimes to the degree though that the native population's cultural traditions are overshadowed by the newly introduced customs and traditions of the immigrant. The narrative reveals that while Christmas and Easter were typically the only holidays observed in schools, in the spirit of inclusion today schools observe, "Christmas, Ramadan, Chinese New Year, Diwali, Yom Kippur, Hanukkah, the birthday of Haile Selassie, and the death of Dr. Martin Luther King."[4] The school's observance of this many religious holidays is a clear indication of England's move towards cultural diversity even at the expense of their own homogeny. Smith's treatment of multiculturalism differs from standard discussions concerning the effect of immigration. Other texts, especially Black British novels emphasise the racial tensions between Black and white Britons. In *Lara*,[5] a verse-novella about growing up bi-racial in Britain, Bernardine Evaristo describes the verbal assaults of the racist hate groups such as the National Front (NF) who routinely attacked Black families: "Late [19]74 the NF Juggernaut braked in our street, offloaded two teenage brothers at No 49, swastika tattoos, shaved heads, crombies, Union Jack braces. Our windows were smashed soon after, nothing new, my father spent my childhood chasing snot-picking gits who'd missiled our windows and flown down the alley."[6] In the *bildungsroman Every Light in the House Burnin'*,[7] Andrea Levy recounts the kind of racial epithets white children reserve for their Black friends in times of conflict:

"'You're not English-my dad said.' 'He said you come over with
all the other coons. You wanna go back – go back to where you
came from – Blackie....Nig nogs. You're all nig-nogs.'"[8]

Smith does not pretend that racism in England is obsolete. Racial
conflict also occurs in *White Teeth*. For example, when bi-racial Irie
Jones and her Bangladeshi friends bring their harvest festival gifts to
an old war veteran, they are insulted by the veteran who, while
reminiscing about his time in the Congo, says "the only way I could
identify the nigger was by the whiteness of his teeth" and that "there
certainly were no wogs [in the army] as I remember."[9] While the text
includes a number of other racial incidents, Smiths emphasis is on
the larger theme of "ethnicity as the shared problem of a diverse
citizenship…"[10] Throughout the novel Smith drives home the point
that we must move beyond familiar discussions of racism and
prejudice for although these behaviors exist, we should as Paul
Gilroy insists, "destroy raciology, transcend race, and liberate
humankind from race-thinking."[11] Smith persuades us to accept that
racial categories in Britain have transformed into alternative modes
of representation and therefore a new discourse is required to discuss
identity. The following description of a typical schoolyard
emphasises Smith's point that racial homogeneity is on the verge of
extinction:

This has been the century of strangers, brown, yellow, and white.
This has been the century of the great immigrant experiment. It is
only this late in the day that you can walk into a playground and
find Isaac Leung by the fish pond, Danny Rahman in the football
cage, Quang O'Rourke bouncing a basketball, and Irie Jones
humming a tune. Children with first and last names on a direct
collision course. Names that secrete within them mass exodus,
cramped boats and planes, cold arrivals, medical check ups. It is
only this late in the day, and possibly only in Willisden, that you
can find best friends Sita and Sharon, constantly mistaken for each
other because Sita is white (her mother like the name) and Sharon
is Pakistani (her mother thought it best – less trouble).[12]

The passage indicates then that racial mixing has become deeply
embedded and rooted in the society. Rather than simply focusing on
the cohabitation between Blacks and Whites, Smith forces us to
recognise that interracial unions have crossed racial *and* ethnic lines.

And thus in today's world, it is the immigrant who must recognise that their ethnic identities are in jeopardy. She writes:

> It makes an immigrant laugh to hear the fears of the nationalist, scared of infection, penetration, miscegenation, when this is small fry, peanuts, compared to what the immigrant fears – dissolution, disappearance. Even the unflappable Alsana Iqbal would regularly wake up in a puddle of her own sweat after a night visited by visions of Millat (genetically BB; where B stands for Bengaliness) marrying someone called Sarah (aa, where a stands for Aryan), resulting in a child called Michael (Ba), who in turn marries somebody called Lucy (aa), leaving Alsana with a legacy of unrecognizable great grandchildren (Aaaaaaa!), their Bengaliness thoroughly diluted, genotype hidden by phenotype.[13]

Alsana's fear that her family might loose their "Bengaliness" is somewhat exaggerated, but to some extent her concerns are valid. Smith questions how can one maintain an authentic ethnic identity in a culturally diverse society especially when you constantly adopt the cultural practices of others? Smith demonstrates that although in past times ethnic identity could be signified and maintained by cultural markers such as dress, food, specific cultural traditions or even language, today these distinctions are nebulous.

To highlight the murkiness of ethnic identity, Smith demonstrates how English speech, perhaps one of the more recognisable signifiers of Englishness, has become hybridised. *White Teeth* skillfully captures an array of vernaculars and dialects (Standard English, Cockney, Jamaican Patois, and Bengali) which are spoken by many of the country's inhabitants. Smith's appropriation of this polyglot of voices is unique. To underscore the hybridisation of the society Smith demonstrates that specific speech patterns are not relegated to a single ethnic group for Arabs speak with cockney accents and Jamaican patois is as likely to be spoken by a Bengali as it is to be spoken by an Englishman: For example, when playing a game of taxing, "whereby one lays claim...to items in a street that do not belong to you," Millat says "Cha, man! Believe, I don't want to tax dat crap," [invoking] the Jamaican accent that all kids, whatever their nationality, used to express scorn."[14] Linguistic differences are also indicated when Smith contrasts the characters dialects: Abdul-Mickey's coarse expletive ridden cockney accent, for example, is juxtaposed with Samad's gentleman like standard English vernacular:

"oi"

"Hello Mickey, how are you?"

"Same old, same old. But enough about me. What's the fucking
matter wiv you, mate? Eh? Eh? I've been watchin you, Sammy,
since the minute you stepped in here. Face as long as shit.
Tell you uncle Mickey."[15]

In another scene, Smith contrasts Abdul-Mickey's cockney with
Denzel and Clarence's Jamaican patois:

"Dat Pattie look strange," said Clarence.
"Im try to poison us, said Denzel.
"Dem mushroom look peculiar," said Clarence.
"Im try to infiltrate a good man with de devil's food," said Denzel.
Mickey slapped his spatula down on Denzel's fingers,
"Oi Tweedledum and fucking Dee. Get a new fucking routine, all
right?"[16]

In *Lara*, Evaristo also attempts to capture the multilingual voices of
contemporary English society. In addition to presenting different
regional English dialects, she also describes the southern Irish dialect
of the protagonist's great-grandmother whose:

honeyed Rs and Irish vowels once lyrical as a trickling stream,
coarsened by stunted desires, nasalised by city concrete, 'You'll
do better than I did, then, and you could do worse.....'You're a
cheeky wrench aren't yer! Love's a ladder, Edie. He's suitable,
first and foremost, and Lord knows if you're lucky real love will
follow. Just work hard so's your children enter the professions,
or marry into 'em."[17]

In contrast to Smith and Evaristo, other Black writers work on
capturing the nuance and cadence of Black speech. The adoption of
these distinctive Black speech patterns separates Black writing from
the mainstream. Kadija Sesay points out, that the contemporary
Black British writer is far more experimental than older generations
in their approach to Black speech. Diran Adebeyo, for example,
"adeptly employs various styles of language in an attempt to
exemplify the hybridity that exists *within* Blacks in Britain. The
protagonist, Dele, is an Oxford graduate of Nigerian parentage, and
we watch how he straddles three different cultures – African, British,

and Caribbean."[18] Sesay goes on to note that writers like Adebeyo "use a tri-composite language in their work, that is, Jamaican English, African English, and Standard English."[19] This diverse employment of Black speech is also represented in *White Teeth*. Smith describes the younger generation speaking a fusion of Standard English, Jamaican patois, and Bengali: "'we've taken it too long in this country. And now we're getting it from our own, man[standard English]. Rhas clut! [Jamaican patois] He's fucking bador[Bengali slang], white man's puppet.'"[20]

In addition to exposing us to the hybridised nature of English linguistics, Smith also reveals other forms of cultural synthesis. For example, in one scene Alsana is described as wearing a mix of traditional Indian dress, western athletic apparel, and African garb. Her husband (Samad) criticises Alsana's ensemble because her clothing selections betray her assimilation into the mainstream:

> "Look at how you dress. Running shoes and a sari? And what is that?" It was one of Clara's African headscarfs, a long, beautiful piece of orange Kente cloth with which Alsana had taken to wrapping her substantial mane."[21]

As he ostracises Alsana, Samad fails to remember that he is also guilty of "crossing over": "And that is a beautiful lungi you have on, Samad Miah," [Alsana] said bitterly, nodding in the direction of his blue terry cloth jogging suit topped off with Poppy's LA Raider's baseball cap."[22] What this passage shows is that as Alsana and Samad trade Eastern tradition for Western comfort, both "have their two feet in two different continents" Bangladesh and England.[23]

The image of the immigrant straddling two cultures was a popular motif in early Black British writing and Smith's treatment of the theme of exile and alienation is similar to what others have presented. In *White Teeth*, Samad Iqbal is the archetypal migrant living in exile. After living in England for eighteen years Samad realises that migrating to England was a mistake. He knows he cannot return home to Bangladesh, it is a foreign to him as England:

> "Cold, wet, miserable; terrible food, dreadful newspapers – who would want to stay? In a place where you are never welcomed, only tolerated. Just tolerated...[Y]ou are unsuitable to return, your children are unrecognizable, you belong nowhere."[24]

While Black texts focus on how migrant groups grapple with rootlessness, Smith explains that rootlessness is not limited to the Black experience. In *White Teeth*, British born Archie Jones feels as alienated and displaced as Samad. Archie's failed relationship with his Italian wife and her extended family leave Archie feeling suicidal and rootless. The narrator notes:

> "At nights he looked out through the windshield into the monstropolous sky and had the old realization of his universal proportions, feeling what is was to be tiny and rootless. He thought about the dent he might make on the world if he disappeared, and it seemed negligible, too small to calculate."[25]

Thus Archie's experience of rootlessness differs from Samad's for although there is no disconnect from home, he still experiences an emotional disconnect that leaves him feeling vulnerable and alienated.

While almost all of the early writing in Britain published before 1970 dealt with this theme of exile (Sam Selvon's *Lonely Londoners*, Joan Riley's *Unbelonging*) most contemporary writers have moved beyond this subject. Sesay maintains that contemporary Black British writers characterise Britain as home. The characters in these novels "see themselves, growing up, as being part of British society and are only made aware as they get older that they may constitute another blend."[26] Although in Levy's second novel *Fruit of the Lemon* the protagonist returns home to find her roots, in *Every Light*, the characters are told to overlook their differences and accept England as their home:

> 'You come from here. But we're different – we're coloured,'
> I said. 'Look child,' my mum said. 'You were born here. That's what matter.' My mum always say to me, 'You're not Black and you're not white.' That's what we are – we're not Black and we're not white. 'What are we then?' my brother asked.
> 'Cha, child – you're just you?'[27]

While others have abandoned the theme of homelessness, Smith returns to this subject because feeling of rootlessness continue to be a part of contemporary Black British experience, especially for bi-racial characters like Irie Jones. For obvious reasons half-Jamaican, half-English Irie Jones has difficulty defining her identity. She is both

British and Jamaican and yet she identifies with neither of these cultures: "There was England, a gigantic mirror, and there was Irie, without reflection. A stranger in a stranger land."[28] Confused about her ancestry at one point in the narrative she wishes to become as English as the Chalfens (who as we learn are not English but in fact Jews "third generation, by way of Germany and Poland, ne Chalfenovsky."[29] Later she decides that in order to forge a true sense of identity she must return to Jamaica in search of her roots. But by the end of the novel Irie accepts Abdul-Colin's announcement that "we're all English now mate like it or lump it." Pregnant with her own multiracial child (Jamaican, English, and Bengali) Irie knows that her child will never fit neatly into any racial category "will never be mapped exactly nor spoken of with any certainty."[30] Her child symbolises the promise of a multicultural raceless British society, where "roots won't matter anymore because they can't because they mustn't because they're too long and they're too tortuous and they're just buried too damn deep."[31] By the end of the novel then, the reader understands Smith's point that Englishness no longer exists. As the character Alsana points out "you go back and back and it's still easier to find the correct Hoover bag than to find one pure person, one pure faith, on the globe. Do you think anybody is English? Really English? It's a fairy tale."[32]

The various discussions involving the identity politics of Smith's multicultural cast of characters serve as telling examples of the text's essential Britishness. But at the same time, in some sense the text is as much Black British as it is British: that is Smith achieves a fusion of British and Black British literature, reforming both literatures and proving the two to be mutually exclusive. Smith creates a new Black/British text, a story that includes the experiences of characters from diverse ethnic backgrounds, whose racial differences actually account for the commonality of their shared experiences and their Britishness.

NOTES AND REFERENCES

[1] Brennan T. "Writing from Black Britain." *The Literary Times Review*, 34, 1 (Fall 1990): p.5-11

[2] Smith Z. *White Teeth*. New York: Random House. 2000

[3] Hall S. "New Ethnicities" in Procter, James (Ed.) *Writing Black Britain 1948-1998: An Interdisciplinary anthology.* Manchester: Manchester University Press, 2000. p.274

[4] Smith Z. *White Teeth*. New York: Random House. 2000. pp.108-109

[5] Evaristo B. *Lara*. Kent: Angela Royal Publishing Ltd. 1997

[6] Ibid. p.70

[7] Levy A. *Every light in the house burnin'*. London: Headline Book Publishing. 1994

[8] Ibid. p.57

[9] Smith Z. *White Teeth*. New York: Random House. 2000. p.144

[10] Head D. "Zadie Smith's *White Teeth:* Multiculturalism for the Millennium" in Richard L, Mengham R and Tew P. (eds.) *Contemporary British Fiction*. London: Polity Press, 2003, p.10, pp.106-119

[11] Gilroy P. *Against Race: Imagining Political Culture Beyond the Color Line*. Cambridge: Harvard University Press, 2000. p.12

[12] Smith Z. *White Teeth*. New York: Random House. 2000. p.271

[13] Ibid. p.272

[14] Ibid. p.140

[15] Ibid. p.154-155

[16] Ibid. p.160

[17] Evaristo B. *Lara*. Kent: Angela Royals Publishing Ltd. 1997. p.14

[18] Sesay K. "Transformations Within the Black British Novel." In Arana V. and Ramey L. (eds.) *Black British Writing*. New York: Palgrave Macmillan. 2004. pp.99-108

[19] Ibid. 104

[20] Smith Z. *White Teeth*. New York: Random House. 2000. p.193

[21] Ibid. p.166

[22] Ibid. p.166

[23] Sesay K. "Transformations Within the Black British Novel." In Arana V. and Ramey L. (eds.) *Black British Writing*. New York: Palgrave Macmillan. 2004. p.103

[24] Smith Z. *White Teeth*. New York: Random House. 2000. p.336

[25] Ibid. p.10

[26] Sesay K. "Transformations Within the Black British Novel." In Arana V. and Ramey L. (eds.) *Black British Writing*. New York: Palgrave Macmillan. 2004. p.103

[27] Levy A. *Every light in the house burnin'*. London: Headline Book Publishing. 1994. p.59

[28] Smith Z. *White Teeth*. New York: Random House. 2000. p.222

[29] Ibid. p.273

[30] Ibid. p.437

[31] Ibid. p.437

[32] Ibid. p.196

Marginalia: Black Literature and the Problem of Recognition

"we walk invisible"
- Shakespeare, Henry IV Part I

Mahlete-Tsigé Getachew

INTRODUCTION

Black writers want recognition: recognition through inclusion in publisher lists and subsequent marketing efforts; in review coverage and discussions in arts programmes; in bookshop sales figures and publicity events; in the shortlists for literary awards; in the canon, the national consciousness, and the national curriculum. To an extent, this recognition, or recognition like it, is something that all writers want. But in this regard Black authors don't seem to enjoy the same success as their non-Black counterparts. A few Black authors have received this recognition, it is true – literary stars like Ben Okri, Grace Nichols, and Caryl Phillips; and more recent constellations like Courttia Newland, Bernardine Evaristo, and Mike Gayle. There are others; but are there enough? If not, we must entertain two disturbing conclusions: either that recognition is not deserved, or that it is denied. The Hegelian scholar Axel Honneth argues that recognition comes with contribution to a shared goal, and where there is no shared goal or no contribution to that goal, then recognition cannot be achieved.[1] But equally, "denied recognition can be a form of oppression"[2] and if a contribution to a shared goal is not acknowledged, then clearly some sort of injustice is occurring. We must seriously consider whether Black literature shares a goal with wider literary activity, if it successfully contributes to this collective goal, and if this contribution is being systematically marginalised.

In this paper I shall defend three claims.

1) Traditional conceptions of Black literature are only justifiable from a political rather than aesthetic point of view; therefore 'Black literature' as it is traditionally conceived does not share a goal with more general literature.

2) These political considerations have led to a commercial segregation of Black literature, and the comparatively devalued cultural status of Black literature reflects the perceived commercial

weakness of its target market. This situation can only be improved as the target market increases its influence by increasing its spending and widening its membership.

3) The development of an apolitical but linguistically innovative Black literature would meet the criteria for aesthetic and commercial success and would overcome both the limitations of traditionally conceived Black literature and the segregation associated with this form.

I WRITING IN BLACK

> "Happiness writes white."
> - Henri de Montherlant

A typical definition of Black art is:

> art produced by Black people, largely and specially for the Black audience, and which, in terms of its content, addressed Black experience.[3]

This conception of Black art is also applied to Black literature: Black literature is literature produced by Black people, for the Black audience, and which addresses Black experience. On the basis of these conditions I shall ask whether Black literature is a suitable candidate for literary recognition. Thomas Carlyle once observed that "of insinuations, by assent or contradiction, potent if you know the nature of the beast; of these we need not speak."[4] But I think these potent insinuations should not exist unnoticed and unchallenged; and so there is a need to speak, and to consider the nature of the beast.

I.1 BLACK AUTHORSHIP

If we assert that Black literature is any literature produced by a Black person, then we have to concede that should a Black person sit down and write a dark comedy about conspiracy and paranoia (like Pynchon's *The Crying of Lot 49*), or a short story about a man's transformation into an insect (like Kafka's *Metamorphosis*), or a poem about superseding one's parents (like Heaney's *Follower*), these would *all* count, equally, as 'Black literature'. This doesn't seem to correlate with the sorts of works we associate with the category 'Black literature', implying that there is more to Black literature than Black authorship.

This criterion for Black literature also encounters problems when we try to use it to explain why Black literature deserves aesthetic recognition. To claim that works by Black authors deserve aesthetic recognition as a *category* of literature, is to claim that an ethnic or racial quality about the author confers a literary or aesthetic quality onto the work. This could only be true if one's ethnicity gave one a unique perspective on a general experience – if, for example, the Black experience of 'enjoying the Summer' was different from the White or the Asian experience of 'enjoying the Summer'. This is a difficult claim to believe, let alone defend, though I shall investigate this notion of a 'Black Experience' further in I.4. Of course it might be useful or interesting from an academic perspective to categorise literature by the social category of the author – for example, 19th Century Literature, Russian Literature, and so on. But the existence of *these* literary categories does not guarantee the aesthetic merit of their works, and when individual works within these categories do achieve commercial and literary success, they *do* so as individual works and not as examples of the category.

Defining 'Black literature' by its authorship is also motivated by the belief that Black authors are not being encouraged, published, or recognised within the general literary tradition. By segregating the work of Black authors into the category 'Black literature', it is thought that the profile of these authors is raised within the Black and non-Black community so that their works are brought to the attention of the wider public and can inspire future generations of Black writers.

These are admirable goals, but I think certain conditions would need to be met for Black literature to achieve this sort of success. In the first place, in order for the works of Black authors to gain a wide readership, they should appeal to a broad range of people or to a substantial segment of the UK population. Black authorship *in itself* is not a guarantee that this will be the case. Moreover, the publishers of Black literature should be able *and* willing to invest in decent marketing campaigns to raise the profile of these authors. Such campaigns cannot be based on Black authorship alone; for a legacy that endures, the literature should possess aesthetic qualities that present and future generations can hold in high regard. These are issues that I shall examine in sections 2 and 3 of this paper.

Initiatives like the Saga Prize, founded by Marsha Hunt in 1994 to encourage unpublished Black novelists born in the UK and the Republic of Ireland, are intended to raise the profile of Black authors. In order for these initiatives to be successful they must have a public legitimacy and they must endorse works of the appropriate literary merit; the former often follows the latter, and neither can be based on Black authorship alone. When the Orange Prize for women novelists was established in 1996, substantial controversy surrounded it until it became clear that many of the books it honoured were works whose literary merit was recognised by other award-making panels and by popular sales, so that comparatively unknown books it selected were given credibility[5]. This sort of commercial and literary success by Black authors is certainly possible: as recent examples of outstanding performance, I would cite Zadie Smith's *White Teeth* (Hamish Hamilton, 2000), Malorie Blackman's *Noughts and Crosses* (Corgi, 2002), and Andrea Levy's *Small Island* (Headline Review, 2004). Any prize for Black authors must aspire to similar standards, otherwise there are no *aesthetic* reasons why the reading public should pay attention to the deliberations and decisions of the prize-making panel.

Black authorship might, therefore, be a necessary condition for defining 'Black literature', but it doesn't fully describe the category, and doesn't provide aesthetic justification for the recognition of this category of literature. Moreover, there is doubt about whether *any* piece of literature produced by a Black author counts as 'Black literature'. It seems we must look to the work's readership and content to find a better account of Black literature.

I.2 BLACK READERSHIP

The conception of Black literature as 'literature for Black people' is perhaps even more problematic than the conception of it as 'literature by Black people'. It seems inconsistent to claim that a literary category has such a restricted audience and yet deserves wider literary recognition. We must also ask: *why* is Black literature 'for' Black people? It seems to me that the answer to this lies in the subject matter of such work. Black literature is for Black readers either because it is literature that resonates with their own experience, or because it is literature where they can identify with the Black characters. We can witness a similar phenomenon in Black American literature:

> African-Americans still seem to hunger for fiction and nonfiction
> that reflects their experience ... For a very long time now African-

> Americans had very few books that spoke to their unique
> experience. Now there are many, and they love that, and many
> say reading such books is not a luxury but a necessity.[6]

This socialisation role of the literature is certainly useful and important in doing things like cultivating self-confidence and self-affirmation within the Black community; but this is primarily a social rather than aesthetic goal, and does not *in itself* provide justification for the general and aesthetic recognition of Black literature. Moreover, when such literature remains outside the mainstream, or markets itself as being of minority interest, resonance or identification with such literature might actually *reinforce* the marginal status of the readers rather than countering it, and might also play a part in segregating the Black *community* from the mainstream.[7]

It is one thing for a literature to *attract* a certain type of reader, and another thing for a literature to be *targeted* at a certain type of reader. I must confess, I'm uncomfortable with the idea that a literary category can exist *for* a specific readership. Aristotle praises literature for engaging with "the universal"[8] and since literature is meant to be an imaginative enterprise, it seems odd to deliberately restrict its audience on social grounds, as if these social grounds determine a reader's imaginative capacity and then to assert that this socially restricted art-form possesses unique literary merit. In defining Black literature as 'literature *for* Black people', it seems to be of little or no interest whether the literature has a non-Black readership. But I think the literary and commercial benefits of having a non-Black readership far outweigh the benefits – and disadvantages – of having an exclusively Black readership. I shall examine these factors in section 2.

1.3 BLACK CONTENT

Black authorship and Black readership have proved comparatively unsuccessful as criteria for describing and defending Black literature as a separate literary category that also merits general literary recognition. It seems that the actual content of so-called works of Black literature might prove a more fruitful approach. Mike Phillips, in his history of Black Britain, remarks that "[a]lthough Black people have an undeniable historical presence in Britain, their absence from the image of the nation's culture is equally undeniable."[9]

As a consequence of this, literary works that prominently feature a plurality of developed Black characters are generally regarded as different from *ordinary* contemporaneous literary works – different enough to merit the label 'Black literature'. This is somewhat startling; startling that the omission of developed Black characters is ordinary, and startling that the inclusion of developed Black characters can earn a book mention in a literary *sub*-category. Perhaps these categories should be reconsidered; the existing hierarchy does little to suggest that omitting Black characters is injudicious.

Despite the apparent misnomer, Black literature, defined as something like 'literature featuring a plurality of developed Black characters', is clearly a suitable candidate for general literary recognition. But even this account of Black literature is not without its problems. I'm not sure that *segregating* works that do and do not feature Black characters is the best way for an inclusive society and an inclusive literature to develop. Keeping 'ordinary' and 'Black' literature apart will only legitimate the current trend instead of countering it; it would be like instituting a separate body of literature for lefthanders, or tall people, and saying that this isn't divisive but rather helps *integrate* them into wider society.

Moreover, due to the widespread absence of Black characters in 'ordinary' literature, the few depicted in any literary work are suddenly taken as representative of a whole section of British society. Initially this opportunity to represent – or re-present – the Black community was seized by writers from the colonies who "felt a need and duty to represent colonial societies, to reveal the humanity of the people to a British society maliciously ignorant of that humanity."[10] In the 1980s, the problem was not ignorance but demonisation, and so non-colonial Black British writers produced a literature that was "[part] of an attempt to take control of representation of Black Britishness at a time when they were becoming increasingly unsavoury within the national media."[11]

This kind of re-presentation through literature is admirable but it does not necessarily entail literary merit or even the appropriateness of *literary* recognition. And when the representation of the Black community is seen as the 'duty' of authors writing about Black characters, the danger is that literary considerations will come second to political duty. This much is evident from the reception of ER Braithwaite's *To Sir With Love*:

Though both the book and the film were beautifully done in their popular vein, Braithwaite's name seems to be mud among Black people today. The book is not thought to be angry enough by today's Black Briton, and it is accused of telling the success story of one Black, in apparent isolation from the struggles of the other Blacks.[12]

What would the reading public or the Black community make of a novel where Black characters were the perpetrators of racist crimes? Or where the Black characters were, in a refreshingly nonstereotypical way, persistently lazy, dishonest, violent, and daft? Black people are not immune to these personal qualities; and one need only consider the race-related hostility sometimes manifest between Black British Africans, between Black British Caribbeans, between Black British Africans and Caribbeans, and the race-related hostility that Black Britons sometimes demonstrate against non-British immigrants or non-Black Britons, to realise that in this world Black Britons are not just the victims of racism[13]. Literature reflecting *this* social reality would be, I believe, unwelcome in the canon of Black literature. This is in part because it would contradict the monolithic narrative of 'the Black Experience' (see I.4), and also because Black literature in its current incarnation is preoccupied with the political duty of positively representing the Black community.

In addition to the literary dangers, this emphasis on representation also has *political* disadvantages. Whether positively represented or not, the fact that a few individuals *can* represent a community reiterates the comparative weakness of that community:

> [W]hat is at stake in the debates on 'Black representation' is …
> a broader problematic in cultural politics shaped, as Paul Gilroy
> suggests, of depiction and representation as a practice of
> *delegation* … [that] reinforces the perceived secondariness of
> that community.[14]

Black literature may try to counter ignorance and the demonisation of Black people by stopping Black people from being reduced to a few negative associations; but it doesn't try to stop Black people from being reduced to a few associations in the first place. In focussing on *controlling* representation of the Black community through the portrayal of some fictional characters, Black literature does not challenge the idea that the Black community *can* be represented by some fictional characters. Of course this kind of tokenism is unconscious, and an unfortunate result of the scarcity of Black characters in literature. But the weight of this disproportion is not going to be alleviated by putting these works in a whole separate literary category – in fact, it will make the pressures of representation even worse.

Finally, I believe this duty of positive representation is *not* best served by encouraging the segregation of Black literature from general literature. If Black literature is regarded as separate from mainstream literature, and becomes primarily identified as literature that positively represents Black people, then it risks its efforts being redundant because it's unlikely such literature will be sought out, or even casually picked up, by readers who are not interested in the positive portrayal of Black people.

I.4 BLACK EXPERIENCE

The pervasive conception of how Black literature differs from other literature is that it describes, or otherwise engages with, the experience of being Black. This 'Black experience' is usually described from the perspective of a Black person.

> British ethnic minority literature is, understandably,
> autobiographical to an extent which is untypical of
> 'mainline' British literature. This is as true for white
> minorities as it is for Black ones.[15]

Already Black literature seems comparatively restricted in goal and content; if descriptions of the Black experience are predominantly autobiographical, then there is less opportunity for imaginative engagement with this experience by Black writers[16], and even less opportunity for non-Black writers, which is bound to constrain the literature's artistic potential. Moreover, the casual assumption that Black literature is unusually but 'understandably' autobiographical implies that the Black experience, whatever that is, is so profound that Black authors have little else to write about. This is a view echoed by some Black authors:

> [I]n different circumstances, it would be possible to put our Blackness
> into perspective. White writers are hardly distracted by their
> whiteness, since for them, its practical consequences are trivial.[17]

'Practical consequences' is a lovely euphemism for the effects of race-related marginalisation on Black Britons. As another author puts it:

> Afro-Caribbean and British Black writing displays outrage at abuse and exclusion; it expresses resistance and outcry ... It exposes the experience of a merely-to-be-human survival struggle.[18]

This gives us the beginning of a definition of 'The Black Experience' as the experience of racial oppression that comes with being Black; it is this experience that supposedly motivates Black literature and is Black literature's principal narrative.

I am sceptical that a single and unifying Black Experience, shared by all Black Britons, exists. To propose an essential Black Experience is to disregard the range and subtle diversity of ethnic and cultural experiences that make up contemporary Britain.[19] It could be argued that these subtle differences are not as important as the common experience, amongst ethnic minorities, of being subject to racial oppression. Stuart Hall informs us that:

> [t]he term 'Black' was coined as a way of referencing the common experience of marginalisation in Britain and came to provide the organising category of a new politics of resistance among groups and communities with, in fact, very *different* histories, traditions, and ethnic identities.[20]

So there is a political motive behind the demarcation of the Black Experience; the Black Experience is an account of racial victimisation that both *unifies* and *characterises* the lives of Britain's ethnic minorities.

Since the Black Experience is a political category, it follows that literature about this experience will be politically defined – irrespective of whether its authors intend it as such. This has serious implications for the marketing of Black literature, as I shall discuss in section 2. It also has implications for the relevance of Black literature to wider literature. Literature *may* be, but *need not* be, concerned with politics; and for as long as Black literature exists as a *political* category of literature, then its relevance to the general *literary* community will be undermined.

Unity comes at a price; the British ethnic minority community initially used the term 'Black Experience' to resist Anglo-Saxon cultural dominance by recognising difference, and now the term is developing a similar kind of cultural dominance within the ethnic minority community:

> [P]olitically speaking, the 'Black Experience' as a singular and unifying framework ... became 'hegemonic' over other ethnic/racial identities ... [W]hat is at issue here is the recognition of the extraordinary diversity of subjective positions, social experiences, and cultural identities which comprise the category 'Black'.[21]

As well as *unifying* the range of ethnic minority experiences, the Black Experience *characterises* them. For the sake of unity, a plenitude of stories is replaced by just one narrative – the narrative of 'the' Black Experience; and this single narrative, with its focus on race, is used to characterise Black Britons. This implies that there is only one thing Black Britons want to write about, the race-related "experience of a merely-to-be-human struggle", and there is only one thing to say about this one thing. This is the complaint the literary critic Harold Bloom is making when he writes of such literature that it includes:

> by no means the best writers who happen to be women, African, Hispanic, or Asian, but rather the writers who offer little but the resentment they have developed as part of their sense of identity.[22]

Such a narrow conception of Black literature – and indeed, of 'Blackness' – is often reinforced, ironically, by initiatives like the Saga Prize intended to *develop* Black literature. For example, the 1996 Saga Prize winner, *Some Kind of Black* by Diran Adebayo, chronicles the struggles of a young Black Oxford graduate to reconcile his privileged background with the racism and race riots he encounters in London; *Canteen Culture* by Ike Eze-Anyika, the 2000 Saga Prize winner, is about racism in the Metropolitan Police.

It is obvious that this politically-motivated conception of Black literature as 'literature about the Black Experience' risks ignoring and even eroding the subtle range of British ethnic minority experiences. This erosion inevitably creates political, cultural, and literary paucity, and besides which, being a *politically* motivated literature, does not in itself offer adequate grounds for receiving *literary* recognition. Nevertheless it is this conception of the Black Experience and Black literature that dominates all the analyses of Black literature's style, content, and purpose. I shall now look at the implications of this view of Black literature for its commercial status and how it has been marketed.

II: COMMERCE AND CULTURE

"I write the songs / that the whole world sing."
– Jay-Z feat. Jermaine Dupri, *Money Ain't A Thang*

So far I have examined the literary credibility of 'Black literature' as it is traditionally conceived. In this section, I shall examine its commercial credibility. In particular, I shall look at the effects of the literature's politicisation and segregation on how it is marketed. The implicitly political nature of 'Black literature' often limits the potential market of the literature – or at least the *perceived* potential market – to just Black readers. Within this market, there are two prevalent myths: the majority of Black people don't read, and that the minority who *do* read want to read Black literature. The consequence has been that Black people have little or no influence on mainstream literature, and this commercial invisibility may have undermined the efforts of Black writers to attain mainstream commercial recognition. After all,

> ... art is a profession. It has an economic base ... While the Black community has no economic power to support its artists, then the Black artist is lost.[23]

In this section of the paper, I shall look at strategies to counter this.

II.1 Strengthening the market

> Although the general conception is that Black people are poor readers, national statistics reveal that [e]thnic minorities comprised 8.2% of library user visits in 2000... against their 5.9% share of the total population.[24]

Visiting a library is not the same as being interested in literature – especially as the modern local library will frequently offer services like internet access, photocopying, and DVD/CD/video rental. However, within these library user visits, the same statistics indicate that 83% of Black library users borrowed books, compared with 77% of White users. These are clear grounds for holding that the Black community is interested in literature, and that their interest matches and even exceeds the interest of the non-Black community[25]. Moreover, the most recent government survey shows both that Black people spend more time reading than any other ethnic group in

Britain (weighted percentages: Black 103, White 100, Indian 93, Pakistani/Bengali 76), and that reading is the favoured home-based leisure activity for Black people[26].

There is obviously a clear commitment to literature within the Black community. How can this commitment best be harnessed to the advantage of Black writers and Black literature as a whole? One outstanding success story is The X Press, the publishing company set up by Dotun Adebayo and Steve Pope in 1993 to publish 'Black populist fiction' like Victor Headley's *Yardie* and Patrick Augustus' *Baby Father* books. The X Press is now the foremost Black publisher in Europe, and has sold some of its titles to American publishers too. This is one model of success, but it is not the only model, and my concern is that it invites the kind of *political* and *cultural* segregation that makes it difficult for such literature to achieve mainstream recognition as *literature*. Percival Everett's 2001 novel *Erasure* is a devastating satire telling how a Black college professor writes a parody of 'Black literature' that becomes a huge success and is hailed by the Black and White community alike as an "authentic record" of the "ghetto experience", rather than it being treated as art or even as fiction.

Nevertheless, the commercial viability of Black publishers, coupled with the impressive library usage and reading preference figures, demonstrates the incredible capacity of the Black community to impact publishing.[27] And yet nowhere has this potential been recorded, or even estimated. Apparently:

> [t]he shortage of commercial data on Black consumers is
> largely due to the fact that noone has yet *bothered* to carry out
> a more definitive national survey on the market... most of the
> data collected on Black and other ethnic minorities tends to have
> political overtones.[28]

The commercial cost of the politicisation of 'Blackness' is now made clear. Consequently, I believe there are immense advantages to be gained if it is seen that the Black market is interested in more than just so-called *Black* literature. If Black readers are vocal, active, and demonstrative in their appreciation of literature, attending generalist (and not just Black) reading groups, getting involved in general library projects and literary ventures, and so on, then should they praise or criticise a book, or a literary approach, their opinions will be accorded more significance within the mainstream, and will therefore have more commercial influence. By demonstrating that 'the Black Pound' can be spent on Black *and* non-Black literature, mainstream publishers are more likely to try to woo Black consumers instead of consigning them to the efforts of specialist Black publishers.

Political history of the New Social Movements in Europe and America in the 1960s and 1980s teaches us that minority groups and their interests can influence the mainstream by being incorporated in it, not by existing in parallel to it. The counter-cultural movements and protest-groups like civil rights activists, eco-warriors, and feminists did not enjoy their political success as independent groups, but rather were co-opted by the dominant political parties because these parties realised that they would lose support if they didn't accommodate these alternative movements.[29] Crucially, however, according to neo-Marxist and Frankfurt School interpretations of this phenomenon, the assimilation is motivated by economics rather than ethics or politics; the dominant groups incorporate the minorities not because of an essential concern for the values of such minorities, but because the dominant group doesn't want to be excluded from the burgeoning minorities' economic potential.[30] Similarly, I believe that the Black literary community – including readers – are more likely to have their interests catered to by being incorporated into the mainstream instead of being segregated from it, and by demonstrating the sort of economic commitment to literature that will earn them the attention of the rest of the mainstream.

II.2 WIDENING THE MARKET

As stated earlier (in section 1), I said that if Black literature is to achieve widespread recognition, it must either appeal to a broad range of people or to a substantial segment of the UK population. In addition to strengthening the economic influence of Black literature's target market, I believe that *widening* this target market to include non-Black readers would improve the commercial credibility of Black literature. A parallel can be drawn with Black music – in the contemporary incarnations of hiphop and RnB – which is the most dominant form of music at the time of writing, and, significantly, has been imitated and co-opted by non-Black performers and listeners. This is despite the fact that hiphop began in America in the 1970s as a specifically Black cultural practice, and which, like punk in Britain, was a music of rebellion and protest[31]. But, as hiphop group Lords of the Underground put it in *Tic Toc*:

> Well, times have changed / not only for the urban / but also for suburban / We get props, we're deservin'.

> From Black kids, to white kids / I see them bob their heads, / from the blond hair, to redhead / I even seen a dread.

> So now it doesn't matter / as the clock winds down / with the tic and the toc / because they love the sound. ['props' = proper respect; 'dread' = dreadlocks]

It would be naïve to attribute the success of the form purely to its musical qualities, as this would imply it was essentially superior to other music like rock or classical or modern electro-acoustic. Although the music must possess the aesthetic qualities that merit recognition, a more probable explanation for hiphop's success can be found in the economic potential of hiphop and RnB, and the extra marketing this potential attracts which both generates and insulates the success of the form.

> [w]here hiphop once attacked the mainstream, to all intents and purposes, it now is the mainstream. It has become the hub at the centre of America's cultural wheel. It is the vehicle which sells Coca-Cola, Sprite, and clothing lines ranging from Hilfiger and Gap to Fubu and Phat Farm. It has been customised and redefined, not only in the ghettos, but throughout white suburbia and beyond, paying no heed to geographical or linguistic boundaries ... its domination of fashion has been unprecedented. Even a young man as insulated against the wider world as Prince William, the future King of England, knows it's cooler to wear your baseball cap backwards.[32]

Whether one takes a neo-Marxist or a capitalist interpretation of this, the story is the same: the economic potential of hiphop began in the Black community and was successfully exported to other sectors of society with disposable income including, now, the White middle classes (and often the gatekeepers of modern culture).

This transfer from Black origins to commercial acceptance is possible, I believe, *precisely* because hiphop and RnB do not try to define themselves as 'Black art': they are not defined by the performers and composers being Black; they are not defined by being targeted at the Black market, and there is no single narrative of 'Black Experience' that pervades hiphop. Internationally successful hiphop can be about race-related hostility and marginalisation (Method Man 'Perfect World'), the staple narrative of the 'Black Experience'. But hiphop can also be about success (Puff Daddy 'Can't Nobody Hold Me Down,' Notorious B.I.G. 'Mo Money, Mo Problems'), and it can be critical of commercial success (Ms Dynamite 'It Takes More'). Internationally well-known hiphop can reject social institutions like marriage (50 Cent 'P.I.M.P.', Nelly 'Playa'), or it can reinforce them (Ma$e 'Tell Me What You Want', Missy Elliott 'All 'N My Grill'); or it can be about other things entirely (The Roots 'You Got Me', Pharcyde 'Passin' Me By'). In fact, hiphop's range turns out to be just as broad as forms like opera and folk music; and what hiphop seems to celebrate and prize well above its racial content, or the ethnicity of its performers, is linguistic and aesthetic *innovation*, be it through free-styling, sampling, breakbeats, or the idiosyncrasy of delivery. In doing so, this distinctively Black music has opened itself up to both aesthetic and commercial recognition, and to acceptance by the non-Black community. The results have been phenomenal, and provide an illuminating – and inspiring – model for Black literature.

III: BLACK AESTHETICS

> "I have crossed an ocean / I have lost my tongue / from the root of the old one / a new one has sprung."
> – Grace Nichols, *Epilogue*

Some of Black music's success can be attributed to the Black community's economic investment in it. But the form would not have spread into the non-Black community if it didn't also possess qualities that made it aesthetically and commercially attractive. In addition to galvanising the Black community to extend a similar economic investment to literature, I believe Black literature could benefit from a change of strategy in how it defines and orientates itself. As with hiphop, I think the key to success is not political content but linguistic innovation.

III.1 THE OLD

Traditionally, a Black writer using classical 'White' discourse risked both inauthenticity and wholesale rejection by the Black reading community, "for how could a Black writer be true to his Blackness using the language of his/her colonial master?"[33] Moreover, this writer also risked rejection by the White reading community too, despite using White paradigms.

> Francis Williams [a Black man in the first half of the 18th Century] ... studied classics at an English grammar school then mathematics at Cambridge University, where he also became famous for his composition of Latin odes, a practice he continued on his return to Jamaica. Francis Williams' classical attainments were however disputed by David Hume who declared that "In Jamaica indeed they talk of one Negro as a man of parts and learning, but it's likely he is admired for very slender accomplishments, like a parrot, who speaks a few words plainly." Literature written by Blacks in European classical vein could therefore only be hollow mimicry.[34]

It would appear that the Black writer should instead write in the 'Black discourse' of African and Caribbean languages. African and Caribbean languages do not presently have the cachet in Europe and America of the European languages, it is true. But the Kenyan writer Ngũgĩ Wa'thiong'o reminds us that this is a situation that is subject to change.

> If we turn to history and look at a language like English, we note that most English writers wrote in Latin during the fifteenth century, because they considered their native language barbaric. It could not express philosophy or religion, they argued, and lacked the vocabulary to create stimulating literature or compose poetry. Writers like Chaucer and later Shakespeare refuted these claims. Today they rank amongst the world's most renowned writers. John Milton wrote his early poetry in Latin but later changed to his own language, English. His Latin poetry is today hardly mentioned.[35]

He goes on to describe how Boccaccio and Dante demonstrated the value of the Italian language at a time when it was neglected in preference to Latin, and how Pushkin and Tolstoy redeemed Russian from the 'cultural superiority' of French and German, and so on. Thus the African and Caribbean languages are adequate and worthy media with which to produce fine literature. But for Black British writers the historical voice of an overseas African/Caribbean people is, in many ways, as distant in time and space from the contemporary Black Briton as some of the European canon are purported to be. It seems the only recourse available to the Black British writer would be to imitate in English the discourse of a Black African or Caribbean. But this would also be a kind of mimicry and inauthenticity. And yet, disturbingly, it is this kind of 'exotica' which institutions within the book trade have:

> no difficulty in honouring ... as long as [it] could be conveniently distanced from the practice of native English writing ... [A]nd for a long time it was easier for a Black writer living in the Commonwealth to be published in Britain than for a person born and brought up in London or Birmingham ... the key to success depending on the extent to which Black artist could impersonate 'alien' voices, the content and style of much of the work we produced had to be derivative or frank imitations of foreign success.[36]

In fact, this institutional desire for the exotic has already affected contemporary Black British art for the worse. Stuart Hall, in an interview with Maya Jaggi, alludes to several Black British artists:

> who he says have been "quietly written out of the record; not British enough for the Tate, not international enough for Bankside".[37]

The challenge Black writers face is to develop a mode of expression, a new language, which resists these pressures, transcends these expectations, and makes Black literature a distinctive and aesthetically valuable enterprise.

III.2 THE NEW

Consider this extract from a 1960s novel:

> We yeckated back townwards, my brothers, but just outside, not far from what they called the Industrial Coast, we viddied the fuel

needle had like collapsed, like our own ha ha ha needles had, and the auto was coughing kashl kashl kashl. Not to worry overmuch, though, because a rail station kept flashing blue – on off on off – just near. The point was whether to leave the auto to be sobiratted by the rozzes or, us feeling like in a hate and murder mood, to give it a fair tolchock into the starry waters for a nice heavy loud plesk before the death of the evening.[38]

This is Nadsat, a language invented by Anthony Burgess in *A Clockwork Orange*, and which combines Slav argot, Cockney, rhyming slang, gypsy's bolo, and neologisms. It is startling and provocative but also eminently comprehensible, despite the initial unfamiliarity, and successful at conveying ideas and images. *A Clockwork Orange* is now a significant part of our cultural and intellectual landscape. Burgess is not the only canonical British author to experiment with linguistic innovation: James Joyce experienced enormous literary success with *Ulysses*,[39] which distorts language and literary convention to explore consciousness, and his 1939 novel *Finnegans Wake* begins:

> riverrun, past Eve and Adam's, from swerve of shore to bend of
> bay, brings us by a commodious vicus of recirculation back to
> Howth Castle and Environs.[40]

The aesthetic and commercial potential of developing new linguistic techniques is something that has also been used by non-white writers like Salman Rushdie and Arundhati Roy, both of whom have won the Booker (Rushdie in 1981 for *Midnight's Children*, which subsequently won the 1993 Booker of Bookers, and Roy in 1997 for *The God of Small Things*, which became an international bestseller).

This emphasis on linguistic innovation is also at the core of hiphop, and has not been an obstacle to hiphop's wider assimilation. In fact, hiphop neologisms like *jiggy*, *phat*, and *bling-bling* have all been included in the OED, that careful observer of the English language. Not everyone will be pleased with this institutional acceptance of Black culture. Chef, a Black character in the TV series *South Park*[41], explains:

> Black people used to always say "I'm in the house" instead of
> "I'm here." But then white people all started to say "in the house"
> so we switched it to "in the hizzouse." Hizzouse became

hizzizzouse, and then white folk started saying *that*, and we had to change it to hizzie, then "in the hizzle" which we had to change to "hizzle fo shizzle," and now, because white people say "hizzle fo shizzle," we have to say "flippity floppity floop".[42]

But, of course, it is this *consistent* innovation that keeps hiphop fresh and maintains the aesthetic potential of Black music.

I cannot, of course, develop a new Black language here. Nor can I dictate to other Black writers the form that such a language should take. This is a responsibility and a pleasure that each writer must discover for themselves. However, I would like to suggest two principles that emerge in the history of successful Black art, and that might prove significant in the renaissance of Black literature.

Some contemporary Black writers are beginning to fuse Creole, African, Caribbean, and European languages with an originality and sensitivity that illuminates the content of their works. It seems to be more widespread in poetry, and in particular in 'dub poetry' as established by Linton Kwesi Johnson, and amongst the heirs to this tradition – for example, Merle Collins' poignant 'Quality Time', which ends:

> Bowler runs in, crowd leaning forward
> ball hit timber, wicket done scatter and
> suddenly so, sun get swallowed by sea.

Moreover, this *artistic* use of synthesis is not merely a result of the neophilia of the nineties and noughties. James Baldwin traces the creation of Black English to "that bitter hour of the world's history" when:

> Blacks came to the United States chained to each other, but from different tribes: Neither could speak the other's language ... [B]lack English began to be formed. This was not, merely, as in the European example, the adoption of a foreign tongue, but an alchemy that transformed ancient elements into a new language.[43]

Thus it could be argued that this tradition of fusing elements of the old to create the new reflects an essential aspect of the historical marginalisation of Blacks – the 'Black Experience'.

There is also a well-established tradition of *improvisation* in Black art – perhaps, even, a defining characteristic of Black art.

> If European-derived art is shaped by restrictions of form and
> propriety, made into definitive, finalized 'texts', then African-derived
> art is looser, freer, more improvisational, and closer to an oral
> tradition that never totally fixes or finalizes the artwork. (You could
> think, maybe, of the difference between 'classical' music and jazz.)[44]

Indeed Toni Morrison once expressed a desire that Black literature
develop a voice as distinctive as jazz is in music, and Black poetry in
the form of *performance* poetry (with all the mutability and variation
that implies) is experiencing a remarkable renewal at this time.[45]

These two techniques – fusion and improvisation – could form the
basis of a distinctive Black language with which one could produce
Black literature. According to Bloom, who did not recognise
traditionally-conceived 'Black literature' as canonical, the mark of a
canonical literary work is "strangeness, a mode of originality that
either cannot be assimilated, or that so assimilates us that we cease
to see it as strange."[46] I believe linguistic innovation would qualify as
a "mode of originality", and this is a view reinforced by Bloom
himself who includes writers like Shakespeare, Dante and Joyce in
the canon – writers we have already encountered in this paper, who
experimented in language with lasting effect on our literature. And
just as linguistic innovation has been the engine and trademark of
hiphop's success, I believe it could play the same role in the rise of
Black literature.

Although this distinctiveness would be an *aesthetic* feature of
Black literature, it would not represent a total disregard for Black
literature's political origins either. Simply by virtue of *being* a
different language, it would be making an adequate political
statement. After all "language is also a political instrument, means,
and proof of power. It is the most vivid and crucial key to identity."[47]

CONCLUSION

Black literature may presently occupy the margins of modern British
literature. But I think the way that the form can gain widespread
recognition is through being assimilated into the mainstream instead
of being segregated from it. There must also be a demonstrable
economic commitment within the Black community to *all* literature,
in order for the wishes of the Black market to become a matter of
concern to mainstream publishers and not just a marginal detail.
And amongst the practitioners of Black literature, linguistic

innovation should be given priority over political content in the development of a distinctive 'Black literature'. These strategies would keep Black literature open to development, and available to anyone to read or write; there would be no preconceptions about the subject-matter or 'message' of the literature, and therefore no constraints in the minds of writers and readers. Such a literature would nurture creativity, and would be an asset both to general literature and to the development of an inclusive society.

Thomas De Quincey once remarked that Coleridge's infamous marginalia "enriched books" with notes "from such a cornucopia of discursive reading, and such a fusing intellect, commentaries so many-angled and so many-coloured". This same dynamism and versatility has been observed in Black fashion, leading the curators of a recent exhibition of Black British Style to conclude:

> What is exciting is that there is always a new order of Black style: there will always be new ways of 'being Black'.[48]

Sometimes the greatest things happen in the margins.

NOTES AND REFERENCES

[1] Axel. (trans. Joel Anderson), *The Struggle For Recognition: The Moral Grammar of Social Conflicts* (Polity Press, 1995)

[2] Charles Taylor, *The Ethics of Authenticity* (Boston: Harvard University Press, 1991), p.50

[3] Remark by Eddie Chambers from Rasheed Araeen 'Black Art: A discussion with Eddie Chambers', in Owusu, Kwesi ed. *Black British Culture and Society: A Text Reader* (London: Routledge, 2000, pp.239-249), p.240

[4] Carlyle, Thomas, *History of Friedrich II of Prussia* Vol 5 Chapter VI

[5] For a succinct history of the Orange Prize and a discussion of the debate surrounding it, see Sarah Ridgard, "The Orange Prize for Fiction: is it really necessary?" in *The Culture of Publishing: 5* (Oxford Brookes, 1997)

[6] Arnold, Martin."Black Americans are Still Buying" *The New York Times* 13 December 2001. More is said on the Black Experience and Black characters in I.3 and I.4.

[7] "Blacks and Asians were funded and supported in organising separate cultural artefacts, which ... offered a clear and unambiguous delineation of Black otherness." Phillips, Mike *London Crossings: A Biography of Black Britain* (Continuum, 2001) p150; "If Black artists are only going to address the Black community, and White artists address White society, it seems to me to be a recipe for cultural Bantustan." Remark by Rasheed Araeen from Araeen p.240

[8] Aristotle, "...poetry is something more philosophic and of graver import than history: for poetry tends to express the universal, history the particular." *On Poetics* IX.3-4

[9] Phillips, Mike p.147

[10] Dabydeen, David & Wilson-Tagoe, Nana *A Reader's Guide to West Indian and Black*

British Literature (Hansib & University of Warwick, 1988), p.83. The quotation goes on: "The urgent task was to address and convince a British readership of the human values that resided in Black communities. The writer was thus a missionary in reverse, coming to Britain to educate and civilise the ignorant."

[11] Procter, James. "Literature" in Alison Donnell ed. *Companion to Contemporary Black British Culture* (London: Routledge, 2000), p.180

[12] Guptara, Prabhu. *Black British Literature: An Annotated Bibliography* (Warwick: Dangaroo Press, 1986), p.23

[13] Claire Alexander, commenting on Hall's "Frontlines and Backyards", highlights his: "implication of boundaries and oppositions between Britain's 'Black' communities, emotively symbolised as 'frontlines'. This latter, tensely loaded image suggests particularly a move not only towards fragmentation but also towards mutual competition and antagonism.", p555 from Claire Alexander "Beyond Black: re-thinking the colour/culture divide" in *Ethnic and Racial Studies* Vol 25 no 4 July 2002 pp552-571; Stuart Hall "Frontlines and Backyards: The Terms of Change" in Owusu ed. pp.127-129

[14] Julien, Isaac & Mercer, Kobena. "De Margin and De Center" in Baker, Diawara & Lindeberg eds. *Black British Cultural Studies: A Reader* (Chicago 1996), pp.194-209; quotation pp.197-198, my emphasis

[15] Guptara, Prabhu. p22

[16] Leone Ross in an interview remarks "The story of a young woman, mixed race, born in England, grow inna Jamaica, doesn't interest me as a fictional process. I live that. Regurgitating it would be boring to me." Kirk Henry, "All the blood is red" in *The House of YAD* July 2001

[17] Phillips, Mike. p.147

[18] Guptara, Prabhu. p.100

[19] Regarding the view that countries have a single culture, Guptara remarks: "There is little factual evidence for [it] in any country, but there is probably even less (if such a thing is possible) evidence in the case of the countries that are most relevant to the term Black British ... All of these have wellknown cultural differences between their various regions, classes, and so on." p.15

[20] Stuart Hall "New Ethnicities", reprinted in Baker, Diawara & Lindeberg, p.163

[21] Hall, Stuart. pp.163-166

[22] Bloom, Harold *The Western Canon: The Books and School of the Ages.* (Oxford: Harcourt, 1994)

[23] Remark by Rasheed Araeen from R Araeen p.253

[24] Seldwood, Sara. ed. *Cultural Trends Issue 42* (London: Policy Studies Institute, 2002)

[25] It has been pointed out to me by Prof. Laura Chrisman (University of York) that these figures may also reveal an economic disparity between the Black and non-Black communities, such that non-Black readers can afford to buy books more often than Black readers, who rely more heavily on libraries. Whether this is a consequence of economic disparity or the consequence of a choice about how Black and non-Black readers allocate their disposable income, is something Kadija Sesay has suggested I investigate. These are good points that I have not been able to address, due to absence of data (see Endnotes 27 & 28); but they are worth bearing in mind should the figures become available.

[26] Church, Jenny & Summers, Carol eds. "Social Habits and Health" in *Office for National Statistics: Social Focus on Ethnic Minorities.* (Government Statistical Service 1996). Data taken from Table 5.16 *Participation in selected home-based leisure activities, 1990-1994.* Weighted percentages for home-based leisure activities for Black people as follows: Reading 103, watching V 99, listening to the radio 99, visiting/entertaining friends 98, listening to records 93, DIY 90, needlework 76, gardening 54.

[27] "The huge potential of Black culture as a money-spinning commodity in the entertainment industry has not yet been realised." Karen St-Jean Kufour "Black Britain's Economic Power, Myth or Reality?" p.329 in Owusu ed. And "[T]he UK's ever-growing Black middle class has a lot of money to spend, on things other than Afro-combs or ghetto-blasters." Etom Phillips-Eteng, *A Guide To Afro-Caribbean and Asian Markets in the UK*, p.12

[28] Black British Consumer Markets vol 1 (London, 1988), my emphasis

[29] Mayer, Magit and Roth, Roland "New Social Movements and Post-Fordist Society" in Mary Darnovsky, Barbara Epstein and Richard Flacks eds. *Cultural Politics and Social Movements*

[30] See, for example, Horkheimer, Max &. Adorno, Theodor W *Dialectic of Enlightenment*, (Continuum, 1944/1996)

[31] Light, Alan ed. *The Vibe History of Hiphop* (Canada: Three Rivers Press, 1999), p.246

[32] Ogg, Alex with David Upshad, David, *The Hiphop Years: A History of Rap* (Channel 4 Books, 1999), p.8

[33] Dabydeen & Wilson-Tagoe, p.169

[34] Dabydeen & Wilson-Tagoe, pp.167-8

[35] Wa'thiong'o, Ngũgĩ "Literature in African Languages" (trans. from Gĩkũyũ by Wangũi Wa'Goro) in K Owusu ed. *Storms of the heart: An Anthology of Black Arts and Culture* (Camden Press 1988), pp225-321, quotation p.225

[36] Phillips, Mike. p.148, my emphasis

[37] Maya Jaggi "Prophet at the margins", The Guardian Profile: Stuart Hall *The Guardian* 8 July 2000

[38] Burgess, Anthony, *A Clockwork Orange* (London: Penguin, 1962), chapter 3

[39] Joyce, James. *Ulysses* (Shakespeare & Company 1922)

[40] Joyce, James. *Finnegans Wake* (London: Penguin/Viking Press, 1939)

[41] Chef is one of two Black characters in *South Park*, the other being a schoolboy called Token who is the Token Black child at the school. This brings to mind the problem of Black characters and representation discussed in section 1, a fact *South Park*'s writers Matt Stone and Trey Parker satirise wonderfully by having Chef voiced by Isaac Hayes and being something of a "Love Doctor" to the children.

[42] *South Park* Episode 708 – South Park is Gay. My thanks to Willie Westwood for referencing this for me.

[43] Baldwin, James. "If Black English Isn't a Language, Then Tell Me, What Is?" in *The New York Times* 29 July 1979

[44] doCarmo, Stephen. De Sales University *Black Cultural Movement / Contemporary Literature* course notes 2001

[45] "Fred D'Aguiar, a poet and novelist of Guyanese descent who has had occasion to track such trends, calculates that there are at least sixty poets of Afro-Caribbean or Asian descent currently living and working in the UK; many of them – including John Agard, Valerie Bloom, Jean Binta Breeze, Merle Collins, Lemn Sissay, and Benjamin Zephaniah – are "primarily performers." Michael Eldridge "The Rise and Fall of Black Britain" in *Transition* No 74 (1997), pp.32-43; quotation pp.32-34

[46] Bloom, Harold.

[47] Baldwin, James.

[48] Exhibition Guide notes, *Black British Style* at the Victoria & Albert Museum, London, Autumn/Winter 2004/2005: curated by Carol Tulloch (Senior Research Fellow in Black Visual Culture, University of the Arts/V&A) and Shaun Cole (V&A Contemporary Programmes)

Prelude to a Brand New Purchase on Black Political Identity: A Reading of Bernardine Evaristo's *Lara* and Diran Adebayo's *Some Kind Of Black*

Koye Oyedeji

> 'The really important thing is to see connections. It is only when we see real connections that we can meaningfully talk about differences, similarities, and identities. So the border, seen as a bridge, is founded on the recognition that no culture is an island unto itself. It has been influenced by other cultures and other histories with which it has come into contact. This recognition is the basis of all the other bridges that we want to build across our various cultural borders.'
>
> *Borders and Bridges* – Ngugi Wa Thiong'o[1]

There are three paradigms that represent the post-Second World War relationship between Britain and its West African colonies. Writers such as Ama Ata Aidoo, Chinua Achebe and Ngugi wa Thiong'o deal with a response to problems of post-colonialism and a need to create national discourse in the wake of independence. Migrant writers such Ben Okri and Buchi Emecheta continue to consider themselves Nigerian and maintain in their work a strong sense of Nigerian identity. Younger writers such as Bernardine Evaristo and Diran Adebayo represent the legacy of colonialism, a generation of people of west-African descent in Britain who may or may not have visited the country of their parents birth but yet are faced with re-imagining the borders of cultural space and national identity.

For contemporary writers of migrant descent the concept of cultural identification remains an ongoing and problematic debate. The complex politics of Black identity in Britain are self-effacing. Daily we are asked to mis-manage our lives by placing ourselves into neat and convenient categories. These categories at times serve as nothing more than political chains, becoming ever more appropriate restraints for a nation struggling to deal with an emerging generation of Blacks who possess the confidence to claim their culture inheritance now from various backgrounds. As with all that are restrained, there will come a time where patience is lost and captives seek to free themselves. There is a generation that has seen their mothers and grandmothers fight and in some cases die for the right to call themselves 'British' and to have the nation grudgingly accept them. The argument has shifted. Yesterday the racist dealt an emotive blow to our mothers with the words, "Go back to Africa", the racist uttering such words today would (hopefully) feel the weight of their own contrived ignorance.

In two debut novels, Diran Adebayo's *Some Kind Of Black*[2] and Bernardine Evaristo's *Lara*[3], the authors allow us to perceive that the term Black British is not sufficient nor adequate to represent the protagonists of the text nor the writers themselves, all of which have an influence from at least one Nigerian parent, an influence which assists to disrupt the flow of cultural assimilation into British nationality. At the same time the absorption of many aspects of cultural hybridity (that includes a British influence) in present Britain, leaves them at odds with contemporary notions of a unified Black Diaspora where race is assumed as cultural markers. These books speak of a need for Blacks to come together to carefully articulate and reinvent our global, society and political identification. Adebayo and Evaristo highlight our growing need to place a new purchase on these new identities and to celebrate the paradox of collective individualism. Only with a clear understanding of the present state of identity can we mobilise ourselves towards the future.

Britain has a fervent need to hold onto a national identity that belies what it truly is today. For nationalists in the 21st century, race politics hides itself in many guises. In one façade it's about stemming the flow of migrants, in another it is concerned with the politics of assimilation. Behind all of this, the country remains institutionally and inherently racist, concerned with what it is generally thought Britain should be as opposed to what it is.

The problems of identity lie, in part, in our need to maintain tradition or to at least create new stable 'traditions' for ourselves, and quite often, the refusal to come to terms with the face of modernity where both true national and cultural identities no longer exist. Hip-hop culture, channeled through voices of those such as the late Tupac Shakur and the Notorious B.I.G. have had a huge influence on the youth culture in the streets of Lagos as the Yoruba

Ijala poetry of hunters takes a central role in my 'British' academic education in London. With such ambiguity one needs to initially ask age-old questions: what does it mean to be Black in terms of identity politics? What does it mean to be British? Can the two ever really sit together with genuine duality? *Some Kind Of Black* and *Lara* help us to embark on a precarious rejection of the term 'Black British', the process of which initially leads one to question what it means to define Black identity and then to define British identity, and to merge these two distinctions together for assessment. The problem for writers such as Adebayo and Evaristo are two-fold because, at least for a generation of Blacks that share their background, the only factor that is not redundant about the term Black-British writer, is the 'writer'. Both Evaristo and Adebayo, in respective interviews with Alistair Niven and Monica Ali in *Writing Across Worlds* admit that their novels draw on and can contain a semiautobiographical aspect of their lives4. A writer of mixed parentage, Evaristo draws on her childhood in Woolwich to shape Lara's experiences. The voyage Lara takes through Europe mirrors that of the author's travels between 1988 and 1990. Adebayo, like Dele shares a Nigerian background and studied for an undergraduate Law degree at Oxford.

Bernardine Evaristo was born in London to a Nigerian father and English mother. *Lara* is a novel-inverse that traces the ancestral line of two families to one child, Omilara or Lara for short. It is a narrative that on one hand takes us through the generations of Yoruba enslavement in 19th century Brazil, a return to colonial Nigeria and the dreams of the Nigerian post-war migration. This is contrasted with the historical sentiment of Irish Catholics at the turn of the twentieth century, their aspirations in 1920s London and the disruption of war. The narrative is charted through the voice of multiple characters: from ancestral spirits to Lara's parents, grandparents and friends.

As it charts the emergence of what we view as multi-culturalism today, *Lara* examines the desire to conform to culture and the problem of identity explored through the tensions of a Black and white couple in an intransigent Britain. Subsequently, the offspring of this union, Lara and her siblings growing up in 1960 and 1970s London, are to come to terms with society that doesn't quite know how to respond to them.

Diran Adebayo was born in London to Nigerian parents. *Some Kind Of Black* centres on the protagonist Dele, his relationship with his sister Dapo and how he attempts to juggle the life of a Black student in the white world of Oxford University with that of the fundamentalist expectations of his father's strict doctrine and a Black world within London. In juggling these worlds, a savvy Dele plays the race card in a variety of ways: in Oxford his race and London background gives him an authority on the latest trends and measures of style, whereas in London that very same race and background gives him the ability to sink into a street culture where he can perceive himself as a more rounded person than his peers, standing at two points as that educated but street smart individual. However his self-reflective nature and insightfulness begins to show him how he has often exploited people with the way in which he combines his intellectual position with that of what is expected of him from his peers and parents. Dele is a man influenced by many cultures, the danger lies in methodically playing with these cultures with what is perceived as inconsistent 'switches' in identity. When his sister Dapo falls into a coma after an altercation with the police, Dele is forced to come to terms with radical Black politics and begins to genuinely question just what a Black person is expected to be in Britain.

So we revisit age-old questions: What does it mean to be Black? The argument has come down to one of examining the tension between that of an essentialist position in which the argument is that identity is fixed and there is something inherent that links all Black people in the world today, and the non-essentialist position which is to believe that societies and distinct cultural influences help us to inherit identities that are never fixed but fluid and ever changing with the politics of modernity and the path that the world is taking towards globalisation.

The essentialist notion of a Black identity serves its use as a reaction to the discourse of national identities. Black identity holds onto the idea of a 'shared past', the historical trauma of race serves to offer a communal sense of security for the Black diaspora to use in continually withstanding the rejection from the national identities of the western territories in which they are located. "At least we belong to something," we say. We forge cultural representations and use them as signifiers, codes that as Black people we inherit globally. Then we say, "At least Rhythm and Blues belongs to us."

The civil rights movements, anti-apartheid movements and their like, the lessons of Pan-Africanism and of Negritude –

conceptualised by the likes of W.E.B. Dubois, Marcus Garvey, Frantz Fanon, Amiee Cesaire and Leopold Senghor – have trickled down to the Black masses and filtered into easy manageable everyday messages that individuals attach themselves to. And while these individuals in the diaspora are constantly being reminded that national identity is linked to the idea of territory, they too look for borders in which to claim their own, Black identity, intrinsically tied to a global African identity becomes such a territory.

Nigerian novelist and critic Isidore Okpewho believes that essentialism in diaspora discourse is "an ugly label for any tendency to see the imprint of the homeland or ancestral culture in any aspect of the lifestyles or outlook of African-descended peoples in the western Atlantic world[5]. He argues that the influence of Africa cannot be denied in regards to the ways in which Blacks in the New World have chosen to "address the realities before them".

Is such an influence an essential part of being Black in the western world? While cultural theorist Paul Gilroy acknowledges the shared experience of the horrors of slavery as being fundamentally behind the basis of the Black Diaspora he also rejects the idea of an inherit essentialism to our Black identity and instead views the Black diaspora in terms of "intercultural embodiment". In his text, *The Black Atlantic*, Gilroy[6] argues that Black identity in today's modern world is in a process of constant travel and exchange across the Atlantic where there is a variety of cultural influence. He believes there is a "quiet cultural nationalism which pervades the work of some radical thinkers. This crypto-nationalism means that they are often disinclined to consider the cross catalytic or transverse dynamics of racial politics as a significant element in the formation and reproduction of English national identities".

Within Evaristo's text we see a Lara at the age of ten really beginning to interrogate her identity. While playing, she places a stick in the snow and conquers new icy terrain for her Britain, conscious of her appearance she studies the size of her lips in the mirror and concludes they are not too big and thus not too Black, "Still, she'd suck them in from now on, just in case"[7]. Influenced by her peers she accepts and perceives that her difference is negative and remains in awe of her friend Susie and the crown of blonde hair she wears. We are privy to how notions of origin are addressed naively as these complex identities begin to emerge in Britain:

'Where'you from, La?' Susie suddenly asked
one lunch break on the playing fields.' 'Woolwich.'
'No, silly, where are you from, y'know originally?'
'If you really must know I was born in Eltham, actually.'
'My dad says you must be from Jamaica,' Susie insisted.
'I'm not Jamaican! I'm English!' 'Then why are you coloured?'
Lara's heart shuddered, she felt so humiliated, so angry.
'Look, my father's Nigerian, my mother's English, alright?'
'So you're half-caste!' Lara tore at the grass in silence.
'Where's Nigeria then, is it near Jamaica?' 'It's in Africa.'
'Where's Africa exactly?' 'How should I know, I don't
bloody well live there, do I!' [8]

What appears as an innocent conversation of ignorance between the children belies the educative failure of the adult community in Britain to breed a climate that interrogates these questions. Susie cannot accept that Lara is English, after all Lara's colour contradicts what she knows to represent Britishness, she pushes for a suitable answer and upon not receiving one draws her own conclusion based on the ignorance of her father. Post-war migration to Britain was primary undertaken by West Indians answering Britain's call for manual labour; West African migration has often been overlooked in studies as Blacks are lumped together and associated by colour. Lara is already noticing and feeling the sense of difference between those of colour. She is not Jamaican, she is English and furthermore her father is Nigerian. The response that Lara is 'half-caste', albeit somewhat a derogatory term in modern times, is true but it wields a disappointing response from Lara for Susie represents the nation that has won the war of words and in doing so successfully excluded Lara when she so badly wants to be accepted. What the conversation also reveals is Lara's ignorance to where her father's background lies.

Critics of Gilroy view his theories as attempts to naturalise our hybridity. Michael J. C. Echeruo (in Okpewho et al 1999) argues: "It does seem odd, to say the least, that our theoreticians would want to see our "modernity" in these terms, and, further, that they would suggest that this condition (of mulattoism) is our natural and peculiar condition in the modern world." He goes on to add: "'European" and "Black" does immediately underscore the kind of blindness of vision required to understand the predicament. For the problem apparently is striving to be "white" and "Black" at the same time, to be simultaneously "European" and "African".

Phrased in such equal terms, the problem would be utterly insane."[9]

Paradoxically, given the ever-expanding fields of identity and Africa's continual embrace of American culture,' it is becoming increasingly difficult for those within the Black Atlantic to identify with what in some cases tend to remain nothing more than idealistic ideas of 'roots'. Evaristo's *Lara* turns to this idea of roots following her constant rejection from British society, with Dele there is an antagonism between him and those that expect him to project the perceived utilitarian values of the Black community.

While Dele and Lara remain conscious of what it is to be Black, this Blackness as Gilroy asserts, is not defined by nation (Britain in Lara and Dele's case) and it does not necessarily hark back to Africa either, as Echeruo asserts. The influence of the western world on Blacks within Britain strangles ontological ideas. Perhaps there is a need to reclaim our roots, yes, but not in an idolised fashion.

Adebayo revisits this problematic in *Some Kind Of Black*. Throughout the text Dele is constantly faced with an antagonism from Black people that suggest that he is not behaving in a manner appropriate of their race. "The one thing that gets me is all these jokers on a "Blacker than You" tip. Its like they're telling you there are only so many ways to stay true to the race"[10] Dele asserts and no sooner has he done so his racial integrity is called into question by Celia, one of the two women he and his colleague Gabriel pick up at a bar.

The expectations that Dele is felt to have to conform to as a Black person troubles him. He had come to college open minded but while dancing to the Smiths, an indie rock band by, he encountered fellow student Jonathan, the only other person that shared a similar background to Dele's own in being "of West African descent, inner-city (albeit Liverpool), elevated post-GCSE's to a state grammar school."[11] Dele was keen to be associated with Jonathan however, his colleague fosters the belief that there are things expected of a Black person and when he sees Dele next he flies into a mock rendition of a Smiths song with slightly altered lyrics:

I would go out tonight
but I haven't got a stitch to wear
My name is Dele
and I may be Black
but I don't care – aa-are![12]

The opinions of others around him matter, particularly those of his Black contemporaries. Jonathan's comment may have been delivered in humour but Dele confesses that it stings him and as a reactionary move, he soon found himself on the Black Students Discussion Group at Oxford.

However, at the African Society meetings Dele feels out of place amongst other Black men who "carried the sombreness of folk whose sponsors were paying untold pounds sterling in overseas fees for graduate places, and who were still too near to their homeland's tragedies to lighten up even in an ivory tower half the world away."[13] In being "a Londoner yet to set foot in his home country" Dele was acknowledging the influence of Nigeria in calling it home but at the same time realising that unlike the others he is not "too near" the homeland, he is different, a half a world away from such concerns, so removed that he is concerned that his style, his haircut fostered on a Black diasporic style: "a short fade with razor cuts at the back, had introduced an unwelcome note of levity to the proceedings."[14]

Adebayo has identified that for the Black writer an identity born of politics becomes increasingly problematic when taking into account the different ideologies that the individual brings to each work. Identification, it seems, is a way of life, but a myriad of multi-generic texts fuelled with multitude of different intents has created a diverse body of material where colour is not sufficient enough criteria in which to group us. The focus has shifted from one of race to varying struggles of economics, religion, culture, gender, class and more.

Novelist Courttia Newland encountered and acknowledged this problem in looking for a title to an anthology co-edited with Kadija Sesay, *IC3: The Penguin Book Of Black Writing in Britain*.[15] In trying to find a term that accurately described Black people in collective terms Newland recognised that Black Britain was not sufficient and wrote:

> "I was searching for a name that defined Black British people as a whole. Lo and behold, there was nothing. I was born here. I've been to the Caribbean once – so I in no way consider myself Afro-Caribbean, or any of the other titles thrown our way. This is what the new generation of kids born here feel too. Hear us, listen to us, take these things on board. The fact that IC3, the police identity code for Black, is the only collective term that relates to

our situation here as residents (Black British is political and refers
to Africans, Asians, West Indians, Americans and sometimes even
Chinese) is a sad fact of life I could not ignore.[16]

To the behest of cultural purists who may argue that there is a
'cultural essence' to be lost, individuals are much more self-defined
and seek to be represented with as much individuality as possible.
Lemn Sisay, poet and editor of *The Fire People*, speaking to Peter
Kennedy in *The Voice* newspaper expressed such anxieties: "When
I first started writing, there were people like Linton Kwesi Johnson
and Benjamin Zephaniah – beautiful poetry, but it seemed like
everybody had accent. And, if I didn't, then I wasn't a Black poet.
Then Black poets started coming through with Mancunian, Cockney
and Scottish accents. They were poets just as concerned with love as
with revolution, or with food as with fighting. They had grown into
a second generation, developing a duality between cultures."[17]
Anything else is but to hang onto idealised notions of Black
essentialism.

Our culture is neither submissive to British nationalities nor
homeland ones; by homeland I mean the land of our parents and
grandparents. Although there are elements of both our parent's
homeland and British culture within our writing, this new
generation has got its tentacles in a multi-cultural society and has
also taken influence from other shores, as for example the United
States. Author Stephen Thompson himself makes no attempt to hide
his admiration of writers such as James Baldwin, and Newland
publicly points to the writings of Chester Himes as the spark that set
him off into exploring the genre of the detective novel in his third
work *Snakeskin*. We only need to look at how hip-hop and in
particular the lyrics of the Wu-tang Clan features heavily in
Adebayo's second novel *My Once Upon a Time*.

Gilroy notes the processes of development that culture in Britain
has gone through: "Britain's Black settler communities have forged
a compound culture from disparate sources. Elements of political
sensibility and cultural expression transmitted from Black America
over a long period of time has been reaccentuated in Britain. They
are central, though no longer dominant, within the increasingly
novel configurations that characterize another newer Black
vernacular culture. This is not content to be either dependent upon
or simply imitative of the African diaspora cultures of America and
the Carribean."[18]

Adebayo pays homage to these influences in *Some Kind Of Black*.
Dele's world is one in which he flips over "U.S hip-hop fairytales,
U.K. hardcore and garage raves,"[19] a world in which he can speak as
he sees fit with a Jamaican ragamuffin dialect or the Queen's
English. This fusion is definitive of a Black youth sub-culture in
1990s Britain and Dele uses it to rebel against his father's notions
that he should behave and dress how a Nigerian child abroad would
dress: "The red and green patched Click suit, over Caterpillar lug
boots and topped with a matching woolly hat, was his pride and joy.
It was one of only three pieces of his wardrobe in which he actually
liked the look of himself. And it was the first ever rudebwoy gear he
had brought home, slipped, and gone downstairs in, looking at his
father as if to say, 'So wha'cha gonna do?'"[20] The Click suit was
amongst the height of fashion amongst young Black boys in the early
90s, a style of clothing appropriated from the trends of Jamaican
clothing, marketed and produced for a mass market. The rebellion
is not in the style of clothing that the narrator attributes to the
'rudebwoy' (a term used to describe the urban London Black boy
associated with street culture) but in the confrontation with his
father in which Dele celebrates and exerts who he is.

The more and more qualified our texts may become in regards to
the experiences we live today, doesn't mean that they will lack any
more importance or relevance than the great volume of work
produced by Black writers such as George Lamming or Buchi
Emecheta who we often feel had a clear sense of Black nationality
having been born on shores elsewhere. Such nationalism at times
seems to blatantly neglect to acknowledge the legacy of imperialism
which manifests itself two-fold: firstly, in the adoption of language
and culture in parts of Africa and the West Indies, secondly, in the
direct part that post-war immigration policy allowed Nigerians, the
likes of the protagonists fathers in Adebayo's and Evaristo's text, to
come to Britain. In a sense the purity of these cultures themselves are
in continual question.

For many of a Black generation born in Britain, a knowledge of
Africa remains no more than facing The Unexamined River. A
rippling river across which you can see Africans on the other side.
Seldom is anything learned about them from what can be shouted
across the river. Intimate conversations cannot be engaged in. No
infrastructure has been set up on British education curriculum
enabling you to build bridges or make meditative boat trips across
this river, at least nothing to enable you to make anything remotely

like a natural course of travel. In time, for Blacks in Britain wanting to learn about Africa, they realise they have to learn swim, to make a personal effort in educating themselves, in discovering Africa. This is what Lara does when, at 29, she makes her first trip to Lagos. It is motivated by the voices of spiritual ancestors urging her to take her father home for the first time in thirty years.[21]

If Nigeria is to be Lara's home she is again plagued with insults as she was as a child in 1960s London. She is called "Oyinbo" by Nigerian children, a term that means: "white" in Yoruba. She is once again perceived as being different, attracting stares in 90s Lagos just as she would in the London streets of the 70s. "This is the land of my father, she mused, I wonder if I could belong."[22]

Lara's narrative is one that informs us of the problems with trying to affirm fixed identities. Lara initially resents her appearance, her colour and herself as it is felt that it does not reflect who she is and only garners negativity. She is constantly reminded of her colour, singled out in assembly to deliver a contralto of Luther King's 'I Have A Dream,' to an assembly hall of 500 white people as well as being pulled aside on a school field trip and asked to tone down her clothing so as to not attract unnecessary attention.[23] She is mistaken as her grandmother's nurse and tenses when people pass her in the street as she anticipates hostility.[24]

Such events placed on the adolescent cause her to withdraw. Lara is in denial about what her colour means politically when her cousin Beatrice confronts her:

> 'What's so funny about being Black?'
> Lara smirked, 'I'm not Black, I'm half-caste, actually.'[25]

Its left for her older Cousin, who is also mixed race, as a member of the family somewhat removed from them (in Liverpool where she too experiences polarisation) to be brutal with her frank honesty:

> 'Lara, lovey, so long as you're of negroid stock, diluted or not, you're Black, ask me how I know?'
> 'How d'ya know, Miss Africa?'
> 'The P word, prejudice. So it's about time you learnt some African ways, eh? I know the difference between yam and cassava. Do you?'[26]

With this the seeds of re-evaulation are planted, but this is just what it is; a re-evaluation. Lara was not born with any sense of her political Blackness, it is a painstaking transition she has gone through based on a prejudice that lead her to hate what she is *on the outside*. Now with a confidence she can re-address her inner-self, no longer ashamed of what she is, she confronts her father for knowledge of Nigeria knowing that he is to blame for not instilling her with a sense of where he came from. As she learns from him, her father asks her why she should be so excited as to learn that her grandfather was Brazilian, for knowing his daughter's previous complexes, he believes she would rather be anything than an African.[27] Lara soon begins to make teenage foray's into Brixton an area of South London known for a strong Black community, "awed by the vivacious tableaux of Atlantic faces" she was elated, and noticed by men that paid her compliments in their very own indelible way, "Yuh look nice, gyal." With this discovery of self, Evaristo has shown us that a Black identity is not something inherent, but something often worked upon in response to white hostility. However just as Evaristo makes this argument she points out the danger in Lara confusing this identity for an African one.

When Lara's Nigerian boyfriend Josh addresses her it is done so from a position of difference and exclusion: "Well, you know how we Nigerians are",[28] he states when he says to her that she has more educational choices and that she is not bound by the expectations of a Nigerian family like he is. When they have an argument he shouts, "You'll not marry a Nigerian if you can't obey me". It is clear that there is some cultural tension; she does not conform to the stereotypes and practices associated with a Nigerian woman, and Josh is of the belief that his relationship with her is founded on her hope to attain some Nigerian culture. He notes that she cannot cook Jolof rice, a staple dish in the Nigerian household. She replies in a derogative manner suggestive of an English culture re-aafirming his suggestions that she is not a Nigerian woman: "You are such a wanker."[29]

Josh's betrayal[30] is significant. It acts a conduit for her anger. At this point we witness an explosion of angst: she denounces her father for his misguided and authoritative approach to fatherhood and she divorces her "honky" mother for the sins of white people and in "deconstructing" her childhood in an almost regretful way, she begins to search trendy markets for "cowries, batiks and sculptures." Still, misguided in thinking that these items make her any more Black in any way, the betrayal is still perhaps the baptism of fire. She has taken Josh's advice to grow up and come to terms with the real world.[31] The last trace of her innocence, her naïveté, in which she believed she could be judged as just an individual, where people could look beyond the cultural, race and gender politics of Britain, is lost and this has caused her to take a political stance with an anger that has driven her to extremes in which she sees "the rapist in every homme, worms in every phallus, the bigot in all whites...London has become the war zone in which the globe is rubbished for 'its self-destruct sins.'"[32]

It is in her travels, in crossing borders to territories neutral to her like Turkey, that she feels Britain offers her some sought of home and at the same time becomes less aware of the race politics. Under Asian sun her "armour roasts, rusts, falls off in bits, is swept out by the tide."[33] As a tourist she is born anew, a reflection on the notion that it is only as cultural tourists, constantly in transit that we do not have to deal with the problematic of identity, the skin that she originally "warily dipped into like a wet suit"[34] is now dried out.

How should we define it then, our "localised brand of Black Atlantic literature", a conglomeration of not only culture, but the transcendence of the history of past generations borne on other shores, the frustrations of living as The Other, the aspirations that writers often allude to from their subversive positions, how should we describe it? As British culture? No. The notion of Britishness has implied meaning that is of no benefit to Black people and as a result of which they are beginning to reject. There may be Black people standing up in Britain but there aren't any Black people in what Britain stands for.

Gilroy saw the distinction between Blackness and Englishness as a brand of racism that is a product of nationalist and ethnic absolutist understandings of culture. Instead of seeing culture as something fluid and divided and given fixed identities: "The politics of 'race' in this country [Britain] is fired by conceptions of national belonging and homogeneity which not only blur the distinction between 'race' and nation, but rely on that very ambiguity for their effect...The new racism is primarily concerned with mechanisms of inclusion and exclusion. It specifies who may legitimately belong to the national community and simultaneously advances reasons for the segregation or banishment of those whose 'origin, sentiment or citizenship' assigns them elsewhere."[35]

The differences in which the narrator describes between Dele and the other Blacks at Oxford make him the "undisputed number one negro" on the campus.[36] Dele is the connoisseur on the games that

Black folk play on whites. He lords it as an authority on trend: "So it was with something of the world-weariness of the dab old hand that Dele strolled to the stereo situated at the back of Tabitha's cavernous sitting-room. The Motown selection had just played out and the punters parted and smiled expectantly at the brother as he moved through the crowd to exercise his inalienable prerogative."[37] He continuously toys with his race in this fashion, dropping "ghetto jive" for humour and playing with misguided stereotypes.[38] In trying to woo the white girl Helena, he considers changing tack thinking that, "Perhaps he should drop the dress of his Queen's grammar and go for pure ragga blather."[39] In contrast, he knew he "could do little wrong by coming overly cerebral with Cheryl. She said she'd never heard a brother so softly-spoken and polysyllabic before. At college he broke everything down with a little ragga blather. Now here he was buttering it up on the smoother side. Different strokes for different folks."[40]

Throughout the majority of the text Dele celebrates the manner in which he shifts his "cultural capital", having accused his close friend Concrete of having a ghetto mentality, Concrete retorts that he is "a blood chameleon", shifting representations of race to suit his circumstances be it London or Oxford. "And Dele had smiled at the time and thought 'That's right. Nothing can contain me!'"[41] The 'reality check' begins with the police towing Concrete's car away for illegally parking, an altercation between Concrete and the officer-in-charge ensues, and in referring to each other by their surnames, a more sinister act, a personalised act, is revealed. Furthermore the officer, makes no attempt to diffuse the situation by immediately calling for backup on his radio, referring to Concrete, Dele and Dapo as suspects and threatening the latter with arrest. The PC is unsettled as Dapo insinuates that the action being carried out is fused by racism: "You stop us the most and we have the least cars, isn't it?" and as Dele warns that he'll put in a complaint "I've got the numbers of these fools and we'll speak to their boss-man later,"[42] PC Daniels violently restrains Dapo even though she has done nothing wrong, the backup arrives and the police are brutal in their handling of the three citizens.

Here Adebayo reflects the experiences of Black youth in Britain, as the three are arrested (without a stipulation of the crime) they are referred to as 'Black cunts',[43] in reading Dele's name on his ID, PC Daniels asserts that he is not British but a 'Fuckin' NI-gerian', they are then subjected to some 'bunny bashing',[44] referred to as a beating particularly reserved for Black youths. The attack his sister receives at the hands of the police has grave results: she is and as a sickle cell sufferer and she lapses into a coma. Dele reflects that, "He had been so crazily casual; about Dapo's health, about London, about life – where bad things happened to Black people."[45] The attack thrusts him into politics and he is soon addressing an audience reflective of a disaffected Black community. However in addressing them, his "Blackness" is called into question once again, this time by old family acquaintance Chris Makanje: "It's interesting that the speaker himself admits that his time at one of Anglo-Saxon England's great seats of learning taught him nothing at all about the real world outside...Maybe if he and others of his sort paid more respect to those Afrikan warriors who cleared the way instead of dancing on their graves, all this would come as less of a shock! But what does he know of the situation facing the *urban Black man in Britain today?*"[46]

Dele is left to seek solace from Makanje's verbal attack from new found Gabriel,[47] a new found friend who is present at the gathering and who he had earlier identified as a Black man willing to embrace different cultures and not conform to racial expectations and simplifications. However despite the constant antagonism Dele receives from members of the Black community and his ideologies towards the space that Black people occupy in Britain, is still notably interrogated. The analogy of white people taking up a different seat at the end of the carriage away from the seats that he and his Black colleagues occupy is tantamount to his recognition of the arena of race politics in Britain that he had either not been aware of or had surreptitiously ignored.

"The white world increasingly seemed to represent a combination of indifference and hostility. It seemed right, as he settled securely into his seat, that your space should be guaranteed, one way or the other."[48] Adebayo identifies that if this polarisation is what it takes, then so be it, but at least a seat on the underground, a place and space in which to safely sit within the British nation, should be guaranteed for his kind. History had dictated it.

The Conservative politics of the 1980s, Thactherism and the attack on left wing governing bodies, the outspoken and notorious comments of Norman Tebbit that Pakistani's ought to get behind the England cricket team and not Pakistan, did little to give ethnic minorities a sense that there was a willingness to assimilate the ideas and cultures of other races into that of Britain. The far right movements of the 70s and early 80s and the tense relationship between Black communities and the police force was tested, culminating in the Brixton riots of 1981. At the same time, a disproportionate number of Black deaths in police custody was being noted along with the high profile murder of Black teenager Stephen Lawrence. Almost twenty years later, The Brixton, Soho and Brick Lane nail bombings of 1999, which left a total of 110 injuries and three deaths was a reminder of the underlining racial tension that still exists in modern Britain.

A seminal moment in Black British history took place on the night of 22nd April 1993 when two Black youths, Stephen Lawrence and his friend Duwayne Brooks were on their way home in Eltham, South East London. A racially motivated assault occurred when a group of five to six white youths attacked Stephen.[49]

The brutal and unprovoked murder was well publicised. There was a strong outcry from amongst the Black community and Black media. The press closely followed the investigation and Stephen's parent's tireless campaign for justice. The collapse of the prosecution in 1996, the coroner's verdict of unlawful killing and the Police Complaints Authority investigation into the case in 1997, coupled with the continual pressure of Black community groups and organisations, led the then Home Secretary Jack Straw to call for a public inquiry into the murder of Stephen Lawrence.

He appointed William MacPherson to the Public Inquiry and the report was published in February 1999[50] pointing to the mishandling of the investigation by the police, the withholding of information and the collusion in covering up between officers: The Macpherson Inquiry brought to the public attention the institutional racism that runs deep in the echelons of the political landscape of British society:

> *Paragraph 6.39.* Given the central nature of the issue we feel that it is important at once to state our conclusion that institutional racism, within the terms of its description set out in Paragraph 6.34 above, exists both in the Metropolitan Police Service and in other Police Services and other institutions countrywide.

This was not the first time an inquiry had came to these conclusions. In the inquiry into the Brixton riots of 1981 Lord Scarman wrote[51] "All the evidence I have received, both on the subject of racial disadvantage and more generally, suggests that racialism and discrimination against Black people – often hidden, sometimes unconscious – remain a major source of social tension and conflict". However as journalist Gary Younge noted in *The Guardian*[52], the "Macpherson [inquiry] emerged from an incident prompted by a group of white racists louts, bungled by an overwhelmingly white police force, which sparked an investigation presided over by a white lord. This was no longer a debate about how to contain the problems that Black people cause by their very presence. This was white people talking to other white people about the problems engendered by their racism."

White Britain was faced with re-examining its very nature; the problems facing ethnic minorities for decades were now open for new debate with the hope that there might be a broader understanding of the problems facing people of colour in the country. The inquiry pointed out that racism was not just displayed in acts of violence by mindless thugs but also lay undetected and indirect within the very organisations that are expected to shape our society: Policing, Education, Employment.

Right Wing Britain came out to defend its "good" name: Gerald Howarth, the Conservative MP for Aldershot of whom the BBC profile as being "anti-European-union" and a "standard bearer for Thatcherism" was reported to have: "bemoaned the dispiriting effect the report had on the white psyche."[53] Others trivialised the Macpherson inquiry by almost ignoring its significant findings and reducing the argument to that of the recommendations compromising police power. Once again it became an argument between those that remain in denial to protect imaginary borderlines and those that accept that the face of Britain is no longer an exclusively white one.

In the wake of the September 11th attacks Muslims are being alienated and persecuted. Migrants and asylum seekers are prejudiced against and attacked in communities such as Dover where they arrive and are expected to remain with generally little support for neither old nor new residents to the effective change this brings to British society. Newspapers such as the *Daily Mail* have held a long running stance against them. (Although, ironically, they came out in full force against the youths who attacked Stephen Lawrence). Often failing to project the immigration issue from a rounded perspective, their headlines report that: 'Sickly Immigrants add 1bn pounds to NHS bill'[54] and attribute the rise of AIDS and hepatitis to migrants: 'Migrants blamed for diseases.'[55] An online poll conducted by the *Daily Mail* on the 24th of September last year reported that a "staggering 92% of *Daily Mail* online [readers] believe that Britain needs immigration quotas, a policy outlined by Conservative leader Michael Howard." Just five months prior to the poll, in an editorial commentary on the 6th April 2004, the *Daily Mail* sought to vindicate its position writing that "For years, the Mail has been denounced by a canting, smug liberal elite for expressing the concerns felt by millions over Britain's asylum shambles. And now the whole conspiracy of politically correct silence has collapsed. Immigration has been thrust to the top of the political agenda. Mr Blair's "summit" today is billed as the opportunity to get a grip on the abuses that have turned official policy into such a demeaning farce." In the response to the *Daily Mail* headline on the European Convention on the Future of Europe in May 2003 that read: "the end of everything we understand by the terms Britain and Britishness", Nick Clegg Member of European Parliament, wrote in *The Guardian* on the 16th May 2003[56] that "The barrage of wilful misinformation and prejudice is difficult to stomach" and called their headline "a gloriously over-the-top front page declaration". Hari Kunzru, author of the prize winning debut *The Impressionist* rejected the £5,000 prize winnings of the John Llewellyn Rhys award sponsored by the *Daily Mail* and its sister paper *The Mail on Sunday*, citing his disliking of the "papers' consistent hostility towards Black and Asian British people."[57] Kunzru, whose father is Kashmiri said that they, "pursue an editorial policy of vilifying and demonising refugees and asylum-seekers ... As the child of a migrant, I am only too aware of the poisonous effect of the Mail's editorial line". The attitudes of the *Daily Mail* and much of Britain's race politics today are formed on the basis of protecting "the nation", claiming that traditions and nationalities are in danger of being lost: 'The process of national decline is presented as coinciding with the dilution of once homogenous and continuous national stock by Alien strains. Alien cultures come to embody a threat which, in turn, invites the conclusion that national decline and weakness have been precipitated the arrival of Blacks.'[58] Madeleine Bunting commenting in *The Guardian*[59] on *The Sun* newspaper's 2004 campaign to 'Save Christmas' which was apparently in danger of being lost behind "the political correctness of local government's multicultural policies", noted that, "There's a curious phenomenon in the complex politics of identity that is increasingly evident...it is how the established majority inverts its status to one of victimhood." (Bunting, 2004)

An illuminating example of the attitudes that still lie in the underbelly of 'Great' Britain was the response towards the Commons Public Administration Committee's report into the legitimacy of the British Honours System. In the 2004 Report "A Matter of Honour", the Committee found that titles and name changing honours such as knighthoods and damehoods were preoccupied with rank and class. The Honours, made under the Order of the British Empire, were also criticised for their association with an imperialistic past.

Sections of the Black media commenting on the report spoke of the need for reform citing the public rejection of the OBE awards by writers such as Benjamin Zephaniah, Graham Greene and pop star David Bowie because of its symbolised colonialism.

The Commission on the Future of Multi-Ethnic Britain was set up in 1998 by the Runnymede Trust, an independent think-tank. They published a report in October 2000 which concluded that the term 'British' had 'racial connotations and would no longer serve as a description of the UK's multicultural society'. It also concluded that the UK should be "formally recognised as a multicultural society" and that its history needs to be "revised, rethought or jettisoned."[60]

The report stated that 'Britishness, as much as Englishness, has systematic largely unspoken racial connotations'. Not all agreed and the report was subject to a large amount of criticism, particularly from Conservative MP's who regarded it as an attempt at 'social engineering'. Speaking in *The Guardian* newspaper, Lord Tebbit, the former Tory party chairman, said interestingly, "The best way forward is integration rather than separation into cultural ghettoes."[61]

The Runnymede report concluded that: "Hybrid cultural forms have emerged, especially in music and the arts". Alan Travis, home affairs editor for *The Guardian*, reported on how Tories saw this report as an "affront to the native British". What does "native British" mean exactly? Is this not to suggest that the white British man today has more in common with its history than with its present multicultural society? That what it means today is an identity that has remain fixed and uninfluenced by other races and nationalities including those such as the French and Americans?

The novelist Caryl Phillips was born in St Kitts and raised in Yorkshire, North England. In an essay recently published in *The Guardian*,[62] Phillips has written on how the race politics of Britain caused him to seek shores elsewhere in order to enable him to intricately recognise and re-examine his identity, for Britain

"...seemed determined to offer me only unpalatable, and racially determined, stereotypes as models for my own identity."

For Phillips and for many Blacks in Britain, the nation rejects the authentic individualism and heterogeneity within the country in order to protect its ideas of nation. Therefore Britain relies on stereotypical notions and representations in order to distinguish what the country is as well as what it is not. And this is where Evaristo and Adebayo become increasingly significant in revealing the true disparity between the pedagogical and performative concepts in the narrative of nation, as outlined by Homi K. Bhabha in his essay 'DissemiNation'[63], in which he states that the idea of a nation is paradoxically hinged on an imagined concept of a homogenous sociological entity with the reality of a heterogeneous mix of people living under such a concept.

How can minorities in Britain ever truly feel part of a country that perpetuates the stereotypes that represent this homogenous entity? Britain is a proud nation that still has not got over the loss of its empire nor has it come to terms with dealing with the legacy of colonialism. "Britain is a deeply class-bound society, with a codified and hierarchal structure that locates the monarchy at the top, with a roster of increasingly 'marginal' people as one filters down to the bottom. It is a largely inflexible system whose survival is dependent upon the maintenance of the status quo, and any societal change or development, such as immigration, is likely to cause instability."[64]

However far the politics of assimilation may take an ethnic minority there are always borders that cannot be passed. Colour has been written into the criteria of British nationality. How we appear to be consciously aware of our difference, respond to it and what it means on day to day terms is often illustrated within our work. For example Adebayo alludes to the tension between races in given locations as Dele and his white colleagues are chased out of Sussex by the locals. It is his only other experience outside of London bar his time at Oxford: "Dele urged them to hurry to the car. Just in time, as the pack suddenly ran at them and beer bottles rushed in the air past them and smashed against the ground and the wall, to the sounds of 'niggerlovers!'[65]

Why would an emerging generation of Black Atlantic youth want to identify themselves with a history of Britain and British literature that has been at best elitist, at worst imperial? The diaspora (as we know it I hasten to add) is in continuous struggle with the inherent nationalism and unflattering connotations possessed in what it means to be British. The term 'Britain' still throws up notions of an empire, rule, colonialism, neo-colonialism. Knowing this, new groups of people are refusing to attach notions of 'British nationality' to the corpus of their conglomerate work.

We perpetuate a notion of 'whiteness' as being a norm that we must measure ourselves against by setting our identities up with arbitrary codes and signifiers. The issues of identity are continuingly coming to the fore in our Black 'British' texts, from the painstaking emotions felt on the Greenside estates of Courttia Newland's *The Scholar* to the marginalisation of Jazz, the sole Black man in the white patriarchal dominated space of the police force in Ike Eze-anyika's *Canteen Culture*. Still, the problem of identity only helps to unveil the fact that the idea of a common voice is now non-existent. Black writing as a subculture is an imagined community much like national identity in which we identify with people we'll never meet or not share a single view with.

The truth is we have multiple identities in an inclusive society. It is time to look to other things for a sense of belonging. Contemporary Black writers in Britain would be limiting themselves to idolised notions of essentialism in arguing that their texts were any more African, or West-Indian etc. than they were British and vice versa. As generations spring forth it seems safe to surmise that what is emerging is something quite different, a hybrid that, as new generations having been born and raised here, feel no direct attachment to the work of diaspora as we know it, or rather *knew* it.

What I'll argue for is that younger generations of Black people are increasingly rejecting what both the identities associated with Black diaspora and Britain mean in their connotative forms. In continuing to categorise ourselves in this fashion we run the risk of confining ourselves to walking, to inflect on the parable, the narrow road *often* taken. Black British writing will continue to be termed on the basis of being Black, to be politicised and considered in the first hand on its non literary merit, as ethnographic accounts of how Black people in Britain negotiated their way. Mike Phillips, in his criticism of Sukhdev Sandhu's study on Black writing in London, *London Calling: How Black and Asian Writers Imagined a City*, exposed how such views can be huge oversights. In considering Sandhu's comparative look at the writing of Caryl Phillips and Hanif Kureishi, Phillips observes that, "Contrasting *The Final Passage* [Phillips] and *My Beautiful Laundrette* [Kureishi's screenplay] merely underlines the futility of comparing the experiences of a Black urban migrant family in the 1950s with that of the relatively prosperous British born child of an English and Asian union, moving to London from the suburbs in the 1980s."[66] Here are two texts by authors of great merit that bare no similarities but are lumped together under the redundant term of Black British writing maintained by the status quo. In an interview with Sarah Hughes, Percival Everett shares similar frustrations at being grouped by skin colour, recognising that this grouping strips our ethnicity of any pluralism, in stating that he finds it "ridiculous that Black writers are constantly asked to reflect their community – as though when you are Black you can't write a novel which addresses other issues or ideas,"[67] Everett acknowledges that there is a huge savvy of actors writing outside of the box.

Things are not just Black or white, while a lot of what I embrace is western by design, a lot of what the west is, (no pun intended), *taken* from a host of other nations. Different familial identities have emerged – Lara's mixed race parentage gives her another dimension, as would 'class', and 'location' as Dele's date Cheryl notes of the Black boys from Preston: "Black folk be going round saying 'Got a light, Chuck?', 'Ta, cock!' and 'Our Kid' as native as the natives."[68] Because of this cultural traffic the very maintenance of national identity (in which there is security) is dependent on the rejection of the Other. A nation in denial, Britain turns a blind eye towards the streets, the mosques, the Pentecostal churches practicing their own brands of syncretic Christianity, the Caribbean take-away and the Kurdish community halls. Adebayo and Evaristo play an important role in re-writing the nation. The spirits embrace Lara on her trip to Lagos, but she cannot rest there, she has one more step to make: To Brazil where her great grandfather was enslaved. In Rio she realises she is "a poor relation" in a "rainbow metropolis" but still she hopes she will find the past there and although she acknowledges the retention of Yoruba she does not find anything personal to her in the city, she observes a Palm Sunday tradition being carried out and realises she is observing a way of the world's future, "witness to one culture being orchestrated by another, yet the past is gone, the future means transformation."[69]

Evaristo points here to further problems with identity, where even your skin can be a non-determinate, further proof that what we all have 'third positions' now, hybrids not just in race but in cultural inheritance. There's retention of tradition when Lara's father Taiwo names his first grandchild, the daughter of his eldest daughter, Iyabo. There's a double irony at play here in that Iyabo means 'Mother returns' in Yoruba, a tribute to his recently passed mother-in-law who despised him because of his Black skin but at the same time would be proud of her great granddaughter who has "hazel eyes, straight nose, blonde hair, ivory skin."[70]

The language Dele uses reflects the hybridity of his culture, too. He speaks in terms that are part of a general youth culture as Black, white and Asian . Youths refer to clubbing as "raving"[71](a term that has become appropriated from Black culture) but at the same time he uses terms that are associated with Black British youth culture such as "spar" to refer to a close friend and "belled" to mean to have called someone by phone. Its reflective of what the narrator does, switching language when they feel it's appropriate, from describing Dapo as "creasing up" (laughing) and describing that Dele "bucked up" (met up) with Concrete.[72] Adebayo is asserting that his narrator is either himself, someone informed or someone privy to a language that is born of young Black people on British shores. This narrator even uses the cockney rhyming slang of east London to reinforce this idea of hybridity: "it gave him six with size twelve's in his boat race."[73] In Dele's father stating that "You can lead a horse to water, but you cannot make him drink." and "But for your mother, I would throw you and your complexes out of the house, until you understand that you're an African, not some Follow-Follow boy!"[74] we can see that his father is concerned and therefore is in admittance that Dele is not living in tradition with the Nigerian child, instead he recognises that Dele is complex, influenced by a myriad of cultures, a contrast to his "young cousins with impeccable manners and impeccable ambitions – one eye turned toward home."[75] His cousin Timi is the product of parents who like his father, came to London in the sixties but chose to return to Nigeria. Timi is Dele's reflection representing the product of Nigerians who came to post-war England and succeeded in their studies while Dele is the product of those who failed and remained in the country. 'His Dad [Dele's] was speaking forcefully in Yoruba, so Dele couldn't catch the whole drift, but he was using both his name and Timi's in a way, contrasting the latter, who conducted his affairs in the family tradition, with the errant ways of doing of "this boy, this boy…" '[76] His cousin is not sympathetic to his ways either, mouthing 'Jamo' to him on account of what he saw as Dele's West Indian manner. What it is in fact is the strong influence of West Indian on a culture that occupies a new place within the politics of identity.

As a writer, but first and foremost as a human being, I am concerned with identity and take an interest in those writers whose personal background or literary work mirror my own understandings. Those that spring foremost to my mind are Diran Adebayo and Bernardine Evaristo. The trouble with our 'condition' is that we are raised in semi tradition, meaning a 'double standard' manner in which it is the legacy of colonialism that will have our parents wanting their children to take on an English education, an English accent (for this is proper) and often neglect the need to speak and thus teach us, their native language but at the same time to observe customs when they see fit. It leaves an uncertainty in the child that is present and knows no other locality than the mother country of those that were formerly colonised to deal with managing two worlds – a 'Third Space'. It is a condition of cultural hybridity that in critiquing Salman Rushdie's *The Satanic Verses* Homi K. Bhabha described 'Third Space' in the following terms:

> "...for me the importance of hybridity is not to be able to trace two original moments from which the third emerges, rather hybridity to me is the 'third space' which enables other positions to emerge. This third space displaces the histories that constitute it, and sets up new structures of authority, new political initiatives, which are adequately understood through received wisdom."[77]

"The intervention of the Third Space of enunciation, which makes the structure of meaning and reference an ambivalent process, destroys this mirror of representation in which cultural knowledge is customarily revealed as an integrated, open, expanding code. Such an intervention quite properly challenges our sense of the historical identity of culture as a homogenizing, unifying force, authenticated by the originary Past, kept alive in the national tradition of the People. In other words, the disruptive temporality of enunciation displaces the narrative of the western nation."[78]

The reason why Lara and Dele are being called into question is because they are being real to themselves, that there is something else going on, they occupy third spaces. The cultural hybridity is perceived as a threat, a threat that if Black people become like this then the imagined community, in this case the global diasporic identity, will be called into question.

It is fundamental that as Black writers we continue to address and re-address the question of identity: "I was still in a struggle to recognise and protect my own identity, in all its intricacy, for I knew that I had to view it as unique, complicated, open to inspection and re-examination, and binding me not just to a particular tribe, clan, or race, but to the human race. I always understood that recognising this would be a prerequisite of writing well, for the more vigorously one resists a narrow view of self, the more one sees."[79] There is a dangerous ambivalence at play when the writer does not reflect the true face of the nation. Frantz Fanon warns us of this: "The artist who has decided to illustrate the truths of the nation turns paradoxically towards the past and away from actual events. What he ultimately intends to embrace are in fact the cast-offs of thought, its shells and corpses, a knowledge which has been stabilized once and for all. But the native intellectual who wishes to create an authentic work of art must realize that the truths of a nation are in the first place its realities. He must go on until he has found the seething pot out of which the learning of the future will emerge."[80]

Fanon urges us to simply tell the truth about our identities/nationalities, only then can we progressively move forward into the future. Our Blackness as a political entity may well be suitable in mobilising us as a people but we need to bring the tool into the 21st century, re-invent it and toss aside the romanticised, archaic and idolised notions of afro-centricity that remain a chain around our necks.

A Black 'British' individual in Britain can never be white. This much is unquestionable. Can they ever be African and can they ever be British? I believe the answer is also no. To the question of being African is one in most cases, which requires the individual to scale a language barrier, then perhaps a religious one, followed by practiced customs. To make the task harder these are barriers that, having experienced colonialism and experiencing globalisation, are continually shifting. To truly be considered British? Again the answer is no. To be British is to carry a burden of representation, Blacks do not fit into the national identity of Britain, our very difference maintains its identity, and the texts of Evaristo and Adebayo serve to remind us of the tensions and obstacles of which we face as we negotiate the differing dominant ideology of the territory we call home. In a bid to maintain imagined borderlines it apparent that we have got a purchase on almost every other culture that there is. So in essence what we call Black British is not very British at all; 'Black' is not enough to group it in anything else but simple terms and playing with the term 'British' and its meaning is a growing issue continually expounded upon. To be tagged British but not to contribute to British national identity is an antagonism that a new emerging generation of Black writers will not want to be attached to.

Evaristo and Adebayo's texts offer us preludes to a brand new purchase on identity. The shackles of 'Post-Colonialism' used to restrain Black writing have slipped loose. Writing by Blacks in Britain has already moved beyond the post-colonial. Where Bhaba's Third Space conceptualised the movement to which writers *arrived* in, Adebayo and Evaristo represent writers *birthed* in the 'Third Space.' These writers have no basis or as much basis in the cultural imperialism of America as they do in the cultural legacy of colonialism. The creative culture of the Black diaspora in Britain is dominant above these other forms and thus renders the post-colonial theoretical framework as insufficient in dealing with these writers, far less the future Black writers of British shores. Such are the antagonisms in Britain experienced by ethnic minorities that the framework in which to place Black people will be in need of constant examination and re-evaluation as the cultural exchange across continents is continued and remains enslaved to the political and economical dynamics of the world and globalisation.

NOTES AND REFERENCES

[1] Ngugi Wa Thiong'o in *The Pre-Occupation Of Postcolonial Studies* eds. Afzal-Khan, Fawzia and Seshadri-Crooks,Kalpana 'Borders and Bridges: Seeking Connections Between Things', Durham: Duke University Press, 2000, p.124

[2] Adebayo, Diran, *Some Kind Of Black,* London: Abacus, 1996

[3] Evaristo, Bernardine, *Lara,* Kent: Angel Royal Publishing, 1997

[4] See "Bernadine Evaristo with Alastair Niven" p.285 and "Monica Ali with Diran Adebayo" p346 in Nasta, Susheila (ed.) *'Writing Across Worlds: Contemporary Writers Talk'* (London: Routledge 2004)

[5] Isidore Okpewho pXV in "Introduction" to Okpewho, Isidore, Boyce Davies, Carole and Mazrui, Ali A (eds.), *The African Diaspora: African Origins and New World Identities,* Indiana: Indiana University Press, 1999

[6] Gilroy, Paul, *The Black Atlantic: Modernity and Double Consciousness* (London: Verso, 1993) p.4

[7] Evaristo, Bernardine *Lara* p.60

[8] Ibid. p.65

[9] Okpewho, Isidore, Boyce Davies, Carole and Mazrui, Ali A (eds.), *The African Diaspora: African Origins and New World Identities,* Indiana: Indiana University Press, 1999. For an interesting critique of Gilroy see "An African Diaspora: The Ontological Project" by Michael J. C. Echeruo p.3-18, p.5

[10] Adebayo, Diran, *Some Kind of Black,* p.105

[11] Ibid. p.20

[12] Ibid. p.20

[13] Ibid. p.28

[14] Ibid. p.28

[15] Newland, Courttia, and Sesay, Kadija (eds.), *IC3: The Penguin Book of New Black Writing In Britain*, London: Hamish Hamilton, 2000, p.X

[16] Ibid. p.X

[17] Pete Kennedy's interview in The Voice Newspaper with Lemn Sissay Kennedy, Peter, 'In Search Of Collective Identity', *The Voice*, 31st July 2000

[18] Gilroy, Paul, *The Black Atlantic: Modernity and Double Consciousness,* London: Verso, 1993 p.15

[19] Adebayo, Diran, *Some Kind of Black* p.60

[20] Ibid. p.26

[21] Evaristo, p.103

[22] Ibid. p.104

[23] Ibid. p.72

[24] Ibid. p.85

[25] Ibid. p.76

[26] Ibid. p.76

[27] Ibid. p.81

[28] Ibid.p.89

[29] Ibid.p.90

[30] Ibid.p.92

[31] Ibid. p.91

[32] Ibid. p.91

[33] Ibid. p97

34 Ibid. p.87

35 In Gilroy, Paul, *There Ain't No Black in the Union Jack,* London: Hutchinson, 1987 p.45

36 Adebayo, p.19

37 Ibid. p.17

38 Ibid. p.26

39 Ibid. p.39

40 Ibid. p.53

41 Ibid. p.30

42 Ibid. p.74

43 Ibid. p76

44 Ibid. p.77

45 Ibid. p.86

46 Ibid. p.92

47 Ibid. p.95

48 Ibid. p.100

49 For a more details on the murder of Stephen Lawrence, the campaign for justice and the subsequent Macpherson report see, for a biographical account: Brooks, Duwayne with Hattenstone, Simon, *Steve and Me,* London: Abacus, 2003. For an analysis of the media account see: Cottle, Simon, *The Racist Murder of Stephen Lawrence: Media Performance and Public Transformation,* London: Greenwood 2004. For a theoretical approach see Hall, Stuart, 'From Scarman to Lawrence' in *Connections,* Spring, 2000

50 *The Stephen Lawrence Inquiry,* Report of an Inquiry by Sir William Macpherson of Cluny, London: The Stationary Office, February 1999

51 The Brixton Disorders, April 10-12, 1981: Inquiry Report. Chairman Lord Scarman London: The Stationary Office, November 1981 (Para 6.35, p 110)

52 "A Year Of Reckoning" by Gary Younge in *The Guardian,* 21 February, 2000

53 Ibid.

54 Doughty, "Sickly immigrants add £1bn to NHS bill" by Steve Doughty in the *Daily Mail,* 23 June, 2003

55 "Migrants blamed for diseases" by Edward Heathcot Amory in the *Daily Mail,* 5 August, 2003

56 "Don't EU believe it" by Nick Clegg in *The Guardian,* Friday 16 May, 2003

57 see Fiachra Gibbons and Claire Armitstead report Author rejects prize from 'anti-migrant' newspaper in *The Guardian,* Friday 21 November, 2003.

58 Gilroy, Paul, *There Ain't No Black in the Union Jack,* London: Hutchinson, 1987 p.46

59 "This is about real victims" by Madeleine Bunting in *The Guardian,* Saturday 11 December, 2004

60 See the report by the Commission on the Future of Multi-Ethnic Britain, Bhikhu Parekh (chair), published as "The Future of Multi-Ethnic Britain: The Parekh Report" London: Profile Books 2000

61 "British tag is 'coded racism'" By Alan Travis, *The Guardian,* 11 October, 2000

62 "Necessary Journeys" by Caryl Phillips, *The Guardian,* 11 December, 2004

63 See Bhaba, Homi K. (ed.) Nation and Narration, London: Routledge 1990, pp.291-320 *"DissemiNation: time, narrative, and the margins of the modern nation"* by Homi K. Bhabha

64 "Necessary Journeys" by Caryl Phillips, *The Guardian,* 11 December, 2004

65 Adebayo, Diran, p.153

66 Mike Phillips "From Slaves to Straw Men", *The Guardian,* 30 August, 2003

[67] Sarah Hughes, "Redefining Black Literature", *New Nation* Newspaper, 19 April 2004

[68] Adebayo, Diran p.54

[69] Evaristo. Bernardine p.139

[70] Ibid. p.101

[71] Adebyo p.2

[72] Ibid. p.12

[73] Ibid. p71

[74] Ibid. p5

[75] Ibid. p115

[76] Ibid. p.116

[77] See Homi K. Bhaba 'The Third Space', an interview with Jonathan Rutherford in Rutherford, Jonathan (ed), *Identity: Community, Culture, Difference,* London: Lawrence & Wishart 1990

[78] See Bhabha, Homi K., *The Location Of Culture,* London: Routledge, 1994 p.37

[79] *"Necessary Journeys"* by Caryl Phillips, The Guardian, 11 December, 2004

[80] Fanon, Frantz, *The Wretched Of The Earth,* London: Penguin Books Edition, 1967

Author Biographies and Bibliographies

Chapter 1 – DIRAN ADEBAYO

Diran Adebayo was born in London in 1968 to Nigerian parents. He read Law at Oxford University and worked as a journalist at *The Voice* newspaper, before working in television as a researcher and assistant producer. The manuscript of his novel *Some Kind of Black* won the inaugural SAGA Prize, set up by actress and novelist Marsha Hunt for Black British writers. The prize included a publishing contract with London publishers Virago, who published the book in 1996. The book centres on Dele, a young Black student living in Britain, and his attempt to reconcile his experiences at university in Oxford, his Nigerian roots, and his exploits in urban London, where he explores the music scene, experiments with drugs and becomes involved in black activism after his sister is arrested. The book also won the Author's Club Best Novel of the Year award, a Betty Trask Award and a Writers' Guild Award (New Writer of the Year) in 1996. His second novel, *My Once Upon a Time* (2000), is a modern day fable set in London's near future. Diran Adebayo is currently working on a screenplay, 'Burnt', for FilmFour, his third novel, 'The Ballad of Dizzy and Miss P' and a collection of essays, 'Here is a Protest'. He was recently appointed to the National Council of Arts Council England in which his role will be to discuss policy issues for artists in Britain. He lives in London.

PRIMARY WORKS
Novels: Some Kind of Black (Virago, 1996); My Once Upon a Time (Abacus, 2000).
Anthologies: New Writing 12 (Picador, 2003), (co-editor with Jane Rogers and Blake Morrison).
http://www.contemporarywriters.com/authors /?p=auth5

Chapter 2 – JACKIE KAY

Jackie Kay was born in Edinburgh, Scotland in 1961 to a Scottish mother and a Nigerian father. She was adopted by a white couple at birth and was brought up in Glasgow, studying at the Royal Scottish Academy of Music and Drama and Stirling University where she read English. The experience of being adopted by and growing up within a white family inspired her first collection of poetry, *The Adoption Papers* (1991). The poems deal with an adopted child's search for a cultural identity and are told through three different voices: an adoptive mother, a birth mother and a daughter. The collection won a Scottish Arts Council Book Award, the Saltire Society Scottish First Book of the Year Award and a commendation by the Forward Poetry Prize judges in 1992. The poems in *Other Lovers* (1993) explore the role and power of language, inspired and influenced by the history of Afro-Caribbean people, the story of a search for identity grounded in the experience of slavery. The collection includes a sequence of poems about the blues-singer Bessie Smith. *Off Colour* (1998) explores themes of sickness, health and disease through personal experience and metaphor. Her latest collection is *New and Selected Poems* (2004). Her poems have appeared in many anthologies, and she has written widely for stage and television. Her first novel, *Trumpet*, published in 1998, was awarded *The Guardian* Fiction Prize and was shortlisted for the International IMPAC Dublin Literary Award. Inspired by the life of musician Billy Tipton, the novel tells the story of Scottish jazz trumpeter Joss Moody whose death revealed that he was, in fact, a woman. Kay develops the narrative through the voices of Moody's wife, his adopted son and a journalist from a tabloid newspaper. *Why Don't You Stop Talking* (2002), is a collection of short stories. She has also published a novel for children, *Strawgirl* (2002). Jackie Kay lives in Manchester.

PRIMARY WORKS
Poetry: The Adoption Papers (Bloodaxe,1991); Twice Through the Heart (English National Opera, 1991); Other Lovers (Bloodaxe, 1993); Bessie Smith (Absolute, 1997); Off Colour (1998); Sick Bag (Bloodaxe, 1998); New and Selected Poems (Bloodaxe, 2004).
Fiction: Trumpet, First Published 1998 (Picador 2002); Why Don't You Stop Talking (Picador 2002); Borders (Picador, forthcoming 2005); Children and Young People: That Distance Apart (Turret, 1991); Iwo's Company (Blackie, 1992); Three Has Gone (Blackie, 1994); The Frog Who Dreamed She was an Opera Singer (Bloomsbury, 1999); Strawgirl (Macmillan, 2002); International Connections: New Plays for Young People (contributor) (Faber and Faber, 2003).
Audio: Kay, Agard, D'Aguiar, Berry (audio-cassette) Bluefoot Cassette (British Library National Sound Archive, 1990); Hearsay: Performance Poems Plus (57 Production, 1994); Teeth (57 Production, 1998).
Plays: Chiaroscuro (Methuen, 1986); Gay Sweatshop: Four Plays and a Company – includes 'Twice Over' (Methuen, 1989).
Anthologies: A Dangerous Knowing: Four Black Women Poets (Sheba, 1984); Penguin Modern Poets 8 – Merle Collins, Jackie Kay and Grace Nichols (Penguin, 1996); North: The Scotsman and Orange Short Story Award 2004 (editor) (Polygon 2004).
www.contemporarywriters.com/authors/?p=auth54

Chapter 3 – ANDREA LEVY

Andrea Levy was born in London, England in 1956 to Jamaican parents. She is the author of three novels, each of which explore – from different perspectives – the problems faced by black British-born children of Jamaican emigrants. Her first novel, the semi-autobiographical *Every Light in the House Burnin'* (1994), is the story of a Jamaican family living in London in the 1960s. Her second, *Never Far from Nowhere* (1996), is set during the 1970s and tells the story of two very different sisters living on a London council estate. In her most recent book *Fruit of the Lemon* (1999), Faith Jackson, a young Black Londoner, visits Jamaica after suffering a nervous breakdown and discovers a previously unknown personal history. Andrea Levy has been a judge for the Saga Prize and the Orange Prize for Fiction. In 2004, her fourth novel, *Small Island*, won the Orange Prize for fiction, and consequently, the Whitbread Novel Award and the Whitbread Book of the Year and the Commonwealth Prize for Eurasia. She lives with her partner, a graphic designer, in north London.

PRIMARY WORKS
Novels: Every Light in the House Burnin' (Headline Review, 1994); Never Far from Nowhere (Headline Review, 1996); Fruit of the Lemon (Headline Review, 1999); Small Island, (Headline Review, 2004).
http://www.andrealevy.co.uk/

Chapter 4 – COURTTIA NEWLAND

Courttia Newland was born and still lives in West London. He is the author of three acclaimed novels, *The Scholar*, *Society Within* and *Snakeskin*. Short Stories have appeared in several anthologies and he has a forthcoming collection of short stories entitled, *Music for the Off Key*. He is also the co-editor of *IC3: The Penguin Book of New Black Writing in Britain*. Newland is also an accomplished playwright and the On My Bookshelf Editor for *Sable* LitMag.

PRIMARY WORKS
Novels: The Scholar: A West Side Story (London: Abacus, 1997); Society Within (London: Abacus, 1999); Snakeskin (London: Abacus 2002).
Anthologies: 'The Great White Hate' In Afrobeat: New Black British Fiction, ed. Patsy Antoine. (London :Pulp Faction, 1999); 'A Hard Crossing to Bear' In Playing Sidney Poitier and other stories, ed. Catherine Johnson (London: S.A.K.S. Publications, 1999); 'Complexion Does Not Maketh the (Black) Man' In New Writing 8, eds. Tibor Fischer and Lawrence Norfolk (London:

Vintage, 1999); 'Piece of My Mind' In Disco 2000 (London: Sceptre, February 1998); 'His Healing Hands' In Rites of Spring: New London Writing (London: 4th Estate, 2001); 'Suicide Note' In The Time Out Book of London Short Stories, Volume 2 (London: February 2001); 'Sound of the Drums In England Calling (London: July 2001).

Plays: Estates of Mind. First staged at The Post Office Theatre, London, Summer 1998; Women of Troy 2099. First staged at The Post Office Theatre, London, Summer 1999, second run at The Pleasance, Edinburgh Festival, 1999; The Far Side. First staged at The Tricycle Theatre, second run at The Tricycle Theatre, Summers 2000/2001; also, The Tabernacle Community Centre, London, October 2001; Mother's Day. First staged at The Lyric Theatre, Hammersmith, September 2002; B is for Black. First staged at the Oval Theatre, London, October 2003. Courttia Newland (http://www.myvillage.com/ urbanfactor/courttianewland.htm)

Chapter 5 – LEONE ROSS

Leone Ross was born in Coventry, England, on 26 June 1969. She grew up in Jamaica, and studied at the University of the West Indies and at the City University in London. She has worked as a journalist for *The Voice* newspaper in London and as a researcher for LWT as well as contributing to a wide range of magazines and newspapers in Britain and America, including *The Guardian* and *The Sunday Times*. In 2000, she received a London Arts Board Writers' Award. Leone Ross has taught creative writing as an Associate Lecturer at Cardiff University, Birkbeck College and the City Literary Institute and was a Fellow at Trinity College Dublin in 2001. She was the Fiction Editor for Sable LitMag and she presently teaches creative writing (fiction and life writing) at Roehampton Institute. She is the author of two novels, *All the Blood is Red* (1996) and *Orange Laughter* (1999) and she is presently working on her third novel, 'Faith is Seven' and a collection of short stories.

PRIMARY WORKS

Novels: All the Blood is Red (Angela Royal Publishing 1996); Orange Laughter (ARP 1995, Anchor Books, 2000).

Anthologies: Creation Fire: A CAFRA Anthology of Caribbean Women's Poetry (Sister Vision Press – Canada, 1988); Born Fi Dead: A Journey Through the Jamaican Underworld (Introduction) (Canongate, 1995); Burning Words, Flaming Images (SAKS Publications, 1996); Wild Ways: Stories of Women on the Road (Sceptre, 1997); Dark Matter: A Century of Speculative Fiction from the African Diaspora (Warner, 2000); IC3: The Penguin Book of of Black British Writing (Penguin, 2000); Time Out London Short Stories, Volume 2 (Penguin, 2000); Brown Sugar: A Collection of Black Erotica (Dutton/Plume, 2001); England Calling: 24 Stories for the 21st Century (Weidenfeld & Nicolson, 2001); Whispers in the Walls: New Black and Asian Voices from Birmingham (Co-editor with Yvonne Brisset) (Tindal Street Press, 2001); Brown Sugar 2: Great One Night Stands (Simon & Schuster, 2003); Brown Sugar 3: Opposites Attract (Penguin, 2004). http://members.tripod.com/leoneross/leone.htm

Chapter 6 – ZADIE SMITH

Novelist Zadie Smith was born in North London in 1975 to an English father and a Jamaican mother. She read English at Cambridge, graduating in 1997. Her acclaimed first novel, *White Teeth* (2000), is a vibrant portrait of contemporary multicultural London, told through the story of three ethnically diverse families. The book won a number of awards and prizes, including *The Guardian* First Book Award, the Whitbread First Novel Award, and the Commonwealth Writers Prize (Overall Winner, Best First Book). It also won two EMMA (BT Ethnic and Multicultural Media Awards) for Best Book/Novel and Best Female Media Newcomer, and was shortlisted for the *Mail on Sunday*/John Llewellyn Rhys Prize, the Orange Prize for Fiction and the Author's Club First Novel Award. *White Teeth* has been translated into over twenty languages and was adapted for Channel 4 television for broadcast in autumn 2002. Her tenure as Writer in Residence at the Institute of Contemporary Arts resulted in the publication of an anthology of erotic stories entitled *Piece of Flesh* (2001). More recently, she has written the introduction for *The Burned Children of America* (2003), a collection of eighteen short stories by a new generation of young American writers. Zadie Smith's second novel, *The Autograph Man* (2002), a story of loss, obsession and the nature of celebrity, won the 2003 Jewish Quarterly Literary Prize for Fiction. In 2003 she was nominated by Granta magazine as one of 20 'Best of Young British Novelists'. She was a Radcliffe Fellow at Harvard University and is married to poet, Nick Laird.

PRIMARY WORKS
Novels: White Teeth (Hamish Hamilton 2000); The Autograph Man (2002).
Anthologies:
Speaking with the Angel (contributor) Penguin, 2000; Piece of Flesh (editor) (Institute of ContemporaryArts, 2001); The May Anthologies (editor) (Varsity Publications, 2001); Best of Young British Novelists 2003 (includes short story 'Martha, Martha') Granta, 2003; The Burned Children of America (Introduction) (Hamish Hamilton, 2003).
http://www.contemporarywriters.com/authors/?p=auth257

Chapter 7 – PATIENCE AGBABI

Patience Agbabi is a poet, performer and workshop facilitator. She was born in London in 1965 to Nigerian parents and spent her teenage years living in North Wales. She was educated at Oxford University and has appeared at numerous diverse venues in the UK and abroad over the last twelve years. (Full biographical details appear before the chapter on Patience Agbabi).

PRIMARY WORKS
Poetry: Raw (Gecko Press, 1995); Transformatrix (Payback Press, 2000).
Anthlogies: The Virago Book of Wicked Verse (Virago, 1992); Bittersweet: Contemporary Black Women's Poetry (Women's Press, 1998).
Oral: poems, sonnets, lyrics and the like (Sceptre, 1999); IC3: The Penguin Book of New Black Writing in Britain (Hamish Hamilton, 2000).

Chapter 8 – BERNARDINE EVARISTO

Bernardine Evaristo was born in London to a Nigerian father and English mother. She is the author of a poetry collection, *Island of Abraham* (1994), and of two novels-in-verse: *Lara* (1997) and *The Emperor's Babe* (2001). Lara traces the roots of a mixed-race Nigerian/English family over three continents and seven generations. The Emperor's Babe is set in Roman London in 211AD and follows the tragi-comic adventures of Zuleika, a girl of Sudanese parents who ends up having an affair with Emperor Septimius Severus. Evaristo's writing is widely published in anthologies, magazines and newspapers and she has written for theatre and radio. She has completed 31 worldwide tours since 1997, including writers' residencies at Binghamton University, New York, the University of the Western Cape, Cape Town, and at universities in Palestine, Bosnia and Herzegovina and Zimbabwe. In 2002 she was Writing Fellow at the University of East Anglia and at Barnard College/Columbia University in New York. Evaristo has featured in several television programmes internationally, was The Poetry Society's Poet in Residence at the Museum of London in 1999, and was one of two British writers who took part in the Literaturexpress Europa 2000 tour, which took 105 European writers through 11 European cities over six weeks by train. She received a NESTA Fellowship Award in 2003 and was elected a Fellow, Royal Society of Literature in 2004. Her latest novel, *Soul Tourists* (2005), is a comic tale of two twentieth-century misfits and their adventures across Europe.

PRIMARY WORKS
Poetry Island of Abraham (Peepal Tree Press, 1994); Lara (ARP, 1997: Hamish Hamilton, 2001).
Novels in Verse: The Emperor's Babe: A Novel (Hamish Hamilton, 2001); Soul Tourists (Hamish Hamilton, 2005). http://www.bevaristo.net/bio.asp

Chapter 9 – DOROTHEA SMARTT

Dorothea Smartt is of Barbadian heritage. Dubbed 'Brit-born Bajan international' [Kamau Brathwaithe], her work receives critical attention in Britain, Europe, the Caribbean, and the USA. She is acknowledged as tackling multi-layered cultural myths and the real life experiences of Black women with searing honesty. She was Brixton Market's first Poet-in-Residence, and a former Attached Live Artist at London's Institute of Contemporary Arts. Described as "accessible & dynamic", her work was recently selected to promote the best of contemporary writing in Europe today [www.liffey.net]. Her poetry collection *Connecting Medium* [Peepal Tree Press, 2001] contains a Forward Poetry Prize 'highly commended poem'. With her 'unique and penetrating voice' she's considered, "...a master artist who sculpts both Standard English and Caribbean English into a wide variety of poetic forms...capable of boldly crossing cultural boundaries in order to borrow from the past as she shapes poems for twenty-first century readers." [*Caribbean Times*]. "Connecting Medium", includes poems from her performance works "Medusa" and "From You To Me To You" (an ICA Live Arts commission). Other collaborative performances include "fo(u)r women"; and "Triangle" (a Black Arts Alliance commission). Her solo work, "Medusa", is considered a seminal and outstanding example of Black British Live Art. Her "medusaplay project", an on-going live art work-in-progress, premiered at the British Festival of Visual Theatre. Recently she collaborated with Hungarian artists to produce a multi-media performance in Budapest based on her collection. In 2000 she was commissioned to write her first play, 'fall out', which successfully toured primary schools. Most recently she's produced her first short films, for her installation/performance "Just A Part" commissioned by AFFORD (African Foundation for Development) and "Bringing It All Back Home", inspired by Sambo's grave, on Sunderland Point, a Lancaster LitFest commission. She has read and performed her work globally and she regularly goes into schools to inspire and motivate, as a visiting or resident poet, and provides workshops in varied settings. She is the poetry editor of *Sable* LitMag and she is currently working on her second poetry collection.

PRIMARY WORKS

Poetry: Connecting Medium (Peepal Tree Press, Leeds, 2001).
Anthologies: Intimate Wilderness (Eighth Mountain Press, 1991); Moving Beyond Boundaries (Pluto Press, London, 1995); Burning Words, Flaming Images (SAKS Publications, London, 1996); Bittersweet (Women's Press, London, 1998); The Fire People (Payback Press, Edinburgh); Love Shook My Senses (Women's Press, London, 1998); The Forward Book of Poetry 2002 (Forward/Faber & Faber, 2001); IC3: The Penguin Book of New Black Writing in Britian (London, Hamish Hamilton, 2000); Mythic Women/Real Women (Faber & Faber, London, 2000); Voice Memory Ashes (Mango Publishing, London, 1999). http://www.dorotheasmartt.com

Chapter 10 – BENJAMIN ZEPHANIAH

Poet, novelist and playwright Benjamin Zephaniah was born on 15 April 1958. He grew up in Jamaica and the Handsworth district of Birmingham, England, leaving school at 14. He moved to London in 1979 and published his first poetry collection, Pen Rhythm, in 1980. He has been Writer in Residence at the Africa Arts Collective in Liverpool and Creative Artist in Residence at Cambridge University, and was a candidate for the post of Professor of Poetry at Oxford University. He holds an honorary doctorate in Arts and Humanities from the University of North London (1998), was made a Doctor of Letters by the University of Central England (1999), and a Doctor of the University by the University of Staffordshire (2002). In 1998, he was appointed to the National Advisory Committee on Creative and Cultural Education to advise on the place of music and art in the National Curriculum and in 1988 Ealing Hospital in London named a ward after him. His second collection of poetry, *The Dread Affair: Collected Poems* (1985) contained a number of poems attacking the British legal system. *Rasta Time in Palestine* (1990), an account of a visit to the Palestinian occupied territories, contained poetry and travelogue. In addition to his published writing, Benjamin Zephaniah has produced numerous music recordings, including 'Us and Dem' (1990) and 'Belly of de Beast' (1996), and has also appeared as an actor in several television and film productions, including appearing as Moses in the film Farendg (1990). His first television play, 'Dread Poets Society', was first screened by the BBC in 1991. His play 'Hurricane Dub' was one of the winners of the BBC Young Playwrights Festival Award in 1998, and his stage plays have been performed at the Riverside Studios in London, at the Hay-on-Wye Literature Festival and on television. His radio play 'Listen to Your Parents', first broadcast on BBC Radio 4 in 2000, won the Commission for Racial Equality Race in the Media Radio Drama Award and has been adapted for the stage, first performed by Roundabout, Nottingham Playhouse's Theatre in Education Company, in September 2002. Many of the poems in *Too Black, Too Strong* (2001) were inspired by his tenure as Poet in Residence at the chambers of London barrister Michael Mansfield QC and by his attendance at both the inquiry into the 'Bloody Sunday' shootings and the inquiry into the death of Ricky Reel, an Asian student found dead in the Thames. His most recent book is *We Are Britain!* (2002), a collection of poems celebrating cultural diversity in Britain. He is also well known for his animal rights and human rights activism work.

PRIMARY WORKS

Poetry: Pen Rhythm (Page One Books, 1980); The Dread Affair: Collected Poems (Arena, 1985) Rasta Time in Palestine (Shakti, 1990); City Psalms (Bloodaxe, 1992); Propa Propaganda (Bloodaxe, 1996); A Little Book of Vegan Poems (A. K. Press, 2000); Too Black, Too Strong (Bloodaxe, 2001).

Plays: Black Plays: Two (includes 'Job Rocking' by Benjamin Zephaniah) (Methuen, 1987).

Anthologies: Inna Liverpool (Africa Arts Collective, 1988); Out of the Night: Writings from Death Row (editor with Marie Mulvey Roberts) (New Clarion Press, 1994); The Bloomsbury Book of Love Poems (editor) (Bloomsbury, 1999); Children and Young People: Talking Turkeys (Viking, 1994); Funky Chickens (Viking, 1996); School's Out: Poems Not for School (AK Press, 1997); Face (Bloomsbury, 1999); Wicked World (Puffin, 2000); Refugee Boy (Bloomsbury, 2001); We Are Britain! (with photographs by Prodeepta Das) (Frances Lincoln, 2002).

Benjamin Zephaniah (http://www.contemporarywriters.com/authors/?p=auth105)

OTHER WRITERS IN PART THREE

Vanessa Walters

Vanessa Walters is best known as the teenage novelist discovered to be writing a novel as hobby to share with her school friends. When discovered by teachers, the journal was passed over to an agent who quickly had her signed to a publishing company with a five-figure book deal even before she'd left. The book, *Rude Girls*, made her a success, but instead of diving head long into the literary world she continued her studies, progressing to University. Whilst studying law, Vanessa found time to spend a year in Paris and continue her fictional writing. *The Best Things in Life* was published in 1998 and explored the lives of young Black women struggling to balance friendship, work and relationships. Vanessa lives in East London with her mother and sister.

Novels: Rude Girls (Pan Paperback,1996); The Best Things in Life (Pan Paperback, 1999).

(http://www.blackinbritain.co.uk/AZfiles/VanessaWalters.htm)

Stephen Thompson

Born and and raised in Hackney, East London Thompson was educated at the notorious Hackney Downs Comprehensive. His teenage years were spent, like many, hanging out with friends and comrades and having fun. It wasn't long until Thompson started to deal marijuana on the Sandringham Road (the old 'front line') and it wasn't long after that that he developed an addiction of his own, fast turning into a full time occupation. In 1989, when Thompson was only 23, he arrived at the height of his addiction realised then that he couldn't go on and after a particularly bad period, checked himself into rehab in Notting Hill and began to slowly climb the ladder back to sanity – and become an author!

Novels: Toy Soldiers (Sceptre 2000); Missing Joe (Sceptre 2001).
(http://www.bbc.co.uk/arts/books/author/thompson/pg2.shtml)

Alex Wheatle

Alex Wheatle, of Jamaican origin was born in South London. He is a founder member of The Crucial Rocker sound system where he wrote lyrics, jingles etc for performance on sound systems. Alex is now working with The Book Trust to introduce literature for those who are dispossessed. He organises and holds workshops in prisons and young adult institutions. He is the author four novels: *Brixton Rock*, *The Seven Sisters*, *East of Acre Lane* and *Checkers* (co-written with Mark Parkham).

PRIMARY WORKS
Brixton Rock (BlackAmber Books, 1999, 2004); East of Acre Lane (Fourth Estate 2001); The Seven Sisters (Fourth Estate 2002).
(http://www.blackamber.com/authors/alex_wheatle.html)

Biyi Bandele-Thomas

Biyi Bandele-Thomas was born in Kafanchan, in Nigeria, in 1967 where he studied drama at Obafewi A. Awolowo University. He was awarded the Commonwealth Prize in the Black Young Writers Competition. His poetry has been published in a variety of magazines and journals, as well as in a BBC anthology of African poetry, *The Fate of Vultures*. He has written several plays, including 'The Female God and other Forbidden Fruits', which was broadcast on the BBC World Service in 1991 and on Radio 5 in 1993, 'Marching for Fausa', which was performed at the Royal Court Theatre in 1993, and 'Death Catches the Hunter'. His film and television work includes 'Not Even the Gods are Wise Enough' and 'Bad Boys'. He has received several fellowships and awards including a Royal Literary Fellowship. He was most recently a judge for the 2004 Caine Prize for African Writing and his forthcoming novel, *White City* will be published by Jonathan Cape in 2006.

PRIMARY WORKS
Novels: The Man Who Came in from the Back of Beyond (Publishing Co., 1991); Man Who Came in from the Back of Beyond (AfricanWriters Series – Heinemann International Literature and Textbooks1992); The Sympathetic Undertaker and Other Dreams
(AfricanWriters Series Heinemann International Literature and Textbooks, 1993); The Street (Picador).
Plays (Staged and Published): "Brixton Stories" and "Happy Birthday, Mister Deka D" (Methuen Publishing Ltd 2001); Marching for Fausa (Plays) (Amber Lane Press Ltd 1993); Resurrections (Plays) (Amber Lane Press Ltd 1994); Death Catches the Hunter (Amber Lane Press Ltd 1995); Oroonoko (Amber Lane Press 1999).
http://www.africanwriters.com/Writers/WriterTop.asp?cPK=Bandele-ThomasBiyi